Automated Sudoku

Sudoku Puzzles Made Easy

Alan Ross

Trafford
Bloomington

Order this book online at www.trafford.com
or email orders@trafford.com

Most Trafford titles are also available at major online book retailers.

Note for Librarians: A cataloguing record for this book is available from Library and Archives Canada at www.collectionscanada.ca/amicus/index-e.html

Printed in Victoria, BC, Canada.

ISBN: 978-1-4269-1654-0 *(Soft)*

Our mission is to efficiently provide the world's finest, most comprehensive book publishing service, enabling every author to experience success. To find out how to publish your book, your way, and have it available worldwide, visit us online at www.trafford.com

Trafford rev. 10/19/2009

www.trafford.com

North America & international
toll-free: 1 888 232 4444 (USA & Canada)
phone: 250 383 6864 • fax: 812 355 4082

ABOUT SUDOKU

Sudoku needs no introduction; a puzzle is in every daily newspaper. But most people just try it and after a time give up especially the hard ones since they only arrive at the answer by guesswork. This is what this book seeks to address.

All the puzzles in this book have been made by a computer program developed by the author. They contain twenty seven numbers and are arranged in five symmetrical ways. For those mathematically minded, here are some of the formulas used.

north-south: y:=9*((81-x)DIV 9)+((x-1)MOD 9)+1
east-west: y:=9*((x-1)DIV 9)+((x*8)MOD 9)+1;
north-east/south-west diagonal: y:=9*((x-1)MOD 9)+((x-1)DIV 9)+1;
north-west/south-east diagonal: y:=9*((81-x)MOD 9)+((81-x)DIV 9)+1;

They have been tested by a special program to make sure they are really difficult. I hope you really enjoy doing them, and are able to finish them without having to look at the answers. The difficult puzzles in newspapers and magazines are usually made by taking out an extra number, usually one with only two possibilities, and therefore one has to try the one, and then if unsuccessful the other. I prefer puzzles where no guesswork is involved and are intellectually stimulating and these I have provided here. I would like to hear from you, if you liked this book and also if you think it can be improved. My phone number is 0207 502 6339. I hope to print more books where your views will be taken into consideration.

The puzzles here contain twenty seven numbers and if two more are taken out (to keep the symmetry) they will likely be unsolvable. That leaves 54 numbers to find. To help the process along I have included in the blank squares the possible numbers. Like there are different ways of solving a crossword and one needn't start at the beginning, the same is with sudoku. The order of the answers given (go from left to right not downwards) may not be in the same order as you find them. But after a time especially with these hard puzzles one arrives at a point where one has to find a certain pair or twin and this will occur whichever way you have used to solve so far. For instance you have found say ten numbers and now you are stuck. The answers given will have found the same ten numbers even though it has been in a different order.

My puzzles have the innovation of providing you with the possible answers in each square. Since this has to be done to be able to solve the puzzle and is most tedious, it should come as a welcome relief.

There is a grid of 9 by 9 containing all the numbers 1 to 9 in each Row, Column and Box. A block consists of 3 rows or 3 columns. A row consists of 9 squares containing all the numbers 1 to 9. Each block contains 3 sets of nine numbers. That means 3 one's, 3 two's etc. and in different columns. A set are the small possible numbers in each square.

One first looks at the puzzle and sees if there are already 2 of the same numbers given in the block. Let us say two nines. Then one looks at the third row for another nine. In my puzzle it will be in the small numbers. There is definitely one there but there may be up to three. If you find just one, then you overwrite the small numbers with a big nine, and cross out all the small nines in the same row, column and box. This is denoted in my answers as (a). This is most important not to forget to cross out any. One carries on like this until the puzzle is finished. This is normally termed an easy puzzle.

As each number is found, either by that being the only possible one to complete the row column or box (denoted by (a) in my answers) or if there is only one left in the square (denoted by (b) in my answers) one has to cross any others off (of the same answer) in the same row, column or box. First make sure you have crossed them all off. It is best to cross them off with a colored pen not a black one, and the 'found' ones to write with big numbers overwriting the square.

The way the answers work, like (D3Ba4). D3 is the square, like in chess notation the rows are labeled A-J (J instead of I) and the columns 1-9. Afterwards it may be an R, B or C. This means now you are going to fill a Row, Box or Column. That means this is the only number left in the possibles of that Row, Box or Column. The (a) denotes that that is the reason. If a (b) follows, that means that this is the only number left in the square and the R, B or C in front has no relevance. Afterwards follows of course the answer.

Having exhausted all the possible reasons why a number can be found and the puzzle is still not finished, one must use the rules and it is not termed an easy puzzle anymore.

Rule one is pairs or twins. (This book does not contain any triplets). An example is something like this.

1246789, 24567, 37, 12368 , 34569, 37.

One can see straight away there are two squares with only two numbers and both are the same so one can cross out all the other threes or sevens in the other squares since they, the numbers with 3 or 7 can only be them, and nothing else. These are easy to find. But beware! 78, 79, 89 is not a twin. Now look at this!

6	2~~4~~7~~9~~	49	149	8	149	5	~~1~~27	3

What can one do about them! So here comes rule 2. If you look carefully you will notice that only two numbers contain a two and seven. These are called hidden pairs. So one can cross out all the rest since they are the only possible ones for a two and a seven. These are usually not very easy to spot and it means looking at each set, first to find a number which is only twice in the row (in only two sets) and then another one again which is only twice and in the same set. Writing them down until you find them can help. It is a good idea to follow the answers given, which use all the rules to cross out the numbers every time a new one is found, to make sure you understand and know how to apply them although there may be a simpler way to do the puzzle.

This is usually termed a medium puzzle but may still not solve it, so one has to turn to rule 3.

In the following puzzle the second row has two squares with a possible 2 in them, in the first block. The third row has also 2's in the second block. Therefore one crosses out the ones in the first block of row 3 which leaves only one 2 in the first column on the second row.

1678	136	13678	78	5	9	13678	2	4
2789	39	23789	1	4	6	378	378	5
12678	4	5	278	27	3	1678	678	9

X-wing, swordfish, and jellyfish.

If we have two columns let us say far apart (to make things simple) each with two of the same small number on it, in the same rows, then one from each column has to be correct and one can discard any other of the same number in that row. The same applies to rows and columns.

9	~~9~~			~~9~~				9
			9			9		
				9				
	9							
						9		
9	~~9~~		~~9~~		~~9~~			9
x						9		x

This also applies to three or four columns or rows.

9	~~9~~			9				9
						9		
9		~~9~~		9			~~9~~	9
	9							
						9		
9	~~9~~		~~9~~	9	~~9~~			9
x				x		9		x

Although this is a 333 set it will also be the same if it was 332 or even 222 as long as there were two in one column and in the same row.

2	2	2
2	2	2
2	2	2

2	2	2
2	2	2
2	2	

2	2	2
2		2
2	2	

2	2	
2		2
	2	2

Most of the puzzles in this book are hard puzzles and most will have to use all three rules to be able to solve them. Please remember that it may look unsolvable but it definitely can be solved. All the puzzles have been checked by my computer program and cannot contain print mistakes since they are printed directly from the computer program. If you must look at the answer try to find out where you went wrong, it does give a clue. It is usually because you have not crossed out all the small numbers each time and of course if you have made a mistake by crossing out the wrong ones. That is the only way, by learning from mistakes, to progress into becoming an expert which you will no doubt become. Once you have mastered the art you will find doing a sudoku a real pleasure, which uses your brain power giving you a sense of achievement and not just guessing!

About the author and programs used to make the puzzles.

I was born in Manchester and studied computer science in Westminster University and live in London with my wife. I have already written many books and supplied puzzles for magazines. But this is my first book which I hope will develop into a series which provides step by step answers plus the small numbers. First a program makes the puzzles using random numbers. Then another program checks the puzzles and grades them. After that they are converted to a Microsoft word document with the small numbers in a dark yellow. This then is converted to a PDF file using an excellent free program called pdf995; it does not seem to convert grayscales very well but will convert colours like yellow into a light shade of black. Afterwards the PDF files are combined into a book and paginated using Adobe. Microsoft word is not good at combining documents and Adobe is not good at converting colours or grayscales and pdf995 is not good at pagination so all three programs are used.

All the programs are written in Modula2 except the one which makes random numbers for which I have to use the original Pascal since Modula2 does not have a proper random number maker.

6	2589	3	24	124	7	1245	12589	259
7	29	1	5	8	1246	1234	12369	2369
1258	258	4	3	9	126	125	125678	2567
358	3568	9	248	245	234	7	2356	1
358	1	578	2789	6	239	235	4	2359
4	3567	2	79	15	139	8	3569	3569
12389	23489	18	249	7	5	6	123	23
1259	25679	1567	269	3	8	125	1257	4
235	234567	567	1	24	246	9	2357	8

H4Ca6 C9Ca7 G4Ba9 B3Rb1 F4Rb7 G3Cb8 H1Ca9
J3Ca6 E3Ra7 G2Ra4 G1Ba1 H3Rb5 J8Ra5 H8Ba7
H2Rb2 J1Cb3 B2Cb9 H7Cb1 J2Bb7 C1Ca2 C7Rb5
C2Cb8 A2Bb5 A8Ca8 A5Ra1 A9Ra9 C8Ba1 F6Ba1
F8Ba9 C6Rb6 F5Rb5 E6Ca9 E9Ca5 D1Ra5 E7Ra3
E1Ba8 D6Ba3 D8Ba2 D2Rb6 D5Rb4 E4Rb2 F9Rb6
G8Rb3 F2Cb3 A4Cb4 D4Cb8 J5Cb2 B8Cb6 G9Cb2
B6Bb2 A7Bb2 B9Bb3 J6Bb4 B7Ca4

489	5	24	278	6	289	1	3	249
1389	2689	1236	4	1389	5	29	26	7
1349	269	7	12	139	1239	2459	246	8
47	1	246	9	37	23	8	5	2346
578	2678	256	12578	4	1238	2379	267	2369
4578	3	9	2578	578	6	247	1	24
2	79	135	158	1589	1489	6	478	1345
6	9	15	3	1589	7	245	248	1245
1357	4	8	156	2	1	357	9	135

J4Ca6 G6Ca4 A4Ra7 C7Ra5 H2Rb9 J6Rb1 G2Cb7
G8Bb8 E8Ca7 E4Ra1 G5Ra9 H5Ra8 J7Ra7 A6Ba8
G4Ba5 C4Rb2 C2Cb6 F4Cb8 C8Bb4 F5Ca5 C6Ca9
E7Ca3 B8Ca6 E9Ra9 F1Ra7 B7Ba9 D5Ba7 D9Ba6
A9Rb2 D1Rb4 E6Rb2 H8Rb2 A1Cb9 E2Cb8 A3Cb4
D3Cb2 D6Cb3 H7Cb4 F9Cb4 B2Bb2 E1Bb5 F7Bb2
B1Ca8 H3Ca5 E3Ca6 H9Ra1 J9Ra5 G3Ba1 G9Ba3
B3Rb3 J1Rb3 C1Cb1 B5Cb1 C5Bb3

1268	3	4	178	2678	1268	2679	5	12679
12568	9	256	178	2678	4	267	167	3
126	7	26	9	236	5	8	146	1246
23578	258	2357	4	23568	268	1	9	25678
234578	258	23579	358	1	2689	23467	467	245678
23458	6	1	358	23589	7	234	4	2458
157	15	8	6	4579	3	479	2	1479
9	15	567	2	4578	18	467	3	1467
12367	4	2367	17	79	19	5	8	1679

E3Ca9 C5Ra3 F5Ra9 J6Ba9 F8Rb4 J5Rb7 J4Cb1
H6Bb8 J9Bb6 E1Ca4 A6Ca1 C9Ra4 H3Ra6 G1Ba7
C3Rb2 B3Cb5 J3Cb3 D3Bb7 J1Bb2 D1Ra3 F1Ca5
E4Ca5 D9Ra5 E7Ra3 F4Ba3 E8Ba6 C8Rb1 E6Rb2
F7Rb2 C1Cb6 E2Cb8 D6Cb6 B8Cb7 F9Cb8 A1Bb8
B4Bb8 B7Bb6 D2Bb2 D5Bb8 E9Bb7 B1Ca1 A4Ca7
A5Ca6 H7Ca7 A9Ca2 A7Ra9 B5Ra2 H5Ra4 G5Ba5
G7Ba4 G9Ba9 G2Rb1 H9Rb1 H2Cb5

123	12	4	1378	13	78	6	9	1235
12369	7	1369	1349	13469	5	234	8	123
5	19	8	2	13469	469	7	134	13
124689	12489	169	5	7	469	2348	1346	123689
14689	3	1569	49	2	469	458	7	15689
24679	249	569	349	8	1	2345	3456	23569
18	18	2	178	15	3	9	56	4
13489	5	139	6	149	4789	38	2	378
3489	6	7	489	459	2489	1	35	358

F1Ca7 J6Ca2 H9Ca7 A9Ra5 G8Ra6 G4Ra7 A6Ba7
F4Ba3 J8Ba5 F8Rb4 D2Ca4 G5Ca5 H6Ca8 B7Ca4
A4Ra8 B9Ba2 H5Ba1 J9Ba8 A5Rb3 H7Rb3 H3Cb9
H1Bb4 G2Ca8 B3Ca3 B4Ca1 G1Ra1 J1Ra3 B1Ba6
A1Rb2 B5Rb9 A2Cb1 J5Cb4 C2Bb9 C5Bb6 J4Bb9
F2Ca2 E4Ca4 C6Ra4 D7Ra2 F9Ra9 E7Ba8 E1Rb9
F7Rb5 D1Cb8 F3Cb6 E6Cb6 D3Bb1 D6Bb9 E9Bb1
E3Ca5 C8Ca1 D9Ca6 C9Ra3 D8Ra3

1	2359	29	23579	4	2379	8	3567	356
2356	7	2	2358	1358	1238	9	3456	3456
35	4	8	6	3579	379	1	2	35
23478	23	247	234789	3789	5	3467	1	34689
9	135	147	3478	6	3478	3457	3457	2
234578	6	247	1	3789	234789	3457	3457	34589
47	8	3	457	157	6	2	9	145
247	129	6	34579	13579	13479	345	8	1345
4	19	5	3489	2	13489	346	346	7

B1Ca6 E3Ca1 A3Ca9 A8Ba7 B3Rb2 J1Rb4 G1Cb7
H1Bb2 D2Ca2 J8Ca6 A9Ra6 F6Ra2 A4Ba2 D7Ba6
A6Rb3 J7Rb3 A2Cb5 C1Bb3 E2Bb3 F1Ca5 D1Ba8
C9Rb5 E8Ca5 F9Ca8 F5Ra9 C6Ba9 D9Ba9 H7Ba5
C5Rb7 D5Cb3 H5Bb1 J2Ca1 H4Ca3 B5Ca8 B6Ca1
G9Ca1 B9Ca3 B8Ra4 B4Ra5 F8Ra3 G4Ra4 H6Ra7
H2Ra9 J4Ra9 E6Ba4 G5Ba5 J6Ba8 H9Ba4 D4Rb7
E7Rb7 D3Cb4 E4Cb8 F7Cb4 F3Bb7

23569	1356	1359	8	1357	23567	4	679	179
568	1568	4	156	157	9	3	67	2
2369	7	139	1236	4	236	169	8	5
3589	1358	135789	1235	13589	4	12579	2579	6
589	2	15789	15	6	58	1579	3	14789
4	13568	13589	7	13589	2358	1259	259	189
7	9	358	3456	2	3568	56	1	34
1	345	6	9	357	357	8	2457	347
358	3458	2	3456	3578	1	5679	45679	3479

E9Ra4 F2Ra6 H8Ra2 F9Ba8 J8Ba4 G9Rb3 H9Cb7
J9Bb9 H2Ca4 G4Ca4 A6Ca7 A9Ca1 A1Ra2 B8Ra7
J5Ra7 G6Ba8 E6Rb5 G3Rb5 E4Cb1 H6Cb3 G7Cb6
C7Bb9 F6Bb2 H5Bb5 J7Bb5 C4Ca2 B4Ca5 B5Ca1
D5Ca8 C6Ca6 D7Ca2 A8Ca6 A2Ra5 A3Ra9 B1Ra6
C3Ra1 D3Ra7 F8Ra5 J4Ra6 C1Ba3 B2Ba8 A5Ba3
D2Ba1 D1Ba5 F5Ba9 F7Ba1 E7Ba7 D8Ba9 D4Rb3
E3Rb8 F3Rb3 J1Rb8 J2Rb3 E1Cb9

147	179	6	13457	2	47	39	8	1379
1478	5	3	9	1478	4678	26	127	1267
178	179	2	13578	13578	678	369	1579	4
9	367	78	2	178	5	4	17	1378
2378	4	578	178	9	78	238	6	12378
278	27	1	6	478	3	289	279	5
5	23679	479	3478	3478	24789	1	249	2689
246	269	49	458	458	1	7	3	2689
12347	8	479	347	6	2479	5	249	29

H1Ca6 E3Ca5 C8Ca5 A4Ra5 D2Ra6 F5Ra4 G9Ra6
J1Ra1 E1Ba3 G2Ba3 H5Ba5 H9Ba8 H4Rb4 H3Cb9
H2Bb2 F1Ca2 D3Ca8 C5Ca3 D9Ra3 F7Ra8 J4Ra3
A7Ba3 F2Ba7 F8Ba9 E7Rb2 B7Cb6 C7Bb9 A2Ca9
C6Ca6 J9Ca9 A9Ra1 G6Ra9 C2Ba1 D8Ba1 J6Ba2
D5Rb7 E9Rb7 J8Rb4 J3Cb7 G5Cb8 E6Cb8 G8Cb2
B9Cb2 B5Bb1 B8Bb7 E4Bb1 G3Bb4 G4Bb7 C4Ca8
A6Ca7 A1Ra4 B1Ra8 C1Ra7 B6Ba4

8	4679	5	2	3467	36	1	369	379
2	4679	1	45678	34567	368	567	35689	3579
7	67	3	9	1567	168	4	2568	257
1349	1349	2	1456	14569	7	56	13456	8
1349	5	4	146	8	1269	6	7	123
6	1478	48	3	1245	12	9	1245	125
134	13468	9	1678	1367	5	2	1	17
135	1236	6	167	123679	12369	8	159	4
15	128	7	18	129	4	3	159	6

C1Ca7 H3Ca6 F3Ca8 B7Ca7 A5Ra7 F2Ra7 G9Ba7
C2Rb6 E3Rb4 E7Rb6 G8Rb1 E4Cb1 D7Cb5 F6Bb2
H4Bb7 J4Bb8 G1Ca4 G2Ca8 B4Ca5 C8Ca2 F9Ca1
A2Ra4 C9Ra5 C6Ra8 E9Ra2 F5Ra5 G5Ra3 B2Ba9
C5Ba1 B5Ba4 B8Ba8 D8Ba3 G4Ba6 B9Rb3 D2Rb1
D4Rb4 E6Rb9 F8Rb4 D1Cb9 E1Cb3 J2Cb2 D5Cb6
B6Cb6 H6Cb1 A9Cb9 A6Bb3 A8Bb6 H1Bb5 H2Bb3
J5Bb9 J1Ca1 H5Ca2 J8Ca5 H8Ca9

67	246	8	347	7	5	267	9	1
579	3	1	47	2	6	78	4578	457
567	2456	24567	147	9	178	2678	245678	3
15679	1569	35679	2	17	4	13679	3567	8
15789	12589	23579	17	6	1789	12379	23457	24579
4	12689	2679	5	178	3	12679	267	2679
2	15689	569	167	4	17	36789	3678	679
68	468	46	9	3	27	5	1	267
3	7	569	8	15	12	4	26	269

```
A4Ca3 G4Ca6 J5Ca5 F5Ca8 E6Ca9 A2Ra4 B1Ra9
J6Ra1 C4Ba1 C6Ba8 G2Ba1 H3Ba4 H6Ba2 A5Rb7
E4Rb7 G6Rb7 A1Cb6 B4Cb4 D5Cb1 G9Cb9 A7Bb2
G3Bb5 H1Bb8 E1Ca1 E2Ca8 E9Ca4 C8Ra4 E8Ra5
F7Ra1 H9Ra7 J3Ra9 B9Ba5 C7Ba6 D7Ba9 H2Ba6
D2Rb5 E7Rb3 D1Cb7 C2Cb2 E3Cb2 G7Cb8 C1Bb5
C3Bb7 B7Bb7 F2Bb9 F3Bb6 D8Bb6 G8Bb3 D3Ca3
F8Ca7 B8Ca8 J9Ca6 F9Ra2 J8Ra2
```

3	468	1	9	5	24678	267	2467	247
4567	2	567	348	3678	1	567	45679	4579
4567	456	9	24	267	2467	3	8	12457
1	56	2567	2458	278	3	9	2457	2457
8	359	2357	245	1	2479	257	23457	6
2579	359	4	6	279	279	1257	2357	8
2569	7	8	123	2369	269	4	2569	259
24569	34569	2356	7	23689	2689	256	1	259
269	169	26	12	4	5	8	2679	3

```
J2Ca1 A2Ca8 F7Ca1 C9Ca1 G4Ra1 J8Ra7 J4Rb2
J3Cb6 C4Cb4 E4Bb5 J1Bb9 H2Ca4 B4Ca3 E6Ca4
H6Ca8 B5Ra8 D2Ra6 E2Ra9 G5Ra3 B1Ba4 D4Ba8
H3Ba3 C2Rb5 F2Cb3 B3Cb7 C1Bb6 E3Bb2 F1Ca7
D3Ca5 H5Ca6 E8Ca3 E7Ra7 F8Ra5 G8Ra6 H9Ra9
A6Ba6 A9Ba7 B8Ba9 D5Ba7 G6Ba9 A7Rb2 B9Rb5
C5Rb2 F6Rb2 F5Cb9 C6Cb7 B7Cb6 H7Cb5 A8Cb4
G9Cb2 D8Bb2 D9Bb4 G1Bb5 H1Bb2
```

17	123	4	1379	9	179	8	5	1367
6	138	5	134789	2	14789	134	3479	137
9	1238	12378	6	45	14578	1234	2347	137
2	458	6	458	7	458	345	1	9
1458	14589	18	24589	3	245689	45	478	57
3	7	8	4589	1	4589	6	48	2
1457	1245	127	124579	4569	3	125	26	8
157	1235	1237	1257	8	12567	9	236	4
1458	6	9	1245	45	1245	7	23	135

```
E2Ca9 G5Ca6 B8Ca9 A9Ca6 A2Ra2 D7Ra3 E6Ra6
G4Ra9 H8Ra6 J1Ra8 E4Ba2 F6Ba9 A5Rb9 F3Rb8
G8Rb2 E3Cb1 F8Cb4 J8Cb3 C8Bb7 F4Bb5 E7Bb5
G3Bb7 A1Ca7 H3Ca2 C7Ca2 E8Ca8 J9Ca5 E9Ca7
A4Ra3 D2Ra5 E1Ra4 H2Ra3 J6Ra2 C3Ba3 B7Ba4
G2Ba4 H6Ba5 G7Ba1 A6Rb1 C9Rb1 G1Rb5 H1Rb1
J5Rb4 C2Cb8 H4Cb7 J4Cb1 C5Cb5 B9Cb3 B2Bb1
B4Bb8 C6Bb4 D4Ca4 B6Ca7 D6Ca8
```

7	1	23	9	6	2348	23458	3458	24
8	23	236	12345	245	1234	234569	34569	12467
9	4	5	7	28	1238	2368	368	126
23	2389	2389	24	2479	6	1	3489	5
125	6	1289	1245	3	1249	2489	7	24
4	2359	7	8	259	129	2369	369	26
236	239	23469	2346	249	5	7	1	8
12356	23578	123468	2346	248	2348	456	456	9
56	589	4689	46	1	7	456	2	3

```
H2Ca7 D5Ca7 B9Ca7 F6Ra1 B3Ba6 B4Ba1 C9Ba1
G5Ba9 E4Ca5 E6Ca9 F9Ca6 F2Ra5 B5Ba5 D4Ba4
F5Rb2 J4Rb6 J1Cb5 C5Cb8 H5Bb4 J7Bb4 G3Ca4
H6Ca8 E9Ra4 G1Ra6 E7Ba2 A9Rb2 E1Rb1 A3Cb3
E3Cb8 B2Bb2 A6Bb4 J3Bb9 J2Ca8 D2Ca9 H3Ca1
C6Ca2 A7Ca8 B8Ca4 A8Ra5 B7Ra9 D8Ra8 G4Ra2
B6Ba3 D1Ba3 F8Ba9 H1Ba2 H4Ba3 H7Ba5 D3Rb2
F7Rb3 G2Rb3 H8Rb6 C7Cb6 C8Cb3
```

7	468	1	5	249	3	2689	24689	269
569	3456	3456	8	12479	1279	1269	124679	1269
89	48	2	9	1479	6	189	5	3
2	135678	35678	369	35679	79	1569	1369	4
56	356	9	1	8	4	7	236	256
4	13567	3567	2369	235679	279	12569	12369	8
3	9	568	7	126	12	4	1268	1256
168	124678	4678	2369	12369	5	12689	12689	1269
156	1256	56	4	1269	8	3	1269	7

```
B8Ca7 C5Ra7 A8Ba4 G9Ba5 C4Rb9 C1Cb8 A5Cb2
A2Bb6 C2Bb4 B6Bb1 C7Bb1 B1Ca9 H3Ca4 B5Ca4
H9Ca1 A7Ra8 G5Ra1 H2Ra7 A9Ba9 J2Ba2 G3Ba8
G6Rb2 H1Rb6 E1Cb5 J3Cb5 H4Cb3 G8Cb6 B3Bb3
E2Bb3 D4Bb6 J1Bb1 H5Bb9 J8Bb9 B2Ca5 D2Ca8
F3Ca6 F4Ca2 J5Ca6 H8Ca8 D8Ra1 E9Ra6 F6Ra7
H7Ra2 B9Ba2 B7Ba6 F2Ba1 D3Ba7 D6Ba9 E8Ba2
F8Ba3 D7Rb5 F5Rb5 D5Cb3 F7Cb9
```

5689	356	4	2	356	135	158	7	1568
2568	356	1	458	7	345	458	2568	9
25678	567	268	1458	56	9	3	2568	124568
478	9	5	6	2	37	8	1	378
1678	1367	368	579	4	357	589	23589	23578
7	2	3	579	1	8	6	4	357
124569	1456	7	3	59	1245	14589	5689	14568
3	1456	69	14579	8	1457	2	569	1456
12459	8	29	1459	59	6	7	359	1345

```
A5Ca3 G6Ca2 A1Ra9 B2Ra3 D1Ra4 F4Ra9 C5Ba6
D7Rb8 F1Rb7 F3Rb3 F9Cb5 E7Bb9 C2Ca7 A9Ra8
B8Ba6 G8Ba8 A2Ra6 B1Ra2 G5Ra9 C1Ba5 J3Ba2
C3Rb8 C8Rb2 E2Rb1 J1Rb1 J5Rb5 G1Cb6 E3Cb6
J4Cb4 E8Cb3 C4Bb1 E1Bb8 D9Bb7 H3Bb9 J8Bb9
J9Bb3 B4Ca8 H6Ca1 D6Ca3 B6Ca4 H8Ca5 E9Ca2
H9Ca6 A7Ra1 B7Ra5 C9Ra4 G2Ra5 H2Ra4 H4Ra7
A6Ba5 E6Ba7 G9Ba1 G7Ba4 E4Rb5
```

2	78	789	1	34789	5	468	49	4689
3	578	6	249	24789	2789	1	2459	2489
458	1	589	249	2489	6	7	2459	3
5678	4	23578	269	26789	1	2358	2359	289
178	9	2378	24	5	278	2348	6	1248
1568	2568	258	3	24689	289	2458	7	12489
9	2356	1	7	236	23	2346	8	246
568	23568	4	256	1236	23	9	123	7
67	2367	237	8	12369	4	236	123	5

```
C1Ca4 H4Ca5 A5Ra3 G2Ra5 J5Ra9 C3Ba5 H5Ba1
A3Ca9 D4Ca6 J8Ca1 A2Ra7 B8Ra5 C5Ra8 B2Ba8
F6Ba9 G5Ba6 A8Rb4 E6Ca8 A9Ca6 A7Ra8 H1Ra8
D5Ba7 J7Ba6 D1Rb5 J1Rb7 E1Cb1 F1Bb6 H2Ca6
E3Ca7 B6Ca7 F7Ca5 F9Ca1 E7Ra3 F5Ra4 F3Ra8
B4Ba4 D3Ba3 E4Ba2 E9Ba4 D9Ba8 H8Ba3 B5Rb2
C4Rb9 D7Rb2 F2Rb2 G9Rb2 H6Rb2 J3Rb2 J2Cb3
G6Cb3 G7Cb4 C8Cb2 D8Cb9 B9Cb9
```

467	2689	5	2478	247	2478	489	3	1
47	1	4789	234578	6	24578	489	2789	2489
3	28	478	2478	9	12478	48	6	5
8	569	14679	45679	457	3	2	19	469
1467	3	14679	24679	8	24679	1469	5	469
456	569	2	1	45	4569	34689	89	7
9	7	68	24568	1	24568	568	28	3
156	568	168	256789	3	256789	15689	4	2689
2	4	1368	5689	5	5689	7	189	689

```
J3Ca3 B4Ca3 A5Ca2 C6Ca1 F7Ca3 B8Ca7 B9Ra2
B6Ra5 C2Ra2 F8Ra8 J8Ra1 E7Ba1 G8Ba2 B1Rb4
D8Rb9 J5Rb5 F5Cb4 D5Bb7 H1Ca1 D4Ca5 D3Ra1
G7Ra5 E3Ba4 H2Ba5 D2Rb6 E9Rb6 E1Cb7 F1Cb5
F2Cb9 D9Cb4 A1Bb6 A2Bb8 F6Bb6 C3Ca7 B3Ca9
H7Ca6 A7Ra9 B7Ra8 J4Ra6 C4Ba8 C7Ba4 G3Ba6
G4Rb4 H3Rb8 A4Cb7 G6Cb8 H9Cb9 A6Bb4 H4Bb2
J6Bb9 J9Bb8 E4Ca9 E6Ca2 H6Ca7
```

3678	346	5	9	1246	237	1248	248	1248
1	46	4679	24567	8	257	2459	3	249
389	2	3489	145	145	35	14589	7	6
356	7	2	8	59	4	69	1	39
3568	1346	13468	125	7	259	24689	2468	23489
8	9	148	3	12	6	7	5	248
4	5	1367	267	26	278	1268	9	1278
2679	8	1679	2467	3	279	1246	246	5
2679	6	679	24567	24569	1	3	2468	2478

E2Ca1 G6Ca8 F5Ra1 G3Ra3 C4Ba1 H3Ba1 F1Rb8
J2Rb6 B2Cb4 F3Cb4 A2Bb3 E3Bb6 F9Bb2 A1Ca6
C3Ca8 C6Ca3 H8Ca6 A6Ra7 B4Ra6 D7Ra6 B3Ba7
G5Ba6 B9Rb9 C1Rb9 J3Rb9 D9Cb3 D1Bb5 E1Ca3
D5Ca9 E7Ca9 H6Ra9 A7Ca8 A9Ra1 G7Ba1 G9Rb7
G4Cb2 E4Bb5 A5Ca2 B6Ca5 A8Ra4 B7Ra2 C7Ra5
E6Ra2 J5Ra5 C5Ba4 E9Ba4 J8Ba2 E8Rb8 H7Rb4
J1Rb7 J9Rb8 H1Cb2 H4Cb7 J4Cb4

347	6	137	1245	9	2345	234	35	8
348	348	9	2456	358	7	1	356	2345
5	2	138	146	138	3468	9	36	7
369	139	123	8	7	3569	236	4	12359
36789	13789	12378	569	4	3569	23678	356789	12359
346789	5	378	69	2	1	3678	36789	39
1	3789	4	579	58	589	378	2	6
789	789	6	3	18	2489	5	789	49
2	3789	3578	4579	6	4589	3478	1	349

B2Ca4 J3Ca5 F1Ra4 H5Ra1 H6Ra2 A7Ba4 A4Ra2
H9Ra4 C4Ba1 B9Ba2 J4Ca4 A3Ra1 C6Ra4 A1Ba7
B4Ba6 G4Ba7 F4Rb9 E4Cb5 F9Cb3 J9Bb9 G6Ca9
E8Ca9 D9Ca5 C8Ra6 D2Ra1 G5Ra5 A6Ba5 D1Ba9
E9Ba1 J6Ba8 A8Rb3 H1Rb8 B1Cb3 G2Cb3 B8Cb5
H8Cb7 C3Bb8 B5Bb8 E1Bb6 F8Bb8 H2Bb9 J2Bb7
G7Bb8 J7Bb3 E2Ca8 C5Ca3 D6Ca6 D3Ra3 F7Ra6
E3Ba2 E6Ba3 E7Ba7 D7Rb2 F3Rb7

2589	35689	25689	2679	125679	1256	134589	23459	1489
259	3569	7	8	12569	4	1359	2359	19
4	1	2589	3	259	25	7	6	89
1	579	59	467	34567	356	459	8	2
3	57	25	1	8	9	45	457	6
6	4	2589	27	257	25	159	579	3
79	2	3	469	469	8	469	1	5
89	689	14689	5	13469	7	2	349	489
5789	56789	145689	2469	123469	1236	34689	3479	4789

J9Ca7 E3Ra2 F7Ra1 F3Ra8 G1Ra7 C9Ra8 F8Ra9
E8Ba7 J7Ba8 E2Rb5 D3Cb9 E7Cb4 C3Bb5 D2Bb7
D7Bb5 J1Ca5 G7Ca6 C5Ra9 H9Ba9 A3Rb6 B9Rb1
C6Rb2 G5Rb4 H1Rb8 H2Cb6 A4Cb7 G4Cb9 F6Cb5
A9Cb4 A6Bb1 F4Bb2 J2Bb9 A2Ca8 D4Ca4 J5Ca2
F5Ca7 B5Ra6 J3Ra1 B2Ba3 A5Ba5 D6Ba6 H3Ba4
H5Ba1 B7Rb9 D5Rb3 H8Rb3 J4Rb6 J6Rb3 B1Cb2
A7Cb3 A8Cb2 J8Cb4 A1Bb9 B8Bb5

16	3	5	1678	167	4	168	69	2
126	267	12679	123678	12367	123568	13568	4	1389
4	8	126	9	1236	12356	1356	356	7
9	1	234678	2367	5	236	2346	36	34
236	5	2346	1236	8	12369	12346	7	1349
236	267	2367	12367	4	12369	1236	8	5
8	4	134	134	139	7	345	2	6
12356	9	12346	123468	1236	12368	34578	35	348
7	246	2346	5	236	2368	9	1	348

H1Ca5 D3Ca8 B3Ca9 G5Ca9 H7Ca7 A8Ca9 D4Ra7
F6Ra9 G7Ra5 B2Ba7 C8Ba5 E3Ba4 E9Ba9 G2Rb4
H8Rb3 D8Cb6 F3Ca7 H4Ca4 A5Ca7 B6Ca5 D7Ca4
B9Ca1 D6Ra2 J9Ra4 H9Ba8 D9Rb3 A1Ca1 B4Ca2
J6Ca8 B7Ra8 C3Ra2 B1Ba6 A4Ba8 C7Ba3 J2Ba2
A7Rb6 B5Rb3 F2Rb6 J5Cb6 C5Bb1 J3Bb3 H6Bb1
G3Ca1 H3Ca6 E4Ca6 H5Ca2 E6Ca3 C6Ra6 E7Ra1
F1Ra3 G4Ra3 E1Ba2 F4Ba1 F7Ba2

24678	2346	248	5	39	1	247	2367	23467
12456	123456	1245	26	3	7	1245	9	8
9	12356	125	8	4	36	1257	123567	23567
1245	12459	6	7	1359	345	8	125	259
125	8	7	9	6	5	3	4	259
145	1459	3	49	1589	2	6	157	579
456	4569	459	46	2	8	4579	3567	1
3	7	24589	1	5	456	2459	2568	24569
124568	12456	12458	3	57	9	2457	25678	24567

A1Ca7 B4Ca2 J5Ca7 F5Ca8 A3Ra8 A5Ra9 E1Ra1
G8Ra3 C6Ba6 D5Ba1 J1Ba8 G7Ba7 B5Rb3 E4Rb9
E6Rb5 H5Rb5 F4Cb4 H6Cb4 E9Cb2 F1Bb5 D6Bb3
D8Bb5 G4Bb6 D1Ca2 B1Ca6 H7Ca9 H8Ca8 D2Ra4
F8Ra1 H3Ra2 H9Ra6 B3Ba4 A8Ba6 F2Ba9 F9Ba7
J2Ba6 D9Rb9 G1Rb4 G2Rb5 J8Rb2 B2Cb1 G3Cb9
J3Cb1 C8Cb7 C3Bb5 B7Bb5 C7Ca1 J9Ca5 C2Ra2
J7Ra4 A2Ba3 A7Ba2 A9Ba4 C9Rb3

3689	7	3469	1	348	3468	469	2	5
169	12459	4569	46	45	7	3	49	8
1368	12458	3456	3468	9	23468	46	47	167
379	9	2	3789	378	5	1	6	4
1379	149	3479	34789	6	1348	2589	3589	239
5	6	8	2	134	134	7	39	39
6789	589	5679	34678	2	13468	45689	345789	3679
4	89	1	5	378	368	2689	3789	23679
2	3	567	4678	478	9	4568	1	67

F5Ca1 B5Ca5 C6Ca2 C9Ca1 B2Ra2 C8Ra7 F6Ra4
G6Ra1 B1Ba1 D2Rb9 H2Cb8 G2Bb5 E2Ca1 C3Ca5
E4Ca9 E8Ca5 E3Ra4 J7Ra5 C2Ba4 E7Ba8 C7Rb6
E6Rb3 E1Cb7 H6Cb6 E9Cb2 A6Bb8 D1Bb3 C1Ca8
A3Ca3 B4Ca6 H7Ca2 G8Ca8 A1Ra6 B8Ra4 C4Ra3
B3Ba9 A5Ba4 A7Ba9 H5Ba3 G7Ba4 G1Rb9 G4Rb7
H8Rb9 G3Cb6 D4Cb8 J5Cb8 F8Cb3 H9Cb7 D5Bb7
F9Bb9 J3Bb7 J4Bb4 G9Bb3 J9Bb6

1267	12689	278	134789	12478	1389	2456	23459	2346
4	5	28	6	28	389	1	7	23
1267	1269	3	5	1247	19	8	249	246
9	12	6	178	3	4	2	128	5
12357	1234	2457	178	9	158	246	12348	123468
8	134	45	2	6	15	9	134	7
256	2468	9	148	1458	7	3	12458	1248
35	7	1	348	458	2	45	6	9
2356	23468	2458	13489	1458	135689	2457	12458	1248

J6Ca6 J7Ca7 B6Ra9 D4Ra7 J4Ra9 H4Ba3 C6Rb1
D7Rb2 H1Rb5 D2Cb1 F6Cb5 H7Cb4 F3Bb4 E6Bb8
D8Bb8 E7Bb6 H5Bb8 A1Ca1 E3Ca5 A4Ca8 A6Ca3
A7Ca5 B9Ra3 B3Ra8 E1Ra7 F8Ra1 A3Ba7 E2Ba2
E4Ba1 E8Ba3 B5Rb2 E9Rb4 F2Rb3 G4Rb4 J3Rb2
G1Cb6 J1Cb3 A5Cb4 J8Cb5 C1Bb2 C5Bb7 G2Bb8
J5Bb1 G8Bb2 J2Ca4 G5Ca5 C8Ca4 G9Ca1 A9Ca2
J9Ca8 A2Ra6 C2Ra9 C9Ba6 A8Ba9

2469	269	2469	1	7	3489	2468	5	268
3	27	8	45	5	6	9	124	127
45679	1	4569	4589	2	4589	4678	3	678
2467	267	246	245678	156	12458	3	9	12568
246	5	2346	2468	9	12348	2468	7	1268
24679	8	1	24567	356	2345	2456	246	256
12569	3	2569	2569	4	1259	2567	8	25679
25689	269	7	3	56	259	1	26	4
12569	4	2569	2569	8	7	256	26	23569

H1Ca8 E3Ca3 D5Ca1 F5Ca3 B8Ca1 J9Ca3 A6Ra3
B4Ra4 E9Ra1 F1Ra9 J1Ra1 G6Ba1 G9Ba9 B5Rb5
H5Cb6 H8Bb2 F8Ca4 F4Ra7 G7Ra7 H6Ra5 D4Ba5
J4Ba9 J7Ba5 C4Rb8 F6Rb2 G4Rb2 H2Rb9 J8Rb6
J3Cb2 E4Cb6 C6Cb9 F7Cb6 C7Bb4 F9Bb5 A3Ca9
A1Ra4 D3Ba4 D6Rb8 E1Rb2 E6Cb4 E7Cb8 D9Cb2
A7Bb2 B9Bb7 B2Ca2 D2Ca7 A9Ca8 A2Ra6 C1Ra7
D1Ra6 C3Ba5 C9Ba6 G3Ba6 G1Rb5

356	156	7	4	6	35689	189	2	13568
3456	1456	9	35678	2	35678	18	13568	13568
8	256	2356	3569	1	3569	9	4	7
346	146	8	1267	5	2467	147	137	9
7	1456	13456	168	9	468	148	1358	2
2	1459	145	178	3	478	6	1578	158
1	7	256	23569	8	23569	29	69	4
4569	245689	2456	2569	7	24569	3	1689	168
469	3	246	269	46	1	5	6789	68

H2Ca8 J5Ca4 G7Ca2 D7Ca7 F2Ra9 J8Ra7 E7Ba4
J9Ba8 A5Rb6 C7Rb9 C2Ca2 A6Ra9 C3Ra6 G3Rb5
J3Rb2 H3Cb4 F3Bb1 E3Ca3 A7Ra8 D8Ra3 F6Ra4
E2Ba5 F4Ba7 E8Ba1 A2Rb1 B7Rb1 F9Rb5 B2Cb4
F8Cb8 A9Cb3 A1Bb5 B9Bb6 D2Bb6 B1Ca3 D1Ca4
D4Ca1 B6Ca7 B8Ca5 H9Ca1 B4Ra8 D6Ra2 E6Ba8
H4Ba2 E4Rb6 J4Cb9 J1Bb6 G4Bb3 H1Ca9 C4Ca5
C6Ca3 G8Ra9 H6Ra5 G6Ba6 H8Ba6

1	469	5	269	7	2469	8	3469	346
3478	2	6789	1569	149	14569	367	345679	34567
47	4679	679	2569	3	8	267	1	4567
6	157	4	8	1	13	9	37	2
278	178	278	12369	5	123469	1367	3467	13467
9	1	3	126	14	7	5	46	8
2578	3	2789	4	6	159	17	578	157
4578	456789	6789	13579	189	1359	1367	2	13567
578	5678	1	357	2	35	4	35678	9

B1Ca3 H5Ca8 C7Ca2 B3Ra8 D2Ra5 F4Ra2 A6Ba2
D5Rb1 F2Rb1 F5Cb4 D6Cb3 B5Bb9 D8Bb7 F8Bb6
J6Bb5 B6Ca4 A8Ca9 A9Ra3 B4Ra1 J2Ra6 C3Ba6
C4Ba5 C9Ba4 A2Rb4 A4Rb6 B8Rb5 C1Rb7 E9Rb1
J1Cb8 C2Cb9 E4Cb9 E7Cb3 G8Cb8 E1Bb2 E6Bb6
E8Bb4 H2Bb7 J8Bb3 H1Ca4 E2Ca8 G3Ca2 E3Ca7
H4Ca3 J4Ca7 G6Ra9 H9Ra5 G1Ba5 H3Ba9 H6Ba1
H7Ba6 B7Rb7 G9Rb7 G7Cb1 B9Cb6

1359	8	135	4	2356	369	235679	15679	23679
1359	4	135	2369	7	8	23569	1569	2369
2	6	7	1	35	39	3459	59	8
345	2357	2345	8	2346	34679	1	679	234679
6	237	2348	2379	1	3479	23479	789	5
1348	1237	9	2367	2346	5	23467	678	23467
7	359	356	36	36	2	8	4	1
1348	13	13468	5	9	3467	67	2	67
4589	259	24568	67	468	1	5679	3	679

J5Ca8 C7Ra4 G2Ra9 H6Ba4 J7Ba5 J1Rb4 J2Rb2
J3Cb6 J4Bb7 D2Ca5 E3Ra4 G3Ra5 J9Ra9 D3Ba2
F1Ba8 D1Rb3 H1Cb1 E2Cb7 F2Bb1 H2Bb3 H3Ca8
D6Ca7 E8Ca8 D8Ra9 C8Rb5 C5Cb3 C6Bb9 G5Bb6
E4Ca9 A5Ca5 E6Ca3 A6Ca6 B1Ra5 D9Ra6 E7Ra2
G4Ra3 A1Ba9 B4Ba2 F4Ba6 F9Ba4 H7Ba6 B9Rb3
D5Rb4 F5Rb2 F8Rb7 H9Rb7 B3Cb1 A7Cb7 B7Cb9
F7Cb3 A8Cb1 A9Cb2 A3Bb3 B8Bb6

17	123	8	123	12	5	6	9	4
145	12359	12469	1234	8	7	35	135	13
1457	1359	14679	134	169	13469	358	1357	2
14	6	14	1235	125	123	7	8	9
3	189	19	1278	4	12689	2	12	5
2	7	5	138	19	1389	34	6	13
6	1258	127	124578	1257	1248	234589	23457	378
1578	1258	127	9	3	1248	2458	2457	678
9	4	3	6	257	28	1	257	78

H1Ca8 C5Ca6 G7Ca9 H9Ca6 A1Ra7 B3Ra6 C7Ra8
E6Ra6 E4Ra7 F7Ra4 C6Ba9 C8Ba7 E2Ba8 F9Ba3
B9Rb1 E7Rb2 H7Cb5 E8Cb1 B7Bb3 E3Bb9 J8Bb2
B2Ca9 F5Ca9 D6Ca3 G8Ca3 B8Ca5 B4Ra2 H3Ra7
J5Ra5 A2Ba2 C4Ba4 D5Ba2 D4Ba5 G2Ba5 G5Ba7
H8Ba4 A5Rb1 B1Rb4 C3Rb1 G9Rb8 H2Rb1 J6Rb8
C1Cb5 D1Cb1 C2Cb3 D3Cb4 G3Cb2 A4Cb3 G4Cb1
F6Cb1 H6Cb2 J9Cb7 F4Bb8 G6Bb4

1568	568	7	468	2	146	1569	3569	1356
126	9	126	67	3	5	4	26	8
12568	4	3	9	178	16	1567	256	12567
7	23568	24689	1	5	2369	568	23568	23456
235689	1	2689	356	4	2369	568	7	2356
2356	2356	246	3567	57	8	156	2356	9
13689	368	1689	358	158	7	2	4	56
4	378	5	2	6	3	789	1	7
1268	2678	1268	458	9	14	3	568	567

A8Ca9 D9Ca4 A9Ra3 B4Ra7 F7Ra1 F3Ra4 H7Ra9
C9Ba1 F5Ba7 J8Ba8 C5Rb8 C6Rb6 D5Rb5 H6Rb3
H9Rb7 H2Cb8 A4Cb4 G5Cb1 A6Bb1 J4Bb5 J6Bb4
J2Ca7 G4Ca8 C7Ca7 E9Ca2 A1Ra8 G9Ra5 D6Ba2
J9Ba6 E6Rb9 G1Ca9 F2Ca2 D3Ra9 G2Ra3 E3Ba8
G3Ba6 D2Rb6 A2Cb5 D7Cb8 D8Cb3 C1Bb2 A7Bb6
B1Ca6 J3Ca2 E7Ca5 B8Ca2 F8Ca6 B3Ra1 C8Ra5
E4Ra6 F1Ra5 J1Ra1 E1Ba3 F4Ba3

8	1259	124569	1569	1456	3	2456	7	246
7	59	4569	5689	456	2	1	3456	346
12345	125	12456	156	7	146	8	9	2346
9	18	14	136	1346	5	346	2	7
1245	1257	12457	1369	8	14679	3456	13456	346
6	3	1457	2	14	147	45	1458	9
125	4	3	1568	9	168	267	68	268
25	2579	8	4	2356	6	23679	36	1
12	6	129	7	123	18	2349	348	5

C1Ca3 D2Ca8 E6Ca9 G9Ca8 B4Ra8 F8Ra8 G7Ra7
J6Ra8 A4Ba9 F6Ba7 E8Ba1 H2Ba7 G8Rb6 H6Rb6
G6Cb1 H8Cb3 C6Bb4 G4Bb5 J8Bb4 J1Ca1 E1Ca4
B2Ca9 E3Ca7 B8Ca5 B9Ra3 E2Ra2 G1Ra2 H1Ra5
H7Ra9 J5Ra3 A5Ba5 F3Ba5 J3Ba9 H5Ba2 J7Ba2
A2Rb1 B5Rb6 D3Rb1 E9Rb6 F7Rb4 C2Cb5 B3Cb4
C4Cb1 E4Cb3 D5Cb4 F5Cb1 A7Cb6 D7Cb3 C9Cb2
A3Bb2 C3Bb6 A9Bb4 D4Bb6 E7Bb5

5789	4	3	178	6	5789	1258	258	15789
5789	258	1	78	589	4	2568	3	56789
5789	6	789	1378	13589	2	1458	458	15789
13678	9	5	2368	38	368	168	68	4
4	38	68	9	7	1	568	568	2
2	138	68	368	3458	3568	7	9	13568
35689	2358	2689	4	389	36789	2568	1	568
1368	7	2468	5	138	368	9	2468	68
15689	158	4689	168	2	689	3	7	568

C3Ca7 D4Ca2 F5Ca4 C7Ca4 F9Ca3 D1Ra7 E2Ra3
F2Ra1 F6Ra5 G6Ra7 J3Ra4 B2Ba2 D7Ba1 H8Ba4
G3Ca9 C4Ca3 A8Ca2 G7Ra2 H3Ra2 J6Ra9 A6Rb8
B4Cb7 A7Cb5 A1Bb9 A4Bb1 C8Bb8 H5Ca1 E7Ca8
E8Ca5 C9Ca1 A9Ca7 B1Ra8 C5Ra9 D5Ra8 E3Ra6
J1Ra1 C1Ba5 B5Ba5 B9Ba9 F3Ba8 D6Ba3 D8Ba6
J4Ba8 B7Rb6 F4Rb6 G5Rb3 H6Rb6 J2Rb5 G1Cb6
H1Cb3 G2Cb8 H9Cb8 J9Cb6 G9Bb5

129	6	3	589	5	5789	1279	4	1279
1249	249	8	3469	46	3679	1279	129	5
49	459	4579	1	2	5679	8	3	679
14689	489	1469	456	3	2	1579	1589	14789
5	7	149	4	8	1	129	6	3
123468	248	146	7	9	156	125	1258	1248
689	1	2	35689	7	4	359	589	89
7	589	569	235689	156	135689	4	12589	1289
489	3	459	2589	15	1589	6	7	1289

F1Ca3 C3Ca7 B5Ca4 G7Ca3 C9Ca6 E7Ra2 C2Ba5
F2Ba2 A5Rb5 B2Rb9 C6Rb9 E4Rb4 E6Rb1 C1Cb4
H2Cb8 E3Cb9 A4Cb8 J5Cb1 A6Bb7 D2Bb4 J1Bb9
H5Bb6 D1Ca8 J3Ca4 J6Ca8 F9Ca4 D9Ca7 B7Ra7
F8Ra8 G1Ra6 J4Ra5 F6Ba5 H3Ba5 H4Ba2 G9Ba8
D4Rb6 F7Rb1 G4Rb9 H6Rb3 J9Rb2 D3Cb1 F3Cb6
B4Cb3 B6Cb6 A7Cb9 G8Cb5 A9Bb1 D7Bb5 D8Bb9
B1Ca1 H8Ca1 B8Ca2 H9Ca9 A1Ra2

6	1479	1479	12579	125789	125789	159	3	129
5	8	1379	123679	1279	123679	19	269	4
13	139	2	13569	159	4	7	569	8
7	459	49	259	3	2589	6	1	29
123	13459	1349	12579	6	125789	34589	24589	239
123	6	8	1259	4	1259	359	259	7
4	137	5	8	179	13679	2	9	139
9	13	13	12345	125	1235	1348	7	6
138	2	1367	134679	179	13679	13489	489	5

J1Ca8 J3Ca6 A5Ca8 D6Ra8 G6Ra6 H7Ra8 E8Ba8
G2Ba7 G8Rb9 G5Cb1 J8Cb4 G9Bb3 H4Ca4 E7Ca4
A9Ca1 J7Ra1 B8Ba2 F7Ba3 B7Rb9 F8Rb5 B5Cb7
A7Cb5 C8Cb6 J5Bb9 A3Ca7 B4Ca6 H5Ca2 A2Ra4
H6Ra5 C2Ba9 D3Ba4 C5Rb5 D2Rb5 E3Ca9 E4Ca5
E6Ra7 D9Ba9 J4Ba7 D4Rb2 E9Rb2 J6Rb3 A4Cb9
B6Cb1 B3Bb3 A6Bb2 C4Bb3 F4Bb1 F6Bb9 F1Ca2
E1Ca3 H3Ca1 C1Ra1 E2Ra1 H2Ra3

5	489	7	2	68	68	49	1	3468
129	1289	3	16789	4	5	279	289	2678
1249	6	1289	3	78	178	2479	24589	24578
12369	7	5	16	236	1346	8	2349	234
8	23	26	567	9	3467	24	2345	1
1239	1239	4	158	2358	138	6	7	235
12347	12348	128	578	3578	9	1247	6	2478
23679	2389	2689	4	1	3678	5	28	278
1467	5	168	678	678	2	3	48	9

B4Ca9 G7Ca1 A9Ra3 B9Ra6 C6Ba1 D8Ba9 J3Ca1
E8Ca3 B7Ra7 E4Ra5 C5Ba7 E6Ba7 F9Ba5 G5Ba5
E2Rb2 E3Cb6 E7Cb4 A7Bb9 D9Bb2 F5Ca2 D6Ca4
C7Ca2 C8Ca5 A2Ra4 B1Ra2 B2Ba1 C9Ba4 H6Ba3
H8Ba2 B8Rb8 C1Rb9 F6Rb8 C3Cb8 F4Cb1 A6Cb6
J8Cb4 A5Bb8 F1Bb3 D4Bb6 G3Bb2 H3Bb9 D1Ca1
G1Ca4 G2Ca3 F2Ca9 D5Ca3 J5Ca6 H1Ra6 J4Ra8
J1Ba7 H2Ba8 G4Ba7 G9Rb8 H9Rb7

5	4	2789	6	137	17	2379	1237	1239
3	9	679	2	157	1457	8	167	19
678	1	2678	3478	9	47	23467	2367	5
89	7	2389	3459	2356	24569	1	236	2389
4	6	1239	139	8	129	239	5	7
189	2389	5	1379	12367	12679	2369	4	2389
2	359	13679	1579	4	15679	357	8	13
179	359	4	1579	1257	8	2357	1237	6
1678	58	1678	157	12567	3	257	9	4

F2Ca2 C4Ca8 C7Ca4 A3Ra8 B6Ra4 C8Ra3 C3Ba2
A5Ba3 B5Ba5 B8Ba6 D4Ba4 B2Rb9 C6Rb7 D8Rb2
C1Cb6 B3Cb7 D5Cb6 A6Cb1 B9Cb1 A8Bb7 F6Bb9
G9Bb3 H2Ca3 J2Ca8 E6Ca2 G6Ca6 F7Ca6 H8Ca1
A9Ca2 A7Ra9 D3Ra3 D6Ra5 F4Ra3 J3Ra6 F5Ba7
E7Ba3 D9Ba9 G2Ba5 D1Rb8 E4Rb1 F9Rb8 G7Rb7
H5Rb2 F1Cb1 E3Cb9 G4Cb9 J5Cb1 H7Cb5 G3Bb1
J1Bb7 H4Bb7 J7Bb2 H1Ca9 J4Ca5

9	6	245	1247	3	1247	578	578	78
7	1	235	8	6	269	3569	569	4
4	38	34	4679	5	4679	1	6789	2
2	279	2679	5	468	24689	246789	3	1
125	2359	123569	12469	7	124689	245689	5689	689
8	4	125679	1269	16	3	25679	5679	679
3	579	8	1467	2	1467	679	1679	679
6	79	1479	147	148	5	789	2	3
12	27	127	1367	9	1678	678	4	5

C1Ca4 E1Ca5 C2Ca8 J4Ca3 B7Ca3 G8Ca1 C3Ra3
G2Ra5 E2Ba3 H3Ba4 B5Rb6 D1Rb2 J1Cb1 F5Cb1
H5Bb8 J2Ca2 E3Ca1 D5Ca4 A6Ca1 A4Ra4 C8Ra6
E7Ra4 H4Ra1 J7Ra8 B6Ba2 B8Ba9 F7Ba2 H2Ba9
G6Ba4 B3Rb5 D2Rb7 E8Rb8 H7Rb7 J3Rb7 A3Cb2
J6Cb6 A7Cb5 A8Bb7 E6Bb9 G4Bb7 E4Ca2 C4Ca9
C6Ca7 D6Ca8 F8Ca5 F9Ca7 A9Ca8 E9Ra6 F3Ra9
D3Ba6 F4Ba6 D7Ba9 G7Ba6 G9Rb9

12348	2458	1245	2358	13	9	345	6	7
1346	45	1456	357	1367	156	8	2	3459
2368	7	9	4	36	2568	35	1	35
4679	45	4567	1	2	46	34569	8	34569
12469	24	8	39	5	46	7	34	123469
12469	3	12456	9	8	7	24569	45	124569
2478	6	247	2578	47	3	1	9	2458
2478	1	3	25789	479	2458	2456	457	24568
5	9	247	6	147	1248	234	347	2348

A2Ca8 H5Ca9 B9Ra9 C6Ra8 A4Ba2 A7Ba4 E4Ba3
E8Rb4 F4Rb9 E2Cb2 E6Cb6 F8Cb5 D6Bb4 E9Bb1
H8Bb7 B2Ca4 D7Ca9 J8Ca3 A3Ra5 C1Ra2 D9Ra3
E1Ra9 J9Ra8 C7Ba3 D2Ba5 C5Rb6 C9Rb5 J7Rb2
J6Cb1 F7Cb6 G9Cb4 B6Bb5 F9Bb2 G5Bb7 H7Bb5
H9Bb6 D1Ca7 G3Ca2 G4Ca5 B4Ca7 J5Ca4 H6Ca2
D3Ra6 G1Ra8 H1Ra4 J3Ra7 B1Ba6 F3Ba4 H4Ba8
B3Rb1 F1Rb1 A1Cb3 B5Cb3 A5Bb1

256	125	126	1257	8	127	4	1236	13679
9	1245	124	6	2457	3	127	12	8
7	3	12468	9	24	124	5	126	16
2345	6	7	2358	2345	24	1238	9	134
2345	2459	234	23578	1	24679	2378	2348	347
234	8	1234	237	23479	2479	6	5	1347
3468	4	9	13	3	5	138	7	2
1	27	236	4	2379	8	39	36	5
2348	247	5	1237	6	1279	1389	1348	1349

E2Ca9 C3Ca8 E6Ca6 A9Ra9 G1Ra6 A3Ba6 A8Ba3
B7Ba7 F3Ba1 J1Ba8 H8Ba6 G2Rb4 G5Rb3 G4Cb1
G7Bb8 E8Ca8 C9Ca6 D4Ra8 B3Ba4 H3Ba3 E3Rb2
H7Rb9 E7Cb3 J7Bb1 A1Ca2 F4Ca3 F5Ca9 D7Ca2
J8Ca4 D9Ca1 J9Ca3 D1Ra3 F6Ra2 J6Ra9 E1Ba5
E4Ba7 A4Rb5 D6Rb4 E9Rb4 F1Rb4 J4Rb2 A2Cb1
J2Cb7 B5Cb2 D5Cb5 H5Cb7 C6Cb1 F9Cb7 B2Bb5
A6Bb7 C5Bb4 B8Bb1 C8Bb2 H2Bb2

16	7	23	126	8	146	1249	39	5
16	4	9	126	1256	7	8	3	12
18	1258	258	3	1245	9	6	7	1247
16789	1689	78	12689	1256	1568	12579	4	3
2	169	4	169	7	13456	159	569	8
5	3	478	12689	1246	1468	1279	679	12679
789	589	1	4	36	2	579	56789	679
4789	89	6	5	1	18	3	2	479
3	258	24578	678	9	68	457	1	467

H1Ca4 A3Ca3 J4Ca7 G5Ca3 E6Ca3 G8Ca8 B8Ra3
B5Ra5 E3Ra4 G9Ra6 H9Ra7 C8Ba7 D6Ba5 G1Ba7
J6Ba6 G7Ba9 A8Rb9 G2Rb5 H5Rb1 J9Rb4 H6Cb8
J7Cb5 F8Cb6 E7Bb1 E8Bb5 H2Bb9 D1Ca9 C3Ca5
D5Ca6 A7Ca4 F9Ca9 A4Ra2 C5Ra4 E2Ra6 E4Ra9
C2Ba2 B4Ba6 D2Ba1 F5Ba2 F6Ba4 A6Rb1 B1Rb1
C9Rb1 D4Rb8 F7Rb7 J2Rb8 A1Cb6 C1Cb8 D3Cb7
F3Cb8 J3Cb2 F4Cb1 D7Cb2 B9Cb2

79	1379	8	1279	267	4	136	5	167
457	1357	135	127	8	1257	9	1237	167
579	6	2	179	57	3	4	178	178
1	5789	59	2379	2357	6	58	4	5789
3	5789	569	479	1	579	568	789	2
25679	4	569	8	257	2579	156	179	3
89	1389	4	5	37	178	2	6	189
568	1358	7	1234	9	128	1358	138	1458
589	2	1359	6	34	18	7	1389	14589

F1Ca2 B1Ca4 J5Ca4 A5Ca6 B8Ca2 A4Ra2 B9Ra6
E4Ra4 H9Ra4 H1Ra6 C4Ba9 A7Ba3 D5Ba2 H6Ba2
G5Ca3 D4Ra3 G6Ra7 F5Ba7 J6Ba8 C5Rb5 H4Rb1
C1Cb7 B4Cb7 B6Cb1 A1Bb9 J1Ca5 G1Ca8 J3Ca1
F7Ca1 E8Ca7 A9Ra7 D2Ra7 F3Ra6 G9Ra1 H7Ra5
J8Ra3 A2Ba1 C8Ba1 E2Ba8 D9Ba5 E7Ba6 H2Ba3
G2Ba9 H8Ba8 J9Ba9 B2Rb5 C9Rb8 D3Rb9 D7Rb8
F8Rb9 B3Cb3 E3Cb5 F6Cb5 E6Bb9

4	8	27	9	12567	2567	3	17	5
136	1367	9	135678	1567	35678	78	4	2
123	5	237	12378	4	2378	6	1789	89
8	12379	5	123467	12679	234679	279	3679	369
1239	12379	6	12357	8	23579	4	379	39
239	2379	2347	23467	2679	234679	5	36789	1
569	69	1	45678	3	456789	89	2	4689
7	4	23	2568	2569	25689	1	3689	3689
2369	2369	8	246	269	1	9	5	7

```
G1Ca5 F3Ca4 D7Ca2 G9Ca4 A9Ca5 F8Ra8 J4Ra4
D6Ba4 J7Rb9 G7Cb8 B7Bb7 C9Ca8 C8Ra9 A8Ba1
G2Ba9 C3Ca3 J5Ra2 A3Ba7 H3Ba2 A5Rb6 A6Cb2
C6Bb7 C1Ra2 G4Ra7 G6Ba6 C4Rb1 B5Cb5 H5Bb9
D5Ca1 D9Ra9 F4Ra6 E4Ba2 F5Ba7 D8Ba6 D4Rb3
E9Rb3 H8Rb3 D2Cb7 B4Cb8 F6Cb9 E8Cb7 H9Cb6
B6Bb3 E2Bb1 F1Bb3 E6Bb5 H4Bb5 B1Ca1 E1Ca9
F2Ca2 J2Ca3 H6Ca8 B2Ra6 J1Ra6
```

179	5	137	4	2	137	8	6	79
1789	14789	2	6	1579	157	4579	457	3
679	3479	3467	359	3579	8	1	457	2
125789	6	1378	23589	13589	4	2357	12578	1578
125789	134789	13478	23589	6	135	23457	124578	14578
1258	1348	1348	7	1358	135	2345	9	14568
3	78	9	1	578	567	2457	24578	4578
4	178	178	358	3578	2	6	1578	15789
1678	2	5	8	4	9	7	3	178

```
C3Ca6 G6Ca6 B7Ca9 F9Ca6 A1Ra9 H9Ra9 J1Ra6
E2Ba9 A9Rb7 C1Rb7 J4Rb8 J7Rb7 J9Cb1 B6Ca7
G8Ca2 H8Ca8 G2Ra8 B1Ba8 H2Ca7 G5Ra7 H3Ra1
B2Ba1 A3Rb3 B5Rb5 C2Cb4 H5Cb3 A6Cb1 B8Cb4
C5Bb9 C8Bb5 F2Bb3 H4Bb5 D4Ca9 E6Ca3 C4Ra3
D7Ra3 E4Ba2 F6Ba5 F7Ca2 D1Ra2 F3Ra4 E1Ba5
E7Rb4 F1Rb1 F5Cb8 G7Cb5 E9Cb8 E3Bb7 D5Bb1
D9Bb5 G9Bb4 D3Ca8 E8Ca1 D8Ca7
```

1569	129	1269	3	1789	278	79	4	5679
3469	2349	2369	2479	479	5	379	1	8
7	1349	8	6	149	4	2	359	359
2	3489	39	1	34578	3478	6	3579	3579
13469	7	1369	4	2	34	139	8	1359
136	138	5	78	3678	9	137	237	4
139	139	4	789	3789	6	5	379	2
8	6	12379	5	3479	2347	13479	379	1379
39	5	2379	24789	34789	1	34789	3679	3679

```
A1Ca5 D5Ca5 F5Ca6 J7Ca8 F8Ca2 J8Ca6 E9Ra5
C8Ba5 A9Ba6 H7Ba4 C6Rb4 E4Rb4 E6Cb3 B1Ca4
J5Ca4 H9Ca1 B3Ra6 D2Ra4 E1Ba6 F2Ba8 F4Rb7
D6Cb8 D3Ca3 G4Ca8 A5Ra8 F7Ra3 C5Ba1 C9Ba3
E3Ba9 E7Ba1 A3Rb1 C2Rb9 F1Rb1 A2Cb2 B2Bb3
A6Bb7 G2Ca1 G5Ca7 H6Ca2 B7Ca7 A7Ra9 B4Ra2
H3Ra7 J3Ra2 J1Ra3 B5Ba9 G1Ba9 H5Ba3 J9Ba7
D9Rb9 G8Rb3 H8Rb9 J4Rb9 D8Cb7
```

5	126	169	4	1678	12678	3	127	78
8	3	14	125	157	9	127	6	47
24	1246	7	1238	1368	1268	128	5	9
1	9	4568	58	4568	3	25678	247	45678
347	467	34568	1589	2	1568	56789	479	45678
24	246	4568	7	45689	568	25689	3	1
6	8	139	12359	13579	1257	4	179	57
3479	5	1349	6	1379	17	179	8	2
79	17	2	1589	15789	4	15679	179	3

```
A3Ra9 J7Ra6 B9Ba4 G9Ba5 B3Rb1 G3Cb3 H3Bb4
E1Ca3 J2Ca1 C4Ca3 H5Ra3 E2Ba7 B5Ra5 E8Ra4
J4Ba5 B4Rb2 D4Rb8 J5Rb8 B7Cb7 A9Bb8 G6Ca2
C6Ca8 D9Ca7 D5Ra4 E9Ba6 D8Rb2 D7Cb5 A8Cb1
C7Bb2 D3Bb6 F1Ca2 H7Ca1 A2Ra2 C5Ra1 F2Ra4
H1Ra9 C1Ba4 C2Ba6 J1Ba7 G4Ba1 E4Rb9 H6Rb7
J8Rb9 F5Cb6 G5Cb9 A6Cb6 E7Cb8 G8Cb7 A5Bb7
E3Bb5 F6Bb5 F7Bb9 F3Ca8 E6Ca1
```

2	8	479	4679	9	1479	3	1456	4569
3469	3679	5	246789	289	124789	1289	1246	24689
469	69	1	5	3	2489	289	7	24689
589	29	6	289	7	3	259	245	1
1359	4	39	29	6	259	259	8	2579
7	239	389	1	4	2589	6	235	259
389	5	3789	23789	1	6	4	2	28
134689	1369	3489	23489	2589	24589	7	1256	2568
1468	167	2	478	58	4578	158	9	3

F8Ca3 E9Ca7 D8Ra4 E1Ra1 E3Ba3 D1Ba5 A5Rb9
G8Rb2 G9Cb8 D4Ra8 F3Ba8 C2Rb6 J1Ra6 H3Ba4
H1Ba8 A3Rb7 B2Cb3 G3Cb9 G1Bb3 H2Bb1 J2Ca7
H4Ca3 G4Ra7 H6Ra9 J7Ra1 B6Ba7 E4Ba9 H5Ba2
B5Rb8 J4Rb4 A4Cb6 J5Cb5 B4Bb2 J6Bb8 A6Ca1
E7Ca5 C7Ca8 A9Ra4 B8Ra1 C9Ra2 E6Ra2 F6Ra5
C6Ba4 A8Ba5 B9Ba6 D7Ba2 B7Rb9 C1Rb9 D2Rb9
F9Rb9 H8Rb6 H9Rb5 B1Cb4 F2Cb2

2578	2478	2578	3	24589	4589	4579	1	6
357	9	3567	156	1456	456	457	2	8
1	248	2568	25689	245689	7	459	459	3
23578	6	1	4	25789	589	2579	579	279
257	27	4	2569	3	569	8	579	1279
2578	278	25789	2589	25789	1	6	3	2479
6	238	238	7	1489	3489	12349	49	5
9	1	237	56	456	3456	2347	8	247
4	5	378	1689	1689	2	1379	679	179

G2Ca3 F3Ca9 J8Ca6 D1Ra3 E9Ra1 F9Ra4 J7Ra3
B3Ba3 H6Ba3 G7Ba1 C3Ca6 G3Ra2 H7Ra4 C8Ba4
J3Ba8 H9Ba2 G8Rb9 H3Rb7 A3Cb5 J9Cb7 B1Bb7
D9Bb9 A2Ca4 D7Ca2 A7Ra7 C7Ba9 B7Rb5 H4Ca5
D6Ca5 C5Ra5 D5Ra8 F1Ra5 H5Ra6 F2Ba8 F5Ba7
E8Ba5 G6Ba8 A6Rb9 C2Rb2 D8Rb7 E1Rb2 F4Rb2
G5Rb4 A1Cb8 E2Cb7 C4Cb8 A5Cb2 B5Cb1 E6Cb6
B4Bb6 B6Bb4 E4Bb9 J5Bb9 J4Ca1

389	6	1	378	3457	2	4789	478	479
2389	389	34789	6	1347	478	124789	5	1479
28	5	478	178	9	478	6	3	147
7	38	3568	238	234	1	34	9	3456
4	1389	3589	3789	6	789	137	7	2
1369	2	369	5	347	479	1347	467	8
3569	4	2	79	8	5679	379	1	3679
15689	7	5689	129	125	3	489	468	469
13689	1389	3689	4	17	679	5	2	3679

G6Ca5 B7Ca2 D9Ca5 A5Ra5 C1Ra2 D3Ra6 E3Ra5
F8Ba6 H1Ba5 J6Ba6 E8Rb7 G1Ca6 H9Ra6 G4Ba9
A7Ca9 H3Ra9 A8Ba8 J5Ba7 J9Ba9 A1Rb3 F3Rb3
H8Rb4 D2Cb8 J3Cb8 A4Cb7 F5Cb4 H7Cb8 B2Bb9
A9Bb4 F7Bb1 J1Bb1 B1Ca8 F1Ca9 E2Ca1 J2Ca3
F6Ca7 D7Ca4 G7Ca7 G9Ca3 B5Ra3 E6Ra9 C4Ba1
E4Ba8 E7Ba3 B6Rb4 C9Rb7 D5Rb2 H4Rb2 B3Cb7
C3Cb4 D4Cb3 H5Cb1 C6Cb8 B9Cb1

2346	3468	7	4689	89	1	469	5	23469
12346	5	9	467	7	246	8	12367	12346
1246	468	1468	46789	5	3	14679	1267	12469
8	369	356	1	2	7	569	4	3569
134579	3479	1345	9	6	59	159	1238	123589
1569	2	156	3	4	8	1569	16	7
345679	346789	34568	2	1	469	4567	678	4568
4567	4678	2	4678	78	46	3	9	14568
34679	1	3468	5	3789	469	2	678	468

J5Ca3 B6Ca2 E6Ca5 H9Ra1 E4Ba9 B5Rb7 E7Rb1
H5Cb8 F8Cb6 A5Bb9 H4Ca7 H1Ra5 B8Ca3 B1Ra1
C9Ra9 G9Ra5 C8Ba1 F3Ba1 D9Ba3 F1Rb9 D2Cb6
F7Cb5 D3Bb5 D7Bb9 H2Bb4 G2Ca9 E8Ca2 C1Ra2
C7Ra7 E9Ra8 H6Ra6 J6Ra9 A9Ba2 G6Ba4 C2Rb8
G7Rb6 A2Cb3 A7Cb4 J9Cb4 A1Bb6 B9Bb6 E2Bb7
E1Ca4 J3Ca6 C4Ca6 A4Ca8 B4Ra4 C3Ra4 E3Ra3
J8Ra8 G1Ba3 G3Ba8 G8Ba7 J1Rb7

3	4	256	7	1268	9	156	1568	1568
128	12568	256	246	12468	128	7	3	9
189	168	7	5	13468	138	16	2	1468
2479	235	8	1	23569	23	3569	4567	3456
6	135	3459	39	7	38	1359	145	2
1279	1235	2359	2369	23569	4	8	1567	1356
28	7	236	239	1239	5	4	168	1368
5	9	1	234	234	237	236	68	368
24	23	234	8	1234	6	1235	9	7

H6Ca7 C1Ra9 E6Ra8 J7Ra5 C9Ba4 G3Ba6 G1Ba8
H7Ba2 G8Rb1 G9Cb3 F3Ca9 F9Ca1 A3Ra2 B3Ra5
E2Ra1 J5Ra1 B1Ba1 A5Rb6 B6Rb2 E3Rb4 D1Cb7
J3Cb3 B4Cb4 D6Cb3 A7Cb1 E8Cb5 B5Bb8 C6Bb1
A8Bb8 C7Bb6 F1Bb2 E4Bb9 D7Bb9 D8Bb4 D9Bb6
J2Bb2 H4Bb3 J1Ca4 F2Ca3 B2Ca6 C2Ca8 G4Ca2
F4Ca6 C5Ca3 H5Ca4 G5Ca9 E7Ca3 H8Ca6 F8Ca7
A9Ca5 H9Ca8 D5Ra2 F5Ra5 D2Ba5

2	148	3	1468	14689	7	5	468	46
6	458	478	2458	2458	248	378	9	1
1578	9	1478	3	14568	1468	2	4678	467
1358	7	18	12568	123568	12368	4	3568	9
1358	13568	189	124568	7	1234689	368	3568	256
4	3568	2	568	35689	3689	3678	1	567
1378	1348	6	1478	1348	5	79	2	47
9	2	1478	14678	1468	1468	67	4567	3
37	34	5	9	2346	2346	1	467	8

E3Ca9 G7Ca9 E9Ca2 A5Ra9 B7Ra3 H8Ra5 F6Ba9
F9Ba5 B3Ra7 F7Ra7 H7Rb6 E7Cb8 H4Ra7 G5Ba3
F2Ra3 E2Ba6 J1Ba3 E8Rb3 J2Rb4 D8Cb6 J8Cb7
G9Bb4 G1Ca7 B2Ca5 C3Ca4 D6Ca3 C9Ca7 C5Ra5
A8Ba4 A9Ba6 C8Rb8 C1Cb1 A2Bb8 C6Bb6 E1Bb5
D1Ca8 G2Ca1 D4Ca5 F4Ca6 A4Ra1 D5Ra2 F5Ra8
G4Ra8 J5Ra6 B6Ba8 D3Ba1 E6Ba1 H3Ba8 J6Ba2
B5Rb4 E4Rb4 H6Rb4 B4Cb2 H5Cb1

3478	3478	13478	4679	689	3489	13456	2	13568
3478	2	5	467	1	348	9	468	368
9	348	6	24	5	2348	134	7	138
1	3457	2347	8	29	259	3467	469	3679
268	9	28	3	4	7	16	5	168
34578	34578	3478	159	9	6	1347	1489	2
257	1	27	2569	3	259	8	69	4
458	458	9	1456	7	1458	2	3	156
234578	6	23478	12459	289	124589	157	19	1579

E1Ca6 A3Ca1 A5Ca6 E3Ra2 F4Ba1 E7Rb1 F5Rb9
G3Rb7 D5Cb2 E9Cb8 D6Bb5 F8Bb4 J5Bb8 F3Ca8
D7Ca6 J8Ca1 B8Ca8 B9Ra6 C9Ra1 H6Ra1 G8Ba6
D8Rb9 H9Rb5 J7Cb7 A9Cb3 C7Bb4 D9Bb7 F7Bb3
J9Bb9 F2Ca5 H4Ca6 A7Ca5 F1Ra7 A2Ba7 C4Rb2
B1Ca3 B4Ca7 B6Ra4 C6Ra3 J3Ra3 A1Ba4 A6Ba8
D2Ba3 J4Ba4 A4Rb9 C2Rb8 D3Rb4 H1Rb8 J6Rb2
J1Cb5 H2Cb4 G4Cb5 G6Cb9 G1Bb2

2789	289	3	27	25678	4	5689	1	2569
248	248	6	9	1258	125	7	3	25
5	2489	1	3	2678	26	689	24689	269
3	24569	24579	124	124	8	569	25679	125679
12468	2468	24	5	9	7	368	268	1236
12789	2589	2579	6	123	12	3589	25789	4
246	23456	245	247	24567	9	1	567	8
269	7	8	12	1256	3	4	569	569
469	1	459	8	4567	56	2	5679	35679

G2Ca3 F5Ca3 C8Ca4 C5Ra7 J9Ra3 A1Ba7 E7Ba3
G4Ba7 A4Rb2 H4Cb1 C6Cb6 D4Bb4 J6Bb5 F6Ca2
D9Ca7 D5Ra1 F1Ra1 F3Ra7 J8Ra7 B6Ba1 E9Ba1
G3Ba5 G8Rb6 J1Ca9 A9Ca6 J5Ra6 D7Ba6 H1Ba6
G5Ba4 G1Rb2 H5Rb2 J3Rb4 E3Cb2 D3Bb9 E8Bb8
B1Ca8 E2Ca6 D8Ca2 B2Ra4 C7Ra8 D2Ra5 E1Ra4
F2Ra8 C2Ba2 A5Ba8 A2Rb9 B5Rb5 C9Rb9 A7Cb5
B9Cb2 H9Cb5 F7Bb9 H8Bb9 F8Ca5

134789	3578	13489	56789	2	15679	146	56	1456
178	6	18	578	78	4	9	3	125
149	2	149	569	3	1569	8	56	7
23678	4	5	1	67	2367	236	9	2368
236789	378	2389	235679	4	235679	1236	268	12368
2369	1	239	2369	69	8	5	7	2346
5	38	7	23689	1	2369	236	4	23689
238	9	6	4	78	237	237	1	2358
12348	38	12348	236789	5	23679	2367	268	23689

A2Ca5 F5Ca9 A7Ca4 B9Ra2 F9Ra4 H9Ra5 A9Ba1
C8Ba5 A8Rb6 E2Ca7 D5Ca6 C6Ca1 E6Ca5 E7Ca1
B4Ra5 C4Ra6 D6Ra7 F1Ra6 E9Ba6 H1Ba2 A6Rb9
H6Rb3 H7Cb7 H5Bb8 A4Ca8 B5Ca7 A1Ra7 D7Ra2
J4Ra7 A3Ba3 D9Ba3 G4Ba9 J8Ba2 D1Rb8 E8Rb8
F3Rb2 G9Rb8 J6Rb6 B1Cb1 G2Cb3 E3Cb9 F4Cb3
G6Cb2 J7Cb3 J9Cb9 B3Bb8 C3Bb4 E1Bb3 E4Bb2
J1Bb4 J2Bb8 G7Bb6 C1Ca9 J3Ca1

24568	458	1	7	23689	345689	2349	46	2369
2456	457	24567	124569	12369	34569	2349	8	2369
9	3	246	2468	268	468	7	5	1
24	1	8	3	5	69	24	467	267
245	6	2459	289	7	89	1245	3	25
235	57	257	26	4	1	8	9	2567
7	9	3	1568	168	568	15	2	4
14568	2	456	145689	13689	3456789	1359	17	35789
1458	458	45	14589	1389	2	6	17	35789

F1Ca3 E3Ca9 H6Ca7 D6Ra9 E7Ra1 F4Ba6 E6Rb8
G7Rb5 H8Rb1 E4Cb2 G6Cb6 J8Cb7 C6Bb4 E9Bb5
J1Ca1 D9Ra7 E1Ra4 D8Ba6 A8Rb4 C4Rb8 D1Rb2
F9Rb2 G4Cb1 D7Cb4 G5Bb8 B5Ca1 B2Ca4 C3Ca2
B4Ca9 H9Ca8 B7Ra2 B3Ra7 C5Ra6 J2Ra8 A1Ba8
A5Ba2 F2Ba7 A2Rb5 F3Rb5 B1Cb6 J3Cb4 A6Cb3
B6Bb5 A7Bb9 B9Bb3 H1Bb5 H3Bb6 J4Bb5 H4Ca4
H7Ca3 A9Ca6 J9Ca9 H5Ra9 J5Ra3

79	129	4	8	15	156	267	3	25679
38	1238	5	136	9	7	268	26	4
3789	389	6	345	2	345	1	579	5789
34569	13469	13	2	1345	13459	467	8	15679
2	1489	18	1457	6	1459	47	14579	3
34569	7	13	1345	1345	8	246	124569	12569
3468	23468	9	1346	7	1346	5	1246	1268
1	246	27	9	8	456	3	2467	267
34678	5	378	1346	134	2	9	1467	1678

H3Ca2 E4Ca7 B7Ca8 H6Ra5 B1Rb3 E7Rb4 G2Ca3
J3Ca7 F4Ca5 E8Ra5 A5Ba5 D1Ba5 E3Rb8 E2Cb9
C2Bb8 E6Bb1 J5Ca1 D6Ca9 C9Ca5 A2Ra1 J4Ra3
B2Ba2 B4Ba1 C6Ba3 A6Rb6 B8Rb6 C4Rb4 G4Cb6
G6Cb4 J8Cb4 G1Bb8 H8Bb7 F1Ca4 J9Ca8 C1Ra7
D5Ra4 H2Ra4 J1Ra6 A1Ba9 D2Ba6 F5Ba3 H9Ba6
C8Rb9 D7Rb7 F3Rb1 D3Cb3 A7Cb2 F8Cb2 D9Cb1
A9Bb7 F7Bb6 F9Bb9 G8Bb1 G9Bb2

4678	1	478	2	349	5	6789	34689	4679
9	268	2478	1347	134	37	5	3468	12467
247	3	2457	6	149	8	1279	49	12479
5	7	28	4	24689	269	3	1	69
238	289	1	35	7	2369	4	69	569
3	4	6	135	1359	39	79	2	8
23467	26	2347	8	236	1	269	5	2469
124678	2568	9	57	256	267	1268	468	3
12368	2568	2358	9	2356	4	1268	7	126

E2Ca9 D5Ca8 E9Ca5 C3Ra5 D4Ra4 E1Ra8 F7Ra7
D3Ba2 F1Ba3 D9Ba9 D6Rb6 E4Rb3 E8Rb6 F6Rb9
E6Cb2 H6Bb7 B4Ca7 B6Ca3 A8Ra3 G7Ra9 C8Ba9
H4Rb5 F4Cb1 F5Bb5 J2Ca5 A5Ca9 H2Ca8 B5Ra1
J7Ra8 C5Ba4 B8Ba8 A7Rb6 B3Rb4 H8Rb4 J3Rb3
A1Cb7 G3Cb7 B9Cb2 A3Bb8 B2Bb6 C1Bb2 A9Bb4
C7Bb1 G9Bb6 G1Ca4 G2Ca2 G5Ca3 H7Ca2 J9Ca1
C9Ca7 H1Ra1 J5Ra2 J1Ba6 H5Ba6

47	1457	2	145	3	9	6	17	8
3467	8	3567	12456	145	1246	129	1379	12379
9	16	36	126	18	7	5	4	123
24	2459	59	3	1489	148	7	1589	6
3467	45679	35679	1467	2	1468	1489	13589	1359
1	24679	8	467	479	5	249	39	239
267	3	1	8	57	2	9	5679	4
678	679	679	1457	1457	134	189	2	1579
5	27	4	9	6	12	3	178	17

H1Ca8 H6Ca3 G8Ca6 C5Ra8 G5Ra5 G7Ra9 J8Ra8
E7Ba8 H9Ba5 G6Rb2 H7Rb1 G1Cb7 J6Cb1 B7Cb2
J9Cb7 A1Bb4 F7Bb4 J2Bb2 D1Ca2 C4Ca2 D6Ca8
F9Ca2 F8Ra3 C2Ca1 C3Ra6 B1Ba3 H2Ba6 C9Rb3
E1Rb6 H3Rb9 D3Cb5 E6Cb4 B3Bb7 B6Bb6 D2Ca4
A2Ca5 E3Ca3 F4Ca6 E8Ca5 A8Ca7 A4Ra1 B4Ra5
B5Ba4 D5Ba1 D8Rb9 E4Rb7 H5Rb7 E2Cb9 H4Cb4
F5Cb9 B8Cb1 E9Cb1 B9Bb9 F2Bb7

456	456	145	8	2367	2367	12345	1356	9
8	7	149	1269	2369	5	1234	136	2346
569	3	2	169	69	4	158	7	68
1	2	45789	4679	3456789	36789	389	368	368
3	489	6	249	1	289	7	8	5
59	589	5789	2679	2356789	236789	2389	4	1
245	1	458	3	2478	278	6	9	48
469	4689	3489	5	4689	689	1348	2	7
7	45689	34589	2469	24689	1	3458	358	348

G1Ca2 B9Ca2 G3Ra5 H7Ra1 F7Ba2 E8Rb8 F6Ca3
D7Ca9 C4Ra1 D5Ra5 H3Ra3 B5Ba3 B7Rb4 H6Ca6
J2Ra6 E6Ca9 E4Ra2 D4Ba4 J5Ba2 A5Rb7 E2Rb4
J4Rb9 A2Cb5 B4Cb6 A6Cb2 C5Bb9 A7Bb3 B8Bb1
F4Bb7 F1Ca5 A3Ca1 D3Ca7 F5Ca6 G6Ca7 J8Ca5
A1Ra4 B3Ra9 C7Ra5 D6Ra8 J9Ra3 C1Ba6 C9Ba8
F2Ba9 D8Ba3 J3Ba4 G9Ba4 A8Rb6 D9Rb6 F3Rb8
G5Rb8 H1Rb9 H2Rb8 J7Rb8 H5Cb4

8	2	69	3469	1	345	579	49	4579
1569	7	169	2469	24589	2458	3	1249	1459
4	1359	19	7	259	235	8	6	159
23679	369	4	8	279	1	2679	5	379
125679	1569	12679	249	3	247	12679	1289	1789
12379	8	1279	5	279	6	4	129	1379
127	4	3	12	2578	9	15	18	6
1269	169	5	1234	248	2348	19	7	1489
179	19	1789	14	6	4578	159	3	2

J3Ca8 C2Ba3 B8Ba2 H9Ba4 E2Ca5 B5Ca4 A7Ca7
A8Ca4 E9Ca8 B6Ra8 B1Ba5 G8Ba8 H5Ca8 J7Ra5
G5Ba5 H7Ba9 G7Rb1 G4Cb2 G1Bb7 H6Bb3 H1Ca2
A4Ca3 C6Ca2 A3Ra6 C9Ra5 H2Ra6 J6Ra7 A6Ba5
B4Ba6 B9Ba1 J4Ba4 A9Rb9 B3Rb9 C5Rb9 D2Rb9
E4Rb9 E6Rb4 H4Rb1 J2Cb1 C3Cb1 E8Cb1 E1Bb6
F8Bb9 J1Bb9 F1Ca1 D7Ca6 D5Ra2 E3Ra7 F9Ra3
F3Ba2 D1Ba3 F5Ba7 E7Ba2 D9Ba7

1	347	47	8	2356	3456	34567	23457	9
34	349	2	1349	7	13456	3456	3458	346
5	8	6	2349	239	34	347	1	2347
46	2456	145	139	39	7	8	23459	2346
9	67	78	5	4	2	367	37	1
478	2457	3	6	89	18	457	24579	247
3478	1	4789	347	38	348	2	6	5
34678	34567	4578	2347	1	34568	9	347	347
2	34567	457	347	356	9	1347	347	8

B2Ca9 D3Ca1 G3Ca9 J7Ca1 B8Ca8 E3Ra8 F6Ra1
H4Ra2 B4Ba1 F5Ba8 G5Rb3 D5Cb9 C5Bb2 D4Bb3
C4Ca9 F8Ca9 A8Ra2 G6Ca8 D8Ca5 F2Ra5 H1Ra8
D2Ba2 B1Ca3 D1Ca6 A2Ca4 F9Ca2 A3Ra7 D9Ra4
E7Ra6 B9Ba6 F1Ba4 E8Ba3 G1Ba7 E2Rb7 F7Rb7
G4Rb4 J4Cb7 J8Bb4 H3Ca4 H8Ca7 C9Ra7 H6Ra5
J2Ra3 A5Ba5 J3Ba5 H2Ba6 J5Ba6 H9Ba3 A7Rb3
B6Rb4 A6Cb6 C6Cb3 B7Cb5 C7Cb4

157	3	169	157	569	8	4	126	156
1457	2	1468	1357	356	3567	1356	136	9
15	159	169	4	3569	2	8	136	7
1237	6	5	238	4	39	137	137	138
9	478	48	358	1	356	367	3467	2
1234	148	1248	238	7	36	9	5	13468
8	459	3	6	25	1	257	247	45
6	145	124	23578	2358	3457	12357	9	1345
1245	145	7	9	235	345	12356	8	13456

E2Ca7 H5Ca8 D6Ca9 A8Ra2 B3Ra8 G2Ra9 B1Ba4

F2Ba8 E3Rb4 A1Ca7 E4Ca8 G8Ca4 D9Ca8 E6Ra5

F9Ra4 F6Ra6 G7Ra7 D8Ba7 B8Rb1 D7Rb1 G9Rb5

G5Cb2 A9Cb6 A3Bb9 C8Bb3 C3Ca6 A4Ca1 C5Ca9

B7Ca5 E8Ca6 A5Ra5 B5Ra6 E7Ra3 J7Ra6 B6Ba3

H4Ba5 H7Ba2 B4Rb7 H3Rb1 J5Rb3 J6Rb4 H2Cb4

J2Cb5 F3Cb2 H6Cb7 H9Cb3 J9Cb1 C2Bb1 D1Bb3

F4Bb3 J1Bb2 F1Ca1 C1Ca5 D4Ca2

1	34569	34569	4569	2	7	3589	5689	368
346	8	34569	14569	456	34569	2	569	7
236	23569	7	569	8	3569	4	1	36
9	3456	3456	4568	4567	1	3578	45678	2
23468	123456	13456	24568	9	24568	13578	45678	13468
7	12456	1456	3	456	24568	158	4568	9
4	7	8	2459	3	2459	6	249	14
5	1469	2	4689	46	4689	1789	3	148
346	3469	3469	7	1	24689	89	2489	5

E1Ca8 B4Ca1 D5Ca7 G9Ra1 H7Ra7 E8Ba7 H2Ba1

G1Rb4 C1Ca2 J7Ra8 G8Ba9 H9Rb4 H5Cb6 J8Cb2

J6Bb4 A7Ca9 A9Ca8 C9Ba3 E9Rb6 B6Ca3 B3Ra9

F2Ra2 J2Ba9 B1Rb6 J1Cb3 C2Cb5 B8Cb5 B5Bb4

A8Bb6 J3Bb6 D2Ca6 E4Ca4 F5Ca5 A4Ra5 E6Ra2

F6Ra6 C4Ba6 D4Ba8 G4Ba2 G6Ba5 C6Rb9 D8Rb4

E2Rb3 F7Rb1 H4Rb9 A2Cb4 D3Cb5 F3Cb4 H6Cb8

E7Cb5 F8Cb8 A3Bb3 E3Bb1 D7Bb3

5	3468	3468	1348	2	1348	9	7	34
2389	23489	1	3478	6	5	2348	24	234
7	234689	234689	348	9	3489	234568	2456	1
289	7	2489	6	1	489	245	3	2459
123689	234689	234689	458	7	489	12456	124569	2459
169	5	469	4	3	2	146	8	479
4	2369	23569	12357	5	1367	1235	1259	8
2368	2368	23568	9	4	136	7	125	235
239	1	7	235	8	3	2345	2459	6

G5Ca5 C5Ca9 G6Ca7 F9Ca7 B4Ra7 E4Ba5 H3Ba5

H6Ba6 F4Rb4 J6Rb3 J4Cb2 J1Bb9 G4Bb1 A6Ca1

D9Ca5 B2Ra9 F3Ra9 G8Ra9 H8Ra1 C6Ba4 E9Ba9

E6Rb8 D6Cb9 B7Ca8 A4Ra8 C4Ba3 G7Ca3 B9Ca4

A9Ra3 B8Ra2 B1Ra3 H2Ba3 H9Ba2 H1Rb8 D1Cb2

E2Bb4 D7Bb4 C2Ca8 E3Ca3 A3Ca4 E7Ca2 J8Ca4

A2Ra6 C3Ra2 D3Ra8 E1Ra1 J7Ra5 C8Ba5 F1Ba6

F7Ba1 G2Ba2 G3Ba6 C7Rb6 E8Rb6

1	459	45	2	3	59	6	7	489
2369	23579	2567	689	5678	4	1	259	289
2469	8	24567	169	1567	15679	2459	2459	3
24	247	1247	5	1267	12679	3	8	12479
5	237	127	189	4	1279	279	129	6
248	6	9	18	1278	3	2457	1245	1247
7	2459	245	134	125	125	2489	6	12489
2469	2459	8	7	1256	1256	249	12349	1249
246	1	3	46	9	8	247	24	5

B1Ca3 F1Ca8 G4Ca3 G7Ca8 H8Ca3 A9Ra8 E2Ra3

E4Ra8 J7Ra7 B5Ba8 J4Ba4 F4Rb1 J8Rb2 J1Cb6

E8Ca1 D3Ra1 A6Ba5 A3Rb4 A2Cb9 C1Bb2 H1Ca9

B9Ra2 G9Ra9 E7Ba9 H9Ba1 D1Rb4 H7Rb4 C7Cb5

D9Cb7 C3Bb6 B8Bb9 D2Bb2 F7Bb2 F9Bb4 G2Ca4

B2Ca7 G3Ca2 B4Ca6 C4Ca9 D6Ca9 C8Ca4 F8Ca5

B3Ra5 D5Ra6 E6Ra2 F5Ra7 G5Ra5 C6Ba7 E3Ba7

H2Ba5 G6Ba1 H5Ba2 H6Ba6 C5Rb1

3569	3569	4	7	23568	5689	1	69	589
8	1	57	469	456	4569	3	2	579
35679	2	357	1369	3568	15689	567	679	4
1367	346	137	5	9	2	8	13467	137
23567	34568	2357	46	1	46	24567	34679	23579
1256	456	9	8	7	3	2456	146	125
4	359	1235	12369	2356	1569	27	8	1237
1239	7	8	12349	234	149	24	5	6
1235	35	6	1234	23458	7	9	134	123

E2Ca8 A9Ca8 A5Ra2 J5Ra8 C6Ba8 C4Ra1 C5Ba3
H5Rb4 H7Cb2 G7Bb7 J8Ra4 D2Ra4 F7Ra4 C7Ca6
B9Ba5 A8Rb9 B3Rb7 B5Rb6 E7Rb5 C3Cb5 G5Cb5
A6Cb5 C8Cb7 C1Bb9 E8Bb3 G2Ca9 E9Ca9 E1Ra7
F9Ba2 D9Ba7 E3Rb2 J1Ca2 A2Ca3 H6Ca1 A1Ra6
G4Ra2 H4Ra9 J9Ra1 J2Ra5 B6Ba9 F1Ba5 F2Ba6
G3Ba1 J4Ba3 G6Ba6 G9Ba3 B4Rb4 D3Rb3 E6Rb4
F8Rb1 H1Rb3 D1Cb1 E4Cb6 D8Cb6

59	459	24579	3	4578	458	127	1578	6
35	3456	234567	1	45678	458	237	9	378
1	3569	8	579	567	2	37	357	4
4	389	39	7	137	6	379	2	5
35	356	1	2457	9	345	8	3467	37
2	7	3569	8	345	345	3469	346	1
7	13489	349	6	1348	1348	5	1348	2
3589	2	3459	45	13458	7	13469	13468	389
6	13458	345	245	123458	9	1347	13478	378

H1Ca8 C4Ca9 J5Ca2 G6Ca1 H9Ca9 D5Ra1 D2Ra8
E4Ra2 D4Ba7 J2Ba1 G5Ba8 A1Ca9 F3Ca6 E8Ra6
F7Ra9 D3Ba9 F8Ba4 E9Ba7 H5Ba3 H7Ba6 D7Rb3
F5Rb5 G8Rb3 H8Rb1 G3Cb4 F6Cb3 C7Cb7 J9Cb8
C5Bb6 B7Bb2 B9Bb3 C8Bb5 E6Bb4 G2Bb9 H3Bb5
J7Bb4 J8Bb7 E1Ca3 B2Ca6 A3Ca2 J3Ca3 H4Ca4
J4Ca5 A7Ca1 A8Ca8 A5Ra7 B5Ra4 B6Ra8 C2Ra3
E2Ra5 A2Ba4 B1Ba5 B3Ba7 A6Ba5

4567	45789	45678	258	248	3	456	1	457
3	2	457	15	6	1457	9	45	8
4567	1	45678	58	48	9	2	345	3457
12457	4578	3	12589	12489	12458	1458	2458	6
1245	6	2458	12358	7	12458	13458	9	1345
9	458	2458	123568	12348	124568	7	23458	1345
256	5	1	4	2389	268	358	7	359
8	47	9	13	5	1	134	6	2
2456	3	2456	7	1289	1268	1458	458	1459

A2Ca9 F4Ca6 D4Ca9 B6Ca7 A7Ca6 B4Ra1 H2Ra7
D1Ba7 G2Rb5 H4Rb3 H6Rb1 H7Cb4 E1Ca1 J3Ca6
F5Ca3 C1Ra6 F9Ra1 G6Ra6 J1Ra4 B3Ba4 D5Ba1
G1Ba2 J7Ba1 A1Rb5 B8Rb5 J8Cb8 J6Bb2 G7Bb3
A5Ca2 C8Ca3 A9Ra4 C4Ra5 D8Ra2 E9Ra3 G5Ra8
J9Ra5 C5Ba4 A4Ba8 C9Ba7 E4Ba2 F8Ba4 J5Ba9
G9Ba9 A3Rb7 C3Rb8 E3Rb5 F2Rb8 D2Cb4 F3Cb2
F6Cb5 E7Cb8 D6Bb8 E6Bb4 D7Bb5

23579	239	789	378	2389	278	6	4	12789
1	2469	46789	478	289	5	3	289	2789
23479	2349	4789	6	1	2478	79	289	5
246	7	46	135	356	9	8	156	146
69	8	5	17	4	167	2	3	169
469	1469	3	2	568	168	1459	7	1469
8	469	469	145	7	3	1459	12569	12469
467	46	2	9	568	1468	1457	1568	3
34679	5	1	48	268	2468	479	2689	246789

A1Ca5 F2Ca1 A9Ra1 D1Ra2 J1Ra3 D8Ba1 H1Ba7
G9Ca2 C2Ra3 F7Ba5 E1Ca6 D9Ra6 E9Ra9 F1Ba9
F9Ba4 C1Rb4 D3Rb4 B4Ra4 J4Rb8 J9Cb7 B9Bb8
C7Ca7 H8Ca8 B3Ra7 H5Ra5 B2Ba6 D4Ba5 G8Ba5
D5Rb3 G4Rb1 H2Rb4 G2Cb9 E4Cb7 H6Cb6 H7Cb1
A2Bb2 A4Bb3 E6Bb1 F6Bb8 G3Bb6 J5Bb2 G7Bb4
F5Ca6 A5Ca8 C6Ca2 J6Ca4 A6Ca7 J7Ca9 J8Ca6
A3Ra9 B8Ra2 C3Ra8 B5Ba9 C8Ba9

1245679	12567	1469	8	17	149	3	2479	12479
3	127	149	6	5	149	8	2479	12479
12479	1278	1489	123479	137	1349	6	5	12479
8	9	46	345	2	3456	7	1	34
14567	1567	146	13457	9	13456	24	2348	234
147	3	2	147	8	14	49	6	5
1269	4	5	139	136	13689	129	2379	123679
169	16	7	1359	4	2	159	39	8
1269	1268	3	159	16	7	12459	249	12469

C3Ca8 C4Ca2 G6Ca8 E8Ca8 F7Ra9 J2Ra8 C6Ca3
D6Ra5 E6Ba6 G5Ca3 F6Ca1 D3Ra6 H8Ra3 J5Ba6
G9Ca6 G8Ra7 B2Ca2 A8Ra2 B9Ra7 C2Ba7 A9Ba1
A5Rb7 C5Rb1 B3Ra1 E3Rb4 F1Cb7 A3Cb9 E7Cb2
C1Bb4 A6Bb4 F4Bb4 E9Bb3 G7Bb1 D4Ca3 E4Ca7
B6Ca9 J7Ca4 J9Ca2 B8Ra4 C9Ra9 D9Ra4 G1Ra2
J4Ra5 H4Ba1 H7Ba5 J8Ba9 G4Rb9 H2Rb6 J1Rb1
E1Cb5 H1Cb9 A2Cb5 A1Bb6 E2Bb1

345	1359	139	7	34589	48	6	15	2
356	13569	1369	568	35689	2	4	157	15789
2456	8	7	1	4569	46	59	3	59
35678	4	1368	2	568	9	1578	1567	15678
9	1256	1268	4568	7	468	158	12456	3
25678	256	268	3	4568	1	578	9	45678
36	7	369	46	146	5	2	8	1469
2368	236	4	9	1268	678	1357	1567	1567
1	269	5	468	2468	3	79	467	4679

H6Ca7 H7Ca3 E8Ca2 C1Ra2 A1Ba4 B9Ba8 F9Ba4
H1Ba8 A6Rb8 F3Ca2 J8Ca4 A2Ra5 B8Ra7 B4Ba5
A8Ba1 F2Rb6 E2Cb1 H2Cb2 E3Bb8 J2Bb9 B2Ca3
B3Ca1 J4Ca8 J5Ca2 D7Ca1 C7Ca9 A5Ra3 B1Ra6
B5Ra9 C9Ra5 D5Ra8 E7Ra5 G9Ra9 J9Ra6 A3Ba9
F5Ba5 D8Ba6 F7Ba8 G3Ba6 H9Ba1 H8Ba5 J7Ba7
D3Rb3 D9Rb7 F1Rb7 G1Rb3 G4Rb4 H5Rb6 D1Cb5
E4Cb6 C5Cb4 G5Cb1 C6Bb6 E6Bb4

5	24	27	8	1239	2379	6	247	12347
1	28	6	2357	235	4	9	278	237
23478	9	278	1237	123	6	5	2478	12347
248	3	9	125	12458	258	278	6	247
2468	124568	258	12356	7	23589	28	24589	249
2468	7	258	256	245689	2589	1	3	249
26789	2568	3	4	2568	2578	27	1	2679
267	256	1	9	2356	2357	4	27	8
26789	268	4	2367	2368	1	237	279	5

C1Ca3 E2Ca1 J7Ca3 E8Ca5 G9Ca6 G1Ra9 A2Ba4
F3Ba5 J8Ba9 C8Ca4 C3Ra8 A3Ba7 B8Ba8 A8Rb2
B2Rb2 E3Rb2 E7Cb8 H8Cb7 G7Bb2 J1Ca7 G6Ca7
D7Ca7 H1Ba2 F5Ca4 H6Ca5 F9Ra9 G2Ra5 H5Ra3
E6Ba9 D9Ba2 J2Ba8 A6Rb3 B5Rb5 D6Rb8 E9Rb4
G5Rb8 H2Rb6 D1Cb4 E1Cb6 B4Cb7 D5Cb1 F6Cb2
A9Cb1 A5Bb9 C5Bb2 B9Bb3 C9Bb7 F1Bb8 D4Bb5
E4Bb3 F4Bb6 C4Ca1 J4Ca2 J5Ca6

14678	14	9	146	1248	12468	5	3	12678
2	3	678	146	148	5	14678	9	1678
1468	5	68	13469	7	1234689	12468	126	1268
59	6	25	159	158	7	3	4	1289
34579	49	2357	13459	6	13489	1278	12	12789
3479	8	1	2	34	349	67	5	679
1356	1	356	134567	9	12346	126	8	12356
13569	2	356	8	135	136	16	7	4
13568	7	4	1356	1235	1236	9	126	12356

E2Ca9 G4Ca7 G6Ra4 H1Ra9 J1Ra8 D1Rb5 G2Rb1
A2Cb4 D3Cb2 C7Ra4 E4Ra5 G7Ra2 F5Ba4 E1Ca4
C4Ca3 B4Ca4 A5Ca2 C6Ra9 E3Ra3 J6Ra2 F1Ba7
F6Ba3 D4Ba9 G1Ba3 F7Rb6 G9Rb5 H3Rb5 G3Cb6
H5Cb3 H7Cb1 F9Cb9 J9Cb3 C3Bb8 H6Bb6 J5Bb5
J8Bb6 B3Ca7 A4Ca6 A9Ra7 B9Ra6 J4Ra1 C1Ba6
B7Ba8 E7Ba7 A1Rb1 B5Rb1 D5Cb8 A6Cb8 E6Bb1
D9Bb1 C8Ca1 E9Ca8 C9Ra2 E8Ra2

178	1278	5	189	368	1389	2368	4	23679
3	278	289	4589	468	589	268	26789	1
4	18	6	7	38	2	5	389	39
156	12456	124	3	9	7	1246	1256	8
5678	2345678	2348	48	1	8	2346	235679	23679
9	13478	1348	2	5	6	134	137	37
18	138	7	6	238	4	9	1238	5
2	13568	138	1589	378	13589	1368	1368	4
1568	9	1348	158	238	1358	7	12368	236

B3Ca9 B5Ca4 H5Ca7 C2Ra1 J3Ra4 A5Ba6 E4Ba4
E6Rb8 B6Cb5 B4Bb8 C8Ra8 H7Ba8 C5Rb3 C9Cb9
F3Ca8 E8Ca9 F7Ra1 J5Ra8 D7Ba4 D8Ba5 G5Ba2
F2Rb4 D3Ca2 A7Ca3 D1Ra1 D2Ba6 H3Ba1 E3Rb3
G1Rb8 H2Rb5 A1Cb7 J1Cb6 E2Cb7 G2Cb3 H4Cb9
B2Bb2 A4Bb1 A9Bb2 E1Bb5 H6Bb3 G8Bb1 A2Ca8
J4Ca5 J6Ca1 A6Ca9 E7Ca2 J8Ca2 E9Ca6 F9Ca7
B8Ra7 F8Ra3 H8Ra6 J9Ra3 B7Ba6

139	7	139	5	23	6	8	4	12
1468	1458	146	28	278	9	3	256	12567
3689	2	369	8	4	1	5679	569	567
5	1489	12469	1289	1238	7	1246	268	123468
12489	3	1249	1289	6	258	1245	7	12458
12678	18	1267	4	12358	2358	1256	2568	9
1247	14	1247	6	9	258	2457	3	24578
12349	149	5	7	128	28	2469	2689	2468
279	6	8	3	25	4	2579	1	257

B2Ca5 B5Ca7 F6Ca3 D9Ca3 H1Ra3 A5Ba3 H5Ba1
C4Rb8 B4Cb2 B8Bb6 C3Ca3 H9Ca6 A9Ra2 B1Ra8
C1Ra6 B3Ba4 B9Ba1 F2Ca8 D5Ca8 D8Ra2 E9Ra8
H8Ba8 F8Rb5 G9Rb4 H6Rb2 G2Cb1 F5Cb2 J5Cb5
E6Cb5 H7Cb9 C8Cb9 H2Bb4 G6Bb8 J9Bb7 E1Ca4
D2Ca9 C7Ca7 C9Ca5 D7Ra4 E3Ra2 E4Ra9 G7Ra5
J1Ra9 A3Ba9 D4Ba1 F7Ba6 G1Ba2 J7Ba2 A1Rb1
D3Rb6 E7Rb1 G3Rb7 F1Cb7 F3Cb1

2478	2489	478	5	1	2489	3	47	67
5	6	13478	23478	248	2348	148	147	9
3478	3489	13478	34678	4689	3489	14568	2	567
1	3458	2	9	458	3458	7	6	35
6	345	34	1234	7	12345	159	1359	8
38	7	9	138	58	6	2	135	4
23478	1	34678	2468	245689	24589	4569	34579	23567
9	234	3467	246	2456	245	456	8	1
248	248	5	12468	3	7	469	49	26

E6Ca1 A9Ra6 E4Ra2 F8Ra1 H3Ra7 J4Ra1 G3Ba6
J9Rb2 J7Ca6 J8Ca9 C9Ra5 E7Ra9 F5Ra5 G9Ra7
H2Ra3 E8Ba5 G1Ba2 G8Ba3 D9Rb3 E2Rb4 J2Cb8
E3Cb3 C2Bb9 D2Bb5 F1Bb8 J1Bb4 C1Ca3 A2Ca2
G5Ca9 A6Ra9 C4Ra7 F4Ra3 A1Ba7 B6Ba3 C5Ba6
A8Rb4 A3Cb8 B8Cb7 H4Ca6 H6Ca2 B5Ra2 H7Ra5
G6Ba5 G7Ba4 G4Rb8 H5Rb4 B4Cb4 D5Cb8 B3Bb1
C6Bb8 D6Bb4 C3Ca4 C7Ca1 B7Ca8

14679	13469	8	5	234	1349	136	16	13
169	1369	1569	39	8	139	2	7	4
14	134	1245	7	6	134	1358	9	1358
14678	1468	1467	23468	2345	3456	1458	12458	9
2	5	4	1	9	7	48	3	6
3	14689	14679	2468	245	456	1458	12458	12578
1469	2	1469	3469	7	8	134569	1456	135
5	7	3	469	1	469	4689	2468	28
14689	14689	1469	3469	345	2	7	14568	1358

C3Ca2 F9Ca7 A5Ra2 A1Ra7 B3Ra5 E7Ra8 C9Ba8
D3Ba7 J5Ba5 E3Rb4 F5Rb4 H9Rb2 D5Cb3 G9Ca5
C7Ra5 H8Ra8 A6Ba4 A2Rb9 F7Rb1 H6Rb9 D7Cb4
H7Bb6 B4Ca9 G7Ca9 A8Ca6 A9Ra1 F3Ra9 G4Ra3
H4Ra4 A7Ba3 J1Ba9 J4Ba6 J9Ba3 J3Rb1 G3Cb6
J8Cb4 G1Bb4 J2Bb8 G8Bb1 D1Ca8 C2Ca4 C6Ra3
D2Ra1 F4Ra8 B2Ba3 B6Ba1 F2Ba6 D4Ba2 B1Rb6
C1Rb1 D8Rb5 F6Rb5 D6Cb6 F8Cb2

9	67	4	5	1	2	36	8	37
12678	1678	267	9	3467	368	2356	1234567	23457
3	1678	5	467	467	68	269	12467	2479
46	46	8	12346	3456	1356	7	9	2345
5	4679	3679	23467	8	369	236	2346	1
467	2	1	3467	345679	3569	8	3456	345
2467	45679	2679	36	3569	3569	1	2357	8
12678	156789	2679	136	3569	4	2359	2357	23579
1	3	9	8	2	7	4	5	6

E3Ca3 D6Ca1 J1Ra1 J8Ra5 J3Ra9 E2Ba9 H4Ba1
E6Rb6 C6Cb8 E7Cb2 B6Bb3 E8Bb4 D4Ca2 B7Ca5
E4Ra7 F1Ba7 F8Ba6 A7Ra3 C7Ba6 A9Rb7 C4Rb4
H7Rb9 A2Cb6 F4Cb3 C5Cb7 H9Cb2 C2Bb1 B5Bb6
B9Bb4 C9Bb9 D2Bb4 D5Bb5 F9Bb5 G4Bb6 G1Ca4
H3Ca6 F5Ca4 G6Ca5 B8Ca1 D9Ca3 C8Ra2 D1Ra6
F6Ra9 G3Ra2 G5Ra9 H2Ra5 B1Ba2 G2Ba7 H1Ba8
H5Ba3 B2Rb8 B3Rb7 G8Rb3 H8Rb7

137	8	1379	2469	467	24679	1246	126	5
157	156	2	4568	3	45678	9	16	167
57	4	579	2569	1	25679	26	8	3
1345	2	13459	7	456	34569	8	1569	169
6	1359	13579	2359	8	2359	1235	1259	4
345	359	8	234569	456	1	2356	7	269
8	7	145	1456	2	456	156	3	169
12345	135	6	13458	9	3458	7	125	128
9	135	135	13568	567	35678	1256	4	1268

H1Ca2 B2Ca6 A7Ca4 B9Ca7 E3Ra7 G9Ra9 G3Ba4
B8Rb1 B1Cb5 H8Cb5 C1Bb7 C3Bb9 E2Ra1 F2Ba9
D9Ba1 J3Ba1 A3Rb3 H2Rb3 H9Rb8 A1Cb1 J2Cb5
D3Cb5 H6Cb4 B6Bb8 H4Bb1 J4Ca8 F5Ca5 G7Ca1
B4Ra4 E7Ra5 J6Ra3 D5Ba4 F7Ba3 J5Ba7 A5Rb6
D1Rb3 F1Rb4 A8Cb2 A4Bb9 C7Bb6 E8Bb9 E4Ca3
A6Ca7 D6Ca9 J7Ca2 D8Ca6 E6Ra2 F4Ra6 J9Ra6
C4Ba2 F9Ba2 G6Ba6 C6Rb5 G4Rb5

1236	1369	269	346	8	7	134	134	5
1367	4	67	5	16	9	2	138	1368
12356	1356	8	346	1246	236	9	7	136
23467	3679	5	1	2679	2368	37	2389	23789
8	13679	2679	367	5	236	137	1239	4
1237	1379	279	378	279	4	6	123589	123789
4567	2	1	467	467	56	8	3459	379
457	578	3	9	47	1	457	6	27
9	5678	467	2	3	568	1457	145	17

J3Ca4 F4Ca8 D1Ra4 F8Ra5 H9Ra2 H2Ra8 J6Ba8
J8Rb1 J9Cb7 J7Bb5 C2Ca5 G6Ca5 H1Ra5 J2Ra6
E3Ba6 G1Ba7 B3Rb7 H7Rb4 H5Cb7 E4Ca7 A8Ca4
F2Ra7 D7Ba7 F3Ba2 A3Rb9 F5Rb9 A1Ra2 C4Ca3
A4Ra6 C5Ra4 B5Ba1 C6Ba2 G4Ba4 G5Ba6 D5Rb2
E6Rb3 D6Cb6 E7Cb1 A7Bb3 E2Bb9 F9Bb3 B1Ca3
A2Ca1 D2Ca3 E8Ca2 G8Ca3 C9Ca1 B9Ra6 C1Ra6
F1Ra1 G9Ra9 B8Ba8 D8Ba9 D9Rb8

1	379	6	3458	3489	3458	3578	2	357
8	4	357	2	369	1	357	5679	3567
259	39	235	358	7	3568	4	569	1
2467	5	23478	1348	13468	3468	9	1467	23467
46	368	348	9	2	7	135	1456	3456
24679	3679	1	345	346	3456	2357	8	234567
3	1678	9	1478	5	248	127	147	247
457	17	457	6	14	9	1257	3	8
457	2	4578	13478	1348	348	6	1457	9

G6Ca2 A7Ca8 G2Ra6 H7Ra2 H2Ba1 J3Ba8 J8Ba5
H5Rb4 J6Cb3 J5Bb1 E2Ca8 D4Ca1 D5Ca8 G4Ra8
J1Ra4 C6Ba8 J4Ba7 E1Rb6 C8Ra6 B5Ba6 B8Ba9
F5Rb3 A5Cb9 C3Ca2 D3Ra3 E3Ba4 E8Rb1 G7Ca1
G9Ca4 G8Ra7 D8Ba4 F7Ba7 D6Rb6 F2Rb9 F1Cb2
C2Cb3 D9Cb2 A2Bb7 C4Bb5 D1Bb7 F9Bb6 H1Ca5
C1Ca9 H3Ca7 A4Ca3 F6Ca5 B9Ca7 A6Ra4 A9Ra5
B7Ra3 F4Ra4 B3Ba5 E9Ba3 E7Ba5

379	179	17	2	579	1579	4	8	6
6	2479	478	3589	5789	579	27	2357	1
2378	127	5	138	6	4	27	237	9
2457	124567	9	145	245	8	3	1257	257
2458	3	148	7	2459	1259	6	125	258
2578	1257	178	6	3	1259	12789	1257	4
1	8	467	49	2479	3	5	2467	27
4579	45679	2	4589	1	5679	78	3467	378
457	4567	3	458	24578	2567	1278	9	278

G3Ca6 F7Ca9 H9Ca3 A1Ra3 D2Ra6 J7Ra1 J6Ra6
B8Ba5 E9Ba8 H8Ba6 H1Ca9 H7Ca8 C8Ca3 G8Ca4
D9Ca5 B4Ra3 G4Ra9 D5Rb4 H6Rb7 D4Cb1 G5Cb2
B6Cb9 C4Bb8 J5Bb8 G9Bb7 F1Ca8 A2Ca9 E5Ca9
A6Ca1 J9Ca2 A5Ra5 B3Ra8 C2Ra1 B2Ba4 B5Ba7
A3Rb7 B7Rb2 H2Rb5 C1Cb2 J2Cb7 F3Cb1 H4Cb4
C7Cb7 D1Bb7 E3Bb4 F2Bb2 J1Bb4 J4Bb5 E1Ca5
E6Ca2 E8Ca1 F8Ca7 D8Ra2 F6Ra5

1	3	45679	249	479	27	45	2456	8
457	478	4578	234	6	27	9	1	235
469	2	469	1349	8	5	34	7	36
3459	489	1	7	2	8	6	3459	35
34567	467	4567	1356	135	9	2	8	1357
35679	6789	256789	13568	135	4	135	359	1357
4679	1	4679	245689	4579	3	58	256	256
2	46	3	14568	145	168	7	56	9
8	5	679	1269	179	1267	13	236	4

F3Ca2 G7Ca8 C4Ra1 B4Ba3 D8Ba4 J7Ba1 D6Rb8
D2Cb9 B3Ca8 H4Ca8 H6Ca1 F8Ca9 F2Ra8 J8Ra3
J6Ba6 J4Ra2 C7Ca4 C9Ra3 A8Ba6 F7Ba3 A7Rb5
D9Rb5 F5Rb1 H8Rb5 D1Cb3 A3Cb7 E5Cb3 H5Cb4
G8Cb2 B9Cb2 F9Cb7 B2Bb4 A5Bb9 A6Bb2 B6Bb7
E9Bb1 H2Bb6 J3Bb9 G4Bb9 G9Bb6 C1Ca9 E2Ca7
E3Ca5 A4Ca4 G5Ca5 B1Ra5 C3Ra6 E1Ra4 F4Ra5
G1Ra7 J5Ra7 F1Ba6 E4Ba6 G3Ba4

1	579	3579	4	357	38	25789	23578	6
34579	579	34579	2	13567	368	5789	134578	15789
2	6	8	357	1357	9	57	13457	157
8	3	79	1	679	5	4	267	27
45679	2	14579	3679	8	346	57	1567	157
4567	157	1457	67	467	2	578	9	3
579	15789	6	589	459	48	3	2578	25789
359	4	359	35689	2	7	1	58	589
3579	5789	23579	3589	359	1	6	2578	4

J3Ca2 A7Ca2 C8Ra4 F7Ra8 G2Ra1 H4Ra6 J2Ba8
F4Rb7 F2Cb5 G4Ca8 B7Ca9 F3Ra1 B2Rb7 G6Rb4
A2Cb9 F5Ca4 F1Ra6 E6Ca3 E8Ra6 D5Ba6 E9Ba1
A6Rb8 E4Rb9 E1Cb4 B6Cb6 E3Bb7 B3Ca4 C7Ca7
B8Ca1 A5Ra7 B1Ra3 B9Ra8 C5Ra1 D3Ra9 E7Ra5
A3Ba5 C4Ba3 A8Ba3 H3Ba3 H8Ba8 B5Rb5 C9Rb5
J4Rb5 G5Cb9 J8Cb7 H9Cb9 D8Bb2 H1Bb5 J1Bb9
J5Bb3 G9Bb2 G1Ca7 G8Ca5 D9Ca7

1789	179	15789	2	168	3	1569	4	15
128	6	3	1458	148	9	125	25	7
129	1249	1259	1456	7	56	8	2359	1235
4	279	2789	378	5	278	23	1	6
2368	5	28	3468	9	1	7	238	2348
123678	127	1278	34678	3468	2678	2345	2358	9
129	3	6	1589	18	58	12459	7	12458
5	179	4	13789	2	78	139	6	138
1279	8	1279	135679	136	4	12359	2359	1235

C2Ca4 A7Ca6 C8Ba9 B5Ca4 C9Ra3 D7Rb3 E3Rb8
E8Cb2 B8Bb5 E9Bb4 F4Ca4 G7Ca4 J8Ca3 F8Ca8
A3Ra5 B7Ra2 F7Ra5 H4Ra3 A9Ba1 F5Ba3 A5Rb8
E4Rb6 F1Rb6 H9Rb8 J5Rb6 E1Cb3 B4Cb1 G5Cb1
H6Cb7 B1Bb8 C4Bb5 F6Bb2 D2Ca2 D4Ca7 G6Ca5
C6Ca6 D6Ra8 D3Ra9 G4Ra8 J9Ra5 J4Ba9 G9Ba2
G1Rb9 J7Rb1 A1Cb7 H2Cb1 H7Cb9 A2Bb9 F2Bb7
J1Bb2 C1Ca1 C3Ca2 J3Ca7 F3Ra1

6	23478	2347	3478	1	9	278	2358	25
378	23478	5	6	2348	234	2789	1	29
9	2378	1237	378	5	23	4	2368	26
4	5	69	2	689	7	169	69	3
37	1	23679	349	3469	34	5	269	8
38	23689	2369	34589	34689	1	269	7	2469
1357	3679	8	1359	239	235	1269	4	12569
135	349	1349	13459	7	6	1289	2589	1259
2	469	1469	1459	49	8	3	569	7

G6Ca5 F9Ca4 C3Ra1 D7Ra1 D5Ra8 F4Ra5 J8Ra5
A9Ba5 H1Ba5 G5Ba2 G1Ca1 G2Ra7 J4Ra1 H9Ba1
C4Ra7 G4Ra3 A4Ba8 A7Rb7 A8Rb3 E3Ca7 B1Ra7
E8Ra2 F1Ra8 H3Ra3 E1Ba3 D8Ba9 H7Ba2 D3Rb6
E6Rb4 F7Rb6 H8Rb8 E4Cb9 G7Cb9 C8Cb6 B7Bb8
C9Bb2 E5Bb6 F5Bb3 H4Bb4 G9Bb6 J2Ca6 C2Ca8
B5Ca4 J5Ca9 B6Ca2 B9Ca9 B2Ra3 C6Ra3 H2Ra9
J3Ra4 A2Ba4 F3Ba9 A3Rb2 F2Rb2

4	359	356	169	7	156	2356	8	235
5689	7	2	4689	4589	4568	356	4569	1
5689	589	1	3	2	4568	567	45679	457
2578	2358	34578	2468	3458	9	123567	1567	2357
2578	6	3578	28	1	2358	4	57	9
1	2359	345	7	345	23456	8	56	235
25678	4	5678	128	8	1278	9	3	578
578	1	9	48	6	3478	57	2	4578
3	28	78	5	489	12478	17	147	6

B7Ra3 F2Ra9 H6Ra3 J5Ra9 G5Rb8 H4Cb4 C9Ca4
H9Ca8 A4Ra9 E3Ra3 J8Ra4 A2Ba3 A6Ba1 J7Ba1
G4Ca1 D8Ca1 A7Ca2 F9Ca2 A3Ra6 F5Ra3 D9Ba3
G1Ba6 A9Rb5 G9Cb7 G3Bb5 G6Bb2 H7Bb5 J6Ca7
H1Ra7 J2Ra2 D3Ba7 J3Ba8 D7Rb6 F3Rb4 C7Cb7
F8Cb5 F6Bb6 E8Bb7 B4Ca6 B6Ca4 B1Ra8 C8Ra6
D5Ra4 C1Ba9 C6Ba8 B8Ba9 D2Ba8 E6Ba5 B5Rb5
C2Rb5 D4Rb2 E1Rb2 D1Cb5 E4Cb8

279	267	1	24679	679	24679	8	5	34679
579	567	567	3	156789	14679	46	4679	2
4	8	3	2679	5679	2679	6	679	1
2578	2567	5678	1	4	3679	356	36789	36789
178	1467	9	67	2	5	1346	134678	34678
157	3	4567	679	679	8	1456	2	4679
18	14	2	4689	3	1469	7	1468	5
3	147	478	5	1678	12467	9	1468	468
6	9	4578	478	178	147	2	1348	348

D6Ca3 A9Ra3 B5Ra8 C5Ra5 H6Ra2 J3Ra5 B6Ba1
J8Ba3 C7Rb6 B7Cb4 D7Cb5 F7Bb1 B2Ca5 E7Ca3
B3Ra6 C4Ra2 F1Ra5 J5Ra1 D9Ca9 H5Rb6 D2Ca6
A6Ca6 G8Ca6 A4Ra4 D1Ra2 F3Ra4 H8Ra1 A2Ba2
D3Ba7 E8Ba4 G2Ba4 D8Rb8 E2Rb1 G6Rb9 H2Rb7
H3Rb8 E1Cb8 G1Cb1 G4Cb8 C6Cb7 H9Cb4 A5Bb9
C8Bb9 J4Bb7 J6Bb4 J9Bb8 B1Ca9 F4Ca9 F5Ca7
B8Ca7 A1Ra7 E9Ra7 F9Ra6 E4Ba6

7	146	13	2458	23458	23468	12348	1348	9
3469	469	5	248	7	1	2348	348	2368
346	8	2	45	9	346	134	1347	13567
236	267	9	1248	12348	23478	12348	5	1238
23	5	38	12489	12348	23489	7	6	1238
1	27	4	6	2358	23789	2389	389	238
8	1479	17	3	14	5	6	2	17
249	3	17	12489	6	2489	5	1789	178
259	129	6	7	128	289	1389	1389	4

J1Ca5 E3Ca8 C9Ca5 C8Ra7 F5Ra5 G2Ra9 B1Ba9
A4Ba5 B9Ba6 D7Ba4 H1Ba4 B2Rb4 C4Rb4 A2Ca1
A3Ca3 E6Ca4 A8Ca4 A6Ra6 C7Ra1 C6Ra3 E4Ra9
G5Ra4 C1Ba6 J2Ba2 F2Rb7 D2Cb6 D6Ca7 G3Ca1
F9Ca3 F6Ra2 G9Ra7 H3Ba7 H4Ba2 B4Rb8 H9Rb8
D4Cb1 A5Cb2 H6Cb9 B8Cb3 A7Bb8 B7Bb2 E5Bb3
D9Bb2 J6Bb8 H8Bb1 E1Ca2 D1Ca3 J5Ca1 D5Ca8
J7Ca3 F8Ca8 E9Ca1 F7Ra9 J8Ra9

45679	4679	459	78	2	678	3	1578	145789
679	23679	8	1	4	5	2	7	279
1	247	245	9	3	78	248	578	6
4789	134789	1349	3478	1578	134789	168	2	18
2	1789	6	78	178	1789	5	4	3
48	5	134	6	18	12348	7	9	18
3	1248	1245	2478	9	12478	1248	6	124578
4689	124689	1249	5	178	123478	1248	1378	12478
458	1248	7	2348	6	12348	9	1358	12458

D5Ca5 A6Ca6 D7Ca6 B2Ra3 F6Ra2 B1Ba6 B7Rb2
B8Rb7 B9Cb9 H2Ca6 F3Ca3 E6Ca9 F1Ra4 A8Ca1
A4Ra8 C6Ba7 E4Rb7 H5Ca7 G9Ra7 G3Ra5 A1Ba5
A9Rb4 J1Rb8 H1Cb9 A3Cb9 C7Cb8 H9Cb2 A2Bb7
C8Bb5 D1Bb7 D3Bb1 J9Bb5 E2Ca8 D2Ca9 C3Ca2
H8Ca8 F9Ca1 C2Ra4 D9Ra8 E5Ra1 F5Ra8 G6Ra8
H6Ra3 D4Ba3 H3Ba4 J6Ba1 J8Ba3 D6Rb4 H7Rb1
J2Rb2 G2Cb1 J4Cb4 G7Cb4 G4Bb2

9	1278	4	78	567	56	12567	17	3
267	27	5	9	1	346	2467	8	246
167	3	178	478	4567	2	14567	1479	1469
12347	12478	6	5	234	34	9	1347	1248
2347	24789	2378	1	23469	3469	2347	5	248
5	1249	123	234	8	7	1234	6	124
1347	6	137	347	3479	8	134	2	5
12347	12457	9	2347	23457	1345	8	134	146
8	1245	123	6	23459	13459	134	1349	7

C9Ca9 B6Ra3 F2Ra9 G5Ra9 H9Ra6 E6Ba9 J8Ba9
D6Rb4 A6Ca6 E5Ra6 H8Ca4 E7Ca7 D8Ca3 F4Ba3
D5Rb2 H4Ca2 G3Ca7 H5Ra7 J5Ba3 A5Rb5 G4Rb4
J7Rb1 J3Cb2 C5Cb4 J6Cb5 A7Cb2 G7Cb3 B9Bb4
F3Bb1 F7Bb4 G1Bb1 J2Bb4 H6Bb1 E1Ca4 A2Ca1
H2Ca5 E3Ca3 C7Ca5 D9Ca1 A4Ra8 C8Ra1 C1Ra6
D2Ra8 F9Ra2 H1Ra3 C3Ba8 C4Ba7 B7Ba6 A8Ba7
E2Ba2 D1Ba7 E9Ba8 B1Rb2 B2Rb7

12567	9	3	127	27	4	8	156	56
12456	1456	145	8	239	29	7	1456	56
1478	1478	147	179	5	6	149	2	3
579	57	6	2579	4	25789	3	578	1
34579	457	8	2579	279	1	6	457	257
1457	2	1457	3	678	578	45	9	578
56789	5678	2	5679	1	3	5	5678	4
15678	3	157	4	2678	2578	125	15678	9
1456789	145678	14579	25679	26789	25789	125	135678	25678

E1Ca3 J3Ca9 B5Ca3 C7Ca9 J8Ca3 B6Ra9 F5Ra6
G4Ra9 B8Ba4 D1Ba9 E5Ba9 E9Ba2 J4Ba6 G7Rb5
F7Cb4 C3Ca4 A8Ca1 B1Ra2 E2Ra4 C4Ba1 J1Ba4
D2Rb7 C2Cb8 C1Bb7 G2Bb6 A1Ca6 H3Ca7 H8Ca6
A9Ra5 B9Ra6 G8Ra7 F9Ba7 J9Ba8 E8Rb5 F6Rb8
G1Rb8 E4Cb7 D6Cb2 D8Cb8 A4Bb2 D4Bb5 H6Bb5
F1Ca5 H5Ca8 J6Ca7 A5Ra7 F3Ra1 H7Ra2 J2Ra5
B2Ba1 B3Ba5 H1Ba1 J5Ba2 J7Ba1

8	7	23	2	6	1	9	34	5
23569	4	2359	2578	2789	35789	3678	1	6
13569	3569	1359	578	789	345789	34678	3478	2
13459	359	13459	68	89	2	34568	34589	7
259	259	6	3	4	789	258	2589	1
7	8	2349	1	5	69	2346	2349	469
24569	1	24589	25678	3	5678	2457	24579	49
245	25	7	9	128	58	1245	6	3
23569	23569	2359	4	127	567	1257	2579	8

G3Ca8 C6Ca4 A8Ra4 E6Ra7 B6Ba3 A4Rb2 B9Rb6
A3Cb3 H6Ca8 F6Ca9 F7Ra6 D4Ba6 G4Ba7 D5Rb8
F9Rb4 F3Cb2 G9Cb9 F8Bb3 D3Ca4 C7Ca3 B1Ra2
D1Ra1 C3Ba1 D2Ba3 D7Rb5 D8Cb9 J1Ca3 B3Ca5
B5Ra9 C4Ra5 C5Ba7 B4Ba8 B7Rb7 C8Rb8 J3Rb9
J7Cb1 E8Cb2 E7Bb8 J5Bb2 G8Bb5 H7Bb4 G1Ca4
H2Ca2 H5Ca1 J6Ca5 G7Ca2 J8Ca7 G6Ra6 H1Ra5
J2Ra6 C1Ba6 E2Ba5 C2Rb9 E1Rb9

5	6	138	4	129	139	128	7	8
2	48	148	567	157	1567	3	148	9
349	349	7	2359	8	1359	1245	6	5
3489	345789	3458	579	6	2	1589	1389	3578
389	235789	358	1	579	4	6	2389	3578
689	1	568	579	3	5789	2589	289	4
1	3458	9	2356	245	356	7	348	368
346	345	3456	8	14579	135679	49	349	2
7	348	2	369	49	369	489	5	1

E2Ca2 F6Ca8 G9Ca6 F4Ra7 D2Ba7 A9Rb8 C9Rb5
D9Cb3 E9Bb7 C2Ca9 F8Ca2 H2Ca5 B3Ca8 H8Ra3
A3Ba1 H7Ba9 A7Rb2 B2Rb4 F7Rb5 C1Cb3 F3Cb6
A5Cb9 B8Cb1 A6Bb3 C4Bb2 C6Bb1 C7Bb4 F1Bb9
E5Bb5 H3Bb4 J5Bb4 D1Ca4 H1Ca6 E3Ca3 D3Ca5
H5Ca1 G5Ca2 J6Ca9 D7Ca1 G8Ca4 D8Ra8 E8Ra9
G2Ra8 H6Ra7 J4Ra6 B6Ba6 B5Ba7 E1Ba8 D4Ba9
J2Ba3 G4Ba3 J7Ba8 B4Rb5 G6Rb5

2	37	5	1489	1489	6	1378	1378	347
678	67	1678	3	5	128	12678	9	2467
368	4	13689	1289	7	128	123568	12368	2356
1	9	2467	5	24	3	267	267	8
3467	8	23467	12467	124	127	9	5	2367
367	23567	2367	12678	128	9	12367	4	2367
34678	2367	234678	2789	2389	278	235678	23678	1
9	237	2378	1278	6	5	4	2378	237
5	1	23678	278	238	4	23678	23678	9

F2Ca5 C3Ca9 C9Ca5 B9Ra4 G7Ra5 H4Ra1 B3Ba1
F7Ba1 E5Ca1 A8Ra1 C6Ba1 A7Ra8 A2Ca3 A9Ra7
D3Ra6 H9Rb2 H2Cb7 B2Bb6 G1Ca6 G2Ca2 B1Ra7
D5Ra4 G3Ra4 C1Ba8 A4Ba4 E1Ba4 A5Rb9 B7Rb2
C4Rb2 F1Rb3 B6Cb8 D7Cb7 F9Cb6 D8Bb2 E9Bb3
G6Bb7 E4Ca6 G4Ca9 E6Ca2 J8Ca7 E3Ra7 F3Ra2
J5Ra2 J7Ra6 C8Ba6 F4Ba7 G5Ba3 C7Rb3 F5Rb8
G8Rb8 J4Rb8 J3Cb3 H8Cb3 H3Bb8

13	247	124	1478	1467	1468	5	9	12368
6	79	8	157	1579	2	13	13	4
159	249	12459	3	14569	145689	1268	12	7
2	8	469	147	13479	149	13679	5	1369
59	469	3	14578	124579	14589	126789	127	12689
7	1	59	6	2359	589	4	23	2389
19	3	129	145	8	145	1279	6	1259
18	5	7	9	146	3	12	124	12
4	69	169	2	156	7	139	8	1359

A1Ca3 H1Ca8 H8Ca4 E8Ca7 G7Ra7 H5Ra6 G3Ba2
B8Ca1 B7Ra3 J9Ba3 C8Rb2 J7Rb9 J2Cb6 F8Cb3
G9Cb5 E2Bb4 J3Bb1 C1Ca1 A2Ca2 D3Ca6 D5Ca3
C3Ra5 D4Ra7 G1Ra9 J5Ra5 A3Ba4 B2Ba7 B4Ba5
E1Ba5 F3Ba9 D6Ba4 B5Rb9 C2Rb9 D7Rb1 F5Rb2
G6Rb1 G4Cb4 C5Cb4 E5Cb1 H7Cb2 D9Cb9 F9Cb8
A5Bb7 A9Bb6 E4Bb8 F6Bb5 E7Bb6 H9Bb1 A4Ca1
C6Ca6 E6Ca9 C7Ca8 E9Ca2 A6Ra8

15	79	4	567	8	2	1569	169	3
358	2389	2589	3456	1	345	7	2689	2568
1358	6	1258	9	37	357	1258	4	258
2	34	156	8	347	13457	16	167	9
9	38	168	137	237	137	1268	5	4
1458	48	7	145	249	6	3	128	28
468	5	689	2	3467	3478	689	36789	1
7	289	3	16	6	18	4	2689	2568
468	1	268	3467	5	9	268	23678	2678

A2Ca7 F5Ca9 J9Ca7 H9Ra5 E5Ba2 D8Ba7 H5Rb6
H4Cb1 H6Bb8 E4Ca7 B9Ca6 A4Ra6 E2Ca8 E6Ra3
D2Ba3 D6Ba1 D5Rb4 D7Rb6 F2Rb4 D3Cb5 F4Cb5
E7Cb1 E3Bb6 F1Bb1 C3Ca1 A8Ca1 A7Ra9 C7Ba5
H8Ba9 A1Rb5 C6Rb7 G7Rb8 H2Rb2 B2Cb9 G3Cb9
J3Cb8 C5Cb3 G6Cb4 J7Cb2 B3Bb2 C1Bb8 B4Bb4
B6Bb5 G1Bb6 G5Bb7 J4Bb3 B1Ca3 J1Ca4 F8Ca2
G8Ca3 J8Ca6 F9Ca8 B8Ra8 C9Ra2

1	237	9	238	6	5	238	23478	2478
2378	2367	4	12389	12789	138	123568	1235678	278
5	2367	236	1238	1278	4	9	123678	278
39	369	5	368	4	2	7	368	1
237	123467	8	136	1	9	236	2346	5
239	123469	1236	7	158	1368	2368	23468	2489
4	125	12	1258	3	7	1258	9	6
239	8	123	124569	1259	16	125	1257	27
6	1259	7	12589	12589	18	4	1258	3

B1Ca8 H4Ca4 F9Ca9 F5Ra5 H6Ra6 E5Rb1 E1Ca7
A9Ca4 C9Ca8 A4Ra8 F6Ba8 J6Rb1 B6Cb3 J5Ca8
G7Ca8 D8Ra8 J8Rb2 H9Cb7 B9Bb2 A2Ra2 A7Rb3
A8Cb7 E7Ra2 F7Ba6 C3Ca6 B8Ra6 C2Ra3 B2Ba7
B7Ba5 B5Rb9 C8Rb1 H7Rb1 B4Cb1 C4Cb2 H5Cb2
H8Cb5 C5Bb7 H3Bb3 G4Bb5 F1Ca2 J2Ca5 J4Ca9
F8Ra3 G3Ra2 H1Ra9 D1Ba3 D2Ba9 E8Ba4 G2Ba1
D4Rb6 E2Rb6 F2Rb4 F3Rb1 E4Cb3

1248	6	14789	789	1389	179	148	1248	5
128	1258	1589	89	13589	4	6	7	138
148	3	14578	2	158	1567	148	9	148
7	124	6	49	2459	8	1459	3	149
5	1248	148	3	249	79	14789	1468	146789
48	9	348	1	6	57	2	458	478
3	14578	14578	4689	1489	2	145789	14568	146789
1468	1478	1478	5	1489	169	3	1468	2
9	1458	2	468	7	3	1458	14568	1468

H1Ca6 F3Ca3 A4Ca7 A8Ca2 B9Ca3 A5Ra3 C6Ra6
C3Ra7 B1Ca2 F6Ca5 C5Ra5 D7Ra5 F9Ra7 H2Ra7
E6Ba7 G7Ba7 G9Rb9 E7Ca9 B5Ca1 H6Ca1 B4Ra8
H5Ra9 A6Ba9 D4Ba9 G5Ba8 B2Rb5 B3Cb9 G3Ca5
J8Ra5 E3Ca1 D9Ra1 E8Rb6 G8Cb1 G2Bb4 J2Ca1
A3Ca4 J4Ca4 J9Ca6 D5Ra4 G4Ra6 H8Ra4 J7Ra8
C9Ba8 F1Ba4 E5Ba2 E9Ba4 H3Ba8 A7Rb1 C1Rb1
D2Rb2 E2Rb8 F8Rb8 A1Cb8 C7Cb4

4	2367	1	368	5	38	2378	278	9
2359	8	269	1369	136	7	1234	1245	356
359	3567	679	4	2	389	1378	1578	35678
7	2456	2468	12	9	245	148	3	8
13	34	4	137	8	6	5	1479	2
1235	9	248	1237	1347	2345	6	1478	78
8	247	5	23679	3467	2349	2379	279	1
29	1	2479	5	347	23489	23789	6	378
6	27	3	2789	7	1	2789	25789	4

E8Ra9 J8Ra5 D9Rb8 E3Rb4 J5Rb7 E2Cb3 J2Cb2
F9Cb7 E1Bb1 H1Bb9 H9Bb3 G2Ca4 F3Ca8 E4Ca7
H3Ba7 H5Rb4 B8Rb4 B7Cb3 F8Cb1 F5Bb3 D7Bb4
C1Ca3 B5Ca1 F6Ca4 C7Ca1 D4Ra1 F1Ra5 C2Ba5
D3Ba2 F4Ba2 D6Ba5 B1Rb2 C9Rb6 D2Rb6 G5Rb6
A2Cb7 C3Cb9 B9Cb5 B3Bb6 C6Bb8 A7Bb2 A4Ca6
J4Ca8 G6Ca9 G7Ca7 G8Ca2 A8Ca8 A6Ra3 B4Ra9
C8Ra7 G4Ra3 H6Ra2 H7Ra8 J7Ra9

56	5679	1	24569	4567	245679	3	8	2457
2	5678	4	56	5678	3	15	17	9
58	3	89	2459	1	245789	245	247	6
1348	1248	238	7	468	24689	12469	5	2348
9	12458	6	245	458	2458	7	124	2348
458	2458	7	3	4568	1	2469	246	248
346	46	5	8	2	467	46	9	1
1346	12469	239	1456	34567	4567	8	2467	2457
7	12468	28	1456	9	456	2456	3	245

H5Ca3 E9Ra3 F7Ra9 G1Ra3 G6Ra7 D3Ba3 D6Ba9
C8Ra7 H9Ba7 B8Rb1 B7Cb5 B4Bb6 D7Ca1 J9Ca5
D5Ra6 E2Ra1 F8Ba6 H1Ba1 A1Ca6 J4Ca1 H8Ca2
J3Ra2 C7Ba2 J2Ba8 A9Rb4 B2Rb7 D2Rb2 E8Rb4
F5Rb4 H3Rb9 F2Cb5 C3Cb8 B5Cb8 D9Cb8 A2Bb9
C1Bb5 D1Bb4 F1Bb8 E5Bb5 F9Bb2 C4Ca9 A5Ca7
E6Ca8 C6Ra4 E4Ra2 A6Ba2 H4Ba4 A4Rb5 H2Rb6
J6Rb6 G2Cb4 H6Cb5 J7Cb4 G7Bb6

9	2	13458	134	345	1345	1578	6	178
1357	1357	135	6	235	8	9	15	4
145	1458	14568	124	9	7	1258	3	18
1357	13578	1358	37	357	6	4	2	1389
13457	13457	12345	8	23457	23459	6	159	139
6	3458	9	234	1	2345	358	7	38
8	1345	1345	9	23467	1234	137	14	1367
2	1349	134	1347	34678	134	1378	1489	5
134	6	7	5	348	134	138	1489	2

H2Ca9 E3Ca2 C3Ca6 E6Ca9 C7Ca2 G9Ca6 B5Ra2
D9Ra9 H5Ra6 J8Ra9 G6Ba2 J5Ba8 F4Ca2 H8Ca8
A9Ca7 G8Ba4 F7Ca5 B8Ra5 F9Ra8 C9Ba1 A7Ba8
E9Ba3 C4Rb4 E8Rb1 C1Cb5 C2Bb8 D3Ca8 E5Ca4
A6Ca5 A3Ra4 E2Ra5 F2Ra4 A4Ba1 D5Ba5 J1Ba4
G3Ba5 A5Rb3 E1Rb7 F6Rb3 D4Cb7 G5Cb7 J6Cb1
H4Bb3 H6Bb4 J7Bb3 B2Ca7 B3Ca3 H7Ca7 B1Ra1
G2Ra3 H3Ra1 D2Ba1 D1Ba3 G7Ba1

9	12358	125	7	1235	135	1	236	4
1234	6	124	23	1239	8	179	5	12379
7	1235	125	4	12359	6	8	239	1239
1245	1245	6	258	12458	145	3	7	129
1245	12457	124579	2358	12345678	13457	149	2489	129
8	1247	3	9	1247	147	6	24	5
345	3457	8	1	34579	2	4579	3469	3679
6	23457	2457	358	345789	34579	4579	1	379
1345	9	1457	6	3457	3457	2	34	8

A2Ca8 E3Ca9 E5Ca6 H6Ca9 E8Ca8 G9Ca6 A8Ra6
D9Ra9 A7Rb1 E7Cb4 F8Bb2 E9Ca1 A3Rb2 B4Rb2
D5Ca2 C9Ca2 D4Ra8 H2Ra2 E1Ba2 H5Ba8 H3Ra4
B1Ba4 J3Ba7 B3Rb1 C3Cb5 B5Cb9 C2Bb3 C5Bb1
B7Bb7 G7Ca9 H9Ca7 B9Ra3 C8Ra9 G5Ra7 H4Ra3
J1Ra1 E6Ba3 G1Ba3 H7Ba5 A6Rb5 D1Rb5 E4Rb5
F5Rb4 G2Rb5 G8Rb4 E2Cb7 A5Cb3 J5Cb5 D6Cb1
J6Cb4 J8Cb3 D2Bb4 F2Bb1 F6Bb7

6	239	23	2349	234	5	1	7	8
4	379	378	1389	1367	1389	5	3	2
278	5	1	238	2367	238	36	4	9
257	2347	9	6	2345	2348	3478	2358	1
1257	8	23457	12345	9	1234	3467	235	3456
125	1234	6	123458	12345	7	348	23589	345
1258	124	2458	7	12345	6	9	1358	345
1579	14679	457	13459	8	1349	2	135	345
3	1249	2458	12459	1245	1249	48	6	7

H1Ca9 H2Ca6 F8Ca9 E9Ca6 B5Ra6 H3Ra7 C5Ba7
C7Ba6 B8Rb3 B3Cb8 C1Bb2 G1Ca8 B2Ra7 J7Ra8
A2Ba9 D8Ba8 A3Rb3 C6Ca8 E8Ca2 F9Ca5 C4Ra3
F4Ra8 F1Rb1 E3Ca4 H8Ca1 H4Ra5 D5Ba5 G8Ba5
D1Rb7 E4Rb1 G3Rb2 E1Cb5 J3Cb5 B4Cb9 E6Cb3
B6Bb1 E7Bb7 H6Bb4 A4Ca4 G5Ca3 J6Ca9 G9Ca4
A5Ra2 D7Ra4 G2Ra1 H9Ra3 J2Ra4 D6Ba2 F5Ba4
F7Ba3 J5Ba1 J4Ba2 D2Rb3 F2Rb2

8	1247	1457	45	6	57	3	9	45
9	46	456	458	1	3	4568	7	2
3456	3467	34567	4589	5789	2	4568	45	1
456	4678	2	589	5789	5789	1	3	4578
135	1378	1357	12358	4	1578	2578	6	9
1345	13478	9	6	23578	1578	24578	245	4578
1236	5	136	7	2389	4	269	12	6
7	12346	8	12359	2359	1569	24569	1245	456
1246	9	146	125	25	156	24567	8	3

A2Ra2 G5Ra8 J7Ra7 A3Ba1 G9Rb6 G3Cb3 A6Ra7
G7Ra9 D5Ba7 D9Rb8 F9Cb7 G1Ca2 G8Ra1 H6Ra6
J4Ra1 H2Ba1 J6Rb5 J5Cb2 D6Cb9 D4Bb5 F5Bb3
E4Ca2 H4Ca3 C5Ca5 A9Ra5 B3Ra5 C4Ra9 H5Ra9
B4Ba8 C8Ba4 A4Rb4 B7Rb6 C1Rb3 E3Rb7 E7Rb5
F2Rb8 H9Rb4 E1Cb1 B2Cb4 C2Cb7 E2Cb3 C3Cb6
F6Cb1 C7Cb8 H7Cb2 F8Cb2 D2Bb6 F1Bb5 E6Bb8
F7Bb4 J3Bb4 H8Bb5 D1Ca4 J1Ca6

5	9	8	3	1467	47	1267	1247	147
2346	367	23467	678	14678	5	123679	123479	1479
346	367	1	67	2	479	8	34579	479
7	4	35	258	358	1	29	6	89
368	368	9	2678	34678	3478	5	12478	1478
1	2	56	9	45678	478	7	478	3
368	135678	3567	578	9	378	4	1378	2
3489	3578	3457	1	3578	2	379	3789	6
2389	1378	237	4	378	6	1379	13789	5

C6Ca9 C8Ca5 F7Rb7 D9Ca8 D7Ra9 F6Ra8 E8Ba2
F8Rb4 H7Rb3 J7Cb1 A8Cb1 E9Cb1 B7Bb6 G2Ca1
D4Ca2 B5Ca1 A7Ca2 B8Ca3 B9Ca9 A5Ra6 B4Ra8
G4Ra5 A6Ba4 E4Ba6 H2Ba5 A9Rb7 B2Rb7 C4Rb7
F5Rb5 F3Cb6 D5Cb3 C9Cb4 D3Bb5 E6Bb7 C2Ca6
E5Ca4 G6Ca3 C1Ra3 G1Ra6 E2Ba3 E1Rb8 G3Rb7
J2Rb8 H3Cb4 J5Cb7 G8Cb8 B3Bb2 H1Bb9 H5Bb8
J8Bb9 J1Ca2 B1Ca4 J3Ca3 H8Ca7

3	126	5	8	147	167	47	147	9
7	19	149	149	1349	5	2	6	48
149	169	8	2	13479	13679	347	5	47
1258	4	123	17	6	178	378	9	278
189	13679	1369	1479	5	2	34678	347	4678
289	2679	269	3	4789	789	1	247	5
1249	8	1249	1679	1279	1679	5	247	3
1259	12359	7	1569	12389	4	69	2	26
6	2359	2349	579	2379	379	479	8	1

A8Ca1 E8Ca3 A2Ra2 B5Ra3 B9Ra8 D3Ra3 D1Ra5
H5Ra8 C2Ba6 C7Ba3 J6Ba3 H8Rb2 H9Cb6 H7Bb9
H2Ca3 G4Ca6 E7Ca6 D9Ca2 A6Ra6 E1Ra8 F3Ra6
H4Ra5 F1Ba2 D7Ba8 J2Ba5 H1Rb1 F6Ca8 D4Ca1
D6Ra7 J4Ca7 G8Ra7 J7Ra4 C9Ba4 E9Ba7 A7Rb7
C1Rb9 F8Rb4 G1Cb4 B2Cb1 A5Cb4 F5Cb9 C6Cb1
B3Bb4 B4Bb9 C5Bb7 E2Bb9 F2Bb7 E4Bb4 G6Bb9
J5Bb2 E3Ca1 G3Ca2 J3Ca9 G5Ca1

3	16	56	9	7	145	14	124	8
189	18	4	6	1238	138	5	7	139
15789	2	59	1458	13458	13458	1349	6	1349
45678	34678	356	1458	13458	2	134689	1349	13469
4568	3468	1	7	3458	34589	34689	349	2
48	9	23	148	6	1348	1348	5	7
146	5	7	124	9	146	1346	8	1346
1469	146	8	3	145	14567	2	149	1469
2	1346	369	148	148	14678	134679	1349	5

D2Ca7 F3Ca2 G4Ca2 B5Ca2 E6Ca9 J7Ca7 A8Ca2
C1Ra7 H6Ra7 H5Ba5 E1Ra5 D4Ba5 C5Ca3 B9Ra3
F6Ra3 G7Ba3 B6Rb1 B2Cb8 B1Bb9 J3Ca9 J2Ra3
A2Ba1 D3Ba3 A7Rb4 C3Rb5 A3Cb6 A6Cb5 E8Ca3
J6Ra6 G6Rb4 C6Cb8 C4Bb4 F1Ra4 J8Ra4 D1Ba8
D9Ba4 H2Ba4 D5Rb1 E2Rb6 F4Cb8 J5Cb8 E7Cb8
D8Cb9 E5Bb4 D7Bb6 F7Bb1 J4Bb1 H8Bb1 G1Ca1
C7Ca9 C9Ca1 G9Ra6 H9Ra9 H1Ba6

2	3	15678	168	18	18	179	4	19
147	17	17	1234	9	5	8	23	6
146	9	168	123468	7	1348	12	5	12
367	4	3678	2389	5	389	29	1	289
9	1258	158	1248	1248	6	3	7	2458
1356	1258	13568	7	12348	13489	2459	2689	24589
1357	6	2	134589	1348	134789	1459	89	14589
135	15	4	13589	138	2	6	89	7
8	157	1579	1459	6	1479	12459	29	3

J3Ca9 A7Ca7 B8Ca3 F8Ca6 A3Ra5 A9Ra9 B4Ra2
C3Ba8 E3Rb1 J8Rb2 B3Cb7 F3Cb3 B2Bb1 D3Bb6
F1Bb5 C1Ca6 J2Ca7 A4Ra6 B1Ra4 D1Ra7 E9Ra5
G6Ra7 H2Ba5 J6Rb4 C6Cb3 C4Bb4 D4Ca3 E5Ca4
E2Ra2 F2Ba8 F5Ba2 E4Rb8 F9Rb4 D6Cb9 F7Cb9
G9Cb1 C9Bb2 F6Bb1 D7Bb2 G1Bb3 J7Bb5 H1Ca1
G4Ca5 A5Ca1 H5Ca3 A6Ca8 C7Ca1 G7Ca4 D9Ca8
G8Ra9 H8Ra8 J4Ra1 G5Ba8 H4Ba9

1456	3	146	7	2	14	169	689	189
146	126	9	8	14	134	5	267	127
15	1258	7	15	159	6	4	3	1289
14679	1679	146	146	3	5	2	4789	14789
14567	12567	1246	146	14678	9	17	478	3
13479	179	8	2	147	147	179	5	6
2	67	36	9	4567	347	8	1	47
13679	4	136	136	1678	12378	3679	2679	5
8	1679	5	1346	1467	12347	3679	24679	2479

C2Ca8 E3Ca2 C4Ca5 C5Ca9 H6Ca8 A1Ra5 B6Ra3
C9Ra2 F1Ra3 G5Ra5 H8Ra2 B2Ba2 E2Ba5 E5Ba8
J6Ba2 C1Rb1 G3Ra3 G2Ra6 H3Ba1 J4Ca4 G9Ra4
J5Ra1 J7Ra3 A6Ba1 H4Ba3 H5Ba6 B5Rb4 G6Rb7
B1Cb6 F5Cb7 F6Cb4 A3Bb4 B8Bb7 D3Ca6 A7Ca6
B9Ra1 E4Ra6 J8Ra6 D4Ba1 E8Rb4 E1Cb7 D2Bb9
E7Bb1 H1Bb9 D1Ca4 F2Ca1 J2Ca7 H7Ca7 F7Ca9
A8Ca9 A9Ra8 D9Ra7 J9Ra9 D8Ba8

2	158	4	1689	369	13589	38	7	389
578	3	9	478	247	58	6	24	1
6	178	178	14789	23479	1389	2348	5	23489
1579	15679	3	2	8	4	157	169	79
5789	2	578	9	1	6	34578	49	34789
189	4	168	5	39	7	1238	1269	2389
145789	15789	1578	14789	479	2	147	3	6
1479	1679	1267	3	5	19	1247	8	247
13478	1678	12678	14678	467	18	9	124	5

J1Ca3 F5Ba3 E4Rb9 E8Cb4 B8Bb2 C5Ca2 J3Ra2
J8Rb1 J6Cb8 B6Bb5 A2Ra5 D9Rb7 J2Rb7 H7Ra7
H9Ba2 F9Rb8 G7Rb4 E9Cb3 A9Bb9 E7Bb5 H1Ca4
G3Ca5 G5Ca9 F7Ca2 C9Ca4 C6Ra9 D1Ra5 G4Ra7
H2Ra9 A6Ba3 B5Ba7 F1Ba9 D7Ba1 H3Ba6 H6Ba1
A5Rb6 A7Rb8 B1Rb8 C4Rb8 D2Rb6 F3Rb1 F8Rb6
E1Cb7 G1Cb1 C2Cb1 C3Cb7 A4Cb1 B4Cb4 J5Cb4
C7Cb3 D8Cb9 E3Bb8 G2Bb8 J4Bb6

289	48	1	6	3479	2349	234789	23478	5
2589	7	3	2459	459	2459	24689	1	24689
259	456	256	8	134579	123459	234679	23467	24679
15	2	567	34579	8	13459	14679	467	4679
3	58	4	2579	1579	6	12789	278	2789
18	9	678	247	147	124	5	24678	3
7	38	28	349	6	3489	2348	5	1
6	358	258	1	345	7	2348	9	248
4	1	9	35	2	358	3678	3678	678

C2Ca6 A2Ba4 E2Ca8 F8Ra8 D1Ba5 C3Rb5 F1Rb1
G2Rb3 H2Cb5 F5Cb4 F6Bb2 H5Bb3 B4Ca2 D4Ca3
F3Ra6 D3Ba7 F4Rb7 J4Rb5 E4Cb9 J6Cb8 D6Bb1
G4Bb4 C5Ca1 B6Ca5 E7Ca1 E5Ra5 G6Ra9 C6Ba4
A5Ba7 A6Rb3 B5Rb9 B1Cb8 A8Cb2 A1Bb9 E8Bb7
C1Ca2 D8Ca4 H9Ca8 A7Ra8 E9Ra2 G3Ra8 H7Ra4
B9Ba4 H3Ba2 G7Ba2 B7Rb6 C8Rb3 D7Cb9 J8Cb6
C7Bb7 D9Bb6 J9Bb7 J7Ca3 C9Ca9

2349	249	23479	12369	2349	1469	234579	14589	123456789
6	249	5	1239	8	7	2349	149	12349
2349	8	1	2369	5	469	23479	49	234679
1489	149	6	19	7	1589	3459	2	13459
7	129	29	4	29	3	8	6	159
5	3	2489	129	6	189	479	149	1479
1489	1459	489	79	49	2	6	3	4589
23489	7	23489	5	349	469	1	489	2489
2349	24569	2349	8	1	469	2459	7	2459

J2Ca6 A3Ca7 G4Ca7 D6Ca5 A8Ca5 A9Ra8 D1Ra8
E9Ra5 H6Ra6 C9Ba6 F6Ba8 G2Ba5 H5Ba3 J7Ba5
H8Ba8 G1Ca1 J3Ca3 G3Ca8 A4Ca6 A6Ca1 F9Ca7
C7Ra7 E2Ra1 F3Ca2 C4Ca2 E5Ca2 C1Ra3 E3Ra9
B4Ba3 D2Ba4 B9Rb1 H3Rb4 D9Cb3 D7Bb9 A1Ca4
F4Ca9 A7Ca3 F8Ca1 A2Ra2 D4Ra1 F7Ra4 B2Ba9
C6Ba4 B7Ba2 A5Rb9 B8Rb4 C8Rb9 J6Rb9 J1Cb2
G5Cb4 H1Bb9 G9Bb9 J9Bb4 H9Ca2

5789	4	679	89	3	2	1	68	69
3789	1789	1379	6	478	5	3489	2	49
2389	1289	12369	1489	48	1489	7	3468	5
24789	2789	2479	458	4568	468	2456	1	3
347	5	1347	2	9	346	46	467	8
2348	6	234	7	1	348	245	9	24
6	3	2479	14589	4578	14789	24589	4578	2479
479	79	8	3	2	4679	4569	4567	1
1	279	5	489	4678	46789	234689	34678	24679

A1Ca5 A3Ra7 E3Ra1 F7Ra5 C3Ba6 B5Ba7 E8Ba7
B2Ra1 H8Ra5 D5Ca6 D4Ra5 E7Ra6 H6Ra6 G5Ba5
H1Ca4 E6Ra4 H2Ra7 D1Ba7 F6Ba3 D6Rb8 E1Rb3
H7Rb9 C1Ca2 C2Ca8 B3Ca3 B7Ra8 C8Ra3 F1Ra8
B1Ba9 A4Ba8 B9Ba4 J7Ba3 A8Rb6 C5Rb4 F9Rb2
G7Rb2 F3Cb4 G3Cb9 J5Cb8 D7Cb4 A9Cb9 G9Cb7
D3Bb2 J2Bb2 G6Bb1 J8Bb4 J9Bb6 D2Ca9 C4Ca1
G4Ca4 J6Ca7 G8Ca8 C6Ra9 J4Ra9

3679	367	39	2357	1	2567	4	23679	8
367	5	348	23478	3678	9	67	1	267
2	1	3489	3478	3678	678	679	3679	5
179	78	189	1578	2	3	156789	4	1679
5	278	1289	6	78	4	1789	279	3
137	23478	6	1578	9	1578	1578	257	127
136	236	7	9	3568	12568	156	56	146
4	36	135	1357	3567	1567	2	8	1679
8	9	125	1257	4	12567	3	567	167

F2Ca4 G9Ca4 F1Ra3 H9Ra9 B9Rb2 F8Ra2 C8Ca3
C7Ra9 E8Ba9 G8Ca5 J3Ra5 G2Ba2 H5Ba5 G6Rb8
G5Cb3 B5Bb8 E3Ca2 C3Ca8 B4Ca3 C5Ca6 B3Ra4
C4Ra4 E7Ra1 C6Ba7 J9Ba1 E5Rb7 F9Rb7 G7Rb6
J4Rb2 G1Cb1 E2Cb8 A4Cb5 J6Cb6 B7Cb7 J8Cb7
D9Cb6 B1Bb6 A6Bb2 A8Bb6 D2Bb7 H3Bb3 H6Bb1
A1Ca7 A2Ca3 H2Ca6 D3Ca1 H4Ca7 F6Ca5 A3Ra9
D7Ra5 D1Ra9 F4Ra1 D4Ba8 F7Ba8

6	1578	1358	19	1259	1259	35	23579	24579
13	4	135	169	7	12569	35	8	2569
9	57	2	8	3	4	1	567	567
1248	1289	1489	1349	129	1239	6	357	1578
5	3	168	7	12	126	9	4	18
14	169	7	5	8	1369	2	3	1
1378	156789	135689	2	159	135789	4	569	5689
2378	256789	35689	39	4	35789	58	1	25689
1248	12589	14589	19	6	1589	7	259	3

D4Ca4 B4Ca6 H7Ca8 A9Ca4 F1Ra4 J3Ba4 F8Rb3
F9Rb1 E9Cb8 H4Ca3 C2Ra5 D6Ra3 A2Ba7 A3Ra8
B7Ra5 A7Ba3 B1Ca1 B3Ra3 G1Ba3 H1Ca7 G6Ra7
J6Ba8 J1Rb2 D1Cb8 D2Bb2 G2Ca8 A8Ca2 B6Ra2
G5Ra1 H9Ra2 J8Ra5 B9Ba9 E6Ba1 E5Ba2 D9Ba5
J2Ba1 H6Ba5 A6Rb9 D5Rb9 D8Rb7 E3Rb6 G9Rb6
J4Rb9 F2Cb9 D3Cb1 H3Cb9 A4Cb1 A5Cb5 F6Cb6
C8Cb6 G8Cb9 C9Cb7 G3Bb5 H2Bb6

7	1368	9	2356	4	1256	12358	1235	1358
4	5	136	8	237	1267	9	123	13
13	2	138	357	3579	157	13578	6	13458
8	346	3456	234567	1	24567	2356	2359	356
1356	1346	2	3456	8	9	1356	135	7
1356	9	7	2356	235	256	123568	4	13568
135	13478	13458	9	6	4578	135	135	2
23569	368	3568	1	25	258	4	7	356
1256	1467	1456	2457	257	3	156	8	9

H1Ca9 C5Ca9 C7Ca7 D8Ca9 C9Ca4 C3Ra8 J1Ba2
D6Ca4 D4Ra7 E2Ra4 G3Ra4 J4Ba4 D7Ra2 C6Ca1
J7Ca6 C4Ra5 D9Ra6 C1Rb3 D2Rb3 G1Cb5 D3Cb5
J3Bb1 A2Ca1 H3Ca3 H2Ra6 J5Ra5 B3Ba6 F6Ba5
G2Ba8 G6Ba7 H9Ba5 B6Rb2 H5Rb2 J2Rb7 F5Cb3
A6Cb6 H6Cb8 A4Bb3 B5Bb7 E4Bb6 F1Ca6 F4Ca2
A8Ca2 B9Ca3 A7Ra5 B8Ra1 A9Ba8 E1Ba1 E8Ba5
G7Ba1 E7Rb3 F7Rb8 F9Rb1 G8Rb3

2	689	5	469	4689	4679	678	1	367
7	689	89	1	3	569	2	68	4
3	168	148	456	2468	24567	5678	9	567
1589	13589	189	7	1469	134569	145689	2468	2569
1589	2	6	3459	149	13459	14589	7	59
4	1579	179	2	169	8	1569	3	569
1569	1569	3	469	7	12469	469	246	8
1689	4	12789	369	5	12369	679	26	2679
69	679	279	8	2469	2469	3	5	1

D2Ca3 C3Ca4 A9Ca3 B6Ra5 C2Ra1 E4Ba5 C4Rb6
E9Rb9 H4Ca3 E6Ra3 A4Ca4 B3Rb9 G4Rb9 G2Cb5
D1Ca5 H7Ca9 H9Ra7 F2Ba9 C9Rb5 J2Rb7 J3Cb2
F9Cb6 F5Bb1 D9Bb2 J1Ca9 F3Ca7 C5Ca2 F7Ca5
C7Ra8 A5Ba8 A7Ba7 D8Ba8 A2Rb6 A6Rb9 B8Rb6
C6Rb7 D3Rb1 E5Rb4 E1Cb8 B2Cb8 H3Cb8 J5Cb6
D6Cb6 D7Cb4 E7Cb1 H8Cb2 D5Bb9 H6Bb1 J6Bb4
G7Bb6 G8Bb4 G1Ca1 H1Ca6 G6Ca2

9	36	2	36	38	5	4	378	1
368	4	1368	1236	1238	7	5	389	89
358	135	7	9	1348	18	38	6	2
346	8	3469	7	139	19	139	2	5
23457	2357	3459	1235	6	1289	1389	3489	489
1	2356	3569	235	23589	4	7	389	689
23458	1235	13458	1245	12459	129	6	4589	7
245678	9	4568	2456	2457	3	28	1	48
24567	12567	1456	8	124579	1269	29	459	3

J6Ca6 A8Ca7 F9Ca6 A5Ra8 C5Ra4 E6Ba8 C6Rb1
D6Cb9 G6Bb2 A2Ca6 A4Ra3 B3Ra1 B4Ra6 F8Ra8
B5Ba2 F3Ra9 G3Ca8 E3Ca3 F5Ra3 D7Ba3 C7Rb8
D5Rb1 H7Cb2 B9Cb9 B8Bb3 E9Bb4 J7Bb9 B1Ca8
G4Ca1 G5Ca9 E7Ca1 E8Ca9 H9Ca8 J2Ra1 J1Ba2
H4Ba4 E2Ca7 H5Ca5 E4Ra2 F4Ra5 H1Ra7 J5Ra7
F2Ba2 E1Ba5 H3Ba6 C1Rb3 D3Rb4 D1Cb6 G1Cb4
C2Cb5 J3Cb5 G2Bb3 G8Bb5 J8Bb4

459	456	459	8	3	569	2	7	159
1	3578	2579	29	57	4	358	3589	6
235789	35678	2579	269	1	25679	358	3589	4
345789	34578	4579	39	48	1	458	6	258
348	2	14	5	6	38	9	18	7
4589	1458	6	7	2	89	1458	158	3
257	9	8	4	57	23567	13567	1235	125
2457	1457	3	126	9	25678	15678	1258	1258
6	157	1257	123	578	23578	13578	4	12589

D5Ca4 A9Ra1 D9Ra2 J9Ra9 F7Ba4 G9Rb5 G5Cb7
H9Cb8 B5Bb5 G1Bb2 J5Ca8 C6Ca7 H8Ca2 J6Ca2
H6Ba5 G7Ca1 G6Ra6 C4Ba6 J4Ba3 H7Ba6 A6Rb9
D4Rb9 G8Rb3 H4Rb1 J7Rb7 B4Cb2 F6Cb8 E6Bb3
A2Ca6 C3Ca2 F1Ra9 B3Ba9 B8Rb8 B7Cb3 E8Cb1
B2Bb7 C7Bb5 E3Bb4 F8Bb5 H2Ca4 J3Ca1 D3Ca7
D7Ca8 C8Ca9 A1Ra4 E1Ra8 F2Ra1 H1Ra7 J2Ra5
A3Ba5 C2Ba8 D1Ba5 C1Rb3 D2Rb3

7	1246	246	126	3	68	468	1568	9
124	12346	5	9	1268	68	3468	7	2468
129	12369	8	1267	4	5	36	136	26
149	1469	4679	3	679	2	5	689	4678
8	24569	24679	4567	679	4679	1	69	3
459	34569	34679	8	679	1	4679	2	467
59	7	9	16	1689	3689	2	4	568
3	2459	1	2467	26789	46789	6789	5689	5678
6	8	249	247	5	3479	379	39	1

F3Ca3 E4Ca5 A8Ra5 C4Ra7 G6Ra3 C8Ba1 E6Ba4
G3Rb9 G1Cb5 F2Ca5 J8Ca3 H9Ca5 H5Ca2 A4Ra2
J3Ra2 B5Ba1 E2Ba2 H2Ba4 G5Ba8 G9Rb6 H4Rb6
J4Rb4 G4Cb1 C9Cb2 C1Bb9 D1Ca1 B1Ca2 D2Ca9
A2Ra1 A3Ba4 F1Rb4 F9Cb7 B7Ca4 B2Ra3 D9Ra4
C2Ba6 C7Ba3 D8Ba8 B9Rb8 H8Rb9 B6Cb6 H6Cb7
A7Cb6 J7Cb7 E8Cb6 A6Bb8 E3Bb7 F7Bb9 J6Bb9
H7Bb8 D3Ca6 D5Ca7 E5Ca9 F5Ra6

4	23789	28	1579	13579	1359	189	123589	6
237	23679	26	14579	8	13459	149	123459	12345
38	1	5	2	39	6	7	3489	348
1238	2368	2468	19	1269	7	5	123489	12348
1238	2368	268	159	4	12589	189	7	1238
5	278	9	3	12	128	6	1248	1248
9	4	7	6	125	125	3	158	158
8	58	1	4579	3579	3459	2	4568	4578
6	25	3	8	1257	1245	14	145	9

B1Ca7 D3Ca4 D5Ca6 H8Ca6 H9Ca7 F2Ra7 J5Ra7
A4Ba7 J2Ba2 H1Rb8 C1Cb3 H2Cb5 C5Bb9 H5Rb3
J7Ca4 E7Ca8 D2Ra8 F6Ra8 A3Ba8 E2Ba3 D8Ba9
A2Rb9 D4Rb1 E3Rb6 D1Cb2 B2Cb6 B3Cb2 F5Cb2
A7Cb1 A5Bb5 B7Bb9 E1Bb1 D9Bb3 E4Ca5 G5Ca1
G6Ca2 A8Ca2 E9Ca2 A6Ra3 B6Ra1 E6Ra9 J8Ra1
B4Ba4 B8Ba3 F9Ba1 J6Ba5 H4Ba9 B9Rb5 F8Rb4
H6Rb4 C8Cb8 G9Cb8 C9Bb4 G8Bb5

4	6	9	125	235	1235	1237	8	17
8	123	123	1269	2369	7	1239	5	4
23	7	5	12689	23469	123468	1239	369	169
6	1389	13478	579	579	5	135789	2	1789
259	129	1247	3	8	256	1579	4679	1679
2359	2389	2378	4	1	256	35789	3679	6789
239	2389	2368	12678	2367	12368	4	79	5
1	4	28	2578	257	258	6	79	3
7	5	368	68	346	9	8	1	2

C6Ca4 E8Ca4 C4Ra8 D3Ra4 H8Ra9 J5Ra4 G8Ba7
J7Ba8 D6Rb5 J4Rb6 J3Cb3 G3Ca6 H6Ca8 B5Ra6
G2Ra8 H3Ra2 F3Ba8 G1Ba9 B3Rb1 E3Cb7 D9Ca8
A9Rb7 F7Ca7 F1Ra5 E7Ba5 E1Rb2 C1Cb3 E6Cb6
B2Bb2 C8Bb6 F6Bb2 F8Ca3 F9Ca6 B7Ra3 D2Ra3
F2Ra9 E2Ba1 E9Ba9 A7Rb2 B4Rb9 C9Rb1 D7Rb1
D4Cb7 C5Cb2 C7Cb9 D5Bb9 G5Bb3 H4Bb5 G4Ca2
A5Ca5 H5Ca7 A6Ca3 A4Ra1 G6Ra1

4	13568	356	1568	2	1568	7	9	135
9	15678	567	1568	3	4	15	18	2
235	1358	235	7	15	1589	1345	1348	6
267	467	2679	12468	146	3	1249	5	149
1	345	8	245	9	25	234	6	7
23567	34567	235679	12456	1456	12567	8	134	1349
3567	2	1	34569	8	569	34569	347	3459
8	3567	4	123569	156	12569	13569	137	1359
356	9	356	13456	7	156	13456	2	8

F6Ca7 C6Ra9 D4Ra8 A6Ba8 H5Rb5 C5Cb1 G6Cb6
J6Bb1 F4Ca1 E6Ca5 E4Ba2 H6Rb2 D7Ca2 D9Ra1
F9Ba9 H9Rb3 H4Cb9 A9Cb5 A4Bb6 B7Bb1 G9Bb4
A2Ca1 D3Ca9 J4Ca4 B4Ca5 G7Ca9 H8Ca1 A3Ra3
G1Ra5 H2Ra7 B3Ba7 D1Ba7 J1Ba3 G4Ba3 J7Ba5
G8Ba7 B8Rb8 C1Rb2 H7Rb6 J3Rb6 F1Cb6 B2Cb6
C3Cb5 C2Bb8 D2Bb4 F3Bb2 F5Bb4 F2Ca5 D5Ca6
C8Ca4 C7Ra3 E7Ra4 F8Ra3 E2Ba3

6	123	8	2379	5	1379	4	1237	137
1235	7	9	2348	123468	1368	2356	12356	13
1235	4	235	237	1236	1367	8	123567	9
23578	9	2357	6	1238	1358	237	12378	13478
4	236	236	2389	7	1389	2369	12368	5
23578	236	1	23589	238	4	23679	23678	378
2379	8	237	1	3	357	357	4	6
37	5	4	378	368	2	1	9	378
137	136	367	34578	9	35678	357	3578	2

G1Ca9 B5Ca4 D9Ca4 G3Ra2 H5Ra6 J4Ra4 G5Rb3
F4Ca5 F7Ra9 H9Ca8 E8Ra8 H1Ra3 J6Ra8 B4Ba8
D8Ba1 G6Ba5 D6Rb3 G7Rb7 H4Rb7 D7Cb2 D5Bb8
F1Ca8 C5Ca1 E6Ra1 E4Ba9 B6Rb6 F5Rb2 C6Cb7
A6Bb9 E7Ca6 C8Ra6 E2Ra2 F2Ra6 E3Ba3 J3Ba6
C3Rb5 J2Rb1 C1Cb2 J1Cb7 A2Cb3 D3Cb7 B1Bb1
A4Bb2 C4Bb3 D1Bb5 B8Ca2 A9Ca1 A8Ra7 B7Ra5
B9Ba3 F9Ba7 J8Ba5 F8Rb3 J7Rb3

8	6	1345	145	2	1359	3579	359	35
579	379	345	6	34589	3589	2	1	35
159	139	2	15	7	1359	4	8	356
1257	4	9	12578	1568	12568	135	356	1356
157	137	135	1457	14569	1569	8	34569	2
125	128	6	3	14589	12589	159	7	145
4	128	18	9	1358	7	6	235	1358
3	1289	18	1258	1568	4	15	25	7
126	5	7	128	1368	12368	13	234	9

J1Ca6 A7Ca7 F9Ca4 G9Ca8 C9Ra6 H5Ra6 H2Ra9
J8Ra4 A8Ba9 F2Ba8 G2Ba2 H3Ba8 G3Rb1 F7Ca9
H8Ca2 D9Ca1 B6Ra8 C4Rb5 H4Cb1 A4Bb4 J6Bb2
H7Bb5 B3Ca4 D4Ca2 F5Ca1 E5Ca4 J7Ca1 A6Ra1
D1Ra7 D5Ra8 E6Ra9 F1Ra2 G5Ra5 J5Ra3 B2Ba7
C6Ba3 B5Ba9 D6Ba6 E4Ba7 J4Ba8 G8Ba3 B1Rb5
C2Rb1 D7Rb3 D8Rb5 F6Rb5 C1Cb9 E1Cb1 E2Cb3
A3Cb3 E8Cb6 B9Cb3 A9Bb5 E3Bb5

8	1356	9	2	167	7	157	1357	4
4	1236	136	16789	16789	5	12789	1379	3789
125	125	7	189	1489	3	6	159	89
6	7	468	5	489	1	3	2	689
156	14568	2	3	4789	478	1789	14679	6789
9	1348	1348	78	2	6	178	147	5
1367	13689	1368	1678	5	78	4	3679	2
123567	1234568	134568	1678	13678	9	57	3567	367
23567	23569	356	4	367	27	579	8	1

J6Ca2 E6Ca4 B7Ca2 C5Ra4 D3Ra4 F8Ba4 H2Ba4
A6Rb7 D1Rb6 G6Cb8 C2Ca2 H1Ra2 H3Ra8 J3Ca5
D5Ca8 D9Ra9 E5Ba9 C9Rb8 F4Rb7 G4Cb6 G3Bb1
H4Bb1 B3Ca6 B4Ca8 J7Ca9 A5Ra6 B8Ra9 G2Ra9
J2Ra6 B5Ba1 C4Ba9 B9Ba7 B2Rb3 E9Rb6 F3Rb3
H9Cb3 H5Bb7 G8Bb7 J1Ca7 J5Ca3 E7Ca7 A8Ca3
H8Ca6 E2Ra8 G1Ra3 H7Ra5 C8Ba5 E1Ba5 F7Ba8
A7Rb1 C1Rb1 E8Rb1 F2Rb1 A2Cb5

46789	3	46789	4569	245689	4689	1	28	269
2	489	4689	7	4689	1	3689	5	369
1689	89	5	369	2689	3689	4	238	7
45678	4578	1	2	3	46	68	9	456
45689	24589	24689	469	1	7	2368	2348	23456
3	249	2469	8	469	5	26	7	1246
4789	1	4789	3469	46789	2	5	34	349
4579	6	3	459	4579	49	279	124	8
45789	245789	24789	1	45789	3489	2379	6	2349

C1Ca1 H8Ca1 F9Ca1 H7Ra2 J7Ba7 F7Rb6 D7Cb8
E7Bb3 D2Ca7 B7Ca9 B9Ra3 A9Ba6 G8Ba3 C4Ca3
E8Ca4 E9Ca2 D9Ra5 J6Ra3 B3Ba6 B2Ra8 B5Rb4
C2Rb9 E2Cb5 F5Cb9 E4Bb6 D1Ca6 C6Ca6 C8Ra8
D6Ra4 G5Ra6 A6Ba8 A8Ba2 H5Ba7 J5Ba8 A5Rb5
C5Rb2 H6Rb9 A4Cb9 G4Cb4 H4Bb5 G9Bb9 J1Ca5
J9Ca4 H1Ra4 J3Ra9 A3Ba4 E1Ba9 J2Ba2 A1Rb7
E3Rb8 F2Rb4 F3Rb2 G1Cb8 G3Cb7

8	2479	1467	1239	1237	1279	1234679	1679	5
19	3	5	4	1278	6	12789	179	12789
169	2479	1467	12359	12378	12789	12346789	1679	1246789
9	6	8	129	1247	5	1279	3	1279
4	59	2	139	1367	179	156789	15679	16789
7	1	3	8	236	29	2569	4	269
136	7	9	12	5	4	167	8	167
15	4578	147	6	18	3	14579	2	1479
2	458	146	7	9	18	1456	156	3

G1Ca3 H1Ca5 F3Ca3 C4Ca5 D5Ca4 F7Ra5 G4Ra2
E2Ba5 J3Ba6 J8Ba5 D1Rb9 G2Rb7 B1Cb1 D4Cb1
C1Bb6 H3Ca1 J6Ba1 H5Rb8 J7Rb4 H2Cb4 J2Cb8
C6Ca8 C9Ca4 A3Ra4 C3Ba7 C2Ca9 A2Ba2 C8Rb1
A5Ca1 F6Ca2 F9Ra9 H7Ba9 E8Rb6 F5Rb6 H9Rb7
A8Cb7 D9Cb2 A6Bb9 B8Bb9 B9Bb8 D7Bb7 E4Ca9
E6Ca7 E7Ca8 G9Ca6 A7Ra6 B5Ra7 E9Ra1 E5Ra3
G7Ra1 C5Ba2 A4Ba3 C7Ba3 B7Rb2

1	45	8	245	234	7	9	2356	256
249	459	2459	12458	6	23459	137	23578	257
3	7	6	1258	1289	259	1	258	4
5	3469	2349	24	7	1	346	23469	8
2489	3489	2349	248	5	6	347	1	279
24689	14689	7	3	2489	249	46	24569	2569
46	1456	145	9	124	245	8	467	3
7	1345689	13459	1456	134	345	2	469	69
469	2	349	467	34	8	5	4679	1

```
J4Ca7 F2Ra1 G8Ra7 H2Ra8 H4Ba6 C7Rb1 H9Rb9
H8Cb4 J8Bb6 B4Ca1 A9Ra6 B8Ra8 D8Ca9 F8Rb5
C8Cb2 F9Cb2 C6Bb9 A8Bb3 E9Bb7 F5Ca9 G6Ca2
B7Ca7 B9Ca5 B6Ra3 C4Ra5 F1Ra8 A2Ba5 C5Ba8
D2Ba6 E4Ba8 H6Ba5 F6Rb4 G2Rb4 G1Cb6 J1Cb9
B2Cb9 D4Cb2 G5Cb1 F7Cb6 A4Bb4 D3Bb4 E2Bb3
G3Bb5 J3Bb3 H5Bb3 B1Ca4 H3Ca1 E3Ca9 A5Ca2
J5Ca4 D7Ca3 E7Ca4 B3Ra2 E1Ra2
```

1236	1239	12369	19	8	5	7	1349	1249
12368	1239	4	7	126	269	2359	1359	1259
5	1279	1279	3	12	4	8	19	6
247	24579	279	458	24	1	6	4589	3
1234	8	123	6	9	23	5	45	7
34	6	39	458	7	38	1	2	4589
9	1234	12368	148	1346	368	235	7	1258
134678	1347	13678	2	5	36789	39	13689	189
123678	1237	5	189	136	36789	4	13689	1289

```
D2Ca5 B1Ra8 F4Ba5 E7Rb5 E8Cb4 B8Ca5 A9Ca4
F1Ra4 G9Ra5 H2Ra4 E6Ca2 C5Ra2 F6Ba3 D5Rb4
F3Rb9 D4Cb8 F9Cb8 D8Bb9 G4Ca4 C2Ra9 C3Ba7
C8Rb1 D3Rb2 D1Cb7 A8Cb3 J2Ca7 A4Ra9 B2Ra3
H6Ra7 B5Ba1 J6Ba9 B6Rb6 J4Rb1 G6Cb8 J9Cb2
B9Bb9 G7Bb3 A1Ca2 H3Ca8 J5Ca3 B7Ca2 H7Ca9
H9Ca1 A3Ra6 G2Ra2 H1Ra3 J8Ra8 A2Ba1 E3Ba3
G3Ba1 J1Ba6 G5Ba6 H8Ba6 E1Rb1
```

8	6	23	457	357	9	1	23457	345
357	157	13	2	13567	45678	3579	34579	3459
9	1257	4	157	1357	57	8	2357	6
23	1249	5	8	1269	26	239	12349	7
6	1289	12389	1579	4	257	2359	123589	3589
2	12489	7	159	1259	3	259	6	4589
257	25789	2689	3	25679	1	4	5789	589
4	25789	2689	5679	25679	2567	3579	35789	1
1	3	9	4579	8	457	6	579	2

```
H4Ca6 B6Ca8 B5Ra6 G3Ra6 A4Ba4 D6Ba6 F1Rb2
J3Rb9 D1Cb3 J6Ca4 D5Rb2 D7Cb9 F7Bb5 E2Ca9
H6Ca2 E7Ca2 F4Ra9 G2Ra2 A3Ba2 F5Ba1 H3Rb8
E3Cb1 B3Bb3 D2Bb4 B2Ca1 F2Ca8 C4Ca1 H7Ca3
D8Ca1 C8Ca2 B8Ca4 B9Ra9 C5Ra3 F9Ra4 B7Rb7
B1Cb5 C2Bb7 G1Bb7 H2Ca5 E6Ca7 A5Ra7 C6Ra5
E4Ra5 G5Ba5 J4Ba7 G9Rb8 H5Rb9 J8Rb5 A8Cb3
G8Cb9 H8Cb7 E9Cb3 A9Bb5 E8Bb8
```

8	4579	14579	2469	12346	134569	2357	2345	23457
14	6	3	248	124	1458	9	2458	24578
49	2	459	7	34	34589	1	6	3458
249	1	2479	4689	5	34689	2367	2389	23789
5	8	479	469	3467	2	367	39	1379
3	79	6	1	7	89	4	2589	25789
12469	349	12489	5	1246	146	23	7	2349
246	345	245	246	9	7	8	1	2345
7	459	12459	3	8	14	25	2459	6

```
G3Ca8 E9Ca1 B9Ra7 F5Rb7 F2Cb9 F6Bb8 A2Ca7
B4Ca8 C9Ra8 D8Ba8 H3Rb2 H1Cb6 H4Bb4 D1Ca2
A4Ca2 B8Ra2 F9Ba2 G5Ba2 F8Rb5 G7Rb3 J6Rb1
G2Cb4 J3Cb9 G6Cb6 A7Cb5 H9Cb5 G1Bb1 H2Bb3
J2Bb5 G9Bb9 J7Bb2 J8Bb4 C1Ca9 A3Ca1 C3Ca5
E8Ca9 A9Ca4 A8Ra3 A5Ra6 A6Ra9 B5Ra1 B6Ra5
E5Ra3 B1Ba4 C6Ba3 D6Ba4 D4Ba9 D9Ba3 C5Rb4
D3Rb7 E4Rb6 E3Cb4 D7Cb6 E7Cb7
```

189	289	3	18	18	7	148	6	5
4	578	178	6	1358	2	1378	137	9
1568	25678	12678	1358	4	9	1378	1237	237
7	3489	48	348	38	6	2	5	1
189	23489	5	123478	1238	134	6	379	347
16	2346	1246	9	1235	1345	347	8	347
3	456	46	1245	7	145	159	129	8
568	1	4678	2345	23569	345	3579	2379	2367
2	567	9	135	1356	8	1357	4	367

E4Ca7 H5Ca9 A2Ra2 A7Ra4 D2Ra9 A1Ba9 F3Ba2
E8Ba9 J5Ba6 E5Ca2 G7Ca9 H9Ca6 C9Ca2 H6Ca3
D3Rb4 G3Cb6 G2Ca4 G6Ra5 H4Ra4 F5Ba5 J4Ba1
G4Ba2 A4Rb8 B5Rb3 G8Rb1 C4Cb5 D4Cb3 A5Cb1
D5Cb8 B8Cb7 C8Bb3 H8Bb2 H1Ca5 B2Ra5 H3Ra8
J7Ra5 J2Ba7 J9Ba3 B3Rb1 E9Rb4 H7Rb7 C3Cb7
E6Cb1 B7Cb8 F7Cb3 F9Cb7 C7Bb1 E1Bb8 F2Bb6
F6Bb4 F1Ca1 C1Ca6 E2Ca3 C2Ca8

2346	1	23	8	359	2359	7	2	2346
23678	5	2378	1	37	4	268	9	236
23478	47	9	6	37	237	1248	128	5
234578	479	23578	24579	45789	25789	1245	6	247
1	4679	2578	3	456789	256789	245	257	247
24567	467	257	2457	1	2567	9	3	8
57	2	4	579	56789	156789	3	578	679
9	8	6	57	357	357	25	4	1
57	3	157	4579	2	156789	568	578	679

J3Ca1 C8Ca1 D7Ra1 G6Ra1 H7Ra2 J4Ra4 A8Rb2
A3Cb3 D1Ca3 B9Ca3 J9Ra9 C6Ba2 G4Ba9 B5Rb7
C5Cb3 H5Bb5 H6Ca3 A6Ra5 C2Ra7 H4Ra7 A5Ba9
F2Ca4 F6Ra6 E2Ba6 G5Ba6 B3Rb2 D2Rb9 F1Rb2
G9Rb7 J6Rb8 G1Cb5 F4Cb5 D6Cb7 J8Cb5 F3Bb7
D4Bb2 E6Bb9 E8Bb7 J1Bb7 G8Bb8 J7Bb6 D3Ca5
E7Ca5 E9Ca2 A9Ca6 A1Ra4 B1Ra6 D5Ra8 E5Ra4
C1Ba8 C7Ba4 E3Ba8 D9Ba4 B7Rb8

3	2457	457	9	178	178	1248	148	6
6789	679	1	5	4	2	3	8	9
2689	2469	469	68	1368	1368	7	5	129
69	8	369	46	1369	5	126	7	12
4	5679	5679	678	2	16789	1568	3	15
567	1	2	678	3678	3678	568	9	4
5679	345679	8	1	679	679	4569	2	3579
125679	25679	5679	3	6789	4	1569	16	1579
12679	234679	34679	267	5	679	1469	146	8

J4Ca2 D4Ca4 G9Ca3 H5Ra8 D3Ba3 H9Ba7 B8Rb8
B9Rb9 C1Ca8 J2Ca3 E9Ca5 A6Ra8 F1Ra5 A5Ba7
C4Rb6 H1Ca2 F4Ra7 E4Ba8 J1Ba1 F7Ca8 D9Ca1
D7Ra2 E6Ra1 C5Ba1 C9Ba2 D5Ba9 E7Ba6 A3Rb5
C6Rb3 D1Rb6 G5Rb6 B1Cb7 A2Cb2 F5Cb3 F6Cb6
B2Bb6 G1Bb9 E2Ca7 J6Ca9 E3Ra9 G6Ra7 H7Ra9
J3Ra7 C2Ba9 G2Ba4 H3Ba6 H8Ba1 G7Ba5 A8Rb4
C3Rb4 H2Rb5 J7Rb4 A7Cb1 J8Cb6

679	39	3679	3479	5	24679	123	1234	8
5689	2	369	1	3469	469	7	345	3459
579	4	1	8	2379	279	235	6	359
46789	1389	34679	2	14679	5	136	1347	13467
4679	139	34679	479	8	14679	1356	13457	2
2467	1	5	47	1467	3	8	9	1467
59	7	8	6	1239	129	4	1235	135
1	5	2	3457	347	47	9	8	3567
3	6	49	4579	12479	124789	125	1257	157

F1Ca2 H2Ca5 D2Ca8 J6Ca8 B1Ra8 H9Ra6 C1Ba5
J3Ba4 J4Ba5 F2Rb1 G1Rb9 E7Ca5 F5Ra6 J5Ra9
D7Ba6 D3Ra9 A2Ba9 E2Rb3 E4Ca9 C9Rb9 B6Ca9
C7Ca3 A4Ra4 B3Ra6 A3Ba3 B5Ba3 A6Ba6 E1Ba6
A1Rb7 E3Rb7 F4Rb7 D1Cb4 H4Cb3 F9Cb4 B9Bb5
D5Bb1 E8Bb1 H5Ca4 G6Ca1 B8Ca4 G8Ca5 J9Ca1
A7Ra1 E6Ra4 G5Ra2 G9Ra3 H6Ra7 J8Ra7 C6Ba2
C5Ba7 A8Ba2 D8Ba3 D9Ba7 J7Ba2

678	3	9	24	1	2468	27	5	278
1568	28	12568	9	268	7	123	18	4
1578	4	12578	25	28	3	6	1789	12789
1479	279	1247	6	5	24	8	3	179
34789	5	23478	2347	234	1	79	479	6
13467	7	13467	8	34	9	157	2	17
45789	789	4578	1245	24689	24568	1279	16789	3
2	6	38	13	7	8	4	189	5
345789	1	34578	2345	234689	24568	279	6789	2789

E4Ca7 B7Ca3 F7Ca5 E8Ca4 H8Ra9 C4Ba5 C9Ba9
E7Rb9 F2Rb7 H6Rb8 H3Cb3 F9Cb1 D9Bb7 H4Bb1
J4Ca3 G7Ca1 G4Ca2 D6Ca2 E3Ra2 B2Ba2 E1Ba8
F5Ba4 A4Rb4 D2Rb9 E5Rb3 F3Rb6 F1Cb3 G2Cb8
A6Cb6 A1Bb7 B5Bb8 B1Ca6 C3Ca8 C5Ca2 J7Ca7
A9Ra8 B3Ra5 C8Ra7 G3Ra7 J9Ra2 C1Ba1 B8Ba1
A7Ba2 J8Ba8 D1Rb4 G8Rb6 J3Rb4 D3Cb1 G5Cb9
J6Cb5 G1Bb5 J1Bb9 G6Bb4 J5Bb6

2	4	158	3578	137	9	137	6	357
3	157	15	4567	167	124567	8	145	9
1578	9	6	34578	137	14578	137	2	3457
456	356	345	4679	2	467	3679	34589	1
46	8	7	1	5	3	269	49	4
1456	12356	9	467	8	467	2367	345	3457
16789	1367	138	2	4	1678	5	1389	38
15678	13567	1358	35678	9	15678	4	138	2
14589	1235	123458	358	13	158	139	7	6

J3Ca2 D4Ca9 B5Ca6 B6Ca2 G9Ca8 D8Ra8 E7Ra2
J1Ra4 F2Ba2 D3Ba4 E8Ba9 G1Ba9 E1Rb6 E9Rb4
D1Cb5 D2Bb3 F1Bb1 J7Ca9 B8Ca4 F8Ca5 H1Ca7
B2Ra7 G6Ra7 H3Ra8 B3Ba1 C1Ba8 F4Ba7 G3Ba3
A3Rb5 B4Rb5 D6Rb6 F9Rb3 G2Rb6 G8Rb1 H4Cb6
F6Cb4 D7Cb7 F7Cb6 H8Cb3 A9Cb7 C6Bb1 C9Bb5
C4Ca4 J5Ca1 C5Ca7 J6Ca8 A7Ca1 A4Ra8 C7Ra3
H2Ra1 J4Ra3 J2Ra5 A5Ba3 H6Ba5

1289	29	1289	489	7	12459	3	1259	6
123689	4	1289	689	1258	12569	7	1259	259
1269	2679	5	3	12	1269	19	8	4
249	8	249	5	124	12346	469	3469	379
7	25	6	48	9	234	48	345	1
459	1	3	468	48	7	2	4569	589
14689	679	14789	2	3	49	5	1469	89
24569	3	249	1	45	8	469	7	29
124589	2579	124789	479	6	459	1489	12349	2389

B1Ca3 J4Ca7 D9Ca7 C2Ra7 C1Ba6 G3Ba7 G2Ca6
J9Ca3 H7Ra6 F4Rb6 B6Ca6 D8Ca6 D6Ra3 D5Ba1
E8Ba3 C5Rb2 E6Rb2 E2Cb5 C7Ra9 C6Rb1 D7Rb4
E7Cb8 E4Bb4 J7Bb1 H5Ca4 G9Ca8 A6Ra4 F1Ra4
F5Ra8 G1Ra1 H1Ra5 B5Ba5 J3Ba4 J6Ba5 B9Rb2
G6Rb9 B8Cb1 G8Cb4 H9Cb9 A8Bb5 F9Bb5 H3Bb2
J8Bb2 A2Ca2 A3Ca1 F8Ca9 D1Ra2 J1Ra8 B3Ba8
D3Ba9 J2Ba9 A1Rb9 B4Rb9 A4Cb8

9	2456	26	23457	1	2378	34568	5678	3458
1456	3	8	457	9	7	1456	2	145
1245	1245	7	2345	3458	6	13458	589	134589
1678	1678	5	347	2	1378	9	68	138
128	128	12	39	6	5	1238	4	7
3	9	4	7	78	178	12568	568	1258
258	258	9	6	35	4	7	1	258
245678	245678	26	1	57	279	2458	3	24589
12457	12457	123	8	357	2379	245	59	6

J3Ca3 E4Ca9 C5Ca4 A8Ca7 D4Ra4 E7Ra3 G5Ra3
A6Ba8 D6Ba3 B6Rb7 F4Rb7 B4Cb5 F5Cb8 F6Cb1
E3Ca1 D9Ra1 D8Ba8 B9Rb4 F8Ca6 A2Ra4 J8Ca5
J6Ra9 H6Ba2 H5Ba5 H9Ba9 C8Rb9 H3Rb6 J5Rb7
A3Cb2 A4Bb3 D2Ca6 C4Ca2 C9Ca3 A7Ra6 C7Ra8
D1Ra7 B1Ba6 B7Ba1 A9Ba5 H2Ba7 G9Ba8 F9Rb2
H7Rb4 H1Cb8 F7Cb5 J7Cb2 E1Bb2 J2Bb1 C1Ca1
J1Ca4 G2Ca2 E2Ca8 C2Ra5 G1Ra5

8	12345	1346	7	2456	2456	9	245	1245
457	9	47	58	1	3	6	245	245
457	12457	1467	56	2456	9	1257	8	3
6	1358	138	13589	23589	258	4	7	259
3457	34578	9	3568	23568	25678	235	1	256
2	1357	137	4	3569	567	35	356	8
1	348	2	35689	7	4568	358	3456	456
347	6	3478	358	3458	458	12358	9	1245
349	348	5	2	34689	1	38	346	7

J1Ca9 D4Ca1 C7Ca7 D9Ca9 B4Ra8 F5Ra9 G4Ra9
A9Ba1 H7Ca1 H9Ra2 E7Ba2 B8Ra2 F3Rb1 C2Ca1
C5Ra2 A2Ba2 D6Ba2 A3Ra3 C3Ba6 C4Rb5 D3Rb8
C1Cb4 H4Cb3 B3Bb7 E4Bb6 H1Bb7 E1Ca3 H3Ca4
G9Ca6 A8Ra5 B9Ra4 D5Ra3 E2Ra4 F8Ra6 J5Ra6
B1Ba5 A6Ba6 F2Ba7 F7Ba3 G6Ba4 G7Ba5 A5Rb4
D2Rb5 E9Rb5 F6Rb5 G8Rb3 J7Rb8 G2Cb8 J2Cb3
E5Cb8 H6Cb8 J8Cb4 E6Bb7 H5Bb5

3	4	2	9	125	8	1257	127	6
259	89	28	7	6	12345	12345	123489	249
1	7	268	2345	25	2345	2345	23489	249
467	36	3467	2456	2578	245679	2347	23479	1
8	5	147	24	3	12479	247	6	2479
467	2	9	46	17	1467	347	5	8
24679	3689	5	1	27	2367	2467	247	247
267	16	1267	8	4	2567	9	127	3
2467	136	123467	236	9	2367	8	1247	5

B1Ca5 D5Ca8 G7Ca6 C3Ra6 F7Ra3 G2Ra8 H6Ra5
B3Ba8 B2Ba9 E3Ba1 D4Ba5 G1Ba9 A3Rb2 H3Cb7
C8Ca8 C9Ra9 G6Ra3 C4Ba3 B8Ba3 D8Ba9 E6Ca9
G8Ca4 G5Ra2 J6Ba7 A8Rb7 C5Rb5 G9Rb7 J4Rb6
F4Cb4 A5Cb1 A7Bb5 E4Bb2 F5Bb7 D1Ca7 F6Ca1
B7Ca1 E7Ca7 B9Ca2 B6Ra4 C6Ra2 D7Ra2 E9Ra4
F1Ra6 C7Ba4 D3Ba4 D6Ba6 H2Ba6 D2Rb3 H1Rb2
J3Rb3 J1Cb4 J2Cb1 H8Cb1 J8Bb2

157	178	9	2	7	678	135	1356	4
2457	6	25	3	1	479	8	25	257
1247	1278	3	4678	5	4678	12	9	267
3	1279	1256	45679	8	245679	2459	25	259
2579	4	25	579	2379	1	6	8	259
2569	289	2568	4569	2349	24569	23459	7	1
1269	5	4	189	29	289	7	126	3
129	1239	7	1589	6	2589	1259	4	2589
8	129	126	14579	2479	3	1259	1256	2569

H2Ca3 F3Ca8 A8Ca3 H9Ca8 A6Ra6 B6Ra9 E5Ra3
C9Ba6 F7Ba3 A5Rb7 B1Ca4 A2Ca8 D6Ca7 D7Ca4
B9Ca7 E1Ra7 J4Ra7 C2Ba7 J5Ba4 H4Ca1 G8Ca1
G1Ra6 H6Ra5 D3Ba6 J8Ba6 F2Rb9 J3Rb1 F1Cb5
J2Cb2 F5Cb2 A1Bb1 D2Bb1 E3Bb2 F6Bb4 H1Bb9
G5Bb9 J9Bb5 C1Ca2 B3Ca5 C4Ca4 F4Ca6 G6Ca2
C7Ca1 A7Ca5 J7Ca9 D9Ca2 B8Ra2 C6Ra8 D4Ra9
E4Ra5 G4Ra8 H7Ra2 D8Ba5 E9Ba9

8	1	346	359	69	7	36	2	346
2367	23679	2367	389	4	368	5	67	1
3467	367	5	13	16	2	9	8	346
2356	2356	1236	1238	18	9	4	156	7
9	8	12467	1247	5	14	126	3	26
23457	2357	12347	6	178	1348	128	159	29
2356	2356	9	1458	168	14568	7	146	2346
1	2567	267	4579	3	456	26	469	8
367	4	3678	1789	2	168	136	169	5

B2Ca9 J3Ca8 F5Ca7 A5Ca9 F7Ca8 B8Ca7 F9Ca9
A4Ra5 E3Ra7 D4Ca2 D5Ra8 F6Ba3 J7Ca1 G9Ca3
A7Ra3 E7Ra6 J1Ra3 E9Ba2 H2Ba7 H7Ba2 H3Rb6
H4Rb9 J6Rb6 A3Cb4 J4Cb7 G5Cb1 B6Cb8 H8Cb4
J8Cb9 B4Bb3 C5Bb6 A9Bb6 H6Bb5 G8Bb6 F1Ca4
C1Ca7 D2Ca6 D3Ca3 G4Ca8 E6Ca1 C9Ca4 B1Ra6
C4Ra1 C2Ra3 D8Ra1 E4Ra4 G6Ra4 B3Ba2 F3Ba1
F8Ba5 D1Rb5 F2Rb2 G1Cb2 G2Cb5

389	1359	138	15678	578	4	1378	367	2
7	12	128	1268	3	9	5	4	168
6	1235	12348	12578	2578	78	1378	9	178
29	4	5	679	1	67	279	8	3
39	8	37	45679	4579	2	479	1	45679
239	12379	6	45789	45789	378	2479	27	4579
5	267	2478	3	24789	1	24789	27	4789
2348	237	23478	24789	6	5	1234789	237	14789
1	237	9	2478	2478	78	6	5	478

H1Ca4 G2Ca6 F6Ca3 D6Ca6 A8Ca6 B4Ra6 C3Ra4
E9Ra6 F2Ra1 J2Ra3 E3Ba7 F9Ba5 B2Rb2 C2Cb5
H2Cb7 A2Bb9 A1Ca8 A3Ca3 H8Ca3 B9Ra8 C7Ra3
E1Ra3 B3Ba1 H4Rb9 D4Cb7 H9Cb1 C9Bb7 J6Ca7
A7Ca1 G9Ca9 A5Ra7 C4Ra1 G5Ra4 C5Ba2 A4Ba5
J9Ba4 C6Rb8 E4Rb4 J5Rb8 F4Cb8 J4Cb2 F5Cb9
E7Cb9 F1Bb2 E5Bb5 D7Bb2 D1Ca9 F7Ca4 G8Ca2
F8Ra7 G7Ra7 H3Ra2 G3Ba8 H7Ba8

3579	13579	139	6	3	4	8	135	2359
2	34589	3469	39	7	1	359	3456	34569
3469	13489	13469	5	38	2	139	1346	7
3459	23459	2349	8	2345	359	6	7	1
3456	12345	8	7	2345	35	235	9	235
3579	23579	239	239	1	6	4	35	8
8	6	234	1234	9	357	1357	1345	345
349	2349	5	1234	23468	378	1379	13468	3469
1	349	7	34	34568	358	359	2	34569

D6Ca9 E7Ca2 H8Ca8 A9Ra2 B2Ra8 E2Ra1 E1Ra6
C5Ba8 B4Ba9 A5Rb3 J6Ca8 E5Ra4 C7Ba9 D3Ca4
A8Rb1 B3Rb6 A3Cb9 C3Cb1 C8Cb6 F3Bb2 H2Ca2
G3Ca3 D5Ra2 G4Ra2 E6Ba5 H4Ba1 J7Ba3 B7Rb5
E9Rb3 F4Rb3 G6Rb7 H5Rb6 H7Rb7 J4Rb4 J2Cb9
J5Cb5 H6Cb3 G7Cb1 F8Cb5 B9Cb4 H9Cb9 B8Bb3
F2Bb7 H1Bb4 G8Bb4 G9Bb5 J9Bb6 A1Ca7 F1Ca9
C2Ca4 A2Ra5 C1Ra3 D2Ba3 D1Ba5

2	89	4	6	39	5	13	389	7
5	689	6789	1	3479	489	346	234689	36
6789	3	1	478	479	2	456	45689	56
4	1568	368	35	1356	7	2	356	9
1369	12569	2369	345	8	1469	34567	3456	356
369	7	369	2	34569	469	3456	1	8
13678	1268	5	78	1267	168	9	36	4
1367	1246	2367	9	124567	146	8	356	1356
1689	14689	689	458	1456	3	156	7	2

E7Ca7 B8Ca2 H9Ca1 A7Ra1 E8Ca4 A5Ra3 H8Ca5
C9Ca5 F7Ra5 J5Ra5 E9Ba3 G8Ba3 B9Rb6 D8Rb6
E4Rb5 J7Rb6 D4Cb3 D5Cb1 C7Cb4 B7Bb3 D3Bb8
D2Ca5 J4Ca4 G6Ca1 C1Ra6 H2Ra4 B3Ba7 G4Ba8
C4Rb7 G1Rb7 H6Rb6 J3Rb9 H1Cb3 C5Cb9 G5Cb2
E6Cb9 B5Bb4 C8Bb8 E1Bb1 F1Bb9 F6Bb4 G2Bb6
H3Bb2 H5Bb7 J1Ca8 J2Ca1 E2Ca2 F3Ca3 F5Ca6
B6Ca8 A8Ca9 A2Ra8 B2Ra9 E3Ra6

2	8	356	9	136	1357	167	4	67
456	7	456	126	126	125	9	1268	3
1	36	369	267	8	4	67	5	267
459	1234	123459	124	1249	6	8	137	57
7	1346	134689	5	149	189	2	136	6
4568	1246	124568	3	7	128	1456	16	9
468	1246	124678	124678	123469	123789	567	2678	25678
3	5	24678	24678	246	278	67	9	1
68	9	12678	12678	5	1278	3	2678	4

D1Ca9 F7Ca4 G9Ca8 B8Ra8 C3Ra9 G7Ra5 A7Ba1
C9Ba2 D9Ba5 E9Rb6 F8Cb1 A9Cb7 C7Bb6 E8Bb3
H7Ca7 C2Ra3 C4Ra7 D8Ra7 D3Ba3 J6Ca7 G3Ra7
H6Rb2 F6Cb8 J1Ca8 F2Ca6 E3Ra8 F3Ra2 H4Ra8
F1Ba5 G2Ba2 G8Rb6 J3Rb1 G1Cb4 J4Cb6 J8Cb2
B1Bb6 B4Bb2 H3Bb6 G4Bb1 H5Bb4 B3Ca4 D4Ca4
D5Ca2 A5Ca6 A6Ra3 B6Ra5 D2Ra1 E2Ra4 A3Ba5
B5Ba1 G5Ba3 E5Rb9 G6Rb9 E6Cb1

8	159	19	35	6	4	359	2	7
159	12579	3	2578	1278	1589	4	589	6
4	25679	279	23578	2378	3589	3589	1	3589
3569	3569	89	1	38	2	35689	56789	4
7	2369	2489	3468	5	368	23689	689	1
1356	12356	1248	9	348	7	23568	568	358
2	4	179	5678	178	1568	15689	3	589
139	8	6	23457	12347	135	159	459	59
13	13	5	3468	9	1368	7	468	2

D8Ca7 C2Ra6 G3Ba7 B2Ca7 F5Ca4 E3Ra4 H8Ra4
C3Ba2 H1Ba9 J4Ba4 H9Rb5 H7Cb1 H6Bb3 B1Rb5
F8Ca5 D2Ra5 J6Ra8 J8Ba6 E6Rb6 G5Rb1 G6Cb5
C6Bb9 G4Bb6 B6Ca1 G9Ca9 B8Ra9 G7Ra8 C9Ba8
E8Rb8 F9Rb3 E4Cb3 A4Bb5 D5Bb8 J2Ca3 F3Ca8
B4Ca8 C5Ca3 C7Ca5 A7Ra3 B5Ra2 C4Ra7 D1Ra3
J1Ra1 F2Ba1 F1Ba6 H4Ba2 H5Ba7 A2Rb9 D3Rb9
F7Rb2 E2Cb2 A3Cb1 D7Cb6 E7Cb9

6	1389	139	2	139	34	5	7	18
1358	13578	1357	14567	1367	3457	1268	12468	9
159	2	4	8	1679	57	16	16	3
1589	1589	2	3	4	578	168	1568	15678
4	1358	1356	567	2	9	1368	13568	15678
7	358	356	56	68	1	9	23568	4
12359	13579	8	17	137	6	4	1359	15
12359	6	1359	14	138	2348	7	13589	158
13	1347	137	9	5	3478	1368	1368	2

J2Ca4 H6Ca2 B7Ca2 B8Ca4 A6Ra4 F8Ra2 G1Ra2
H4Ra4 A9Ba8 D9Ca6 D6Ra7 C5Ba7 F5Ba8 E9Ba7
C6Rb5 C1Cb9 B6Cb3 J6Bb8 H3Ca9 G4Ca7 B5Ca6
A5Ca9 D2Ra9 G8Ra9 H8Ra8 J3Ra7 B2Ba7 B4Ba1
J1Ba1 B3Rb5 B1Cb8 D1Bb5 H1Ca3 G2Ca5 E2Ca8
E8Ca5 D7Ra8 E7Ra3 F4Ra5 G5Ra3 H9Ra5 E3Ba1
E4Ba6 D8Ba1 H5Ba1 G9Ba1 J8Ba3 A3Rb3 C8Rb6
F2Rb3 J7Rb6 A2Cb1 F3Cb6 C7Cb1

6	5789	589	1	389	2	45789	479	34579
2589	1	4	3689	7	689	589	29	359
2789	3	289	489	5	489	6	12479	1479
4	569	3569	7	2369	569	19	169	8
1	2	689	4689	689	4689	3	5	479
35789	56789	35689	345689	3689	1	479	4679	2
2359	4	123569	2569	269	5679	1579	8	1579
589	5689	7	5689	4	5689	2	3	159
2589	589	2589	2589	1	3	4579	479	6

G3Ca1 G6Ca7 D5Ra2 E9Ra7 G1Ra3 H9Ra1 C8Ba1
H2Ba6 D7Ca1 B8Ca2 C1Ra7 D3Ra3 G4Ra2 C3Ba2
F2Ba7 G5Ba6 J1Ca2 A9Ca4 A5Ra3 B9Ba3 F4Ba3
C9Rb9 A8Cb7 G9Cb5 G7Bb9 J8Bb4 F7Ca4 J7Ca7
D6Ba5 D2Rb9 D8Cb6 F8Bb9 E5Ca9 A3Ra9 F3Ra6
F1Ba5 H1Ba9 B1Rb8 E3Rb8 F5Rb8 H6Rb8 A2Cb5
J3Cb5 H4Cb5 C6Cb4 B7Cb5 C4Bb8 A7Bb8 E6Bb6
J2Bb8 J4Bb9 E4Ca4 B4Ca6 B6Ca9

2	9	1	78	347	6	3458	3578	48
5	3467	3478	178	1347	2	9	1378	1468
3467	3467	3478	5	13479	34789	13468	2	1468
379	137	379	4	2	789	138	6	5
8	12347	6	79	79	5	1234	139	149
49	245	2459	3	69	1	7	89	489
3469	2346	2349	1269	5	349	168	189	7
4679	8	24579	12679	14679	479	156	159	3
1	3567	3579	679	8	379	56	4	2

E7Ca2 F5Ra6 D6Ba8 F9Ca9 F1Ra4 F8Ra8 E9Ba4
G7Ba8 A9Rb8 A4Cb7 E4Bb9 B4Ca8 B8Ca7 C3Ra8
E5Ra7 J4Rb6 J7Cb5 F2Ca5 D7Ca1 H7Ca6 E8Ca3
A8Ca5 E2Ra1 F3Ra2 H3Ra5 G2Ba2 G4Rb1 H4Cb2
G8Cb9 H8Bb1 G1Ra6 G3Ba4 B3Rb3 G6Rb3 C1Cb7
H1Bb9 D1Ca3 D3Ca9 C5Ca9 C9Ra1 C7Ra3 D2Ra7
H6Ra7 J2Ra3 J6Ra9 B5Ba1 A5Ba3 A7Ba4 B9Ba6
J3Ba7 H5Ba4 B2Rb4 C6Rb4 C2Cb6

578	6	1	459	479	579	2	589	3
578	378	9	1356	1367	2	1578	4	58
257	347	2357	13459	8	1579	1579	159	6
4	19	25	8	1269	3	1569	7	259
26789	1789	278	1269	5	19	3	12689	2489
25689	1389	2358	7	1269	4	15689	125689	2589
1	2	8	459	49	589	45689	3	7
3	789	6	2459	2479	5789	4589	2589	1
789	5	4	1239	12379	6	89	289	289

C2Ca4 E9Ca4 G7Ra6 H7Ba4 G3Rb8 H6Ca8 D5Ra6
J1Ra7 B4Ba6 H2Ba9 H5Ba7 H8Ba5 D2Rb1 H4Rb2
C1Ca2 F5Ca2 A6Ra7 F1Ca9 F8Ra6 E1Ba6 F7Ba1
C8Ca1 B5Ra1 C4Ba3 J4Ba1 C3Rb7 E4Rb9 J5Rb3
B2Cb3 E3Cb2 E6Cb1 D3Bb5 F2Bb8 E8Bb8 E2Ca7
F3Ca3 B7Ca7 J8Ca2 B9Ca8 A1Ra8 B1Ra5 D9Ra2
F9Ra5 J7Ra8 C7Ba5 D7Ba9 J9Ba9 A8Rb9 C6Rb9
A5Cb4 G6Cb5 A4Bb5 G4Bb4 G5Bb9

5	1248	4789	19	479	6	1279	24789	3
149	1234	3479	8	4579	3479	125679	245679	14679
149	6	34789	2	4579	3479	1579	45789	14789
2	348	34689	369	1	3489	3679	36789	5
7	348	1	369	4689	5	2369	23689	689
69	5	3689	7	689	2389	4	1	689
146	7	456	569	2	89	13569	34569	1469
3	1	2	4	5679	79	8	5679	1679
8	9	456	56	3	1	567	4567	2

A4Ca1 F6Ca2 F3Ra3 G6Ra8 B2Ba3 H2Rb1 A2Ca2
C6Ra3 H8Ca5 A7Rb9 G9Ca4 D2Ra8 G7Ra1 H5Ra6
J3Ra4 E2Ba4 G3Ba5 H6Ba7 G8Ba3 C7Rb5 G1Rb6
G4Rb9 H9Rb9 J4Rb5 F1Cb9 D3Bb6 F5Bb8 E4Ca6
B5Ca5 E9Ca8 D6Ra4 E7Ra3 F9Ra6 D4Ba3 E5Ba9
E8Ba2 B6Rb9 B8Rb6 D7Rb7 B3Cb7 B7Cb2 J7Cb6
D8Cb9 J8Cb7 A3Bb8 B9Bb1 C1Ca1 C3Ca9 C8Ca8
C9Ca7 A5Ra7 B1Ra4 C5Ra4 A8Ba4

12789	26789	12479	1567	1567	567	234589	2457	12345789
179	3	179	2	8	4	59	6	1579
5	2678	1247	3	167	9	248	247	12478
279	2579	6	579	457	8	1	3	2457
27	1	8	567	3	2567	245	9	2457
4	2579	23579	1579	157	257	6	8	257
3789	5789	3579	5678	2	1	34589	45	345689
2378	4	2357	5678	9	3567	2358	1	23568
6	2589	12359	4	5	35	7	25	23589

D5Ca4 F3Ra3 J3Ra1 J5Rb5 J6Cb3 J8Cb2 G8Ca5
H3Ra5 H1Ba2 E1Rb7 D1Cb9 B1Bb1 G1Ca3 G2Ca7
F4Ca9 B3Ra7 F5Ra1 A4Ba1 J2Ba8 A1Rb8 G3Rb9
J9Rb9 B9Cb5 B7Bb9 A2Ca9 E7Ca5 C9Ca1 A6Ra5
A5Ra6 C7Ra8 E9Ra4 C2Ba6 C5Ba7 D4Ba5 G7Ba4
C8Rb4 D2Rb2 E4Rb6 H7Rb3 F2Cb5 C3Cb2 G4Cb8
E6Cb2 A7Cb2 A8Cb7 D9Cb7 A3Bb4 A9Bb3 F6Bb7
F9Bb2 H4Bb7 G9Bb6 H6Ca6 H9Ca8

23458	1248	1238	9	1345	145	7	6	34
3457	46	36	35	2	4567	349	1	8
2347	1246	9	13	8	1467	234	23	5
2348	7	12368	12358	1345	12458	1369	389	1369
238	12689	12368	7	13	128	5	4	1369
348	148	5	6	9	148	13	378	2
6	3	2	4	157	12579	8	2579	179
9	28	7	1258	156	3	1246	25	146
1	5	4	28	67	26789	2369	2379	3679

E2Ca9 B7Ra9 F8Ra7 D8Ba8 H2Ba8 G3Rb2 J4Ca8
D9Ra9 A2Ca2 H9Ca4 C7Ra4 C8Ba2 A9Rb3 B3Rb3
H8Rb5 C1Cb7 B4Cb5 G8Cb9 B1Bb4 C6Bb6 J8Bb3
A1Ca5 F2Ca4 B2Ca6 B6Ca7 J6Ca9 A3Ra8 C4Ra3
J7Ra2 C2Ba1 H4Ba2 D4Rb1 D3Cb6 E5Cb3 F6Cb8
E3Bb1 F1Bb3 E6Bb2 D7Bb3 D1Ca2 E1Ca8 H7Ca6
G9Ca1 E9Ra6 F7Ra1 G5Ra7 H5Ra1 J5Ra6 A6Ba1
G6Ba5 J9Ba7 A5Rb4 D6Rb4 D5Cb5

234678	278	2467	13678	134	1378	5	126	9
23567	27	2567	135679	1359	1357	4	8	126
9	8	1	2	45	58	6	3	7
1257	4	3	158	6	1258	78	2579	258
125	6	8	135	7	9	3	245	2345
257	279	257	4	35	2358	1	25679	23568
1247	3	247	157	8	6	9	1457	145
1678	5	9	137	2	4	3678	167	1368
14678	178	467	13579	1359	1357	2	14567	134568

J2Ca1 F2Ca9 C5Ra4 C7Ra6 D8Ra9 C2Rb8 E7Rb3
C6Cb5 E1Ca1 D6Ca1 F6Ba2 E4Rb5 D4Cb8 F5Cb3
A5Bb1 D7Bb7 G3Ca2 J5Ca5 A6Ca8 H7Ca8 B9Ra1
F9Ra8 J1Ra8 J4Ra9 B5Ba9 A8Ba2 D1Ba2 F8Ba6
A2Rb7 D9Rb5 E8Rb4 B2Cb2 J8Cb7 E9Cb2 G9Cb4
G1Bb7 J6Bb3 H8Bb1 A1Ca4 F3Ca7 G4Ca1 B6Ca7
G8Ca5 H9Ca3 A4Ra3 F1Ra5 H1Ra6 H4Ra7 J3Ra4
B1Ba3 B3Ba5 B4Ba6 J9Ba6 A3Rb6

9	247	1247	8	267	1267	267	2567	3
5	2378	1237	12367	267	9	2678	4	178
38	2378	6	1237	4	5	9	278	178
7	2459	2459	24569	2569	8	3	1	49
1	6	2349	23479	279	237	5	78	4789
348	34589	3459	1345679	5679	1367	4678	678	2
2	34579	34579	5679	56789	67	1	3578	4578
46	1	4579	25679	3	267	2478	2578	4578
3	357	8	257	1	4	27	9	6

H1Ca6 G5Ca8 G8Ca3 A8Ra5 J1Rb3 C1Cb8 F1Bb4
F2Ca8 H7Ca4 F8Ca6 F7Rb7 J7Cb2 E8Cb8 A7Bb6
H8Bb7 G6Ca6 B7Ca8 C8Ca2 H9Ra8 G9Ba5 H6Rb2
F4Rb1 C4Cb3 F6Cb3 C2Bb7 E6Bb7 B2Ca3 E3Ca3
G3Ca7 A6Ca1 B9Ca7 A5Ra7 B3Ra1 C9Ra1 G2Ra4
J4Ra7 A3Ba4 H3Ba9 H4Ba5 A2Rb2 F3Rb5 G4Rb9
J2Rb5 D2Cb9 D3Cb2 F5Cb9 E5Bb2 D9Bb4 B4Ca2
E4Ca4 D5Ca5 E9Ca9 B5Ra6 D4Ra6

347	479	3	5	26789	234689	23678	1	23789
37	2	6	379	1	389	378	4	5
13457	14579	8	3679	2679	23469	2367	237	2379
1458	145	7	169	25689	125689	123458	238	12348
6	145	125	17	3	1258	124578	9	12478
9	3	125	4	2578	1258	12578	278	6
2	8	13	136	6	7	9	5	134
1357	157	4	2	59	1359	1378	6	1378
1357	1567	9	8	4	1356	1237	237	1237

D1Ca8 J2Ca6 G9Ra4 A3Rb3 G5Rb6 B1Cb7 G3Cb1
A1Bb4 G4Bb3 C1Ca1 H2Ca7 C6Ca4 F8Ca8 C2Ra5
E6Ra8 A2Ba9 B6Ba3 A5Ba8 B4Rb9 B7Rb8 H9Ca8
C9Ca9 F7Ca1 J8Ca7 J9Ca1 F5Ra7 H6Ra1 J7Ra2
C4Ba7 H5Ba9 H7Ba3 C5Rb2 C7Rb6 E4Rb1 H1Rb5
J6Rb5 J1Cb3 E2Cb4 D4Cb6 D5Cb5 A6Cb6 F6Cb2
A7Cb7 C8Cb3 A9Bb2 D2Bb1 F3Bb5 D6Bb9 D7Bb4
D8Bb2 E7Bb5 E3Ca2 D9Ca3 E9Ca7

238	23458	235	356	7	23568	346	9	1
3789	378	6	139	4	138	2	7	5
1	23457	23579	3569	269	2356	3467	8	346
6789	578	579	2	3	14568	14568	1456	4689
368	1	35	456	68	9	34568	2	7
23689	2358	4	156	168	7	13568	156	3689
5	6	27	8	129	124	147	3	24
237	9	1	3467	5	2346	4678	467	2468
4	237	8	1367	126	1236	9	1567	26

G5Ra9 J8Ra5 G7Ba1 B8Rb7 D1Ca7 H7Ca7 G3Ra7
H9Ra8 J4Ra7 C2Ba7 A2Ca4 D3Rb9 E3Rb3 B1Ca9
F9Ca9 C4Ra9 F7Ra3 C9Ba3 D7Ba8 A7Rb6 D2Rb5
C7Cb4 E7Bb5 E4Ra4 F4Ra5 A4Rb3 A1Cb8 B4Cb1
H4Cb6 B2Bb3 B6Bb8 E1Bb6 H8Bb4 H1Ca3 F2Ca8
G6Ca4 D9Ca4 E5Ra8 F1Ra2 G9Ra2 H6Ra2 J6Ra3
J9Ra6 C5Ba2 J2Ba2 J5Ba1 A6Rb5 C3Rb5 F5Rb6
A3Cb2 C6Cb6 D6Cb1 F8Cb1 D8Bb6

278	2378	2389	1	348	5	347	3478	6
15678	4	13568	9	2	368	1357	3578	138
1568	13568	13568	468	3468	7	1345	9	2
3	1256	7	456	4569	16	8	45	14
158	158	158	4578	34578	2	13457	6	9
9	1568	4	5678	35678	1368	2	357	13
2678	23678	2368	678	678	4	369	1	5
245678	9	2568	3	1	68	46	248	48
14568	13568	13568	2	568	9	346	348	7

A3Ca9 D5Ca9 G7Ca9 H8Ca2 D2Ra2 H1Ra7 A1Ba2
A2Ba7 F2Ba6 J1Ba4 J5Ba5 G3Ca2 G2Ra3 H3Ra5
E7Ca7 B8Ra7 E5Ra3 B6Ba3 B9Rb8 E4Rb4 H9Cb4
D9Bb1 H7Bb6 C3Ca3 F6Ca1 D6Ca6 A7Ca4 J8Ca8
F9Ca3 A8Ra3 A5Ra8 C5Ra4 D8Ra4 H6Ra8 J7Ra3
J3Ra6 C4Ba6 F4Ba8 F8Ba5 J2Ba1 G1Ba8 B3Rb1
D4Rb5 F5Rb7 G4Rb7 C1Cb5 E3Cb8 G5Cb6 B7Cb5
B1Bb6 C2Bb8 C7Bb1 E1Bb1 E2Bb5

235689	234689	1	689	7	345689	58	26	25
256789	24689	245689	689	456	45689	578	3	1
35678	368	3568	168	1356	2	4	9	57
189	7	89	5	2	9	3	14	6
4	1269	269	3	16	679	157	17	8
136	5	36	4	8	67	2	17	9
2359	2349	23459	27	345	1	6	8	247
12689	124689	24689	2678	46	4678	179	5	3
123568	123468	7	268	9	34568	1	124	24

C4Ca1 H7Ca9 A8Ca6 D8Ra4 E7Ra5 A9Ba2 E5Ba1
G9Ba7 A7Rb8 C9Rb5 D6Rb9 E8Rb7 G4Rb2 J7Rb1
J9Rb4 D3Cb8 A4Cb9 E6Cb6 B7Cb7 F8Cb1 J8Cb2
D1Bb1 F6Bb7 C1Ca7 H2Ca1 H4Ca7 C2Ra8 H3Rb2
E3Cb9 E2Bb2 B1Ca2 B2Ra9 C3Ba6 G1Ba9 C5Rb3
F3Rb3 F1Cb6 G5Cb5 G3Bb4 H1Bb8 J6Bb3 A1Ca3
A2Ca4 J2Ca6 B3Ca5 B6Ca8 A6Ra5 B5Ra4 G2Ra3
H5Ra6 J1Ra5 J4Ra8 B4Ba6 H6Ba4

134578	1345	14578	369	2	3469	1357	1359	145789
12348	134	1248	7	5	349	6	139	1489
3457	6	9	1	4	8	357	2	457
1235	8	125	236	167	23567	9	4	125
6	1459	1245	289	148	2459	125	7	3
123459	7	1245	239	14	23459	8	6	125
579	2	3	4	67	1	57	8	5679
1789	19	1678	5	3	267	4	19	12679
14578	145	145678	268	9	267	12357	135	12567

E5Ca8 J4Ba8 C5Rb4 F5Cb1 C7Ca3 J8Ca3 H8Rb1
H2Cb9 B8Cb9 B6Bb3 A8Bb5 F1Ca9 A2Ca3 D9Ca1
G9Ca9 C1Ra5 F4Ra3 G5Ra6 A7Ba1 D1Ba3 C9Rb7
D5Rb7 G1Rb7 H1Cb8 G7Cb5 A1Bb4 E7Bb2 H3Bb6
B1Ca2 A3Ca7 D4Ca2 J7Ca7 B9Ca4 F9Ca5 J9Ca6
A9Ra8 B3Ra8 D6Ra6 F3Ra2 H6Ra7 J6Ra2 B2Ba1
A4Ba6 E6Ba5 H9Ba2 A6Rb9 D3Rb5 E2Rb4 E4Rb9
F6Rb4 J1Rb1 J2Cb5 E3Cb1 J3Cb4

4589	589	3	2568	256	2678	2789	26789	1
2	158	156	568	9	13678	378	4	38
189	7	169	268	1236	4	2389	23689	5
1389	6	19	7	4	29	5	2389	2389
35789	3589	579	1	25	29	6	23789	4
4579	2	4579	3	8	69	1	79	9
139	4	129	2689	1236	5	2389	12389	7
6	139	129	2489	7	12389	23489	5	2389
13579	1359	8	249	123	1239	2349	1239	6

F3Ca4 A1Ra4 F1Ra5 F6Ra6 J1Ra7 E3Ba7 E5Ba5
J2Ba5 F9Rb9 F8Cb7 B3Ca5 A6Ca7 A4Ra5 B4Ra6
B7Ra7 C3Ba6 C4Ba8 G5Ba6 A5Rb2 H6Ca8 A8Ca6
G8Ca1 G7Ra8 B9Ba8 A7Rb9 B2Rb1 C1Cb9 A2Cb8
B6Cb3 C5Bb1 G1Bb3 J6Bb1 D1Ca1 E2Ca3 J5Ca3
J8Ca9 D8Ra8 E6Ra9 H3Ra1 E1Ba8 D3Ba9 D6Ba2
D9Ba3 G3Ba2 E8Rb2 G4Rb9 H2Rb9 H9Rb2 H4Cb4
J7Cb4 C8Cb3 C7Bb2 J4Bb2 H7Bb3

8	239	236	7	12346	5	146	134	136
3567	4	3567	136	8	9	167	135	2
1	2357	23567	346	2346	36	4678	9	35678
456	15	8	1569	169	2	3	7	16
34567	12357	1234567	13568	1367	368	1246	124	9
367	1237	9	136	1367	4	5	8	16
2	13578	13457	3489	349	38	1789	6	13578
37	6	37	389	5	1	2789	23	4
9	1358	1345	2	346	7	18	135	1358

A2Ca9 D1Ra4 F2Ra2 J5Ra6 E7Ca2 E8Ra4 H8Ra2
J3Ra4 A9Rb3 A8Cb1 B8Bb5 E1Ca5 J8Ca3 B4Ra1
D4Ra5 D5Ba9 D2Rb1 D9Cb6 F9Bb1 G3Ca1 E5Ca1
J7Ra1 F5Ba7 C3Ca5 C5Ra2 A3Ba2 A5Rb4 G5Cb3
A7Cb6 B7Bb7 G6Bb8 H1Ca7 J2Ca8 G4Ca4 E4Ca8
C7Ca4 G9Ca7 C2Ra7 C9Ra8 G2Ra5 G7Ra9 H3Ra3
H7Ra8 J9Ra5 B1Ba3 E3Ba7 H4Ba9 B3Rb6 E2Rb3
F1Rb6 F4Cb3 E6Cb6 C4Bb6 C6Bb3

12578	1357	13578	34678	9	134	2568	1258	1256
6	139	1389	2	38	5	89	7	4
12578	1579	4	678	68	1	3	12589	1256
147	2	1367	349	5	8	679	49	67
9	456	56	4	24	7	1	3	8
457	8	357	349	1	6	2579	2459	257
1578	15679	2	35689	368	39	4	158	1357
3	457	578	1	48	2	578	6	9
1458	14569	15689	345689	7	349	258	1258	1235

E5Ca2 C6Rb1 E4Rb4 H5Ca4 A6Ra4 J2Ca4 B2Ca1
A2Ca3 D3Ca1 B5Ca3 D4Ra3 F3Ba3 F4Ba9 G9Ra7
J9Ba3 D9Rb6 J6Rb9 J3Cb6 G6Cb3 E3Bb5 G2Bb9
E2Ca6 B3Ca9 A7Ca6 A9Ca1 B7Ra8 C8Ra9 D7Ba9
D8Rb4 H7Rb5 D1Cb7 H2Cb7 J7Cb2 C2Bb5 F1Bb4
F7Bb7 H3Bb8 A3Ca7 F9Ca5 A8Ra5 C4Ra7 F8Ra2
C5Ba6 C9Ba2 A4Rb8 C1Rb8 G5Rb8 A1Cb2 J4Cb5
G8Cb1 G1Bb5 J1Bb1 G4Bb6 J8Bb8

358	9	568	14678	1378	1468	34578	3456	2
38	368	1	5	2	4689	3478	346	3478
7	23568	4	68	38	68	358	1	9
2458	25678	25678	248	58	3	1	9	47
12349	1237	27	1249	6	1249	347	8	5
134589	1358	58	1489	1589	7	6	2	34
6	258	3	289	589	2589	24589	7	1
1258	12578	9	3	4	12568	258	5	8
1258	4	2578	12789	15789	12589	23589	35	6

B6Ra9 C2Ra2 G7Ra4 H6Ra6 H2Ra7 J7Ba9 C6Rb8
H8Rb5 H9Rb8 C4Cb6 C5Cb3 H7Cb2 J8Cb3 C7Bb5
H1Bb1 B8Ca4 B2Ra6 A8Ba6 D3Ba6 E3Ca7 D9Ra7
J3Ra2 B7Ba7 F9Ba4 B9Rb3 E7Rb3 B1Cb8 E2Cb1
A7Cb8 A3Bb5 F2Bb3 J1Bb5 A1Ca3 D2Ca5 F3Ca8
G6Ca5 D5Ra8 F5Ra5 G4Ra2 F4Ba1 E6Ba2 G2Ba8
J4Ba8 G5Ba9 D4Rb4 F1Rb9 J6Rb1 D1Cb2 E1Cb4
A4Cb7 E4Cb9 J5Cb7 A6Cb4 A5Bb1

2356	4	2356	2569	3569	7	8	1	569
25678	2578	25678	24569	1	2469	3	467	45679
13567	357	9	8	3456	46	2	467	4567
2458	1	2458	246	7	3	5	9	2456
234579	2357	23457	12469	469	2469	157	2467	8
2479	6	247	1249	8	5	17	3	1247
24578	2578	1	3	459	489	6	278	27
345678	3578	345678	4567	2	468	9	78	137
23678	9	23678	67	6	1	4	5	237

C1Ca1 H9Ra1 J9Ba3 D7Rb5 J5Rb6 J4Cb7 B2Ca8
E2Ca2 F1Ca9 B6Ca2 G8Ca2 E7Ra7 G6Ra8 F3Ba7
F7Ba1 G5Ba9 H8Ba8 E5Rb4 G9Rb7 H6Rb4 G2Cb5
F4Cb2 H4Cb5 C6Cb6 E8Cb6 A4Bb9 D4Bb6 E6Bb9
D9Bb2 F9Bb4 G1Bb4 D3Ca4 E4Ca1 B4Ca4 B9Ca9
C8Ra4 D1Ra8 A9Ba6 B8Ba7 J3Ba8 C9Rb5 J1Rb2
C5Cb3 C2Bb7 A5Bb5 H1Ca7 H2Ca3 A3Ca2 A1Ra3
H3Ra6 B1Ba6 E3Ba3 B3Rb5 E1Rb5

9	46	467	246	8	2456	34567	1	234567
14568	3	1468	7	129	124569	4568	45	24568
145678	468	2	46	3	1456	9	457	45678
678	5	6789	1	4	3	67	2	679
24678	24689	346789	29	29	289	34567	34579	1
24	1	349	5	6	7	34	8	349
1468	4689	5	3469	7	1469	2	349	3489
1246	7	1469	8	129	12469	1345	3459	3459
3	2489	1489	249	5	1249	1478	6	4789

G4Ca3 E6Ca8 F1Ra2 J2Ba2 G2Ca9 G8Rb4 B8Cb5
G9Cb8 C8Bb7 C1Ca5 C2Ca8 B7Ca8 H8Ca9 H9Ca5
A6Ra5 A3Ra7 C6Ra1 E7Ra5 H7Ra3 J3Ra8 A9Ba3
D1Ba8 H5Ba1 J7Ba1 E8Rb3 F7Rb4 G6Rb6 J9Rb7
G1Cb1 A7Cb6 F9Cb9 A2Bb4 C9Bb4 F3Bb3 D7Bb7
D9Bb6 E1Ca7 E2Ca6 B3Ca1 D3Ca9 J4Ca4 C4Ca6
B9Ca2 A4Ra2 B6Ra4 B1Ra6 E3Ra4 H6Ra2 J6Ra9
B5Ba9 E5Ba2 H1Ba4 H3Ba6 E4Rb9

139	8	7	4	159	1359	356	23	2356
6	123	1245	358	1578	1357	3457	9	234578
349	39	459	3589	6	2	1	37	34578
5	1369	1689	7	89	369	2	4	13
138	4	128	358	258	35	37	6	9
7	2369	269	1	249	3469	8	5	3
14	167	146	56	3	8	9	127	124567
2	1679	1469	569	14579	145679	34567	8	134567
1489	5	3	2	1479	14679	467	17	1467

E7Ra7 J1Ra8 D9Ba1 F9Rb3 H7Ra3 C4Ca9 A1Ra9
C3Ra5 C9Ra8 C8Ba7 B9Rb4 C2Rb3 J8Rb1 C1Cb4
B7Cb5 G8Cb2 A7Bb6 A8Bb3 G1Bb1 E1Ca3 B2Ca1
J7Ca4 A9Ca2 J9Ca6 B3Ra2 D6Ra3 E3Ra1 G3Ra4
B4Ba3 F2Ba2 D3Ba8 F6Ba6 B6Rb7 D5Rb9 E6Rb5
F3Rb9 D2Cb6 H3Cb6 E4Cb8 B5Cb8 F5Cb4 J5Cb7
A6Cb1 J6Cb9 A5Bb5 E5Bb2 G2Bb7 H4Bb5 H6Bb4
H2Ca9 G4Ca6 H5Ca1 G9Ca5 H9Ca7

457	1	457	9	6	8	2457	2357	234
4679	3	479	7	27	5	124679	126789	12489
2	67	8	37	4	13	15679	135679	139
1568	26	125	4	289	269	3	129	7
1578	9	12357	3578	2378	23	12	4	6
467	2467	2347	1	2379	2369	8	29	5
3	247	6	8	5	9	12479	12789	12489
179	8	1279	36	39	4	125679	1235679	1239
49	5	49	2	1	7	469	3689	3489

E4Ca5 H4Ca6 C6Ca1 B5Ba2 C4Ba3 H5Ba3 G4Ba8
B4Rb7 C9Rb9 G6Rb9 J7Ra6 H7Ca9 H8Ra5 C7Ra5
F2Ca4 C2Ca7 C8Ra6 B1Ba6 A3Rb5 F1Rb7 G2Rb2
H9Rb2 A1Cb4 H1Cb1 D2Cb6 D3Cb1 F5Cb9 B3Bb9
A9Bb3 E1Bb8 D5Bb8 D6Bb2 D8Bb9 F8Bb2 H3Bb7
J1Bb9 D1Ca5 E3Ca2 J3Ca4 E5Ca7 F6Ca6 A7Ca2
J8Ca3 A8Ra7 E7Ra1 E6Ra3 F3Ra3 J9Ra8 B8Ba8
G7Ba7 B7Rb4 G8Rb1 B9Cb1 G9Cb4

8	1	349	5	2349	7	234	24	6
456	359	2	3469	3469	8	345	457	1
7	35	345	12346	12346	1234	9	2458	34
145	6	13457	12349	8	12349	145	14579	479
9	578	14578	146	1456	14	14568	3	2
145	2	13458	13469	7	1349	14568	145689	49
2	589	1589	13489	1349	1349	7	1469	349
1	79	6	12349	12349	5	1234	1249	8
3	4	189	7	129	6	12	129	5

B1Ca6 G4Ca8 E5Ca5 D9Ca7 B8Ra7 C8Ra8 G8Ra6
H2Ra7 J3Ra8 B7Ba5 E3Ba7 E2Ba8 H1Rb1 C5Ca6
F7Ca8 F4Ra6 E7Ba6 G5Ca1 F9Ca9 F6Rb3 F3Cb1
G6Cb4 D3Bb3 E6Bb1 G9Bb3 C4Ca1 B5Ca4 D6Ca9
A7Ca3 C9Ca4 A8Ra2 A3Ra4 C6Ra2 C2Ra3 D4Ra2
E4Ra4 C3Ba5 B2Ba9 B4Ba3 A5Rb9 G2Rb5 G3Rb9
H4Rb9 J5Cb2 H8Cb4 F8Bb5 H5Bb3 H7Bb2 J7Bb1
D1Ca5 D7Ca4 D8Ca1 J8Ca9 F1Ra4

35689	3689	3689	2	4	567	1568	5678	156789
34568	1	7	35	356	9	568	2	4568
24569	2469	69	157	8	567	3	4567	145679
4678	4678	5	47	2	3	9	1	68
13489	3489	1389	6	59	458	7	58	2
6789	6789	2	579	59	1	4	3	568
13689	3689	13689	3459	7	456	2	4568	134568
13678	5	4	3	36	2	168	9	13678
23679	23679	369	8	1	456	56	4567	34567

C4Ca1 D5Ca2 E6Ca8 D4Ba4 G4Ba9 E8Rb5 H4Rb3
B4Cb5 E5Cb9 H5Cb6 B5Bb3 F4Bb7 F5Bb5 B9Rb4
A1Ca5 C9Ra5 A9Ba9 J7Ba5 J6Rb4 G6Cb5 G8Ca4
A7Ra1 C3Ra9 J8Ba6 H7Ba8 B7Rb6 C8Rb7 J3Rb3
B1Cb8 E3Cb1 C6Cb6 A8Cb8 J9Cb7 A3Bb6 A6Bb7
H9Bb1 G1Ca1 E1Ca3 D2Ca7 G3Ca8 G9Ca3 A2Ra3
D9Ra8 E2Ra4 G2Ra6 H1Ra7 C1Ba4 F2Ba8 F9Ba6
C2Rb2 D1Rb6 F1Rb9 J1Cb2 J2Cb9

4679	8	9	24679	4679	3	1	2469	5
1469	13469	39	2469	5	1249	2346	7	8
5	134679	2	46789	146789	1479	346	3469	3469
1289	139	6	3479	479	479	5	12349	349
9	359	4	1	2	8	36	369	7
129	1359	7	34569	469	459	8	123469	3469
3	45679	1	245789	4789	24579	467	456	46
4679	45679	59	4579	3	14579	467	8	2
478	2	58	4578	478	6	9	345	1

B3Ca3 J3Ca8 C5Ca1 B7Ca2 A4Ra2 C4Ra8 D1Ra8
E2Ra5 H6Ra1 J8Ra3 F1Ba2 H3Ba5 G6Ba2 G5Ba8
G8Ba5 A3Rb9 E1Rb9 E8Cb6 A8Bb4 E7Bb3 B1Ca1
F6Ca5 D8Ca2 C9Ca3 D2Ra1 J4Ra5 C7Ba6 C8Ba9
F2Ba3 F8Ba1 D4Ca3 G9Ca6 J1Ca7 C2Ca7 B6Ca9
A5Ra7 C6Ra4 J5Ra4 B2Ba4 B4Ba6 F4Ba4 D6Ba7
H1Ba4 A1Rb6 D5Rb9 F9Rb9 G2Rb9 H7Rb7 H2Cb6
G4Cb7 H4Cb9 F5Cb6 G7Cb4 D9Cb4

1569	3	7	8	569	4569	1469	1246	169
8	269	249	347	1	34679	4679	5	679
1569	1569	1459	2	5679	45679	8	146	3
4	12569	12359	35	8	1359	13569	7	1569
1359	8	1359	6	3579	134579	13459	134	2
7	1569	1359	345	2	13459	134569	8	1569
135	157	1358	9	3567	35678	2	136	4
2	157	1358	357	4	35678	13567	9	15678
359	4	6	1	357	23578	357	3	578

J6Ca2 A8Ca2 J9Ra8 J1Ra9 J8Rb3 H4Ca7 G2Ra7
J7Ra7 B9Ba7 J5Rb5 C8Ca6 B6Ra6 A1Ba6 B4Ba3
G5Ba6 A5Rb9 D4Rb5 G8Rb1 H2Rb1 F4Cb4 C5Cb7
E8Cb4 A9Cb1 A7Bb4 E5Bb3 G1Ca3 C6Ca4 E6Ca7
A6Ra5 B3Ra4 G3Ra5 H6Ra3 B2Ba2 B7Ba9 H3Ba8
G6Ba8 D3Ca2 F6Ca9 D7Ra3 E3Ra9 C2Ba9 F3Ba3
D6Ba1 D9Ba9 C3Rb1 D2Rb6 C1Cb5 F2Cb5 E1Bb1
F9Bb6 F7Ca1 H7Ca6 H9Ca5 E7Ra5

4	1	129	367	5	3679	237	8	137
6	3	258	47	48	1	9	257	457
8	7	1589	2	3489	349	345	6	1345
9	156	4	8	236	23567	3567	1357	13567
78	1568	15678	34567	3469	345679	345678	1357	2
2	568	3	1	469	45679	45678	57	456789
378	2	678	9	136	356	35678	4	35678
5	9	67	346	2346	8	1	237	367
1	468	68	3456	7	23456	23568	9	3568

G1Ca3 J2Ca4 G5Ca1 F9Ca9 A2Rb1 C1Rb8 E1Cb7
E3Ca1 B5Ca8 C9Ra1 D8Ba1 B9Ca4 B4Rb7 D2Rb5
B3Ca5 C7Ca5 B8Ra2 A3Ba2 J7Ba2 C3Rb9 E5Ca9
D6Ca2 A6Ra9 H5Ra2 A4Ba6 F6Ba7 H4Ba4 D5Rb3
F8Rb5 E4Cb5 C5Cb4 E8Cb3 C6Bb3 F5Bb6 J4Bb3
H8Bb7 E2Ca6 G3Ca7 E6Ca4 A7Ca3 A9Ra7 E7Ra8
F7Ra4 G9Ra8 H9Ra3 F2Ba8 D7Ba7 J3Ba8 J9Ba5
G7Ba6 D9Rb6 G6Rb5 H3Rb6 J6Rb6

345678	9	34568	15	135	35	1678	1368	2
2358	1	358	7	6	2359	89	389	4
2367	236	36	8	139	4	1679	5	367
13458	348	7	6	1589	2589	12489	1289	8
168	68	9	12	4	28	3	7	5
14568	468	2	3	15789	5789	14689	1689	68
2368	2368	368	9	3578	1	25678	4	3678
3689	5	368	4	2	3678	678	368	1
123468	7	13468	5	358	3568	2568	2368	9

H1Ca9 J3Ca1 E4Ca2 E1Ra1 J1Ra4 A3Ba4 B6Ba2
D9Rb8 E6Rb8 J4Rb5 E2Cb6 A4Cb1 F9Cb6 B3Ca5
G7Ca5 C7Ra1 C5Ba9 F2Ca8 F7Ra4 D2Ba4 F1Rb5
D1Cb3 B1Bb8 B8Ra3 B7Ba9 G9Ba3 A1Rb7 C9Rb7
D7Rb2 G2Rb2 G1Cb6 C2Cb3 C1Bb2 C3Bb6 G3Bb8
H3Ca3 J5Ca8 H7Ca7 J8Ca2 G5Ra7 H8Ra8 J6Ra3
A5Ba3 A7Ba8 F6Ba7 H6Ba6 J7Ba6 A6Rb5 A8Rb6
F5Rb1 D5Cb5 D6Cb9 F8Cb9 D8Bb1

13456	2	13459	8	34	134	1347	167	13467
1346	7	13489	1349	5	1234	12348	1268	12346
134	1348	1348	134	6	7	5	128	9
8	14	1247	6	47	145	1279	3	127
1237	5	6	137	9	13	127	4	8
9	134	1347	2	347	1348	17	5	167
12347	134	12347	347	8	9	6	127	5
23457	9	234578	347	1	2346	23478	278	2347
12347	6	123478	5	2347	234	1234789	12789	12347

C2Ca8 B4Ca9 J5Ca2 D6Ca5 H6Ca6 F6Ca8 J8Ca9
A3Ra9 C8Ra2 D7Ra9 F9Ra6 A1Ba5 B6Ba2 B1Ca6
H3Ca5 A8Ra6 J3Ba8 J1Ra7 A5Rb3 E7Ra7 A9Ba7
D9Ba2 F7Rb1 A7Cb4 A6Bb1 J7Bb3 G3Ca2 E4Ca1
E6Ca3 J6Ca4 H7Ca2 B9Ca3 B3Ra4 E1Ra2 H8Ra8
J9Ra1 C4Ba4 B8Ba1 B7Ba8 H9Ba4 G8Ba7 G4Rb3
H1Rb3 C1Cb1 H4Cb7 C3Bb3 G1Bb4 F2Ca3 D3Ca1
D5Ra7 F5Ra4 G2Ra1 D2Ba4 F3Ba7

5	12349	2349	7	1369	136	12349	12349	8
7	1239	2389	189	1389	4	1239	6	5
139	6	3489	2	13589	1358	13479	13479	1479
69	9	7	3	1568	2	145689	1489	149
4	8	3569	1	1567	156	135679	1379	2
36	23	1	4	5678	9	35678	378	7
139	5	349	6	123489	138	124789	124789	1479
8	1349	349	19	12349	7	1249	5	6
2	1479	469	5	1489	18	14789	14789	3

J2Ca7 E3Ca5 B4Ca8 C3Ra8 F2Ra2 J3Ra6 F1Ba3
D2Rb9 E4Rb1 F9Rb7 D1Cb6 H4Cb9 E6Cb6 F8Cb8
E5Bb7 F5Bb5 A5Ca6 C6Ca5 D7Ca5 F7Ca6 D5Ra8
C9Ca9 A3Ra9 B3Ba2 A2Ba4 B5Ba9 G1Ba9 C1Rb1
B2Cb3 C5Cb3 A6Bb1 B7Bb1 H2Bb1 G6Ca3 G7Ra8
H3Ra3 G3Ba4 J6Ba8 G8Ba7 C8Rb4 G9Rb1 G5Cb2
C7Cb7 D8Cb1 J8Cb9 D9Cb4 E8Bb3 H5Bb4 J7Bb4
J5Ca1 A7Ca3 E7Ca9 A8Ca2 H7Ra2

13489	123468	12468	236	23468	7	259	246	24569
478	24678	2468	9	5	1	2	3	246
349	5	246	236	2346	236	7	1	8
2	14	3	8	169	56	59	47	4579
458	48	9	237	23	235	6	2478	1
6	18	7	4	1239	235	23589	28	259
178	9	1268	126	1268	268	4	5	3
138	12368	1268	5	7	4	128	9	26
134578	1234678	124568	1236	12368	9	128	2678	267

J3Ca5 E4Ca7 G6Ca8 F7Ca3 C1Ra9 G1Ra7 B2Ba7
A5Ba8 E1Ba5 B7Rb2 C5Ca4 J1Ca4 J7Ra8 H7Ba1
B1Rb8 F6Rb5 H1Cb3 D6Cb6 A1Bb1 A2Ca3 G3Ca1
H3Ca8 J4Ra1 J5Ba3 E5Rb2 G5Cb6 E6Cb3 C6Bb2
G4Bb2 A3Ca2 C4Ca3 A8Ra4 C3Ra6 B3Ba4 A4Ba6
B9Ba6 D9Ba4 D2Rb1 D8Rb7 E8Rb8 H9Rb2 E2Cb4
F2Cb8 H2Cb6 D5Cb9 F8Cb2 J8Cb6 F9Cb9 J9Cb7
A9Bb5 F5Bb1 D7Bb5 J2Bb2 A7Ca9

56789	359	389	2367	23689	4	569	12569	1269
46789	1	2	5	689	6789	3	469	469
4569	3459	349	1	2369	2369	7	24569	8
2	7	5	346	34689	3689	1	689	69
1	49	49	246	7	2689	569	25689	3
3	8	6	2	1259	129	4	2579	279
4	234	134	9	12346	12367	8	13467	5
459	6	7	8	134	13	2	1349	149
489	2349	13489	23467	12346	5	69	134679	14679

F5Ca5 F6Ra1 H1Ra5 F4Rb2 G1Rb4 H6Rb3 A9Ca2
A8Ra1 D6Ra9 E8Ra2 E4Ba6 E6Ba8 E7Ba5 D8Ba8
D9Rb6 C8Ca5 A2Ra5 A7Ca9 B8Ba6 B6Rb7 B9Rb4
J7Rb6 A4Cb3 A3Bb8 D4Bb4 A1Ca7 J1Ca8 J4Ca7
D5Ca3 B5Ca8 A5Ra6 B1Ra9 G8Ra7 C1Ba6 C5Ba9
F9Ba7 G6Ba6 J8Ba3 C6Rb2 F8Rb9 J9Rb1 J3Cb9
H8Cb4 H9Cb9 E3Bb4 J2Bb2 H5Bb1 C2Ca4 E2Ca9
G3Ca1 G5Ca2 J5Ca4 C3Ra3 G2Ra3

6	1578	13589	39	159	2	59	589	4
389	4	3589	7	569	3569	2569	1	5689
179	157	2	8	14569	1569	3	569	5679
129	3	159	4	8	1569	7	2569	569
24789	2578	4589	69	5679	5679	2569	234569	1
1479	6	1459	2	3	1579	8	459	59
1238	128	7	5	269	3689	4	3689	3689
2348	9	3468	1	26	368	56	7	3568
5	18	1368	369	679	4	169	3689	2

C5Ca4 J7Ca1 C9Ca7 A2Ra7 B7Ra2 E8Ra3 J5Ra7
D8Ba2 F8Ba4 J2Rb8 A5Ca1 A7Rb9 D1Rb9 C1Cb1
F1Cb7 A4Cb3 C2Bb5 G2Ca1 B3Ca9 E6Ca7 A8Ca5
A3Ra8 B1Ra3 C6Ra9 J3Ra3 B9Ba8 E1Ba8 F9Ba9
H3Ba6 C8Rb6 E2Rb2 G1Rb2 H5Rb2 H7Rb5 H1Cb4
E7Cb6 J8Cb9 H9Cb3 E4Bb9 D9Bb5 H6Bb8 J4Bb6
G8Bb8 G9Bb6 E3Ca4 B5Ca6 G5Ca9 G6Ca3 B6Ra5
D6Ra6 E5Ra5 F3Ba5 F6Ba1 D3Rb1

458	456	456	3	1	46789	2579	57	25679
7	136	136	5	2	69	8	4	369
2	9	3456	67	678	4678	357	1	3567
145	13457	8	1267	367	123567	123457	9	123457
6	1357	13579	4	379	123579	12357	57	8
145	13457	2	17	3789	135789	13457	6	13457
3	8	14567	167	67	167	14579	2	14579
9	1247	147	8	5	127	6	3	147
15	12567	1567	9	4	12367	157	578	157

A1Ca8 E3Ca9 D4Ca2 J8Ca8 E7Ra2 J6Ra3 A9Ba2
H6Ba2 J2Ca2 F5Ca9 F6Ra8 J3Ra6 C5Ba8 H3Ca7
B3Ca1 B9Ra3 C6Ra4 C3Ba3 C9Ba6 A7Ba9 B2Rb6
C4Rb7 F4Cb1 A6Cb6 B6Cb9 C7Cb5 A8Bb7 G4Bb6
G7Bb4 A3Ca4 D5Ca6 G6Ca1 E8Ca5 G9Ca9 A2Ra5
E2Ra1 G3Ra5 G5Ra7 H2Ra4 E5Ba3 D6Ba5 J1Ba1
J9Ba5 D1Rb4 E6Rb7 H9Rb1 J7Rb7 F1Cb5 F7Cb3
D9Cb7 D2Bb3 F2Bb7 D7Bb1 F9Bb4

5	24	2349	1	79	3789	234679	346	2347
8	124	2349	379	6	3579	1234579	1345	23457
13	7	6	2	59	4	1359	8	35
346	4568	7	346	145	1356	3458	2	9
346	9	2345	3467	8	3567	345	345	1
34	2458	1	349	2459	359	3458	7	6
1467	3	8	5	147	2	1467	9	47
9	1456	45	467	3	167	1245678	1456	24578
2	1456	45	8	1479	1679	134567	13456	3457

G1Ca7 F5Ca2 A6Ca8 H9Ca8 E3Ra2 G7Ra6 H7Ra2
A8Ba6 G9Rb4 G5Cb1 C1Ca1 D6Ca1 A3Ca3 A5Ca7
A7Ra9 B3Ba9 A9Rb2 B4Rb3 A2Cb4 B6Cb5 B2Bb2
C5Bb9 B9Bb7 F4Ca9 D5Ca5 J7Ca7 J6Ra9 F2Ba5
D2Rb8 F6Rb3 J5Rb4 F1Cb4 J3Cb5 F7Bb8 H3Bb4
J9Bb3 B7Ca1 E8Ca3 C9Ca5 B8Ra4 C7Ra3 D1Ra3
E7Ra5 H8Ra5 J2Ra6 E1Ba6 D7Ba4 H2Ba1 J8Ba1
D4Rb6 E6Rb7 E4Cb4 H4Cb7 H6Cb6

23456	234568	1	9	2345	234	2348	7	238
23479	234789	789	1234	1234	6	123489	29	5
23459	23459	59	7	8	1234	12349	6	1239
8	379	6	123	1237	12379	5	4	129
59	59	4	125	1256	1289	129	3	7
1	3579	2	345	3457	3479	6	8	9
2467	12467	7	8	9	12347	237	5	236
2679	126789	789	123	1237	5	23789	29	4
24579	245789	3	6	247	247	2789	1	289

C3Ca5 E5Ca6 E6Ca8 G9Ca6 A5Ra5 F9Rb9 G3Rb7
B1Ca7 F4Ca5 D6Ca9 B4Ca4 B5Ra3 C6Ba1 A6Rb2
B7Rb1 E7Cb2 E4Bb1 D9Bb1 G7Bb3 H5Ca1 F6Ca3
D2Ra3 F5Ra4 G2Ra1 H4Ra3 H7Ra7 F2Ba7 D5Ba7
J5Ba2 D4Rb2 G6Rb4 J9Rb8 G1Cb2 J6Cb7 J7Cb9
A9Cb3 C7Bb4 C9Bb2 H8Bb2 C1Ca3 B2Ca2 A7Ca8
B8Ca9 B3Ra8 C2Ra9 E1Ba9 H2Ba8 E2Rb5 H1Rb6
H3Rb9 A1Cb4 J2Cb4 A2Bb6 J1Bb5

14679	1479	3	1245	124589	12479	24567	1257	457
147	8	2	145	145	6	9	1357	3457
5	1479	1679	124	3	12479	2467	8	47
1468	14	16	7	146	3	58	9	2
12478	5	17	9	124	124	378	37	6
2679	2379	679	8	26	5	37	4	1
3	129	159	1245	7	1249	2458	6	4589
279	6	4	235	259	8	1	2357	3579
1279	1279	8	123456	124569	1249	23457	2357	34579

F2Ca3 G3Ca5 J4Ca6 A5Ca8 G9Ca8 D7Ra5 E7Ba8
H4Ba3 F7Rb7 E8Cb3 D1Ca8 J7Ca3 B9Ra3 G2Ra9
J2Ba2 H1Rb7 J1Cb1 B1Bb4 J6Bb4 D2Ca4 B8Ra7
E5Ra4 E3Ra7 G7Ra4 A8Ba1 D3Ba1 H8Ba2 J9Ba7
A2Rb7 B5Rb1 C9Rb4 D5Rb6 E1Rb2 G4Rb1 J8Rb5
C2Cb1 B4Cb5 C4Cb2 F5Cb2 J5Cb9 A6Cb9 E6Cb1
G6Cb2 A9Cb5 H9Cb9 A1Bb6 A4Bb4 C6Bb7 C7Bb6
H5Bb5 F1Ca9 F3Ca6 A7Ca2 C3Ra9

3789	46789	234678	1	2489	5	23678	2368	678
378	478	23478	48	6	28	9	12358	578
89	5	1	7	3	289	268	4	68
2	1789	78	45689	4789	16789	5678	5689	3
6	3	5	89	2789	2789	4	89	1
4	1789	78	5689	789	136789	5678	5689	2
58	2	9	3	1	68	568	7	4568
378	4678	34678	689	5	6789	1	23689	4689
13578	1678	3678	2	789	4	3568	35689	5689

J1Ca1 F6Ca3 B8Ca1 B9Ra5 F2Ra1 G9Ra4 H8Ra2
D2Ba9 D6Ba1 G1Ba5 A9Ca7 J3Rb6 A2Ca6 B4Ca4
A3Ra4 D5Ra4 B3Ba2 H2Ba4 B6Rb8 H3Rb3 H1Cb7
B2Cb7 G6Cb6 B1Bb3 J2Bb8 H6Bb9 G7Bb8 E4Ca9
F5Ca8 E6Ca7 C9Ca8 J9Ca9 A1Ra8 C7Ra6 C1Ra9
E5Ra2 E8Ra8 F8Ra9 H9Ra6 H4Ra8 J5Ra7 C6Ba2
A5Ba9 A7Ba2 D3Ba8 D8Ba6 A8Rb3 D4Rb5 F3Rb7
F4Cb6 D7Cb7 F7Cb5 J8Cb5 J7Bb3

4	239	7	1258	6	1235	589	2589	258
125	8	1259	12457	2457	1245	4569	259	3
235	6	235	9	23458	2345	7	1	2458
2568	24	2458	12456	245	9	3	7	1458
23568	1	23458	2456	2345	7	458	58	9
357	349	3459	145	345	8	2	6	145
28	7	28	3	2589	256	1	4	2568
1238	5	12348	2468	2489	246	689	2389	7
9	234	6	24578	1	245	58	2358	258

F1Ca7 B5Ca7 G9Ca6 B7Ra6 G5Ra9 J4Ra7 C9Ba4
H6Ca6 E7Ca4 C5Ra8 G6Ra5 H4Ba8 H7Rb9 A6Ca1
A2Ra3 B3Ba9 C6Ba3 J2Rb4 D2Cb2 F2Cb9 J6Cb2
B6Bb4 H5Bb4 H3Ca1 E5Ca2 A8Ca9 A9Ca2 A7Ra8
B1Ra1 H8Ra2 J8Ra3 B4Ba2 B8Ba5 F5Ba3 H1Ba3
J9Ba8 A4Rb5 D5Rb5 E4Rb6 E8Rb8 J7Rb5 E1Cb5
D9Cb1 C1Bb2 E3Bb3 F3Bb4 D4Bb4 F9Bb5 D1Ca6
G3Ca2 C3Ca5 F4Ca1 D3Ra8 G1Ra8

1358	1358	7	9	24	28	123458	248	6
5689	589	4	278	3	1	25789	2789	2589
13689	2	169	78	5	678	134789	4789	1389
2	39	8	4	7	3579	69	1	9
1349	6	19	1238	12	2389	2489	5	7
7	149	5	6	12	289	2489	3	289
14569	7	169	123	8	236	123569	269	12359
1568	158	3	127	9	4	125678	2678	1258
1689	189	2	5	167	367	136789	6789	4

```
F2Ca4 A5Ca4 J5Ca6 D6Ca5 B1Ra6 D2Ra3 D7Ra6
D5Ra7 E7Ra4 F5Ra1 G1Ra4 C6Ba6 C8Ba4 G3Ba6
D9Rb9 E5Rb2 J6Ca7 F6Ca9 H8Ca6 H7Ra7 J7Ra3
C9Ba3 B8Ba7 A1Ca3 C4Ca7 H1Ca5 G8Ca9 H2Rb8
J8Rb8 A8Cb2 A6Bb8 C1Ca8 E4Ca8 G6Ca2 B4Ra2
E6Ra3 G4Ra3 H9Ra2 F7Ba2 H4Ba1 G9Ba1 F9Rb8
G7Rb5 A7Cb1 B9Cb5 A2Bb5 B2Bb9 C7Bb9 J2Ca1
E3Ca9 B7Ca8 C3Ra1 E1Ra1 J1Ra9
```

123568	12368	1256	9	2678	4	12578	18	127
9	12468	7	3	268	5	1248	148	124
1258	1248	125	178	278	127	3	6	12479
123	5	8	4	2349	239	149	7	6
236	7	26	468	1	239	49	349	5
136	9	4	67	3567	37	1	2	8
1278	128	129	147	3479	1379	6	5	123479
4	126	3	5	79	8	1279	19	1279
1578	18	159	2	3479	6	14789	13489	13479

```
A2Ca3 F5Ca5 A7Ca5 C9Ra9 E4Ra8 H2Ra6 A9Ba7
F4Ba6 E8Ba3 D4Rb4 F7Rb1 F1Cb3 D7Cb9 F6Bb7
E7Bb4 B5Ra6 C2Ra4 D1Ra1 E6Ra9 G2Ca2 G1Ra8
B2Ba8 J1Ba7 B7Rb2 G3Rb9 J2Rb1 J7Rb8 J3Cb5
H7Cb7 C3Bb2 H5Bb9 E1Ca2 C1Ca5 A3Ca1 D6Ca2
A8Ca8 J8Ca9 H9Ca2 A5Ra2 A1Ra6 C5Ra8 D5Ra3
E3Ra6 H8Ra1 C4Ba7 B9Ba1 G6Ba3 B8Rb4 C6Rb1
G4Rb1 G9Rb4 J5Rb4 G5Cb7 J9Cb3
```

5679	3	569	4	279	79	25678	1	256789
8	4	169	1237	1279	5	2367	2379	2679
1579	9	2	137	8	6	3457	379	4579
2369	7	3689	168	4	189	128	5	128
56	68	4568	15678	167	2	9	78	3
259	1	4589	578	3	789	2478	6	2478
1369	689	7	1268	5	4	12368	2389	12689
4	2	1689	1678	167	3	15678	789	156789
136	5	1368	9	1267	178	123678	4	12678

```
E3Ra4 C2Rb9 J6Ca1 A6Rb7 C1Ca7 C4Ra1 B3Ba1
B4Ba3 E5Ba1 C8Rb3 D4Rb6 H3Rb9 G1Cb1 J1Ca3
G4Ca2 D3Ra3 G7Ra3 H5Ra6 H4Ba8 G8Rb9 H8Rb7
J5Rb7 B8Cb2 E8Cb8 B5Bb9 A7Bb8 E2Bb6 A1Ca6
G2Ca8 A5Ca2 A9Ca9 A3Ra5 D6Ra8 E4Ra7 G9Ra6
J9Ra8 B7Ba6 E1Ba5 F3Ba8 F4Ba5 F6Ba9 J3Ba6
J7Ba2 B9Rb7 D7Rb1 F1Rb2 D1Cb9 H7Cb5 D9Cb2
F9Cb4 C7Bb4 C9Bb5 F7Bb7 H9Bb1
```

45	3	25	247	6	8	1	9	257
4689	169	7	1234	13	5	2468	246	28
4568	16	12568	9	17	147	245678	24567	3
2	4	39	6	13579	1379	3578	1357	15789
3679	8	369	137	2	1379	3567	13567	4
1	5	369	8	379	3479	2367	2367	279
3789	179	1389	5	13789	1379	2347	12347	6
356789	1679	4	137	13789	2	357	1357	157
357	2	135	137	4	6	9	8	157

```
D5Ca5 F6Ra4 E1Ba7 A9Ra7 B5Ra3 B2Ba1 C2Rb6
H1Ca6 B1Ca9 H5Ra8 J4Ra7 G2Ra7 H2Ra9 J1Ca3
E4Ca3 H9Ca5 G6Ra3 J3Ra5 A1Ba5 G3Ba1 G5Ba9
A3Rb2 F5Rb7 G1Rb8 H4Rb1 J9Rb1 C1Cb4 C3Cb8
A4Cb4 C5Cb1 B4Bb2 C6Bb7 F9Ca2 F3Ra9 D3Ba3
E3Ba6 D9Ba9 B9Rb8 D6Rb1 E7Rb5 E6Cb9 C7Cb2
D8Cb7 E8Cb1 C8Bb5 D7Bb8 G7Bb4 H8Bb3 F7Ca3
H7Ca7 G8Ca2 B8Ca4 B7Ra6 F8Ra6
```

5	4	26789	679	1	3	678	89	789
2679	279	1	4679	8	24679	567	3	79
3679	789	36789	679	567	679	1	4	2
1679	5	4679	2	3467	146789	478	18	13478
8	127	247	1347	347	147	9	125	6
12679	3	24679	5	467	146789	2478	128	1478
1279	12789	2789	1478	47	1478	3	6	5
123	128	5	13468	9	1468	248	7	148
4	6	3789	1378	2	5	8	189	189

C5Ca5 B6Ca2 B7Ca5 E8Ca5 D9Ca3 A3Ra2 B4Ra4
A7Ba6 H7Ba2 J7Rb8 E5Ca3 F8Ca2 H9Ca4 B1Ra6
E2Ra2 G1Ba2 H1Rb3 J3Cb7 E3Bb4 J4Bb3 C3Ca3
G6Ca4 C2Ra8 G3Ba8 G5Rb7 H2Rb1 G2Cb9 G4Cb1
H6Cb6 B2Bb7 C6Bb7 E4Bb7 H4Bb8 C4Ca6 E6Ca1
A9Ca7 A8Ra8 B9Ra9 C1Ra9 A4Ba9 F9Ba8 J8Ba9
D8Rb1 F6Rb9 J9Rb1 D1Cb7 F3Cb6 D6Cb8 D3Bb9
F1Bb1 F5Bb4 D7Bb4 D5Ca6 F7Ca7

8	3678	67	5	69	2	1	3678	4
15	13567	9	8	46	146	2	3567	367
4	12568	1256	3	7	169	5689	568	69
6	1258	3	14	2458	1457	57	9	27
1259	1259	125	149	234569	1345679	567	234567	8
7	2589	4	9	235689	3569	56	1	236
3	24569	256	7	1	459	689	268	269
1259	124579	8	6	459	459	3	27	1279
19	1679	167	2	39	8	4	67	5

A1Ca8 E8Ca4 H9Ca1 A5Ra9 J5Ra3 F9Ba3 F4Rb9
E4Cb1 D4Bb4 E6Ca3 D2Ra1 E7Ra7 F2Ba8 D6Ba7
D9Ba2 F7Ba6 D7Rb5 F6Rb5 D5Cb8 F5Cb2 E5Bb6
H5Ca5 B9Ca7 B5Rb4 H6Ca9 H2Ra4 G6Ba4 H1Rb2
H8Cb7 J8Bb6 G8Ca2 C9Ca6 C7Ra9 G7Ra8 B6Ba6
C8Ba8 G9Ba9 A8Rb3 C6Rb1 B8Cb5 B1Bb1 B2Bb3
E1Ca5 J3Ca1 E2Ra9 J2Ra7 A3Ba7 E3Ba2 J1Ba9
A2Rb6 C3Rb5 C2Cb2 G2Cb5 G3Cb6

23789	37	36789	23569	2356	2569	4	1	2359
12379	137	13679	123569	8	4	579	379	2359
5	4	1389	1239	7	129	89	389	6
134	6	1345	7	35	589	159	2	1459
47	9	2	56	1	56	3	47	8
137	8	1357	4	235	259	1579	6	159
6	2	13589	158	4	158	189	389	7
1478	157	14578	12568	9	3	168	48	14
134789	137	134789	168	6	1678	2	5	1349

H2Ca5 J6Ca7 H7Ca6 D6Ra8 H4Ra2 F6Ba9 J5Rb6
A5Ca5 C6Ra2 F5Ra2 D5Ba3 A6Rb6 E6Cb5 E4Bb6
G6Bb1 B3Ca6 G4Ca5 J4Ba8 A2Ca7 F9Rb5 D3Ca5
B7Ca5 B8Ra7 F7Ba7 E8Rb4 E1Cb7 H8Cb8 D9Cb9
D7Bb1 G7Bb9 A1Ca8 H3Ca7 C7Ca8 C8Ca9 A9Ra2
D1Ra4 G3Ra8 B1Ba2 B9Ba3 J3Ba4 B2Rb1 G8Rb3
H1Rb1 J9Rb1 F1Cb3 J2Cb3 C3Cb3 B4Cb9 H9Cb4
A3Bb9 A4Bb3 C4Bb1 F3Bb1 J1Bb9

24569	2345689	7	139	1259	235	2589	24568	4569
2459	234589	34589	6	259	7	1	2458	459
1	2569	569	4	8	25	3	256	7
8	4579	459	2	4579	6	57	1	345
24569	1245679	14569	39	4579	345	257	234567	8
3	24567	456	8	457	1	257	9	456
7	1489	1489	5	3	48	6	8	2
56	13568	13568	7	126	9	4	358	135
4569	1345689	2	1	146	48	5789	3578	1359

D9Ra3 H5Ra2 J5Ba6 G8Rb8 J4Rb1 G6Cb4 J6Bb8
A5Ca1 A7Ca8 H9Ca1 J7Ca9 J8Ca7 J2Ra3 B3Ba3
J1Ba4 H8Ba3 B2Rb8 H3Rb8 J9Rb5 A2Ba4 E1Ca9
D5Ra9 A4Ba9 A9Rb6 B5Rb5 E4Rb3 B1Cb2 C6Cb2
E6Cb5 F9Cb4 A1Bb5 A6Bb3 B8Bb4 B9Bb9 C8Bb5
F5Bb7 E8Bb6 H1Ca6 E5Ca4 A8Ca2 D3Ra4 H2Ra5
F3Ba5 D2Rb7 E3Rb1 F7Rb2 E2Cb2 F2Cb6 G3Cb9
D7Cb5 E7Cb7 C2Bb9 C3Bb6 G2Bb1

1569	8	4	2369	12369	139	7	129	269
2	1369	139	7	5	13489	168	189	4689
169	7	19	269	12469	1489	1268	5	3
4578	34	3578	1	347	2	9	6	58
456789	3469	235789	359	3479	34579	258	278	1
1579	19	12579	8	79	6	4	3	25
189	5	189	2369	12369	139	1268	4	7
3	19	179	4	8	1579	1256	129	2569
14789	2	6	59	179	1579	3	189	589

E8Ca7 B9Ca4 A1Ra5 J1Ra4 H3Ba7 J6Ca7 G6Ra3
F2Ca9 H7Ca5 F1Ra1 H9Ra6 J4Ra5 D1Ba7 E6Ba5
H8Ba2 F5Rb7 G7Rb1 H2Rb1 H6Cb9 A6Bb1 J5Bb1
C6Ca4 B8Ca1 B3Ra9 C3Ra1 C7Ra8 B2Ba3 B6Ba8
A9Ba2 B7Ba6 D9Ba8 G1Ba9 A8Rb9 C1Rb6 D2Rb4
E7Rb2 F9Rb5 G3Rb8 J9Rb9 E1Cb8 E2Cb6 E3Cb3
F3Cb2 D5Cb3 J8Cb8 A5Bb6 D3Bb5 E4Bb9 A4Ca3
G4Ca6 E5Ca4 C5Ca9 C4Ra2 G5Ra2

8	569	3679	3567	356	2	3679	1	4
1	269	23679	8	4	7	3679	5	379
467	456	3467	9	1356	157	2	378	378
249	3	8	457	1259	6	14579	279	1579
249	1249	1249	457	12589	14579	134579	23789	6
2469	7	5	4	1289	3	149	289	189
24679	2469	24679	1	3569	459	8	379	3579
5	1489	149	2	7	49	139	6	139
3	169	1679	56	569	8	1579	4	2

H2Ca8 A4Ca3 F1Ra6 G5Ba3 B6Rb7 F4Rb4 J4Ca6
C6Ca1 E6Rb9 H6Cb4 G6Bb5 J5Ca9 D9Ca5 E4Ra5
J7Ra5 D1Ba9 D4Ba7 D8Rb2 J2Rb1 H3Cb9 J3Cb7
D5Cb1 A3Bb6 D7Bb4 C1Ca7 G2Ca6 E3Ca1 C5Ca6
B7Ca6 A7Ra7 C2Ra5 F5Ra2 C3Ba4 A5Ba5 B9Ba9
E5Ba8 E8Ba7 A2Rb9 B2Rb2 E7Rb3 G3Rb2 G8Rb9
G9Rb7 G1Cb4 E2Cb4 B3Cb3 H7Cb1 F8Cb8 C8Bb3
E1Bb2 F7Bb9 F9Bb1 H9Bb3 C9Ca8

13678	1678	13678	148	145	2	1678	9	3478
12678	5	12678	3	9	168	12678	1247	2478
4	1268	123689	7	1	168	5	123	238
2378	4	2378	8	6	3578	9	237	1
1237	127	5	149	1347	1379	27	8	6
13678	9	13678	18	2	1378	4	37	5
9	12678	124678	5	17	17	3	1247	2478
1257	3	1247	6	8	179	127	12457	2479
12578	1278	1278	129	137	4	1278	6	2789

C3Ca9 J4Ca2 A5Ca5 D6Ca5 H8Ca5 J5Ra3 J1Ra5
J9Ra9 A4Ba4 H6Ba9 C5Rb1 D4Rb8 F4Cb1 G5Cb7
E4Bb9 E5Bb4 G6Bb1 B8Ca1 B9Ra4 G8Ba4 H3Ca4
C9Ca3 C8Rb2 E7Rb2 G2Ca2 G3Ra6 H9Ra2 F1Ba6
F3Rb8 G9Rb8 A9Cb7 A1Ca8 A3Ra3 C6Ra8 J2Ra8
A2Ba1 B6Ba6 B7Ba8 A7Rb6 C2Rb6 E2Rb7 D3Cb2
E6Cb3 B3Bb7 D1Bb3 E1Bb1 F6Bb7 B1Ca2 H1Ca7
J3Ca1 F8Ca3 D8Ca7 H7Ra1 J7Ra7

1	2678	9	34567	3578	4568	2357	347	2457
3	5	367	13467	9	2	137	1347	8
238	4	378	1357	13578	158	6	1379	2579
7	68	1568	9	15	3	18	2	46
258	9	1568	1256	4	156	178	1678	3
4	26	136	8	12	7	19	5	69
589	1	578	2357	23578	58	4	36789	25679
58	3	4578	2457	6	9	2578	78	1
6	78	2	13457	13578	1458	35789	3789	579

G1Ca9 H3Ca4 D9Ra4 F3Ra3 B1Rb3 G8Ca6 F9Ca6
F7Ra9 F2Rb2 F5Cb1 D5Bb5 C1Ca2 G5Ca2 E4Ra2
G4Ra3 H7Ra2 A9Ba2 E6Ba6 G9Rb7 H8Cb8 H1Bb5
E1Ca8 E3Ca5 D7Ra8 G6Ra5 H4Ra7 D3Ba1 J2Ba7
J5Ba8 D2Rb6 G3Rb8 A2Cb8 C3Cb7 B3Bb6 A6Bb4
C5Bb3 J4Ca4 A4Ca6 A5Ca7 C6Ca8 B8Ca4 A7Ra5
B7Ra7 J6Ra1 C4Ba5 C8Ba1 A8Ba3 E8Ba7 J9Ba5
B4Rb1 C9Rb9 E7Rb1 J7Rb3 J8Rb9

1	34579	3579	8	3459	2349	279	2579	6
45	4589	2	7	6	149	3	1589	58
567	356789	35789	129	1359	1239	12789	4	58
2	19	4	169	139	5	68	38	7
3	157	57	1246	14	8	246	25	9
8	59	6	249	349	7	24	235	1
457	234578	3578	149	14789	149	14789	6	348
467	4678	1	3	2	469	5	789	48
9	34678	378	5	1478	146	1478	1378	2

G2Ca2 G9Ca3 H9Ca4 J3Ra3 A5Ba4 E5Rb1 D2Ca1
F4Ca2 C5Ca5 E8Ra2 F7Ra4 B9Ba5 F2Ba9 E4Ba4
F8Ba5 B1Rb4 C9Rb8 E7Rb6 F5Rb3 B2Cb8 D5Cb9
D7Cb8 D4Bb6 D8Bb3 G1Ca5 J2Ca4 G3Ca8 G6Ra4
H8Ra8 J6Ra6 G4Ba1 J5Ba8 G7Ba9 C4Rb9 G5Rb7
H6Rb9 C3Cb7 B6Cb1 C1Bb6 B8Bb9 E3Bb5 H1Ca7
A2Ca5 H2Ca6 A3Ca9 J8Ca1 A6Ra3 C7Ra1 E2Ra7
J7Ra7 C2Ba3 C6Ba2 A7Ba2 A8Ba7

13569	13569	3569	1268	18	7	4	1356	13568
2	1346	367	1468	5	468	178	9	13678
1567	8	567	3	9	46	157	2	1567
679	269	8	1469	14	5	3	17	1279
3569	23569	1	7	38	3689	589	5	4
3579	359	4	189	138	2	6	157	15789
13689	7	369	5	2	389	19	4	1369
4	12359	2359	9	6	39	1579	8	13579
35689	3569	3569	489	3478	1	2	3567	35679

B2Ca4 H3Ca2 A4Ca2 J5Ca7 D9Ca2 C6Ra4 E2Ra2
J4Ra4 D5Ba4 G6Ba8 B6Rb6 E8Rb5 H4Rb9 H6Cb3
E6Bb9 J1Ca8 D4Ca6 G7Ca9 D8Ra1 E1Ra6 F9Ba9
D2Rb9 E7Rb8 F8Rb7 D1Cb7 E5Cb3 A1Ca9 J3Ra9
F1Ca5 F2Ra3 C1Rb1 G1Cb3 A2Cb6 A8Bb3 G3Bb6
J2Bb5 H2Ca1 B3Ca3 J8Ca6 J9Ca3 C9Ra6 G9Ra1
C3Ba7 B7Ba1 A3Rb5 B4Rb8 C7Rb5 F4Cb1 A5Cb1
H7Cb7 A9Cb8 B9Cb7 F5Bb8 H9Bb5

7	69	12369	4	125	1269	8	126	159
12469	469	124689	1569	125	1269	249	7	3
12469	5	12469	8	3	12679	249	1246	149
3456	2	34567	36	8	3467	1	9	47
3469	8	34679	136	147	5	347	34	2
34	1	347	3	9	2347	6	5	478
12459	3	12459	7	6	1489	249	124	149
12459	479	124579	1359	145	1349	23479	8	6
8	4679	14679	2	14	1349	5	134	1479

B3Ca8 E5Ca7 G6Ca8 A9Ca5 F9Ca8 A3Ra3 C6Ra7
E4Ra1 F6Ra2 F3Ra7 D6Ba4 D9Ba7 F4Rb3 F1Cb4
D4Cb6 D3Bb5 H7Ca7 D1Ra3 G1Ra5 H6Ra3 J2Ra7
J3Ba6 J8Ba3 E3Rb9 E8Rb4 E1Cb6 E7Cb3 C8Ra6
B4Ca9 A2Ra9 B5Ra5 J6Ra9 B2Ba6 A5Ba2 H1Ba9
H4Ba5 A6Rb6 A8Rb1 B6Rb1 H2Rb4 B1Cb2 G3Cb1
H5Cb1 G8Cb2 C1Bb1 C3Bb4 B7Bb4 H3Bb2 J5Bb4
C7Ca2 J9Ca1 G9Ca4 C9Ra9 G7Ra9

1238	123678	13678	5	12368	138	4	1678	9
12348	123468	13468	2468	9	7	156	1568	58
1489	146789	5	468	1468	18	167	3	2
5	2349	349	1	23	6	8	79	34
7	23489	3489	289	238	5	36	69	1
6	1389	1389	7	38	4	2	59	35
1389	135689	2	689	1568	189	135	4	7
13489	1345689	134689	4689	7	2	135	158	358
148	14578	1478	3	1458	18	9	1258	6

A6Ca3 G6Ca9 C7Ca7 J8Ca2 D9Ca4 D8Ra7 E4Ba9
E8Rb6 E7Cb3 F9Bb5 B4Ca2 B7Ca6 F8Ca9 H9Ca3
B8Ra5 A8Ba1 H8Ba8 B9Rb8 A1Ca2 A5Rb6 C1Rb9
C2Cb6 G1Ca8 H3Ca6 B1Ra3 G2Ra3 G4Ra6 H2Ra9
J6Ra8 C4Ba8 D3Ba9 J2Ba5 C6Rb1 D2Rb2 H4Rb4
H1Cb1 C5Cb4 D5Cb3 J5Cb1 F5Bb8 J1Bb4 G5Bb5
H7Bb5 A2Ca7 F3Ca3 E5Ca2 G7Ca1 A3Ra8 F2Ra1
J3Ra7 B3Ba1 E2Ba8 B2Rb4 E3Rb4

14789	12478	1249	269	5	289	246	3	124
458	3	245	1	28	7	9	24568	245
6	1258	1259	4	238	2389	25	1258	7
3459	245	7	23	1	6	8	2459	2459
13459	1245	123459	237	23478	238	2457	12459	6
14	1246	8	27	9	5	3	124	124
2	1467	1346	5	37	139	46	469	8
357	9	356	8	237	4	1	256	235
13458	1458	1345	239	6	1239	245	7	23459

```
A4Ca6 E5Ca4 E7Ca7 B8Ra6 E6Ra8 F2Ra6 F4Ra7
C8Ba8 G7Ba6 H3Ca6 J4Ca9 B5Ca8 G8Ra9 A9Ba1
D9Ba9 E1Ca9 F9Rb2 H8Rb2 C5Ca2 C6Ca3 B3Ra2
C3Ra9 J6Ra2 C2Ba1 A6Ba9 A7Ba2 G6Ba1 A3Rb4
C7Rb5 B1Cb5 G3Cb3 J7Cb4 B9Cb4 H1Bb7 G5Bb7
D1Ca3 A2Ca7 H5Ca3 A1Ra8 E4Ra3 G2Ra4 H9Ra5
J9Ra3 F1Ba4 D4Ba2 J2Ba8 D2Rb5 F8Rb1 J1Rb1
E2Cb2 E3Cb1 J3Cb5 D8Cb4 E8Cb5
```

1368	1368	139	4	5	2	179	16	169
13568	7	1349	138	19	89	1459	12456	12469
2	145	149	17	6	79	14579	3	8
13	134	5	168	149	4689	2	7	134
9	124	8	127	1247	3	6	14	5
137	1234	6	1257	1247	457	8	9	134
4	1256	12	256	3	56	159	8	7
135678	9	1237	2567	247	4567	1345	12456	12346
3567	2356	237	9	8	1	345	2456	2346

```
A2Ca8 B4Ca3 A7Ra7 B6Ra8 G7Ra9 H1Ra8 F1Ba7
D4Ba8 D6Ra6 J3Ra7 D5Ba9 B5Rb1 G6Rb5 C4Cb7
F6Cb4 C6Bb9 F5Bb2 H6Bb7 F4Ca5 H5Ca4 E5Ca7
E2Ra2 D2Ba4 E4Ba1 E8Rb4 H9Rb6 H4Cb2 J8Cb2
A9Cb9 H3Bb3 G4Bb6 J9Bb4 F2Ca3 J2Ca6 G3Ca2
B3Ca9 J7Ca3 B9Ca2 A1Ra3 B7Ra4 D9Ra3 F9Ra1
G2Ra1 J1Ra5 C3Ba4 C2Ba5 B1Ba6 D1Ba1 A3Rb1
B8Rb5 C7Rb1 H7Cb5 A8Cb6 H8Cb1
```

4	2358	12568	7	169	1689	12369	2369	29
36	37	167	2	5	1469	134679	8	479
26	9	12678	168	3	1468	12467	26	5
7	6	259	135	129	12359	239	4	8
259	258	3	568	2469	245689	29	7	1
1	4	289	38	29	23789	239	5	6
2569	1	245679	56	8	256	245679	269	3
2356	235	2456	9	7	2356	24568	1	24
8	2357	25679	4	126	12356	25679	269	279

```
E5Ca4 F6Ca7 H7Ca8 A8Ca3 J7Ca5 C8Rb2 C1Cb6
A9Cb9 B1Bb3 B6Ra9 C6Ba4 B2Rb7 B3Cb1 B9Cb4
C3Bb8 B7Bb6 H9Bb2 E2Ca8 G7Ca4 J9Ca7 A6Ra8
C7Ra7 F4Ra8 G3Ra7 H3Ra4 A5Ba6 A7Ba1 D4Ba3
J3Ba6 C4Rb1 H1Rb5 J8Rb9 H2Cb3 G8Cb6 J2Bb2
G4Bb5 H6Bb6 E1Ca2 A2Ca5 E4Ca6 J6Ca3 F7Ca3
A3Ra2 E6Ra5 E7Ra9 F5Ra2 G6Ra2 G1Ra9 J5Ra1
D3Ba5 D6Ba1 D5Ba9 D7Ba2 F3Rb9
```

68	1689	1	236789	236789	4	1279	123	5
7	689	2	35689	35689	1	49	34	349
3	4	15	2579	2579	29	8	6	179
58	138	9	23568	4	268	125	7	138
2	138	1345	3589	3589	7	145	1345	6
458	378	6	2358	1	28	245	9	348
1	5	47	24679	2679	269	3	8	479
9	267	8	12467	267	3	14567	145	147
46	367	347	146789	6789	5	14679	14	2

```
H2Ca2 A8Ca2 F2Ra7 C3Ba5 A3Rb1 C9Ra1 A7Ba7
A1Ca8 A2Ca9 H7Ca6 E2Ra8 H8Ra5 B2Ba6 D2Ba1
D1Rb5 H5Rb7 J2Rb3 F1Cb4 D7Cb2 H9Cb4 E3Bb3
F7Bb5 J1Bb6 H4Bb1 J8Bb1 C4Ca7 A5Ca3 E7Ca1
B8Ca3 G9Ca7 A4Ra6 B7Ra4 E8Ra4 J3Ra7 B9Ba9
D6Ba6 G3Ba4 J7Ba9 D4Rb3 J5Rb8 F4Cb2 J4Cb4
B5Cb5 D9Cb8 B4Bb8 E5Bb9 F6Bb8 F9Bb3 G4Bb9
E4Ca5 G5Ca6 C6Ca9 C5Ra2 G6Ra2
```

2	7	14689	468	168	3	146	146	5
134568	458	134568	2468	9	148	123467	12346	1236
1346	4	1346	7	16	5	9	8	1236
4568	1	45678	3568	2	78	346	9	36
456	9	2456	356	1356	1	8	12346	7
68	3	2678	689	4	1789	126	5	126
3489	248	23489	1	38	6	5	7	2389
134589	2458	1234589	34589	7	489	1236	1236	123689
7	6	13589	3589	358	2	13	13	4

B4Ca2 B7Ca7 A3Ra9 C9Ra2 C2Rb4 E6Rb1 G2Ca2
J4Ra9 F6Ba9 D6Ca7 F9Ca1 F3Ra7 E3Ba2 F7Rb2
H7Cb6 H8Bb2 H6Ca8 A5Ra8 H4Ra4 J3Ra8 C5Ba1
B6Ba4 G5Ba3 J5Ba5 G9Ba8 A4Rb6 E5Rb6 G3Rb4
H2Rb5 H9Rb9 G1Cb9 B2Cb8 F4Cb8 F1Bb6 D1Ca8
B8Ca6 B9Ra3 C3Ra6 D7Ra4 D9Ra6 C1Ba3 A8Ba4
E1Ba4 E8Ba3 A7Rb1 D3Rb5 E4Rb5 H1Rb1 J8Rb1
B1Cb5 B3Cb1 H3Cb3 D4Cb3 J7Cb3

2	1789	1478	6	149	139	5	13489	1489
489	1589	148	7	12459	1239	123	123489	6
6	3	14	125	8	129	7	1249	149
348	128	9	1238	126	5	136	1346	7
347	127	6	123	1279	12379	8	1349	5
378	178	5	138	1679	4	136	1369	2
5	4	278	128	3	12678	9	12678	18
789	26789	278	4	12567	12678	126	125678	3
1	2678	2378	9	2567	2678	4	25678	8

B2Ca5 J3Ca3 C4Ca5 J9Rb8 G9Cb1 G4Rb2 H3Ca2
J8Ra2 B7Ba2 H8Ba5 C8Rb1 H7Rb6 J5Rb5 C3Cb4
G8Cb7 C9Bb9 G3Bb8 J2Ca6 A3Ca7 H6Ca8 A9Ca4
B5Ra4 C6Ra2 G6Ra6 H5Ra1 J6Ra7 B3Ba1 A5Rb9
E6Rb9 A2Cb8 B6Cb3 B1Bb9 A6Bb1 A8Bb3 B8Bb8
H2Ca9 F8Ca9 F5Ra6 H1Ra7 E5Ba7 D8Ba6 D5Rb2
E8Rb4 E1Cb3 D2Cb1 E2Bb2 F1Bb8 F2Bb7 E4Bb1
D7Bb3 D1Ca4 F4Ca3 D4Ca8 F7Ca1

1257	4	1567	19	8	19	3	56	256
3	158	158	6	2	7	458	9	458
25	258	9	34	45	34	24568	1	7
14579	135789	134578	13489	147	2	145689	45678	45689
6	12789	1478	5	147	1489	12489	478	3
124579	1235789	134578	13489	147	6	124589	4578	24589
4579	579	2	48	46	48	45689	3	1
8	19	14	7	3	5	469	2	469
145	6	1345	1248	9	148	7	458	458

A3Ca6 J4Ca2 C5Ca5 G5Ca6 C6Ca3 A1Ra7 C7Ra6
J3Ra3 C4Ba4 A9Ba2 G2Ba7 J6Ba1 H9Ba6 A6Rb9
A8Rb5 C1Rb2 G4Rb8 C2Cb8 A4Cb1 G6Cb4 E6Bb8
D8Ca6 G1Ca9 E2Ca9 E5Ca1 E7Ra2 G7Ra5 H7Ra9
F2Ba2 J1Ba5 H2Rb1 B2Cb5 H3Cb4 B3Bb1 D2Bb3
E3Bb7 F4Ca3 F8Ca7 D5Ra7 E8Ra4 F9Ra9 F5Ba4
D4Ba9 D9Ba5 J9Ba4 B9Rb8 D3Rb8 F1Rb1 J8Rb8
D1Cb4 F3Cb5 B7Cb4 D7Cb1 F7Cb8

3489	2389	5	7	2469	3469	348	123489	1289
34789	23789	6	239	249	1	3478	234789	5
1	2379	2347	2359	8	3459	6	23479	29
2	1	378	389	479	34789	5	48	6
789	6789	78	2689	5	46789	1	248	3
5	4	38	12368	126	368	9	28	7
6	578	478	1589	3	5789	2	15789	189
378	3578	1	5689	679	2	378	356789	4
378	23578	9	4	167	5678	378	135678	18

E2Ca6 C3Ca2 G3Ra4 J2Ra2 E1Ba9 C9Rb9 A9Ca2
A8Ra1 D5Ca4 C6Ra4 E8Ra4 C4Ba5 F8Ba2 D8Rb8
B5Ca2 E4Ra2 B1Ca7 G2Ca7 B7Ra4 C8Ra7 A1Ba4
B8Ba3 A7Ba8 H2Ba5 B4Rb9 C2Rb3 A2Cb9 B2Cb8
D4Cb3 A5Cb6 A6Bb3 D3Bb7 F5Bb1 F3Ca3 G4Ca1
H5Ca9 E6Ca7 D6Ra9 E3Ra8 G8Ra9 H7Ra7 J9Ra1
J5Ba7 J7Ba3 J8Ba5 G9Ba8 G6Rb5 H8Rb6 J1Rb8
H1Cb3 H4Cb8 J6Cb6 F4Bb6 F6Bb8

14678	9	1478	14	568	14568	2	34578	358
12478	3	12478	124	589	124589	4589	6	589
5	26	248	3	7	24689	489	48	1
1289	12	6	5	4	238	138	38	7
1278	1257	12578	6	38	2378	1358	9	4
478	57	3	9	1	78	568	58	2
3	157	1579	8	2	14579	459	45	6
2679	4	2579	7	3569	35679	3589	1	3589
1269	8	1259	14	3569	134569	7	2345	359

C2Ca6 B4Ca2 H4Ca7 F7Ca6 J8Ca2 A8Ca7 A9Ra3
C3Ra2 D1Ra9 F1Ra4 H1Ba2 H7Ba3 J1Ca6 D8Ca3
H9Ra8 B5Ca8 E5Rb3 J6Ca3 J4Ra4 G6Ba1 A4Rb1
J3Rb1 A1Cb8 A3Bb4 E3Ca8 B1Ra1 B3Ba7 E1Rb7
F2Cb5 E6Cb2 E2Bb1 D6Bb8 F8Bb8 G2Bb7 D2Ca2
F6Ca7 D7Ca1 C7Ca8 G8Ca5 C6Ra9 E7Ra5 G7Ra4
J5Ra5 B6Ba4 A6Ba5 C8Ba4 B9Ba5 H3Ba5 H5Ba9
J9Ba9 A5Rb6 B7Rb9 G3Rb9 H6Rb6

9	578	358	58	78	4	6	238	1
1348	14678	3468	2	1678	1789	49	3489	5
148	14568	2	15689	3	1589	7	489	49
5	148	7	134689	1468	1389	2	1469	469
124	3	4	1469	5	1279	49	14679	8
6	1248	9	148	12478	1278	3	1457	47
234	2456	1	345	9	235	8	4567	467
248	245689	4568	7	1248	1258	459	4569	3
7	4589	3458	3458	48	6	1	459	2

H7Ca5 A8Ca2 A3Ra3 F8Ra5 B8Ba3 G1Ba3 E3Rb4
E7Cb9 B7Bb4 J3Ca5 D6Ca3 C8Ca8 C9Ca9 B6Ra9
D4Ra9 J4Ra3 F6Ca8 D2Ra8 F9Ra7 J5Ra8 A4Ba8
E6Ba7 G8Ba7 A5Rb7 A2Cb5 B2Ca7 E1Ra2 F2Ba1
F5Ba2 F4Rb4 G4Cb5 G6Bb2 H2Ca2 H5Ca4 C6Ca5
H6Ra1 H8Ra9 J2Ba9 G9Ba6 D9Rb4 G2Rb4 H1Rb8
J8Rb4 B1Cb1 C2Cb6 H3Cb6 B3Bb8 C1Bb4 B5Bb6
C4Bb1 E4Ca6 D5Ca1 D8Ra6 E8Ra1

236	123468	468	289	5	69	23689	7	12368
267	2678	5	3	26789	1	4	289	268
9	123678	678	4	2678	67	2368	1238	5
4	3679	2	179	1679	8	367	5	1367
3567	3567	67	127	12467	4567	23678	1238	9
8	5679	1	279	2679	3	267	4	267
1	26789	6789	5	789	79	23789	2389	4
57	45789	3	6	4789	2	1	89	78
257	245789	4789	1789	3	479	25789	6	278

E6Ca5 J7Ca5 E5Ra4 F2Ra5 J4Ra1 D2Ba9 D5Ba1
H1Ba5 J6Ba4 D4Rb7 E4Cb2 F4Bb9 A3Ca4 A4Ca8
A9Ca1 C2Ra1 E8Ra1 H2Ra4 J3Ra9 F5Ba6 E7Ba8
D9Ca3 D7Ra6 B9Ba6 H8Rb9 A7Ca9 A2Ra2 B5Ra9
A1Ba3 C5Ba2 J1Ba2 G6Ba9 A6Rb6 B1Rb7 C7Rb3
E1Rb6 B2Cb8 E3Cb7 C6Cb7 C8Cb8 C3Bb6 B8Bb2
E2Bb3 J2Bb7 G2Ca6 G3Ca8 G8Ca3 F9Ca2 F7Ra7
G7Ra2 J9Ra8 H5Ba8 H9Ba7 G5Rb7

2	389	1389	7	1689	169	4	356	35
1378	38	1378	5	1268	4	2678	9	237
478	6	5	289	289	3	278	1	27
13468	5	1348	2468	1234678	167	127	347	9
1346	349	2	469	5	1679	17	347	8
1348	7	13489	2489	123489	19	125	345	6
3457	1	6	49	479	2	579	8	457
457	4	47	3	4679	8	15679	2	1457
9	248	478	1	467	567	3	4567	457

J2Ca2 J6Ca5 H9Ca1 C1Ra4 G1Ra3 J3Ra8 H1Ba5
H2Rb4 H3Cb7 B1Ca7 A6Ca6 B7Ca6 J8Ca6 H5Ra6
C7Ba8 A8Rb5 H7Rb9 A9Cb3 B9Bb2 G9Ca5 C9Ra7
F7Ra5 D7Ba2 J9Ba4 G7Ba7 E7Rb1 J5Rb7 E1Cb6
D4Ca6 C5Ra9 C4Ba2 G4Ba9 E4Rb4 F4Rb8 G5Rb4
F1Cb1 D1Bb8 F6Bb9 A3Ca9 F5Ca2 D6Ca1 A5Ra1
D8Ra7 E2Ra9 B3Ba1 B5Ba8 D5Ba3 E6Ba7 F8Ba4
A2Rb8 B2Rb3 D3Rb4 E8Rb3 F3Rb3

5679	5679	8	1	2679	269	3	25679	4
15679	145679	2	67	679	3	15789	15679	156
13679	13679	1379	8	4	5	179	12679	16
4	356789	3579	567	35679	1	5	35	2
1357	1357	1357	2457	2357	2	6	8	9
2	13569	1359	456	3569	8	145	1345	7
589	2589	59	3	1	7	459	4569	56
135789	1235789	6	25	258	4	1579	13579	135
1357	1357	4	9	56	6	2	13567	8

B2Ca4 H5Ca8 A6Ca9 B7Ca8 H9Ca3 C8Ra2 D2Ra8
E4Ra4 G2Ra2 A5Ba2 F2Ba6 G1Ba8 H4Ba2 D7Rb5
E6Rb2 F4Rb5 J6Rb6 J5Cb5 D8Cb3 G3Rb5 G9Cb6
C9Bb1 E3Ca1 A8Ca6 B9Ca5 B1Ra1 C1Ra6 H8Ra5
C2Ba9 C7Ba7 B8Rb9 C3Rb3 H7Rb1 H2Cb7 F3Cb9
F7Cb4 G8Cb4 J8Cb7 A2Bb5 D3Bb7 F5Bb3 F8Bb1
H1Bb9 J1Bb3 G7Bb9 E1Ca5 A1Ca7 J2Ca1 E2Ca3
B4Ca7 D5Ca9 B5Ra6 D4Ra6 E5Ra7

389	2	15689	7	1389	1389	4	1359	13569
3489	34689	14689	5	1389	2	169	1379	1369
7	3459	1459	34	6	1349	8	12359	12359
6	459	3	1	27	4	259	8	2459
2	489	489	346	5	3468	19	1349	7
1	458	7	9	238	348	25	6	2345
5	6789	2689	6	4	169	3	129	12689
349	3469	2469	8	139	7	12569	12459	124569
3489	1	4689	2	39	3569	7	459	45689

G2Ca7 D5Ca7 J6Ca5 B8Ca7 F5Ba2 D6Rb4 F7Rb5
G4Rb6 E4Cb3 C4Bb4 F6Bb8 E6Ca6 D2Ra5 F9Ra3
E8Ba4 F2Rb4 J8Rb9 J5Cb3 E7Ra1 C2Rb9 A1Cb8
E2Cb8 E3Bb9 J1Bb4 H1Ca9 B3Ca4 B5Ca8 H9Ca4
B9Ra1 G6Ra9 H2Ra3 H8Ra5 B1Ba3 A5Ba9 H5Ba1
G8Ba1 A8Rb3 B2Rb6 A6Cb1 B7Cb9 C8Cb2 A3Bb5
C6Bb3 C9Bb5 D7Bb2 C3Ca1 H7Ca6 G9Ca2 D9Ca9
A9Ra6 G3Ra8 H3Ra2 J3Ra6 J9Ba8

378	358	3578	2678	9	123468	12678	124678	678
9	2	6	78	134	1348	5	1478	78
1	4	78	5	26	268	26789	26789	3
37	356	3579	1	8	269	2367	23567	4
2	3568	34589	69	46	7	368	3568	1
478	168	1478	3	5	246	2678	2678	9
6	7	138	4	13	13589	1389	13589	2
5	9	2	68	136	1368	4	13678	678
348	138	1348	2689	7	1235689	13689	135689	568

C5Ca2 J9Ca5 G6Ra5 J4Ca2 J6Ba9 E4Ca9 D3Ra9
A9Ca6 C6Ra6 E5Ba6 D6Rb2 H9Rb7 F6Cb4 B9Cb8
B4Bb7 J1Ca4 H4Ca6 B5Ca4 A8Ra4 B6Ra3 C3Ra8
E3Ra4 H6Ra8 A6Ba1 A4Ba8 A7Ba2 J2Ba8 B8Rb1
H8Cb3 H5Bb1 J8Bb6 F1Ca8 F2Ca1 A3Ca5 G5Ca3
F8Ca2 A1Ra7 F7Ra6 J3Ra3 A2Ba3 D2Ba6 F3Ba7
G3Ba1 D1Rb3 E2Rb5 J7Rb1 D7Cb7 E8Cb8 C7Bb9
D8Bb5 E7Bb3 G8Bb9 G7Ca8 C8Ca7

1367	13567	15	3578	9	4	135	2	1357
4	3579	59	357	2	1	8	6	357
12367	123567	8	357	3567	57	9	3457	13457
128	12458	3	6	457	9	145	4578	124578
1268	124568	1245	13457	3457	57	13456	34578	9
169	14569	7	2	345	8	13456	345	13456
12389	123489	6	459	45	25	7	3458	3458
5	3479	49	479	8	6	2	1	34
278	2478	24	457	1	3	456	9	4568

E4Ca1 A4Ca8 C5Ca6 G6Ca2 D9Ca2 A3Ca1 C9Ra1
C8Ba4 C6Ca7 E6Rb5 G5Rb5 G8Cb3 F8Bb5 H9Bb4
B3Ca5 B2Ra9 C4Ra5 D2Ra5 H2Ra3 B4Ba3 F1Ba9
B9Rb7 C2Rb2 G9Rb8 H3Rb9 C1Cb3 G1Cb1 H4Cb7
D1Bb8 G2Bb4 J4Bb4 F2Ca1 J2Ca8 E3Ca4 G4Ca9
E8Ca8 D7Ra1 E1Ra2 E5Ra7 J1Ra7 A2Ba7 E2Ba6
F5Ba3 F7Ba4 D8Ba7 J3Ba2 A1Rb6 D5Rb4 E7Rb3
F9Rb6 A7Cb5 J9Cb5 A9Bb3 J7Bb6

249	14	1249	159	6	8	459	3	7
3479	6	1349	13579	134579	13579	459	2	14589
3479	5	8	2	13479	1379	469	469	149
345	34	6	13579	13579	2	8	4579	3459
1	9	234	3578	357	357	23457	457	6
2358	38	7	35689	359	4	1	59	359
3689	2	5	4	1379	1379	3679	679	39
3469	7	1349	1359	12359	1359	34569	8	3459
349	34	349	3579	8	6	34579	1	2

```
A2Ca1 F2Ca8 F4Ca6 H5Ca2 E7Ca2 B9Ca8 E4Ra8
F1Ra2 G1Ra8 A3Ba2 C9Ba1 D1Ba5 H3Ba1 H1Ba6
J4Ca5 H9Ca5 A7Ra5 H7Ra4 J7Ra7 C8Ba4 G7Ba3
A4Rb9 B7Rb9 G9Rb9 A1Cb4 H4Cb3 C7Cb6 G8Cb6
F9Cb3 B3Bb3 D9Bb4 H6Bb9 J1Ca3 J2Ca4 J3Ca9
B5Ca4 B6Ra5 C1Ra9 E3Ra4 B1Ba7 B4Ba1 D2Ba3
D4Rb7 E6Cb3 D8Cb9 C6Bb7 D5Bb1 E5Bb5 F8Bb5
C5Ca3 G5Ca7 F5Ca9 G6Ca1 E8Ca7
```

1469	146	134	467	14678	468	5	136789	126789
7	146	5	2	1468	3	169	1689	1689
16	2	8	567	9	56	4	1367	167
1456	3	14	4569	4568	7	169	2	14689
8	467	247	1	456	4569	679	4679	3
146	9	147	346	3468	2	167	5	14678
14	5	6	3479	2	49	8	1479	1479
3	47	9	8	4567	1	267	467	24567
124	1478	1247	45679	4567	4569	3	14679	1245679

```
J1Ca2 D1Ca5 A1Ca9 J2Ca8 A3Ca3 F5Ca3 A6Ca8
H7Ca2 A9Ra2 C8Ra3 E3Ra2 F9Ra8 G4Ra3 B8Ba8
D5Ba8 C9Ca1 C4Ra7 C6Ba5 A8Ba7 C1Rb6 H2Rb7
E2Cb6 F3Ca7 J4Ca5 J5Ca7 J6Ca6 G9Ca7 E5Ra5
E7Ra7 H9Ra5 G6Ba9 H8Ba6 E6Rb4 H5Rb4 F4Cb6
B5Cb1 E8Cb9 B2Bb4 A4Bb4 A5Bb6 D4Bb9 F7Bb1
G1Ca1 A2Ca1 B7Ca9 B9Ra6 D3Ra1 F1Ra4 G8Ra4
J8Ra1 J9Ra9 D9Ba4 D7Ba6 J3Ba4
```

3479	5	4789	347	348	2	49	6	1
2349	12349	6	34	5	38	7	2349	2
2347	2347	247	1	346	9	8	2345	25
8	2467	3	24567	1246	167	126	257	9
2679	2679	279	235679	123689	13678	126	2578	4
1	24679	5	24679	24689	678	26	278	3
23679	23679	279	8	12369	4	5	29	26
24569	2469	1	269	7	6	3	2489	268
23469	8	249	2369	2369	5	2469	1	7

```
H1Ca5 B2Ca1 A3Ca8 C9Ca5 H9Ca8 B6Ra8 C5Ra6
G5Ra1 A4Ba7 B9Rb2 H6Rb6 F6Cb7 G9Cb6 D6Bb1
E6Ca3 E7Ca1 J1Ra6 F8Ca8 E5Ra8 J3Ca4 A7Ca4
H8Ca4 A1Ra9 C1Ra4 B4Ba4 B8Ba9 G8Ba2 A5Rb3
B1Rb3 C8Rb3 J7Rb9 G1Cb7 J5Cb2 E1Bb2 D5Bb4
G3Bb9 H4Bb9 J4Bb3 G2Ca3 F2Ca4 C3Ca2 F5Ca9
C2Ra7 E2Ra9 H2Ra2 D2Ba6 E3Ba7 D7Rb2 E8Rb5
D4Cb5 E4Cb6 F7Cb6 D8Cb7 F4Bb2
```

2468	469	2489	2569	3	24569	24568	1	7
24678	4679	5	269	69	1	23468	246	48
1246	3	124	8	7	2456	2456	246	9
9	1467	12347	1236	8	236	1467	5	14
1346	8	134	7	569	3569	1469	469	2
5	167	127	1269	4	269	16789	3	18
378	2	3789	4	1	3579	579	79	6
1347	14579	6	359	59	8	124579	2479	145
147	14579	1479	569	2	5679	14579	8	3

```
B7Ca3 H9Ca5 G6Ra5 A4Ba5 E5Ba5 J2Ba5 H4Ba3
J6Ba7 H5Rb9 J4Cb6 B5Cb6 C7Ca5 J3Ba9 G8Ca7
G7Ra9 E8Ba9 C8Rb6 H2Ca1 H1Ra7 J7Ra1 B2Ba7
J1Ba4 F2Rb6 D2Cb4 A2Bb9 D9Bb1 A1Ca6 F4Ca1
F6Ca9 B9Ca4 B1Ra8 B4Ra9 E7Ra4 F3Ra2 C1Ba2
A7Ba8 D3Ba7 D7Ba6 G3Ba8 H8Ba4 A3Rb4 B8Rb2
C6Rb4 D4Rb2 F7Rb7 F9Rb8 G1Rb3 H7Rb2 E1Cb1
C3Cb1 A6Cb2 D6Cb3 E3Bb3 E6Bb6
```

239	1249	5	1248	24	18	6	123489	7
6	7	13	1248	9	5	2348	12348	12
8	1249	19	12467	2467	3	249	12459	129
379	69	4	23679	8	679	1	269	5
3579	1569	13679	1234679	23467	1679	249	2469	8
9	1689	2	1469	5	169	7	469	3
1	2569	679	356789	367	4	2389	236789	269
4	3	679	56789	1	2	89	6789	69
279	269	8	3679	367	679	5	123679	4

E1Ca5 F2Ca8 A6Ca8 C8Ca5 H4Ra5 J8Ra1 G2Ba5
G4Ba8 F1Rb9 D2Cb6 E2Bb1 F6Ca1 A4Ra1 J5Ca3
G5Rb7 J2Rb2 J1Cb7 C5Cb6 C4Bb7 D1Bb3 A1Ca2
B3Ca3 E3Ca7 E4Ca3 H8Ca7 A8Ra3 B9Ra1 D6Ra7
H7Ra8 C3Ba1 B4Ba2 B8Ba8 G7Ba3 A5Rb4 B7Rb4
D4Rb9 A2Cb9 J4Cb6 E5Cb2 E6Cb6 D8Cb2 C2Bb4
F4Bb4 E7Bb9 J6Bb9 G8Bb9 H3Ca9 C7Ca2 E8Ca4
F8Ca6 C9Ca9 G9Ra2 H9Ra6 G3Ba6

6	12359	259	1235	15	1258	7	4	128
8	1245	245	125	9	7	3	1256	126
1235	12357	25	4	156	12568	2568	12568	9
59	459	7	8	2	14569	456	13569	1346
259	6	3	159	145	1459	2458	12589	7
259	24589	1	7	3	4569	24568	25689	2468
1239	12389	289	6	147	1249	248	238	5
7	259	2569	259	8	3	1	26	246
4	12358	2568	125	15	125	9	7	2368

C2Ca7 B3Ca4 A4Ca3 C5Ca6 G5Ca7 C1Ra3 H9Ra4
F2Ba8 G6Ba4 G1Ca1 D2Ca4 E5Ca4 D9Ca3 F7Ra4
J2Ra3 H4Ba9 G8Ba3 D7Ca6 F6Ra6 F9Rb2 E1Ca2
E4Ca1 J5Ca1 C6Ca1 D8Ca1 A6Ba8 A5Rb5 A9Rb1
B4Cb2 B9Cb6 B8Bb5 J4Bb5 J9Bb8 B2Ca1 H2Ca5
G3Ca8 J6Ca2 E7Ca5 H8Ca6 C3Ra5 E8Ra8 F1Ra5
G2Ra9 H3Ra2 J3Ra6 A2Ba2 A3Ba9 C7Ba8 D1Ba9
D6Ba5 F8Ba9 G7Ba2 C8Rb2 E6Rb9

569	567	5679	35789	39	2	35689	1	4
459	12457	8	13579	6	179	2359	35	239
3	1256	2569	1589	4	189	7	568	2689
7	9	256	268	1	3	2568	4	268
4568	24568	2456	24689	29	489	23568	35678	1
1	3	246	2468	7	5	268	9	268
2	567	35679	1379	8	179	4	367	3679
4689	4678	1	23479	5	479	3689	3678	36789
489	478	3479	13479	39	6	1389	2	5

E5Ca2 J7Ca1 E8Ra7 H4Ra2 E7Ba3 B1Ra4 D7Ba5
C6Ca8 A7Ra8 G8Rb6 H7Cb9 C8Cb5 B7Bb2 B8Bb3
H1Bb6 G9Bb7 C2Ca2 F7Ca6 H8Ca8 H9Ca3 B4Ra5
C4Ra1 B2Ba1 B6Ba7 C9Ba6 G6Ba1 B9Rb9 C3Rb9
G2Rb5 H6Rb4 A1Cb5 H2Cb7 G3Cb3 E6Cb9 A2Bb6
E1Bb8 J3Bb4 G4Bb9 J1Ca9 E2Ca4 J2Ca8 E3Ca5
A3Ca7 J4Ca7 A5Ca9 A4Ra3 E4Ra6 F4Ra4 J5Ra3
D3Ba6 D4Ba8 D9Rb2 F3Rb2 F9Cb8

4	5	9	138	123	1238	127	6	17
7	6	1	89	245	24589	24579	24789	3
8	23	23	1369	7	1234569	12459	1249	1459
157	78	467	2	9	18	3	147	14567
1359	389	36	4	13	7	1569	19	2
1379	2379	2347	5	6	13	8	1479	1479
6	379	37	1379	8	123459	12479	123479	1479
379	4	5	13679	123	12369	12679	12379	8
2	1	8	3679	34	3469	4679	5	4679

B5Ca5 B8Ca8 E2Ra8 G6Ra5 B1Ba7 D6Ba8 B4Rb9
D2Rb7 G3Ca7 A4Ca8 J5Ca4 J4Ca3 G8Ca2 G2Ra3
C3Ba3 H1Ba9 H4Ba7 H8Ba3 C2Rb2 E3Rb6 G4Rb1
F2Cb9 D3Cb4 C4Cb6 H5Cb2 E7Cb5 F3Bb2 D8Bb1
D9Bb6 H6Bb6 D1Ca5 J6Ca9 J7Ca6 F8Ca7 C9Ca5
E8Ra9 F9Ra4 H7Ra1 J9Ra7 A9Ba1 A7Ba7 C7Ba9
G7Ba4 A5Rb3 B7Rb2 C8Rb4 G9Rb9 E5Cb1 A6Cb2
B6Cb4 C6Cb1 E1Bb3 F6Bb3 F1Ca1

1	2	3689	4789	5	689	3469	469	369
349	4689	5	2489	489	2689	23469	1	7
7	469	69	1	49	3	24569	8	2569
2359	1589	12389	289	6	4	1235789	259	12359
259	7	12689	3	189	1289	125689	2569	4
2349	14689	123689	289	7	5	123689	269	12369
8	159	129	6	149	7	12459	3	1259
259	159	4	59	139	19	12569	7	8
6	3	179	4589	2	189	1459	459	159

J3Ca7 A4Ca7 H5Ca3 D7Ca7 H7Ra6 H1Ra2 B6Ca6
B4Ra2 E6Ba2 G2Ca5 J4Ca4 E5Ra1 G7Ra4 H4Ra5
J6Ra8 B5Ba8 A8Ba4 H6Ba1 G9Ba2 A6Rb9 C9Rb5
G5Rb9 H2Rb9 B2Cb4 G3Cb1 C5Cb4 A7Cb3 C7Cb2
A3Bb8 C2Bb6 A9Bb6 B7Bb9 F1Ca4 B1Ra3 C3Ra9
E7Ra8 E3Rb6 F7Rb1 F2Cb8 J7Cb5 D2Bb1 F4Bb9
J8Bb9 D4Ca8 F8Ca6 J9Ca1 D9Ca9 D3Ra3 E1Ra9
F3Ra2 D1Ba5 D8Ba2 F9Ba3 E8Rb5

9	137	357	4	6	127	12378	237	1278
8	137	2	5	7	9	13467	3467	147
17	6	47	18	278	3	124789	5	12478
2357	23789	35789	389	2345789	257	2457	1	6
12357	4	6	138	23578	1257	257	27	9
1257	1279	579	169	24579	12567	2457	8	3
237	5	378	36	3	4	123678	9	1278
6	239	1	7	359	8	2345	234	245
4	3789	3789	2	1	56	35678	367	578

C3Ca4 C7Ca9 A3Ra5 H5Ba9 B5Rb7 G5Rb3 G4Cb6
J6Bb5 F6Ca6 H9Ca5 B9Ca4 H8Ca4 J3Ca3 H7Ra3
J2Ra9 G3Ba8 H2Rb2 G1Cb7 C1Bb1 F2Ca1 D2Ca8
B7Ra1 C9Ra7 A2Ba7 A6Ba1 B8Ba6 G9Ba1 B2Rb3
C4Rb8 F4Rb9 G7Rb2 J8Rb7 J9Rb8 F3Cb7 D4Cb3
C5Cb2 A7Cb8 J7Cb6 E8Cb2 A9Cb2 A8Bb3 D3Bb9
E4Bb1 E6Bb7 E1Ca3 E5Ca8 D6Ca2 D7Ca7 D5Ra4
E7Ra5 F1Ra2 D1Ba5 F5Ba5 F7Ba4

126789	12689	1267	679	4	2679	16	3	5
123569	1269	4	3569	2359	23569	8	7	69
235679	269	2367	1	8	235679	46	246	469
16	7	8	34569	1359	134569	456	456	2
4	5	126	8	12	1267	9	6	3
26	3	9	4567	25	24567	4567	4568	1
13689	14689	136	2	7	134589	3456	456	46
13678	1468	5	34	13	1348	2	9	467
2379	249	237	3459	6	3459	3457	1	8

A7Ca1 C8Ca2 F8Ca8 H9Ca7 E6Ra7 A4Ba7 F7Ba7
E8Rb6 H2Ra6 C2Rb9 B9Ca9 A6Ra9 J4Ba9 A3Rb6
B2Rb1 G1Ca9 D5Ca9 C1Ca5 C3Ra7 B1Ba3 J1Ba7
C6Rb3 J6Cb5 H5Ca3 D4Ra3 H4Rb4 E5Ca1 F6Ca4
D1Ra1 E3Ra2 F1Ba6 F5Ba2 G3Ba1 J2Ba2 A2Rb8
B5Rb5 D6Rb6 F4Rb5 G6Rb8 H1Rb8 J3Rb3 A1Cb2
G2Cb4 B4Cb6 B6Cb2 H6Cb1 J7Cb4 C7Bb6 D7Bb5
G8Bb5 G9Bb6 G7Ca3 D8Ca4 C9Ca4

345	8	135	2569	569	29	1456	13569	7
57	15	2	4	3	8	156	1569	169
9	345	6	1	57	7	2	358	38
45678	14569	1578	689	2	3	1678	1678	168
23678	1236	1378	68	678	17	9	4	5
23678	12369	1378	689	4	5	1678	123678	12368
1	256	9	7	58	24	3	2568	268
258	25	4	3	1	6	578	25789	289
23568	7	358	2589	589	29	1568	125689	4

E6Ca1 G6Ca4 A7Ca4 B1Ra7 C2Ra4 D1Ba4 E5Ba7
C5Rb5 C6Rb7 G5Cb8 J5Bb9 J4Ca5 A5Ca6 A6Ca9
A4Ra2 J6Ba2 E2Ca3 E1Ra2 E3Rb8 F1Cb6 J3Cb3
E4Cb6 J1Bb8 A1Ca3 G2Ca6 G8Ra5 B7Ba5 H2Ba2
A8Rb1 B2Rb1 G9Rb2 H1Rb5 F2Cb9 A3Cb5 J8Cb6
F9Cb3 B8Bb9 C9Bb8 D2Bb5 F4Bb8 F8Bb2 J7Bb1
D4Ca9 D7Ca6 C8Ca3 D9Ca1 H9Ca9 B9Ra6 D8Ra8
F3Ra1 D3Ba7 F7Ba7 H7Ba8 H8Rb7

8	236	1236	5	2679	23679	237	1267	4
3467	2356	23456	23468	2467	1	237	267	9
13467	236	9	2346	2467	2367	8	5	123
39	4	358	29	1	2579	6	278	238
2	1	68	46	3	67	47	9	5
369	7	356	2469	8	2569	1	24	23
146	268	7	1268	256	2568	9	3	128
1369	23689	12368	123689	2569	4	25	128	7
5	2389	12348	7	29	2389	24	1248	6

B2Ca5 H7Ca5 B4Ra8 E3Ra8 G1Ra4 B3Ba4 C5Ca4
G5Ca5 C1Ca7 C9Ra1 A3Ba1 H1Ca1 G4Ra1 J8Ra1
J7Ba4 E7Rb7 E6Cb6 E4Bb4 D6Ca7 F8Ca4 D3Ra5
G2Ra6 B1Ba6 F6Ba5 F3Ca6 H4Ca3 A7Ca2 A8Ca6
A5Ra7 A6Ra9 B5Ra2 B7Ra3 C4Ra6 H5Ra6 J3Ra3
C2Ba2 C6Ba3 B8Ba7 H3Ba2 J5Ba9 A2Rb3 H8Rb8
J2Rb8 H2Cb9 J6Cb2 D8Cb2 G9Cb2 D4Bb9 F9Bb3
G6Bb8 D1Ca3 F1Ca9 F4Ca2 D9Ca8

1	9	4	256	2356	8	256	5	257
3568	2368	2356	12569	7	4	25689	589	258
568	7	256	2569	2569	59	1	4	3
3589	1238	12359	4	1589	7	2358	6	1258
345678	12368	123567	1568	1568	15	23458	1358	9
45689	168	1569	3	15689	2	458	7	1458
39	4	139	1589	1589	159	7	2	6
679	16	1679	125789	4	3	589	1589	158
2	5	8	179	19	6	349	139	14

A5Ca3 A9Ca7 B4Ra1 C1Ra8 H4Ra2 J4Ra7 C5Ba2
A8Rb5 A4Cb6 A7Bb2 B7Ca6 D9Ca2 B8Ra9 C3Ra6
B9Ba8 J7Ca9 J8Ra3 J9Ra4 G1Rb3 J5Rb1 B1Cb5
G3Cb1 D1Bb9 H2Bb6 H3Ca9 F5Ca9 E6Ca1 D2Ra1
F1Ra6 H1Ra7 E1Ba4 E3Ba7 E5Ba6 F9Ba1 E8Rb8
F2Rb8 F3Rb5 H9Rb5 D3Cb3 E4Cb5 F7Cb4 H7Cb8
H8Cb1 B3Bb2 C4Bb9 E2Bb2 D5Bb8 D7Bb5 E7Bb3
B2Ca3 G4Ca8 G5Ca5 G6Ca9 C6Ra5

1	356	56	9	8	2	7	369	4
27	24678	2468	149	469	3	1269	5	1269
9	23456	2456	7	456	15	126	8	1236
25	12569	3	129	2579	4	125689	269	12569
8	12459	12459	6	2359	159	12459	2349	7
25	124569	7	1239	2359	8	124569	23469	123569
4	12389	1289	5	239	9	269	7	269
2357	235789	2589	23489	2349	6	2459	1	259
6	259	259	249	1	7	3	249	8

H1Ca3 H4Ca8 D5Ca7 D7Ca8 G5Ra3 H2Ra7 B1Ba7
F4Ba3 A4Rb9 G6Rb9 C9Ca3 A2Ra3 E8Ra3 A8Rb6
A3Cb5 J2Ca5 J4Ca2 E5Ca2 H3Ra2 J8Ra4 F5Ba9
J3Ba9 H5Ba4 B5Rb6 D4Rb1 F8Rb2 F1Cb5 B4Cb4
C5Cb5 E6Cb5 D8Cb9 B3Bb8 C6Bb1 D1Bb2 D2Bb6
G2Ca8 E2Ca9 C3Ca6 H7Ca5 C2Ra4 D9Ra5 G3Ra1
H9Ra9 B2Ba2 B7Ba9 F2Ba1 E3Ba4 B9Rb1 C7Rb2
E7Rb1 F9Rb6 F7Cb4 G7Cb6 G9Cb2

2568	245689	4569	357	235789	1	234578	478	234578
258	24589	3	6	25789	589	124578	478	124578
7	258	1	4	2358	358	9	6	2358
9	3567	56	8	3456	3456	247	1	2467
1	368	2	3	346	7	48	5	9
4	5678	56	2	1569	569	78	3	678
3	459	7	1	458	458	6	2	458
256	12456	8	9	34567	3456	13457	47	13457
56	14569	4569	357	345678	2	134578	4789	134578

F5Ca1 J8Ca9 F6Ra9 G2Ra9 A3Ba9 E4Rb3 D2Ca3
J3Ca4 B5Ca9 E5Ra6 F3Ra5 D3Ba6 F2Ba7 H6Ba6
E2Rb8 F7Rb8 F9Rb6 E7Cb4 C6Ca3 G6Ca8 C5Ra8
J9Ra8 A5Ba2 B6Rb5 A4Cb7 D6Cb4 D5Bb5 J4Bb5
G9Ra5 A7Ba5 C9Rb2 G5Rb4 J1Rb6 A1Cb8 C2Cb5
J2Cb1 D9Cb7 B1Bb2 A8Bb4 D7Bb2 H2Bb2 H1Ca5
B2Ca4 A2Ca6 B8Ca8 H9Ca4 A9Ra3 B7Ra7 H7Ra1
B9Ba1 J7Ba3 H8Ba7 H5Rb3 J5Rb7

1345	13456	1356	4689	1456	2	7	35689	569
9	14567	1567	3	14567	145678	268	2568	256
357	8	2	679	567	5679	36	4	1
6	1345	135	2	8	45	9	13	7
13457	123457	13579	467	34567	4567	1236	1236	8
8	237	37	1	9	67	5	236	4
15	9	4	68	126	168	1268	7	3
2	1367	13678	5	1467	146789	168	1689	69
157	1567	15678	6789	1267	3	4	125689	2569

E3Ca9 E5Ca3 G1Ra5 C7Ca3 C1Rb7 J1Cb1 E1Bb4
A1Ca3 A4Ca4 A8Ra8 B2Ra4 D6Ra4 B6Ba8 A9Ba9
E6Ba5 H5Ba4 H9Rb6 B5Ra7 C5Ra5 A5Ba1 B3Ra1
G5Ca6 G7Ra2 J5Ba2 H7Ba8 B7Rb6 G4Rb8 G6Rb1
J9Rb5 E7Cb1 J8Cb9 B9Cb2 B8Bb5 D8Bb3 J4Bb7
H8Bb1 D2Ca1 J3Ca8 C4Ca9 F6Ca7 C6Ra6 D3Ra5
E2Ra7 F8Ra6 H6Ra9 J2Ra6 A2Ba5 A3Ba6 F2Ba2
E4Ba6 E8Ba2 H3Ba7 F3Rb3 H2Rb3

4	579	179	2	8	1379	37	1357	6
16789	789	3	16	17	5	4	1278	1278
1678	2	1678	16	4	1367	9	13578	1578
2378	6	478	9	1257	1278	237	234578	24578
2378	378	5	468	27	2678	1	234678	9
2789	1	4789	3	257	2678	267	245678	24578
13789	4	1789	18	6	1238	5	1279	127
13679	379	2	15	135	4	8	1679	17
5	8	168	7	9	128	26	1246	3

A2Ca5 E4Ca4 H4Ca5 H5Ca3 A6Ca9 G1Ra3 J8Ra4
C6Ba3 E2Ba3 J2Rb8 G4Ca8 D5Ca1 B5Ba7 F5Ba5
B2Rb9 E5Rb2 H2Cb7 H9Bb1 A8Ca1 A7Ra3 D8Ba3
A3Rb7 C8Ca5 C9Ra7 D9Ra5 F9Ba4 G8Ba7 G9Rb2
G6Cb1 J7Cb6 B9Cb8 B8Bb2 G3Bb9 J3Bb1 J6Bb2
H8Bb9 F1Ca9 D3Ca4 C3Ca6 B4Ra6 C1Ra8 F7Ra2
H1Ra6 B1Ba1 C4Ba1 D1Ba2 F3Ba8 D7Ba7 D6Rb8
E1Rb7 F8Rb6 E6Cb6 F6Cb7 E8Cb8

1349	5	134	239	239	7	8	1249	6
136789	16789	13678	2389	4	1289	12579	12579	2
14789	1789	2	5	89	6	1479	1479	3
26789	4	678	23789	1	289	26	268	5
12578	178	1578	2478	6	248	124	3	9
12689	3	168	2489	5	2489	1246	12468	7
5678	678	9	1	28	3	2567	25678	4
134568	168	134568	24689	7	2489	2569	25689	28
4678	2	4678	4689	89	5	3	6789	1

A5Ca3 B6Ca1 H9Ca8 D4Ra3 E4Ba7 B9Rb2 G5Ca2
A4Ra2 H7Ca9 A8Ra9 H8Ra2 H6Rb4 H4Cb6 H2Bb1
F4Ca4 E7Ra4 C8Ba4 E2Rb8 E6Cb2 B3Ca8 F8Ca1
B1Ra3 C5Ra8 F6Ra8 G1Ra8 B2Ba6 B4Ba9 C7Ba1
D6Ba9 D8Ba8 H3Ba3 J4Ba8 C1Rb7 F3Rb6 G2Rb7
H1Rb5 J5Rb9 D1Cb2 E1Cb1 C2Cb9 D3Cb7 J3Cb4
F7Cb2 A1Bb4 A3Bb1 E3Bb5 F1Bb9 D7Bb6 J1Bb6
B7Ca7 G8Ca6 B8Ra5 G7Ra5 J8Ra7

28	689	3	4568	1	4569	2468	2458	7
5	4	1678	3678	2	367	368	9	68
28	6789	2678	345678	35689	345679	23468	1	2468
7	3	124	146	6	8	5	24	2469
6	18	1248	9	5	1457	2478	2478	3
9	5	48	3467	36	2	1	478	468
148	1678	145678	12568	5689	1569	24789	3	12489
3	2	1578	158	4	159	789	6	189
148	168	9	12368	7	136	248	248	5

A8Ca5 B3Ra1 D9Ra9 E2Ba1 F9Ba6 B9Rb8 D5Rb6
E5Rb5 F5Rb3 H9Cb1 D4Ra1 G2Ca8 C5Ca8 A1Ra8
H4Ra8 C1Ba2 C9Rb4 G5Rb9 J2Rb6 A2Cb9 H6Cb5
G7Cb7 G9Cb2 C2Bb7 G3Bb5 H3Bb7 G4Bb6 H7Bb9
C3Ca6 J4Ca2 C4Ca5 C6Ca9 A7Ra2 C7Ra3 G1Ra4
J6Ra3 B4Ba3 B7Ba6 J1Ba1 G6Ba1 A4Rb4 B6Rb7
F4Cb7 A6Cb6 E6Cb4 E7Bb8 F3Ca8 J7Ca4 E8Ca7
J8Ca8 E3Ra2 F8Ra4 D3Ba4 D8Ba2

4	58	25	3	678	9	1	2678	268
1359	3589	7	156	2	1458	4	3468	3468
123	38	6	17	1478	148	9	5	2348
23569	1	4	269	689	7	25	2389	2389
8	369	23	1269	5	123	24	2349	7
23579	3579	235	4	89	238	6	1	2389
1567	2	8	1579	1479	145	3	4679	1469
1567	4567	15	12579	3	1245	8	24679	12469
137	347	9	8	147	6	247	247	5

H3Ca1 D7Ca5 J7Ca7 J5Ra1 J8Ra2 A8Ba7 G9Ba1
B7Rb4 J1Rb3 J2Cb4 E7Cb2 E3Bb3 F6Ca3 H9Ca4
E8Ra4 D4Ba2 E6Rb1 H6Ca2 B1Ca9 B4Ra1 E2Ra9
C1Ba1 B6Ba5 A5Ba6 D1Ba6 C4Rb7 E4Rb6 G6Rb4
C5Cb4 G5Cb7 C6Cb8 C2Bb3 G1Bb5 F1Ca2 H2Ca6
H4Ca5 B9Ca6 B8Ra3 C9Ra2 F2Ra7 G8Ra6 H1Ra7
H8Ra9 A3Ba2 A9Ba8 F3Ba5 D9Ba3 G4Ba9 A2Rb5
B2Rb8 D8Rb8 F9Rb9 D5Cb9 F5Cb8

5	4678	469	2	789	4689	67	1	3
4	2467	146	14567	3	1456	567	8	9
389	3678	1369	15678	15789	15689	4	567	2
34	3456	7	9	15	1345	2356	23456	8
3489	3458	2	34578	6	3458	1	3457	47
1	34568	3456	34578	578	2	9	34567	467
7	345	8	1356	1259	13569	236	23469	146
2	1	35	3568	4	35689	3678	3679	67
6	9	34	138	128	7	238	234	5

B2Ca2 G9Ca1 E1Ra9 B1Rb4 D1Cb3 C1Bb8 A6Ra4
A5Ba8 A3Ra9 F5Rb7 D2Ca4 J3Ca4 B7Ca5 B4Ra7
G8Ra4 H8Ba9 J8Rb2 J5Cb1 D8Cb6 C8Bb7 D5Bb5
D7Bb2 F9Bb4 A2Ca7 C4Ca1 E4Ca4 G5Ca2 H7Ca7
H9Ca6 A7Ra6 B3Ra1 C6Ra5 D6Ra1 E9Ra7 G6Ra9
B6Ba6 C5Ba9 G4Ba6 J7Ba8 G7Rb3 J4Rb3 G2Cb5
F4Cb8 H6Cb8 E2Bb8 F2Bb6 E6Bb3 H3Bb3 H4Bb5
C2Ca3 F3Ca5 C3Ca6 F8Ca3 E8Ra5

6	189	18	3	2458	248	125	7	458
2	138	138	7	9	468	1356	134568	34568
5	3789	4	1	268	268	236	3689	368
13	2	9	456	1456	46	8	13456	7
178	1678	1678	245689	3	246789	156	1456	456
4	13678	5	68	168	678	9	2	36
378	35678	23678	268	268	1	4	3568	9
189	15689	168	4689	7	3	56	568	2
3789	4	23678	2689	268	5	367	368	1

E6Ca9 J7Ca7 C8Ca9 A2Ra9 C2Ra7 E4Ra2 H4Ra4
A5Ba5 F6Ba7 J4Ba9 H1Ca9 D4Ca5 D5Ca4 F5Ba1
D6Rb6 F4Cb8 G4Bb6 C5Ca6 D1Ca3 C7Ca3 F9Ca3
C6Ra2 D8Ra1 F2Ra6 A7Ba2 E1Ba1 C9Rb8 E2Rb8
J1Rb8 G1Cb7 E3Cb7 J5Cb2 A9Cb4 A6Bb8 G5Bb8
G3Ca2 B3Ca8 B6Ca4 B7Ca1 E8Ca4 H8Ca8 A3Ra1
B2Ra3 H2Ba1 J3Ba3 G2Rb5 H3Rb6 J8Rb6 H7Cb5
B8Cb5 G8Cb3 B9Bb6 E7Bb6 E9Ca5

24567	567	2467	3457	257	1	248	9	234
8	1	1249	349	29	6	124	7	5
12457	3	12479	4579	8	2479	6	24	124
146	2	3	489	19	5	489	468	7
14567	15678	14678	4789	3	24789	24589	24568	2469
9	578	478	6	27	2478	3	1	24
1267	1678	5	789	4	789	1279	3	1269
3	9	167	2	567	7	1457	456	8
267	4	2678	1	5679	3789	2579	256	269

D5Ca1 J6Ca3 A9Ca3 A7Ra8 B4Ra3 F2Ra5 J3Ra8
E2Ba8 B2Rb1 H6Rb7 B5Ca9 D8Ca8 C9Ra1 C3Ra9
D1Ra6 F6Ra8 G4Ba8 G6Rb9 D4Ca4 C6Ca4 C8Ra2
D7Ra9 A5Ba2 B7Ba4 E4Ba9 J9Ba9 B3Rb2 E6Rb2
F5Rb7 F3Cb4 E7Cb5 E8Bb6 F9Bb2 H7Bb1 A1Ca4
E3Ca1 H8Ca4 E9Ca4 G9Ca6 A4Ra5 E1Ra7 G1Ra1
H5Ra5 J5Ra6 C1Ba5 C4Ba7 J1Ba2 H3Ba6 G2Ba7
J8Ba5 A2Rb6 A3Rb7 G7Rb2 J7Rb7

6	135	9	4	128	128	1358	123	7
25	157	4	3	12789	12789	1589	6	1259
235	1357	123578	12589	12789	6	13589	1239	4
7	4	135	129	1239	129	19	8	6
39	1369	136	12689	5	124789	149	12479	129
8	2	16	169	14679	1479	149	5	3
1	3569	2356	7	24689	2489	34569	349	59
259	8	256	1269	12469	3	7	149	159
4	3679	367	169	169	5	2	139	8

C3Ca8 C4Ca5 D5Ca3 G7Ca6 E8Ca7 D3Ra5 E9Ba2
J3Ca7 E4Ca8 C7Rb3 F3Rb1 C1Cb2 B1Bb5 E1Ca3
G2Ca5 A7Ca5 A8Ca2 A2Ra3 E2Ra9 H9Ra5 B7Ba8
E3Ba6 G3Ba3 H1Ba9 G9Rb9 H3Rb2 J2Rb6 G8Cb4
B9Cb1 B2Bb7 C8Bb9 H8Bb1 C2Ca1 D4Ca2 F6Ca7
J8Ca3 C5Ra7 H5Ra4 E6Ba4 H4Ba6 E7Rb1 F4Rb9
J4Cb1 F5Cb6 D6Cb1 D7Cb9 F7Cb4 A6Bb8 J5Bb9
A5Ca1 G5Ca8 B6Ca9 B5Ra2 G6Ra2

4	1	589	7	59	2368	256	2568	28
58	589	6	24589	459	248	3	24578	1
358	7	2	34568	1	3468	9	4568	48
3578	34589	45789	1	6	478	245	234578	234789
2	4589	45789	489	3	478	145	4578	6
13678	34689	4789	489	2	5	14	3478	34789
56	2456	3	2456	8	1246	7	9	24
9	2456	1	23456	457	23467	8	2346	234
678	2468	478	2346	47	9	246	1	5

F1Ca1 G6Ca1 A6Ra3 B8Ra7 E7Ra1 F2Ra6 J4Ra3
C1Ba3 F7Rb4 D2Ca3 H9Ca3 F8Ra3 H5Ca7 J5Rb4
D7Ca5 A9Ca8 C8Ra5 D8Ra2 A7Ba2 C9Ba4 E8Ba8
A8Rb6 G9Rb2 J7Rb6 H8Cb4 G1Ca6 G2Ca4 B2Ca8
B5Ra9 G4Ra5 J2Ra2 A3Ba9 A5Ba5 H2Ba5 B1Rb5
E2Rb9 E4Cb4 B4Bb2 E6Bb7 D3Ca4 E3Ca5 F4Ca9
H6Ca2 B6Ca4 D9Ra9 F3Ra8 H4Ra6 C6Ba6 D1Ba7
D6Ba8 F9Ba7 J1Ba8 C4Rb8 J3Rb7

4569	8	4569	1346	3467	1347	14567	2	1457
1	3	456	246	4678	247	4567	46	9
246	6	7	9	468	5	146	3	148
34589	59	34589	345	1	6	2459	7	2345
3456	156	2	345	9	347	8	146	1345
34569	7	134569	8	2	34	14569	1469	1345
569	2	1569	7	456	8	3	149	14
7	19	1389	1234	34	12349	1249	5	6
3569	4	13569	12356	356	1239	1279	8	127

C1Ca2 D1Ca8 C9Ca8 B5Ra8 C7Ra1 E6Ra7 H3Ra8
A5Ba7 C2Rb6 C5Cb4 B6Bb2 H5Bb3 J9Ca7 B7Ra7
B4Rb6 B8Cb4 B3Bb5 A9Bb5 D9Ca2 A7Ra6 G9Ra4
G8Ba1 E8Rb6 F8Cb9 D2Ca9 F7Ca5 D4Ra5 E2Ba5
D7Ba4 D3Rb3 H2Rb1 E1Cb4 J3Cb6 A1Bb9 F1Bb6
F3Bb1 E4Bb3 G3Bb9 J5Bb5 J1Ca3 G1Ca5 A3Ca4
H4Ca4 G5Ca6 A6Ca3 E9Ca1 F9Ca3 A4Ra1 F6Ra4
H7Ra2 J6Ba1 J4Ba2 J7Ba9 H6Rb9

1248	6	12458	12345	23459	1235	7	139	1389
9	3	128	7	26	12	5	4	168
124	1245	7	12345	234569	8	2369	139	1369
1347	147	14	8	357	357	349	6	2
23478	247	248	6	1	9	348	357	3458
5	9	1268	23	237	4	38	137	138
2467	2457	2456	9	234578	2357	1	35	3456
14	8	9	1345	345	6	34	2	7
12467	12457	3	1245	2457	1257	469	8	4569

G5Ca8 C7Ca2 D7Ra9 F3Ra6 J9Ba9 J7Ca6 G1Ra6
A3Ca5 F7Ca8 J2Ra5 D3Ca1 D6Ca5 D2Ra4 C1Ba4
H1Ba1 C2Rb1 G3Ca4 H7Ba4 E7Rb3 G9Rb5 G8Cb3
E9Cb4 F9Cb1 C8Bb9 F8Bb7 D1Ca3 A5Ca9 A6Ca3
A8Ca1 E8Ca5 A4Ra4 B6Ra1 C9Ra3 D5Ra7 B5Ba2
B9Ba6 J4Ba1 J5Ba4 A9Rb8 B3Rb8 C4Rb5 F5Rb3
A1Cb2 E3Cb2 F4Cb2 H4Cb3 C5Cb6 H5Cb5 E2Bb7
J1Bb7 E1Ca8 G2Ca2 G6Ca7 J6Ra2

9	1257	2367	8	13456	1357	1246	1236	246
4	1278	23678	367	136	137	5	9	26
1356	15	36	3469	13456	2	7	136	8
12	3	5	4	7	6	289	28	29
7	489	689	34	2	358	689	568	1
26	28	268	1	9	58	3	4	267
8	279	4	5	136	1379	1269	1267	2679
23	6	1	2379	38	3789	2489	278	5
25	2579	279	2679	168	4	12689	12678	3

E2Ca4 E8Ca5 A9Ca4 C4Ra9 D1Ra1 D4Ra4 F6Ra5
F9Ra7 H7Ra4 C5Ba4 E3Ba9 E6Ba8 E7Ba6 H1Ba3
E4Rb3 H5Rb8 A5Ca5 H6Ra9 G9Ca6 B9Rb2 A7Cb1
D9Cb9 C2Ra1 C1Ba5 J1Rb2 F1Cb6 J3Cb7 G2Bb9
J4Bb6 J2Ca5 H4Ca2 B5Ca6 J7Ca9 B6Ra1 H8Ra7
J8Ra8 A6Ba3 D7Ba8 G6Ba7 G8Ba1 A8Rb6 B4Rb7
D8Rb2 G5Rb3 G7Rb2 J5Rb1 B2Cb8 A3Cb2 C8Cb3
A2Bb7 B3Bb3 C3Bb6 F2Bb2 F3Bb8

468	1	346	9	2478	2468	2567	2378	2678
689	5	7	1	28	268	4	2389	2689
2	689	469	5	3	468	1679	789	16789
1	4	269	237	2579	25	8	279	2679
3	2789	29	2478	6	1248	279	2479	5
6789	26789	5	2478	24789	248	2679	1	3
5679	2679	269	268	1	3	279	2789	4
469	269	8	246	24	7	3	5	129
457	237	1234	248	2458	9	127	6	1278

J2Ca3 J3Ca1 D4Ca3 E6Ca1 D6Ca5 A7Ca5 E8Ca4
B8Ra3 G1Ra5 H9Ra1 A3Ba3 A5Ba7 C7Ba1 J5Ba5
C3Ca4 F7Ca6 A6Ra4 D3Ra6 E3Ca9 E2Ra8 F5Ra9
F2Ba2 F4Ba4 F6Ba8 C6Rb6 D5Rb2 E7Rb2 F1Rb7
G3Rb2 J1Cb4 C2Cb9 E4Cb7 B5Cb8 H5Cb4 B6Cb2
J7Cb7 B1Bb6 H2Bb6 G7Bb9 A1Ca8 H1Ca9 G2Ca7
G4Ca6 A8Ca2 D8Ca9 A9Ca6 B9Ra9 D9Ra7 G8Ra8
H4Ra2 C8Ba7 C9Ba8 J4Ba8 J9Ba2

36	239	23569	8	13567	1359	4579	679	569
7	4	569	569	56	2	589	1	3
1	39	8	35679	4	359	579	679	2
368	1238	1236	1369	1368	7	12389	5	4
3468	1378	13467	13569	2	13589	13789	36789	169
9	5	12367	4	1368	138	12378	23678	16
2	137	1347	1357	9	1345	6	3	8
5	6	139	2	138	138	139	4	7
348	13789	13479	1357	13578	6	12359	239	159

G6Ca4 A7Ca4 B7Ra8 G4Ra5 E6Ba5 G8Rb3 C7Ra5
J9Ba5 J2Ca9 C6Ca9 B3Ra9 C2Ra3 H7Ra9 J1Ra8
A3Ba5 J3Ba4 J7Ba1 A1Rb6 A2Rb2 B4Rb6 H3Rb3
J8Rb2 D1Cb3 C4Cb7 B5Cb5 A9Cb9 A8Bb7 C8Bb6
E1Bb4 D7Bb2 J4Bb3 F3Ca2 J5Ca7 E8Ca9 D4Ra9
E7Ra3 E2Ra8 F7Ra7 E3Ba7 F8Ba8 D2Rb1 E4Rb1
G3Rb1 G2Cb7 D3Cb6 F6Cb3 E9Cb6 A6Bb1 D5Bb8
F5Bb6 F9Bb1 H5Ca1 A5Ca3 H6Ca8

6	347	23578	2457	247	1	23459	23459	25
15	14	125	8	3	2459	12459	7	6
9	1347	12357	24567	247	2456	12345	8	25
2	79	789	457	1	458	6	45	3
78	5	678	2347	9	2348	2478	1	278
3	17	4	257	6	258	2578	25	9
157	8	135679	1236	2	236	23579	23569	4
4	2	1369	136	5	7	389	369	8
57	367	3567	9	248	23468	23578	2356	1

E1Ca8 J2Ca6 D2Ca9 J5Ca8 B6Ca9 E9Ca7 A3Ra8
D6Ra8 E3Ra6 F2Ra1 J6Ra4 D3Ba7 F7Ba8 B2Rb4
G5Rb2 H9Rb8 F4Ra7 B3Ca2 B1Ra5 C3Ba1 B7Rb1
J1Rb7 G1Cb1 H4Ca1 G7Ca7 G3Ra5 H8Ra6 H3Ba9
J7Ba5 H7Rb3 J3Rb3 C7Cb4 G8Cb9 J8Cb2 C5Bb7
A7Bb9 A8Bb3 E7Bb2 F8Bb5 C2Ca3 A2Ca7 A5Ca4
C6Ca5 D8Ca4 A9Ra5 C4Ra6 D4Ra5 E4Ra4 F6Ra2
A4Ba2 C9Ba2 E6Ba3 G6Ba6 G4Rb3

1468	7	5	9	126	6	246	3	246
168	28	3	5	4	67	26	289	269
46	24	2469	3	26	8	2456	1	7
134567	9	1467	1246	12356	456	123457	247	8
134568	3458	1468	12468	7	4569	12345	249	123459
2	3458	1478	148	1359	459	13457	6	13459
9	6	248	7	5	1	234	24	234
3457	345	47	46	8	2	9	47	1346
47	1	247	46	69	3	8	5	246

C3Ca9 B6Ca7 B8Ca8 A1Ra8 B1Ra1 B9Ra9 C7Ra5
G5Ra5 G3Ra8 H9Ra1 J5Ra9 C1Ba6 A5Ba1 E8Ba9
J3Ba2 J9Ba6 H8Ba7 A6Rb6 B2Rb2 C5Rb2 F5Rb3
H3Rb4 J4Rb4 J1Cb7 C2Cb4 H4Cb6 D5Cb6 B7Cb6
E3Ca6 F6Ca9 G8Ca4 D8Rb2 D4Cb1 D3Bb7 F4Bb8
E2Ca8 F3Ca1 E4Ca2 F7Ca7 E7Ra1 F9Ra4 A7Ba4
E9Ba5 A9Rb2 D7Rb3 E6Rb4 F2Rb5 D1Cb4 E1Cb3
H2Cb3 D6Cb5 G7Cb2 G9Cb3 H1Bb5

139	13489	1389	5	7	1389	1346	346	2
2	6	1379	13	19	4	1357	357	8
5	1348	1378	1238	168	138	13467	9	167
13	7	1235	9	145	135	8	456	156
6	189	1589	1478	2	1578	14579	457	3
139	1389	4	1378	158	6	1579	2	157
137	5	12367	1478	148	178	2367	3678	9
8	239	2379	6	59	579	2357	1	4
4	19	1679	178	3	2	567	5678	567

G1Ca7 H2Ca2 C4Ca2 C5Ca6 D3Ra2 G7Ra2 E3Ba5
J8Ca8 H3Rb3 J4Rb7 G3Cb6 H7Cb7 G8Bb3 E6Ca7
F9Ra7 B8Ba7 C9Rb1 E8Rb4 A8Cb6 D8Bb5 C3Ca7
G4Ca4 H6Ca5 J7Ca6 J9Ca5 B7Ra5 C6Ra8 D5Ra4
D9Ra6 F5Ra5 H5Ra9 A3Ba8 A6Ba9 G5Ba8 B5Rb1
G6Rb1 B3Cb9 B4Cb3 D6Cb3 D1Bb1 J3Bb1 F1Ca9
A2Ca1 A7Ra4 E7Ra9 F2Ra3 J2Ra9 A1Ba3 C2Ba4
C7Ba3 E2Ba8 F7Ba1 E4Rb1 F4Rb8

238	1	23	6	5	23789	39	3479	3479
236	9	4	1237	7	1237	356	1357	8
5	368	7	13489	49	1389	2	1349	13469
1679	467	169	5	3	79	689	2	1679
23679	2367	8	279	1	279	4	3579	35679
12379	5	1239	2479	8	6	39	1379	1379
36789	3678	5	3789	679	3789	1	349	2
4	238	1239	1389	9	13589	7	6	359
13679	367	1369	1379	2	4	359	8	359

D2Ca4 C5Ca4 G5Ca6 H6Ca5 D7Ca8 F4Ra4 G8Ra4
A9Ba4 B5Rb7 H5Rb9 H9Cb3 B7Ca6 A8Ra7 B8Ra5
C2Ra6 G1Ra9 A1Ba8 E9Ba5 J9Ba9 C9Rb1 J7Rb5
F9Cb7 D9Bb6 J3Ca6 B6Ca1 F8Ca1 E1Ra6 H2Ca2
A7Ca3 E8Ca3 A6Ra9 H4Ra8 B1Ba3 B4Ba2 C6Ba8
C8Ba9 E4Ba9 F7Ba9 G2Ba8 J4Ba1 A3Rb2 C4Rb3
D6Rb7 E2Rb7 F1Rb2 H3Rb1 J1Rb7 D1Cb1 J2Cb3
D3Cb9 F3Cb3 G4Cb7 E6Cb2 G6Cb3

1258	3	1259	4	1289	289	58	6	7
158	569	1569	7	1389	3689	358	2	4
248	246	7	5	238	2368	1	9	38
1235	259	1259	12389	1235789	23789	4	1358	6
12345	2459	12459	12389	6	23789	35789	1358	123589
7	24569	8	1239	123459	239	359	135	12359
45	7	3	689	89	1	2	458	589
9	1	24	2368	2378	5	368	348	38
6	8	25	239	239	4	359	7	1359

B3Ca6 F5Ca4 H7Ca6 E7Ca7 C6Ra6 F2Ra6 G4Ra6
H5Ra7 J9Ra1 D5Ba5 D6Ba7 J3Ca5 H3Ba2 C9Rb3
G1Rb4 H9Cb8 H4Bb3 G8Bb5 E3Ca4 B5Ca3 H8Ca4
F9Ca5 B1Ra1 C2Ra4 G5Ra8 J7Ra3 A5Ba1 D3Ba1
E9Ba2 G9Ba9 A3Rb9 C5Rb2 F7Rb9 C1Cb8 B2Cb5
J5Cb9 A6Cb8 A1Bb2 B6Bb9 A7Bb5 B7Bb8 E2Bb9
J4Bb2 E1Ca5 D2Ca2 D4Ca9 F6Ca2 D8Ra8 F8Ra3
D1Ba3 E6Ba3 E4Ba8 E8Ba1 F4Rb1

1489	5	149	3689	1389	2	3468	7	389
3	7	6	89	4	19	258	9	2589
2489	2489	249	3689	3789	5	1	3469	2389
6	3489	3459	7	159	149	358	2	13589
45789	489	4579	2	6	3	578	19	15789
2579	1	23579	59	59	8	3567	369	4
12579	239	8	4	3579	679	237	13	1237
1457	34	13457	35	2	7	9	8	6
2479	6	23479	1	3789	79	2347	5	237

49	7	249	8	169	156	4569	29	3
39	359	39	3579	2	4	5679	1	8
6	1	23489	3579	379	357	4579	279	2457
134	2	5	1347	13467	13678	34678	378	9
1349	369	7	1349	5	1368	2	38	46
8	369	3469	23479	34679	2367	1	5	467
379	3689	3689	2357	37	2357	35789	4	1
5	4	139	6	8	1237	379	2379	27
2	38	138	13457	1347	9	3578	6	57

D6Ca4 G6Ca6 C8Ca4 B6Ra1 C4Ra6 C5Ra7 J5Ra8
A7Ba6 D5Ba1 J7Ba4 B8Rb9 H6Rb7 B4Cb8 J6Cb9
E8Cb1 G8Bb3 A5Ca3 F8Ca6 G9Ca1 C9Ra3 J3Ra3
A4Ba9 A9Ba8 D2Ba3 H4Ba3 F4Rb5 G5Rb5 H2Rb4
F5Cb9 F7Ca3 D7Ra8 F3Ca7 F1Ra2 G2Ba2 G7Rb7
J1Rb7 G1Cb9 E7Cb5 J9Cb2 C1Bb8 B7Bb2 B9Bb5
D9Bb9 H1Ca5 E2Ca8 C3Ca2 E9Ca7 C2Ra9 D3Ra5
E3Ra9 H3Ra1 A1Ba1 E1Ba4 A3Rb4

G1Ca7 B2Ca5 B7Ra6 C3Ra8 A3Ba2 A8Rb9 G5Rb3
A1Cb4 A7Bb5 F3Ca4 J9Ca5 B4Ra7 C5Rb9 G3Ca6
F5Rb7 F9Cb6 E9Bb4 E2Ca6 H6Ca7 C7Ca4 H3Ra1
J7Ra7 D8Ba7 G2Ba9 G7Ba8 C8Rb2 D7Rb3 F2Rb3
H9Rb2 J3Rb3 D1Cb1 J2Cb8 B3Cb9 F6Cb2 H7Cb9
E8Cb8 H8Cb3 C9Cb7 B1Bb3 E1Bb9 D4Bb4 F4Bb9
G6Bb5 G4Ca2 C4Ca5 J5Ca4 D6Ca8 C6Ra3 D5Ra6
J4Ra1 A6Ba6 E6Ba1 E4Ba3 A5Rb1

345679	345679	2	4789	145	145789	59	1567	156789
579	1	8	79	2	6	4	3	579
45679	45679	79	4789	145	3	59	12567	1256789
179	8	6	49	3	1459	2	145	145
1239	39	5	2469	7	1249	8	146	1346
123	3	4	26	8	125	7	9	1356
146789	4679	179	5	46	2478	39	247	23479
457	2	3	1	9	47	6	8	457
456789	45679	79	234678	46	2478	1	2457	234579

1256	3	1568	125679	26789	1256789	578	258	2458
7	25	568	2356	4	23568	1	2358	9
125	9	4	12357	2378	123578	578	6	2358
159	6	3	579	79	4	2	589	158
8	45	5	23569	1	23569	569	59	7
159	157	2	8	679	5679	3	4	15
12356	8	156	12369	2369	12369	4	7	235
4	127	9	1237	5	12378	8	238	6
2356	257	567	2346789	236789	236789	589	1	2358

G3Ca1 J4Ca3 G7Ca3 D1Ra7 F2Rb3 E2Cb9 A1Ca3
E9Ca3 H6Ba7 B1Ca5 J2Ca5 B4Ra9 H9Ra5 D6Ba9
D8Ba5 A6Rb4 B9Rb7 D4Rb4 H1Rb4 E6Cb1 D9Cb1
E1Bb2 F6Bb5 F9Bb6 F1Ca1 C2Ca4 F4Ca2 E4Ca6
A7Ra9 E8Ra4 C7Ba5 A9Rb8 C5Rb1 A4Cb7 A5Cb5
C9Cb2 A2Bb6 C4Bb8 C8Bb6 G2Ca7 A8Ca1 C3Ra7
J8Ra7 C1Ba9 G8Ba2 G6Rb8 J3Rb9 G1Cb6 J6Cb2
J9Cb4 J1Bb8 G5Bb4 J5Bb6 G9Bb9

E2Ca4 J3Ca7 J4Ca4 E7Ca6 A9Ca4 F2Ba7 J7Ba9
E3Rb5 H7Rb8 E8Cb9 H2Ca1 G3Rb6 B3Cb8 A3Bb1
A1Ca6 B4Ca6 F6Ca5 D8Ca5 B2Ra5 D9Ra8 F5Ra6
C1Ba2 A8Ba8 F9Ba1 J6Ba6 C9Rb3 F1Rb9 J2Rb2
J5Rb8 D1Cb1 C5Cb7 B8Cb2 J9Cb5 B6Bb3 C7Bb5
D5Bb9 J1Bb3 G9Bb2 H8Bb3 G1Ca5 A4Ca5 A5Ca2
G5Ca3 H6Ca7 C6Ca8 A7Ca7 A6Ra9 C4Ra1 D4Ra7
E4Ra3 H4Ra2 E6Ba2 G6Ba1 G4Ba9

247	2479	279	235679	239	8	1	359	35679
127	6	3	2579	4	2579	57	59	8
78	5	789	3679	1	679	4	2	3679
6	23478	12578	2459	289	2459	3578	13589	13579
9	28	258	1	7	3	568	58	4
14578	3478	1578	4569	89	4569	35678	13589	2
278	1	4	2379	5	279	238	6	3
3	28	258	24	6	124	9	7	15
257	279	6	8	239	12479	235	1345	135

J8Ca4 B1Ra1 E7Ra6 J2Ba9 G7Ba8 G9Rb3 J7Ca2
C4Ra3 J5Ra3 A8Ba3 A4Ra5 C6Ba6 A9Rb6 F4Ca6
D5Ca2 C9Ca7 C3Ra9 C1Ba8 B8Ba9 F5Ba8 A5Rb9
B7Rb5 D9Rb9 D4Cb4 D6Bb5 H4Bb2 G4Ca9 B6Ca2
H6Ca4 B4Ra7 F6Ra9 G1Ra2 H9Ra1 J1Ba7 J6Ba1
J9Ba5 A1Rb4 G6Rb7 H2Rb8 F1Cb5 E2Cb2 H3Cb5
A2Bb7 E3Bb8 F8Bb1 F2Ca4 D3Ca1 A3Ca2 E8Ca5
D8Ca8 D7Ra7 F7Ra3 D2Ba3 F3Ba7

7	168	1268	1246	1246	124	3	9	5
1389	135689	12689	12345679	12346	1234579	148	148	128
139	4	129	8	123	12359	6	1	7
1389	13689	5	1236	7	1238	189	18	4
2	7	18	14	9	148	158	3	6
4	13689	1689	136	5	138	2	178	18
5	189	4	1379	138	6	178	2	138
189	189	1789	12345679	12348	12345789	14578	145678	138
6	2	3	1457	148	14578	14578	14578	9

B2Ca5 H3Ca7 D7Ca9 H8Ca6 B9Ca2 C6Ra5 E7Ra5
F8Ra7 J8Ba5 C8Rb1 D8Cb8 B8Bb4 F9Bb1 H4Ca5
B7Ba8 H1Ca8 G9Ba8 H9Rb3 J5Ca8 C1Ca9 F3Ca9
G4Ca3 C5Ra3 G7Ra7 G2Ra9 B1Ba3 H2Ba1 H6Ba9
B6Rb7 C3Rb2 D1Rb1 F4Rb6 G5Rb1 H7Rb4 E3Cb8
B4Cb9 D4Cb2 B5Cb6 H5Cb2 J6Cb4 J7Cb1 B3Bb1
A5Bb4 F2Bb3 D6Bb3 E6Bb1 J4Bb7 A2Ca8 A3Ca6
A4Ca1 E4Ca4 A6Ca2 F6Ca8 D2Ra6

3478	6	478	347	5	9	1	2	48
34578	357	2478	1	2346	2467	568	458	9
145	159	1249	246	246	8	56	3	7
2	159	1689	3469	34689	456	35689	7	3568
578	579	3	2679	1	2567	4	589	2568
578	4	6789	23679	23689	2567	235689	589	1
6	8	147	5	249	124	2379	149	234
9	17	147	246	246	3	2578	1458	2458
134	2	5	8	7	14	39	6	34

B2Ca3 A4Ra3 J7Ra9 B6Ba7 J1Ba3 G5Ba9 J9Rb4
J6Cb1 G8Cb1 A9Cb8 C1Ca1 B8Ca4 A1Ca4 D6Ca4
A3Ra7 G3Ra4 H2Ba7 G6Ba2 G9Rb3 H3Rb1 G7Cb7
D2Ca1 H8Ca5 D9Ca5 D3Ra6 H7Ra8 E9Ba6 H9Ba2
D4Rb9 D7Rb3 E6Rb5 E2Cb9 D5Cb8 F6Cb6 F7Cb2
C2Bb5 F3Bb8 F4Bb7 F5Bb3 E8Bb8 F1Ca5 E1Ca7
B1Ca8 C3Ca9 E4Ca2 B7Ca5 F8Ca9 B5Ra6 C5Ra2
B3Ba2 C4Ba4 C7Ba6 H4Ba6 H5Rb4

7	1259	2349	1259	8	2459	135	13	6
6	1259	239	1259	1259	2579	4	8	357
145	158	48	156	1456	3	157	2	9
34	7	5	23689	269	1	2368	346	38
9	268	23468	23568	7	2568	2368	346	1
13	1268	2368	4	26	268	9	5	378
2	3	69	7	14569	45689	1568	169	58
5	4	1	5689	569	5689	35678	3679	2
8	569	679	12569	3	2569	1567	1679	4

J3Ca7 B6Ca7 C7Ra7 F9Ra7 H8Ba7 H1Rb5 H7Ra3
F1Ca3 F2Ra1 C1Ba1 D1Rb4 E8Ca4 E4Ra3 E6Ba5
G6Rb4 J6Rb2 A6Cb9 C4Ca6 C5Ca4 A3Ra4 C2Ra5
B3Ba3 C3Ba8 A2Rb2 B9Rb5 B2Cb9 A4Cb5 A7Cb1
G9Cb8 A8Bb3 D9Bb3 J2Bb6 J4Bb1 E2Ca8 G3Ca9
B4Ca2 B5Ca1 G5Ca5 G8Ca1 F6Ra8 G7Ra6 J7Ra5
J8Ra9 D8Ba6 D7Ba8 H4Ba8 D4Rb9 E7Rb2 H6Rb6
E3Cb6 D5Cb2 H5Cb9 F3Bb2 F5Bb6

7	6	1359	159	8	19	25	4	259
459	59	2	3	57	4679	578	1	5689
1459	8	159	14579	157	2	57	3	569
12568	25	1568	1458	9	1348	123458	268	7
1568	57	4	1578	2	1378	9	68	1568
3	2579	15789	14578	6	1478	12458	28	12458
289	3	789	6	17	1789	1248	5	12489
289	4	789	12789	137	5	6	289	1289
25689	1	5689	289	4	89	28	7	3

A3Ca3 H5Ca3 B6Ca6 D7Ca3 H8Ca9 B1Ra4 C9Ra6
E6Ra3 C4Ba4 D6Ra4 F2Ca9 G5Ca1 A7Ca5 B9Ca9
A9Ra2 B7Ra8 F8Ra2 H9Ra1 C7Ba7 D2Ba2 E2Ba7
F7Ba1 J7Ba2 G9Ba8 B2Rb5 C5Rb5 E9Rb5 G6Rb7
G7Rb4 G3Cb9 B5Cb7 F6Cb8 F9Cb4 C3Bb1 F3Bb5
E4Bb1 G1Bb2 J6Bb9 D1Ca1 J1Ca5 C1Ca9 H3Ca7
H4Ca2 D4Ca5 F4Ca7 A4Ca9 A6Ca1 H1Ra8 J3Ra6
J4Ra8 E1Ba6 D3Ba8 D8Rb6 E8Rb8

1479	1479	1249	245679	8	245679	467	34567	345679
5	14789	3	4679	1479	4679	2	467	4679
479	479	6	3	4579	24579	47	8	1
4789	4789	489	1	479	46789	5	2	3467
6	3	14	457	2	457	147	9	8
14789	2	5	46789	479	3	1467	1467	467
2	6	48	4578	3457	1	9	457	457
1489	14589	7	4589	459	4589	3	1456	2
13489	14589	1489	245789	6	245789	1478	1457	457

J1Ca3 A3Ca2 B5Ca1 G5Ca3 J7Ca8 A8Ca3 B2Ra8
C6Ra2 D9Ra3 H8Ra6 A9Ba5 J4Ba2 J8Ba1 E3Ca1
G8Ca5 B9Ca9 C5Ra5 D6Ra6 F7Ra1 A7Ba6 F4Ba8
F9Ba6 G3Ca8 B4Ca6 H6Ca8 D1Ra8 B8Ca7 B6Ra4
E7Ra7 C7Ba4 F8Ba4 E6Rb5 H5Rb4 E4Cb4 G4Cb7
A4Bb9 J6Bb9 G9Bb4 A1Ca4 D3Ca9 H4Ca5 A6Ca7
J9Ca7 A2Ra1 D2Ra4 F5Ra9 J2Ra5 F1Ba7 D5Ba7
H1Ba1 J3Ba4 C1Rb9 H2Rb9 C2Cb7

249	469	249	1249	249	7	5	8	3
8	3	1	29	259	6	4	7	29
24579	49	24579	12489	234589	134589	1279	6	129
1479	1489	479	4789	456789	2	3	1457	14568
2347	5	247	478	1	48	267	9	2468
12479	1489	6	3	45789	4589	127	1457	12458
1459	7	459	12489	23489	13489	169	1345	14569
1459	149	3	6	49	149	8	2	7
6	2	8	5	3479	1349	19	134	149

E1Ca3 A2Ca6 D5Ca6 A4Ra1 B5Ra5 B8Ra7 H1Ra5
J5Ra7 C3Ba5 F6Ba5 C1Ra7 F7Ra7 F5Ca8 E9Ra8
D2Ba8 D4Ba9 E7Ba6 B4Rb2 E6Rb4 E4Cb7 C5Cb3
B9Cb9 E3Bb2 G5Bb2 A1Ca2 D3Ca7 C7Ca2 G9Ca6
C9Ra1 F9Ra2 G8Ra5 D9Ba5 J8Ba3 J9Rb4 G6Ca3
C2Ra9 G4Ra8 A3Ba4 C6Ba8 A5Ba9 F1Ba9 H5Ba4
C4Rb4 G3Rb9 H2Rb1 G1Cb4 F2Cb4 H6Cb9 G7Cb1
D1Bb1 F8Bb1 J6Bb1 J7Bb9 D8Ca4

5	379	239	2347	6	237	12379	127	8
278	1	2389	2378	237	23578	6	257	4
2678	4	2368	2378	9	1	237	257	235
68	2	1368	13678	137	4	5	67	69
9	368	368	23678	5	23678	2478	2467	1
468	568	7	9	12	268	248	3	26
267	679	269	5	4	23679	123	8	236
1	5678	4	2367	237	2367	23	9	2356
3	569	2569	126	8	269	124	12456	7

F1Ca4 D3Ca1 J3Ca5 A4Ca4 B6Ca5 A7Ca9 D9Ca9
A8Ra1 B3Ra9 F5Ra1 F2Ra5 G7Ra1 H9Ra5 H2Ra8
C8Ba5 J4Ba1 C3Ca8 B4Ra8 C1Ra6 D1Ra8 B5Ba3
D5Rb7 H5Cb2 D8Cb6 D4Bb3 F9Bb2 J6Bb9 H7Bb3
G2Ca9 G6Ca3 C9Ca3 G9Ca6 F6Ra6 G1Ra7 J2Ra6
A2Ba7 E3Ba6 E6Ba8 G3Ba2 H4Ba6 A3Rb3 A6Rb2
B1Rb2 E2Rb3 E4Rb2 F7Rb8 H6Rb7 C4Cb7 B8Cb7
C7Bb2 E8Bb4 J7Ca4 E7Ca7 J8Ca2

126	3	8	17	79	4	5	127	127
9	5	247	1378	378	1237	2378	6	12347
124	1247	247	13578	6	12357	9	12478	12347
4568	468	456	2	3457	3567	1	478	9
3	2468	246	467	1	679	2678	2478	5
7	1246	9	3456	345	8	236	24	2346
4568	4678	3	145678	2	1567	67	179	167
2456	9	24567	14567	457	1567	267	3	8
268	2678	1	9	378	367	4	5	267

A5Ca9 E6Ca9 G8Ca9 A1Ra6 F2Ra1 C1Ba1 G9Ba1
A8Ca1 A9Ra2 H7Ba2 A4Rb7 J1Ca2 F8Ra2 B5Rb8
D3Ca5 G4Ca8 E7Ca8 C8Ra8 D2Ra6 E4Ra6 E8Ra7
H6Ra7 J2Ra8 D1Ba8 D5Ba7 H3Ba6 G2Ba7 H4Ba1
H5Ba4 B4Rb3 D6Rb3 D8Rb4 F5Rb5 G7Rb6 H1Rb5
J5Rb3 G1Cb4 C4Cb5 F4Cb4 G6Cb5 J6Cb6 B7Cb7
F7Cb3 J9Cb7 C6Bb2 B9Bb4 F9Bb6 E2Ca2 C3Ca7
B6Ca1 C9Ca3 B3Ra2 C2Ra4 E3Ra4

6	4589	45789	2	3	47	1	45	458
24789	1	4789	679	69	5	24689	246	3
2459	23459	3459	8	169	146	24569	7	245
578	358	2	4	1568	136	567	156	9
459	6	3459	35	7	13	245	8	1245
1	458	4578	56	2568	9	3	2456	2457
2459	7	4569	3569	569	8	245	12345	1245
3	2458	4568	1	56	67	24578	9	24578
589	589	1	3579	4	2	578	35	6

F5Ca2 D5Ba8 C5Ca1 F4Ba6 E4Ba5 J8Rb3 G4Ca3
C7Ca9 C6Ra6 A6Ba4 A8Rb5 B5Rb9 H6Rb7 B4Cb7
J4Cb9 F8Cb4 A9Cb8 A2Bb9 E7Bb2 D1Ca7 F9Ca7
A3Ra7 J7Ra7 D7Ba5 H7Ba8 D2Rb3 E9Rb1 G7Rb4
D6Cb1 E6Cb3 B7Cb6 D8Cb6 B8Bb2 C3Ca3 G8Ca1
C9Ca4 H2Ca4 F3Ca5 C1Ra5 F2Ra8 H9Ra2 C2Ba2
G1Ba2 J2Ba5 J1Ba8 G9Ba5 B1Rb4 G5Rb6 H3Rb6
E1Cb9 B3Cb8 G3Cb9 H5Cb5 E3Bb4

4	6789	36789	1689	1789	2	5	79	78
567	2	56789	689	45789	45689	4789	1	3
57	789	1	89	45789	3	6	279	2478
236	1	369	2389	23489	7	24	256	2456
8	5	7	12	6	14	1247	3	9
2367	4679	3679	5	12349	149	1247	8	2467
156	68	4	7	12589	15689	3	2569	2568
9	3	5678	1268	1258	1568	278	4	25678
567	678	2	4	3589	5689	789	5679	1

G1Ca1 F2Ca4 D4Ca3 A3Ra3 D5Ra8 J5Ra3 F1Ba3
E6Ba4 E3Rb7 D1Ca2 D3Ra9 F3Ba6 D7Rb4 C9Ca4
B5Ra4 C8Ra2 A8Ca7 B1Ra7 A2Ba6 C5Ba7 B7Ba9
J2Ba7 A5Rb1 A9Rb8 C1Rb5 G2Rb8 J7Rb8 J1Cb6
C2Cb9 B3Cb8 H3Cb5 A4Cb9 B4Bb6 C4Bb8 H5Bb2
E4Ca2 G5Ca5 H6Ca8 B6Ra5 E7Ra1 G9Ra2 H4Ra1
H9Ra6 J8Ra5 F6Ba1 F7Ba2 D9Ba5 D8Ba6 G6Ba6
H7Ba7 G8Ba9 F5Rb9 F9Rb7 J6Rb9

48	9	248	1	3	24	24578	24578	6
146	126	5	24679	67	8	1247	3	2479
7	12368	123468	2469	5	2469	1248	1248	2489
2	13568	13468	4678	678	346	9	14678	478
9	68	468	5	2	1	478	4678	3
13468	1368	7	4689	68	3469	1248	12468	5
368	23678	2368	268	9	256	234578	24578	1
18	4	1289	3	18	25	6	2578	278
5	12368	12368	268	4	7	238	9	28

D2Ca5 G2Ca7 H3Ca9 H5Ca1 H1Rb8 A1Cb4 A6Bb2
A3Rb8 H6Rb5 G6Cb6 G1Bb3 J7Ca3 G3Rb2 G4Cb8
J4Bb2 J9Ra8 H9Ca7 H8Ra2 F7Ba2 D9Rb4 D6Cb3
C3Ca3 E3Ca4 E8Ra6 F2Ra3 E2Ba8 E7Ba7 A7Rb5
G7Cb4 A8Cb7 B7Bb1 G8Bb5 F1Ca1 C7Ca8 C8Ca4
B4Ra4 C2Ra1 D8Ra1 F5Ra6 B2Ba2 C4Ba6 B5Ba7
D3Ba6 F6Ba4 D5Ba8 F8Ba8 J3Ba1 B1Rb6 B9Rb9
C6Rb9 D4Rb7 F4Rb9 J2Rb6 C9Cb2

145	458	2	457	3	6	1489	147	1479
9	4568	7	245	25	1458	3	1246	1246
146	3	148	247	9	1478	1248	12467	5
4	1	489	4679	67	2	5	3	4679
2345	2459	459	345679	8	34579	1249	12467	124679
2345	7	6	1	5	3459	249	8	249
8	2456	45	23567	1	357	24	9	234
12456	24569	3	2569	256	59	7	1245	8
1257	259	159	8	4	3579	6	125	123

J1Ca7 D5Ca7 D3Ra8 D1Rb4 F5Rb5 B5Cb2 H5Bb6
C1Ca6 G2Ra6 G6Ca7 G3Ra5 H2Ba4 E3Rb9 J3Cb1
C3Bb4 H1Bb2 A1Ca1 E2Ca2 J2Ca9 G4Ca2 E1Ra5
G9Ra3 H8Ra1 F1Ba3 J6Ba3 G7Ba4 J8Ba5 C4Rb7
E6Rb4 E7Rb1 H4Rb9 J9Rb2 D4Cb6 F6Cb9 H6Cb5
C8Cb2 C7Bb8 E4Bb3 D9Bb9 F7Bb2 F9Bb4 B6Ca8
A7Ca9 B9Ca1 A2Ra8 B8Ra6 C6Ra1 B2Ba5 A8Ba4
E9Ba6 A4Rb5 A9Rb7 B4Rb4 E8Rb7

124	257	8	1457	3	157	24	259	6
346	357	567	9	2	567	348	1	3458
12346	9	1256	8	14	156	7	25	2345
1289	4	1279	1236	189	12368	5	267	1237
5	6	12	1234	7	123	123	8	9
1289	278	3	1256	189	12568	126	4	127
268	258	4	127	18	9	1268	3	12578
23689	1	269	237	5	4	268	267	278
7	2358	25	123	6	1238	9	25	12458

C5Ca4 A8Ca9 E4Ra4 J9Ra4 G5Rb8 H1Ra3 H3Ra9
J2Ra8 B2Ba3 G1Ba6 B1Rb4 B7Cb8 B9Bb5 E7Ca3
A7Ca4 J8Ca5 H9Ca8 C9Ra3 G2Ra5 J3Ra2 C3Ba5
C8Ba2 C1Rb1 E3Rb1 A1Cb2 D3Cb7 C6Cb6 E6Cb2
A2Bb7 B3Bb6 B6Bb7 F2Bb2 D8Bb6 F4Ca6 H7Ca6
H8Ca7 D9Ra2 F6Ra5 F9Ra7 G4Ra7 H4Ra2 A4Ba5
D6Ba8 F7Ba1 G7Ba2 A6Rb1 D1Rb9 F5Rb9 G9Rb1
F1Cb8 D5Cb1 J6Cb3 D4Bb3 J4Bb1

379	1	359	3456	346	3569	2	3569	8
23789	25789	6	1235	123	12359	579	4	1379
239	259	4	8	7	123569	59	13569	1369
289	3	1	26	268	7	4	689	5
2489	2689	89	12346	5	12368	789	3689	3679
5	68	7	9	3468	368	1	2	36
178	578	58	12567	9	4	3	158	12
13789	4	3589	12357	1238	12358	6	1589	129
6	589	2	135	138	1358	589	7	149

E1Ca4 J9Ca4 A1Ra7 F5Ra4 G4Ra6 A4Ba4 G2Ba7
H4Ba7 D4Rb2 E2Ra2 F6Ra8 G9Ra2 F2Ba6 D5Rb6
F9Rb3 A5Cb3 H3Ca3 C8Ca3 B1Ra3 B2Ra8 C1Ba2
H9Rb9 D1Ca9 D8Ra8 J2Ra9 A3Ba9 E3Ba8 G3Ba5
J7Ba8 C2Rb5 G8Rb1 J5Rb1 G1Cb8 B5Cb2 C7Cb9
H8Cb5 A8Bb6 E7Bb7 H1Bb1 H5Bb8 H6Bb2 C6Ca6
B6Ca9 B7Ca5 E8Ca9 E9Ca6 B9Ca7 A6Ra5 B4Ra1
C9Ra1 E6Ba1 J4Ba5 E4Rb3 J6Rb3

3	1246	16	1249	8	29	12679	1269	5
12	7	15	129	6	239	4	8	129
9	12468	168	5	14	7	126	1236	126
1278	1268	16789	1278	157	2568	3	124569	12689
5	1268	168	3	9	4	1268	126	7
1278	12368	4	1278	157	2568	125689	12569	12689
478	458	578	6	457	1	2589	259	3
148	9	2	48	3	58	1568	7	168
6	1358	13578	789	2	589	1589	159	4

J3Ca3 D3Ca9 B6Ca3 A7Ca7 C8Ca3 D8Ca4 B3Ra5
F2Ra3 J4Ra7 J6Ba9 A6Rb2 G3Ca7 J7Ra8 G1Ca8
G5Ra4 A4Ba4 H1Ba4 H6Ba5 C5Rb1 G2Rb5 H4Rb8
J2Cb1 B4Cb9 F5Cb7 A2Bb6 D5Bb5 J8Bb5 D1Ca7
C2Ca4 E3Ca6 F7Ca5 F9Ca9 A8Ra9 C3Ra8 E2Ra8
F6Ra8 B1Ba2 B9Ba1 F1Ba1 D6Ba6 D9Ba8 G7Ba9
A3Rb1 D2Rb2 F4Rb2 G8Rb2 H9Rb6 D4Cb1 H7Cb1
E8Cb1 F8Cb6 C9Cb2 C7Bb6 E7Bb2

1	349	4589	259	7	2569	234568	234689	34569
3589	39	2	59	4	569	3568	7	13569
579	479	6	8	1	3	245	249	459
5679	8	579	34579	35	1	346	3469	2
25679	2679	3	24579	8	24579	1	469	4679
4	1279	179	6	3	279	38	5	379
236	2346	4	1	9	8	7	2346	3456
3678	5	1478	347	2	47	9	1346	1346
2379	123479	1479	3457	6	457	2345	1234	8

D5Ca5 A8Ca8 B9Ra1 B1Ra8 E1Ra5 F7Ra8 G9Ra5
A3Ba5 H3Ba8 F5Rb3 G3Rb4 C7Ra5 H8Ra1 C8Ra2
J7Ba2 G1Ca2 D7Ca3 G8Ca3 A9Ca3 B2Ra3 G2Ra6
C9Ba9 D1Ba6 H9Ba6 B7Rb6 C1Rb7 F9Rb7 J8Rb4
H1Cb3 C2Cb4 A7Cb4 D8Cb9 E9Cb4 A2Bb9 D3Bb7
E8Bb6 J1Bb9 J2Ca7 F3Ca9 J4Ca3 H6Ca4 A6Ca6
A4Ra2 D4Ra4 F2Ra1 H4Ra7 J3Ra1 J6Ra5 B4Ba5
E2Ba2 E6Ba7 B6Rb9 E4Rb9 F6Rb2

2	13457	1457	1348	38	1348	9	13458	6
158	1345	6	12348	7	9	134	13458	1348
189	13479	1479	1348	5	13468	1347	2	13478
159	159	8	6	39	135	134	7	2
3	1279	1279	128	4	128	16	169	5
4	6	1259	1235	239	7	8	139	13
159	8	12459	23457	6	2345	12347	134	1347
6	24	24	9	1	2348	5	3468	3478
7	1245	3	2458	28	2458	1246	1468	9

H1Ca6 G4Ca7 C6Ca6 B4Ra2 D7Ra4 H9Ra7 C7Ba7
D5Ca3 F5Ba9 A5Rb8 J5Cb2 E6Ca2 G7Ca2 E8Ca9
E7Ra6 E4Ra8 F3Ra2 D6Ba1 H2Ba2 J8Ba6 A6Rb4
F4Rb5 H3Rb4 J7Rb1 J2Cb5 J4Cb4 B7Cb3 D2Bb9
J6Bb8 A3Ca5 G6Ca5 H8Ca8 A2Ra7 B8Ra5 D1Ra5
H6Ra3 C2Ba3 E3Ba7 A8Rb1 C4Rb1 E2Rb1 B2Cb4
C3Cb9 A4Cb3 F8Cb3 C1Bb8 B9Bb8 F9Bb1 G3Bb1
G8Bb4 B1Ca1 G1Ca9 G9Ca3 C9Ca4

6	28	68	2356	4	2358	9	1	7
9	3	678	1	267	2578	256	568	4
1467	12478	5	23679	23679	23789	236	368	2
147	14579	2	8	379	3479	1345	3459	6
3	1479	14679	24679	5	2479	124	49	8
8	459	469	23469	2369	1	7	3459	259
147	1479	1479	234579	12379	234579	8	45679	159
5	14789	14789	479	179	6	14	2	3
2	6	3	4579	8	4579	145	4579	159

G8Ra6 J8Ba7 A1Rb6 C9Rb2 A3Cb8 A2Bb2 B3Bb7
H2Ca8 E7Ca2 D7Ba1 H7Rb4 J7Cb5 B7Bb6 C7Ca3
F9Ca5 D2Ra5 J9Ra1 B8Ba5 G9Ba9 B5Rb2 C8Rb8
B6Cb8 G6Ca2 F4Ra2 G5Ra3 G4Ra5 A6Ba5 D6Ba3
H3Ba9 H5Ba1 A4Rb3 H4Rb7 F8Ca3 D8Ca4 D5Ra9
E6Ba7 E8Ba9 C6Rb9 D1Rb7 E2Rb1 F5Rb6 C2Cb4
E3Cb6 F3Cb4 C4Cb6 E4Cb4 C5Cb7 J6Cb4 C1Bb1
F2Bb9 G2Bb7 G3Bb1 J4Bb9 G1Ca4

89	3	289	1278	4	178	178	5	6
8	25	1	9	2358	6	78	4	278
468	2456	7	128	258	18	18	9	3
146789	1246	24689	5	3689	34789	136789	23678	12789
3	256	25689	678	1	789	56789	2678	4
146789	1456	45689	4678	3689	2	1356789	3678	15789
5	8	346	146	69	149	2	367	79
16	7	6	3	2689	5	4	68	89
2	9	346	468	7	48	3568	1	58

D6Ca3 B5Ra3 H1Ra1 H5Ra2 C5Ba5 B9Ba2 F4Ba4
B1Rb8 B2Rb5 H3Rb6 A1Cb9 B7Cb7 H8Cb8 A3Bb2
H9Bb9 J9Bb5 C4Ca2 G9Rb7 E3Ca8 E7Ra5 F3Ba5
D3Rb9 D7Cb6 D5Bb8 E8Bb2 J7Bb3 D2Ca2 G3Ca3
F7Ca9 F8Ca3 G8Ca6 F9Ca8 D9Ra1 D1Ra4 E6Ra9
F2Ra1 F1Ra7 G6Ra4 J4Ra6 C2Ba4 E2Ba6 F5Ba6
E4Ba7 D8Ba7 J3Ba4 G4Ba1 J6Ba8 G5Ba9 A4Rb8
C1Rb6 C6Rb1 A6Cb7 A7Cb1 C7Cb8

1459	2	1689	5689	158	3	7	458	458
13459	13458	189	2	7	1589	6	3458	3458
357	3568	68	568	4	568	2358	1	9
1239	138	4	3589	1358	12589	358	3568	7
39	7	5	3489	6	89	1	2	348
6	138	128	34578	1358	12578	9	3458	3458
8	9	16	3567	2	567	345	34567	13456
125	156	7	3568	9	4	2358	3568	123568
245	456	3	1	58	5678	2458	9	24568

C1Ca7 F3Ca2 G8Ca7 C7Ra2 D6Ra2 D8Ra6 J6Ra7
F4Ba7 E4Ca4 C2Ra3 G7Ca4 G3Rb1 H9Ca1 H1Ra2
J9Ba2 J1Ca4 G9Ca6 G4Ra3 J2Ra6 B2Ba4 H2Ba5
H4Ba6 A4Rb9 G6Rb5 A3Cb6 J5Cb8 C3Bb8 A5Bb1
J7Bb5 B1Ca1 B3Ca9 D4Ca8 F6Ca1 C6Ca6 E6Ca9
C4Ra5 D2Ra1 D5Ra5 D1Ra9 E9Ra8 A1Ba5 B6Ba8
E1Ba3 F2Ba8 F5Ba3 A9Rb4 D7Rb3 H7Cb8 A8Cb8
F9Cb5 B9Bb3 F8Bb4 H8Bb3 B8Ca5

6	5	123	347	2347	234	147	8	9
4	2	8	567	2579	2569	3	167	12567
239	7	239	8	23459	1	456	46	256
235	2346	2345	13457	123457	8	14567	9	1567
3589	348	7	1345	6	345	2	134	158
2358	1	2345	9	23457	2345	4567	3467	5678
138	348	134	2	13489	7	169	5	16
1235	23	6	135	1359	359	8	17	4
7	9	145	1456	1458	456	16	2	3

D2Ca6 C3Ca9 G7Ca9 E1Ra9 G9Ra6 H8Ra7 J5Ra8
A3Ba1 J7Ba1 B2Rb2 C1Cb3 H2Cb3 G3Bb4 E2Ca4
C9Ca2 E9Ra8 G5Ra3 H1Ra2 F1Ba8 G1Ba1 J3Ba5
D1Rb5 G2Rb8 B8Rb1 E8Cb3 E6Bb5 D9Ca1 E4Ra1
H5Ba1 H4Rb5 H6Rb9 B6Cb6 B4Bb7 J6Bb4 J4Ca6
B5Ca9 F9Ca7 A7Ra7 B9Ra5 D5Ra7 F7Ra5 C5Ba5
C8Ba4 F8Ba6 C7Rb6 D7Rb4 D4Cb3 A4Bb4 D3Bb2
F6Bb2 F3Ca3 A5Ca2 F5Ca4 A6Ca3

148	89	3	19	7	2	48	5	6
12478	268	12468	135	14568	1456	248	9	1238
1248	5	124689	139	14689	1469	7	348	1238
2458	28	7	6	59	3	2589	1	2589
9	368	68	157	2	157	568	678	4
25	1	26	4	59	8	3	67	2579
138	389	5	179	1469	14679	4689	2	3789
1238	4	1289	12579	1569	15679	5689	3678	35789
6	7	29	8	3	459	1	4	59

B1Ca7 H4Ca2 D1Ra4 E2Ra3 J3Ra2 F1Ba5 F3Rb6
F5Rb9 J8Rb4 E3Cb8 D5Cb5 F8Cb7 D2Bb2 E8Bb6
F9Bb2 C1Ca2 B2Ca6 B4Ca5 B7Ca2 A7Ra4 B9Ra3
E7Ra5 C4Ba3 C9Ba1 H8Ba3 C8Rb8 G1Ca3 B5Ca8
G5Ca1 G6Ra4 C5Ba4 H5Ba6 B6Rb1 C3Rb9 A2Cb8
B3Cb4 H3Cb1 A4Cb9 C6Cb6 E6Cb7 A1Bb1 E4Bb1
G2Bb9 H1Bb8 G4Bb7 H6Bb5 J6Ca9 G7Ca6 J9Ca5
H9Ca7 G9Ra8 H7Ra9 D7Ba8 D9Ba9

2467	8	1247	247	9	24	467	3	5
247	579	234579	6	23458	2348	478	7	1
467	567	3457	4578	3458	1	9	2	468
9	156	125	3	2456	246	1456	8	7
2678	567	2578	24589	1	24689	3456	569	3469
3	4	158	589	568	7	156	1569	2
478	2	6	1	348	3489	3578	579	389
1	79	4789	2489	23468	5	23678	679	3689
5	3	89	289	7	2689	1268	4	689

D2Ca1 F8Ca1 A3Ra1 F4Ra9 J7Ra1 H7Ba2 B8Rb7
G7Ca7 G8Ra5 E7Ca3 B7Ca8 H8Ca6 A1Ra6 J6Ra6
C9Ba6 E2Ba6 J4Ba2 G6Ba9 A7Rb4 E8Rb9 A4Cb7
A6Cb2 E9Cb4 D6Bb4 E6Bb8 G1Ca8 D5Ca2 B6Ca3
C3Ra3 D7Ra6 F3Ra8 G5Ra4 J9Ra8 C4Ba4 F5Ba6
F7Ba5 H3Ba4 H5Ba3 H9Ba9 B5Rb5 C1Rb7 D3Rb5
E4Rb5 G9Rb3 H2Rb7 H4Rb8 J3Rb9 E1Cb2 B2Cb9
C2Cb5 B3Cb2 C5Cb8 B1Bb4 E3Bb7

145679	4679	1456	14	16	1467	3	2	46789
8	3467	13456	124	16	9	467	567	467
4679	2	46	5	8	3	1	67	4679
46	468	468	3	7	168	5	9	12468
345679	346789	34568	189	2	168	4678	13678	134678
3679	1	2	89	4	5	678	3678	3678
136	368	9	7	5	2	68	4	1368
1234	348	1348	6	139	148	2789	1378	5
12346	5	7	1489	139	148	2689	1368	123689

B4Ca2 A6Ca7 B8Ca5 A9Ra8 D9Ra2 A4Ba4 C9Ba9
D6Ra1 H8Ra7 E6Ba6 J4Ba1 C8Rb6 C3Cb4 C1Bb7
E2Ca7 E8Ca1 G9Ba1 A2Ca9 H5Ca3 H7Ra9 J5Ba9
J7Ba2 H1Ca2 D3Ca8 H3Ra1 A1Ba1 A5Rb6 A3Cb5
B5Cb1 E3Bb3 G1Ca3 E1Ca5 B3Ca6 J9Ca3 B2Ra3
E4Ra9 F8Ra3 J1Ra6 D2Ba6 F1Ba9 F4Ba8 E7Ba8
H2Ba4 G7Ba6 D1Rb4 E9Rb4 F7Rb7 G2Rb8 H6Rb8
J8Rb8 J6Cb4 B7Cb4 B9Cb7 F9Cb6

378	1	4	378	6	9	2	35	5
236	23569	35	134	345	145	8	34569	7
3678	356789	358	2	3458	1458	1356	34569	14569
9	3458	1358	6	348	2	7	458	1458
3468	34568	7	348	1	48	9	24568	24568
1468	468	2	5	489	7	16	468	3
12478	2478	18	148	2458	3	56	256789	25689
5	23478	9	148	248	1468	36	23678	268
238	238	6	9	7	58	4	1	258

A4Ca7 F5Ca9 H6Ca6 A1Ra8 H4Ra1 A9Rb5 H7Rb3
A8Cb3 G7Ca5 E8Ca2 H8Ca7 B6Ra1 E2Ra5 J6Ra5
D8Ba5 F8Ca8 C1Ca7 E4Ca8 C6Ra8 E1Ra3 G2Ra7
H2Ra4 F1Ba4 F2Ba6 D5Ba3 J2Ba3 G4Ba4 B4Rb3
C2Rb9 C5Rb5 D2Rb8 E6Rb4 F7Rb1 G1Rb1 J1Rb2
B1Cb6 B2Cb2 B3Cb5 C3Cb3 D3Cb1 G3Cb8 B5Cb4
C7Cb6 D9Cb4 E9Cb6 J9Cb8 B8Bb9 C8Bb4 C9Bb1
G5Bb2 G9Bb9 H9Bb2 H5Ca8 G8Ca6

8	3	12469	7	24569	2456	1249	19	1
127	279	1249	348	23489	2348	12479	5	6
267	5	2469	468	24689	1	3	789	78
167	678	3	1568	1568	9	1567	4	2
5	268	1268	13468	7	3468	16	13	9
9	4	16	2	1356	356	8	137	1357
23	28	7	9	123458	23458	15	6	1358
4	1	25689	3568	23568	23568	579	3789	3578
36	689	5689	13568	13568	7	159	2	4

A9Rb1 A8Cb9 H7Ca7 H3Ra9 B2Ba9 J3Ba5 J7Ba9
E7Rb6 D7Cb5 G7Bb1 D2Ca7 E3Ca8 H4Ca5 C5Ca9
B1Ra7 E2Ra2 G9Ra5 B3Ba1 G1Ba2 C1Rb6 F3Rb6
G2Rb8 D1Cb1 J1Cb3 J2Cb6 C4Cb4 C3Bb2 A3Ca4
D4Ca6 G5Ca4 B7Ra4 D5Ra8 E6Ra4 G6Ra3 A7Ba2
F6Rb5 J5Rb1 J4Cb8 F5Cb3 A6Cb6 A5Bb5 B4Bb3
B5Bb2 E4Bb1 F9Bb7 H6Bb2 H5Ca6 B6Ca8 F8Ca1
C8Ca7 H9Ca3 C9Ra8 E8Ra3 H8Ra8

3568	9	2358	356	368	7	4	168	1356
35678	4	3578	356	368	1	3568	9	2
1	58	358	2	34689	34589	3568	7	356
34578	6	1345789	379	34789	2	1378	148	1347
2	18	13478	367	5	348	13678	1468	9
3478	8	34789	1	346789	3489	23678	5	3467
45	3	1245	579	1279	6	1579	14	8
9	7	158	4	13	35	156	2	156
45	125	6	8	1279	59	1579	3	1457

J2Ca2 F7Ca2 A3Ra2 G5Ra2 H3Ra8 G3Ba1 F2Rb8
G8Rb4 G1Cb5 C2Cb5 E2Cb1 C3Bb3 J1Bb4 D3Ca5
F3Ba9 B3Rb7 C9Rb6 E3Cb4 C7Cb8 A8Bb1 E6Ca8
E8Ca6 D8Ra8 F5Ra6 H7Ra6 H6Ca3 H9Ra5 B7Ba5
J6Ba5 A9Rb3 B4Rb6 F6Rb4 H5Rb1 B1Cb8 A4Cb5
A5Cb8 C6Cb9 F9Cb7 A1Bb6 B5Bb3 C5Bb4 F1Bb3
E7Bb3 J9Bb1 D1Ca7 D4Ca3 D7Ca1 D9Ca4 D5Ra9
E4Ra7 J5Ba7 G4Ba9 G7Rb7 J7Rb9

1568	14578	24568	456	47	467	9	1258	3
35689	4589	345689	1	2	46	568	7	56
1569	1579	2569	569	3	8	256	125	4
4	6	389	289	789	5	1	29	279
1589	2	589	489	6	147	457	3	579
159	159	7	3	49	124	245	6	8
2	489	4689	7	5	346	3468	1489	169
568	3	4568	2468	1	9	245678	2458	2567
7	4589	1	2468	48	2346	234568	24589	2569

B1Ca3 G9Ca1 C2Ra7 D3Ra3 C4Ba9 A4Ca5 E4Rb4
F5Cb9 E1Ca9 E6Ca1 F7Ca4 E3Ra8 F6Ra2 D5Ba7
A5Rb4 D4Rb8 J5Cb8 B6Cb6 A6Bb7 B9Bb5 E7Ra5
C7Ba6 E9Ba7 B7Rb8 G7Cb3 G6Bb4 J7Bb2 H4Ca2
J6Ca3 H7Ca7 D9Ca2 D8Ra9 G3Ra6 A1Ba6 J4Ba6
J9Ba9 A3Rb2 G8Rb8 H9Rb6 G2Cb9 C3Cb5 A8Cb1
A2Bb8 B2Bb4 C1Bb1 C8Bb2 H3Bb4 H1Ca8 F2Ca1
B3Ca9 J8Ca4 F1Ra5 H8Ra5 J2Ra5

2357	6	2359	124579	179	12459	149	1348	1349
1	8	259	24569	3	24569	469	7	49
37	379	4	1679	8	169	2	136	5
245	1259	259	3	19	12589	14579	124	6
6	1259	7	1259	4	1259	3	12	8
8	12359	2359	12569	169	7	1459	124	149
9	357	1	467	2	346	8	346	347
37	4	368	1678	5	1368	167	9	2
237	237	2368	146789	1679	134689	1467	5	1347

D1Ca4 A8Ca8 D7Ra7 D6Ra8 G2Ra5 F7Ba5 A1Ca5
F8Ca4 D3Ra5 F9Ba9 B9Rb4 J1Ca2 J7Ca4 A5Rb7
F3Rb3 A9Ra3 C8Ra6 A7Ba1 G8Ba3 H7Ba6 B7Rb9
G9Rb7 H3Rb8 B3Cb2 J3Cb6 J9Cb1 A3Bb9 J5Bb9
J4Ca8 F5Ca6 D2Ra9 J2Ra7 C1Ba7 H1Ba3 H4Ba7
C2Rb3 D5Rb1 H6Rb1 J6Rb3 F4Cb2 C6Cb9 D8Cb2
A4Bb4 C4Bb1 F2Bb1 E6Bb5 E8Bb1 E2Ca2 B4Ca5
E4Ca9 A6Ca2 G6Ca4 B6Ra6 G4Ra6

24567	247	2567	34568	1	34568	9	257	2357
9	3	256	456	7	456	24	8	125
1457	147	8	2	345	3459	6	57	1357
2378	279	279	369	23	1	5	4	236789
2347	6	279	3459	8	23459	237	1	2379
2348	5	1	7	234	23469	238	269	23689
256	29	4	358	235	7	1	2569	25689
12567	8	2567	15	9	25	27	3	4
1257	1279	3	1458	6	2458	278	2579	25789

B7Ca4 B9Ra1 C6Ra9 B3Ra2 G5Ca5 G4Ra3 D2Rb2
G1Rb2 H4Rb1 H6Rb2 G2Cb9 D5Cb3 H7Cb7 C5Bb4
D1Bb8 G8Bb6 A2Ca4 F5Ca2 A6Ca3 A4Ra8 C9Ra3
G9Ra8 F7Ba8 J6Ba8 F8Rb9 J4Rb4 J7Rb2 E7Cb3
J8Cb5 F9Cb6 C8Bb7 E1Bb4 F6Bb4 D9Bb7 J9Bb9
F1Ca3 J2Ca7 E3Ca7 B6Ca6 A8Ca2 A9Ca5 A1Ra7
B4Ra5 C1Ra5 D4Ra6 E9Ra2 E4Ra9 J1Ra1 C2Ba1
A3Ba6 D3Ba9 E6Ba5 H3Ba5 H1Rb6

369	3469	7	8	1	26	239	5	29
2	1589	19	4	579	3	189	1789	6
35689	135689	169	2569	2579	2567	4	123789	12789
69	169	5	1239	8	12	7	12469	129
4	1789	129	1259	6	1257	1289	1289	3
6789	16789	3	129	4	127	5	12689	1289
35679	345679	8	1256	25	12456	1239	12379	12579
1	356	6	7	25	9	238	238	4
579	2	49	15	3	8	6	179	1579

E3Ca2 J3Ca4 D4Ca3 G6Ca4 D8Ca4 A2Ra4 F8Ba6
G4Ba6 H3Rb6 B2Ra5 J4Ba1 H2Rb3 G5Ca2 H5Ra5
F9Ca8 E2Ra8 C1Ba8 D9Ba2 A9Rb9 C2Rb6 D6Rb1
A1Cb3 D2Cb9 A7Bb2 D1Bb6 F1Bb7 G2Bb7 F2Ca1
A6Ca6 E6Ca7 G7Ca3 H8Ca2 C8Ra3 E4Ra5 F4Ra9
H7Ra8 C6Ba5 B8Ba8 F6Ba2 B7Rb1 C4Rb2 B3Cb9
E7Cb9 C9Cb7 C3Bb1 B5Bb7 C5Bb9 E8Bb1 J9Bb5
G1Ca5 J8Ca7 G9Ca1 G8Ra9 J1Ra9

3	689	4689	7	5	689	2468	1	2469
1468	689	5	129	189	3	2468	7	2469
7	2	1689	19	189	4	368	3589	369
1248	78	12478	6	1348	18	9	2348	5
14568	5678	14678	1459	2	1589	134678	348	1346
9	568	3	145	148	7	12468	248	1246
25	359	29	8	149	159	1234	6	7
268	4	26789	3	179	19	5	29	129
5	1	79	459	6	2	34	349	8

G2Ca3 B4Ca2 D5Ca3 H5Ca7 A6Ca6 E7Ca7 C8Ca5
J3Ra7 D2Ba7 J1Rb5 G1Cb2 G3Bb9 D3Ca2 G6Ra5
C4Rb1 E3Ca1 B1Ra1 D6Ra1 A3Ba4 E6Ba8 G5Ba1
F5Rb4 G7Rb4 H6Rb9 F4Cb5 J4Cb4 J7Cb3 H8Cb2
E4Bb9 F8Bb8 H9Bb1 J8Bb9 E2Ca5 F7Ca1 E8Ca3
B9Ra4 C9Ra3 D1Ra8 F9Ra2 A7Ba2 A9Ba9 E1Ba4
D8Ba4 E9Ba6 H3Ba8 A2Rb8 C3Rb6 F2Rb6 H1Rb6
B2Cb9 C7Cb8 B5Bb8 C5Bb9 B7Bb6

4	1367	167	36	1367	5	9	2	68
5	1267	8	246	124679	1467	16	3	6
123679	12367	1267	236	123679	8	4	1567	56
136	1346	9	7	3456	346	1356	14568	2
367	3467	567	1	8	2	356	4569	34569
8	12346	1256	3456	3456	9	7	1456	3456
1267	12678	3	9	124567	1467	256	456	456
267	9	267	23456	234567	3467	8	456	1
126	5	4	8	1236	136	236	69	7

C1Ca9 G2Ca8 C8Ca7 D8Ca8 A9Ca8 E9Ca9 B5Ra9
C9Ra5 J8Ra9 B7Ba1 J7Ba3 B9Rb6 G9Cb4 F9Bb3
G7Ca2 F8Ca1 E8Ba4 E1Ca3 D2Ca1 F2Ba4 D1Rb6
E2Cb7 D7Cb5 B2Bb2 E3Bb5 E7Bb6 F3Ca2 B6Ra7
A3Ba7 B4Ba4 H3Ba6 C3Rb1 H8Rb5 G8Cb6 G6Bb1
J1Ca1 F4Ca5 A5Ca1 J6Ca6 F5Ra6 G5Ra5 J5Ra2
C4Ba2 H1Ba2 H5Ba7 C5Rb3 G1Rb7 H4Rb3 C2Cb6
A4Cb6 D5Cb4 H6Cb4 A2Bb3 D6Bb3

3	57	9	2	1	468	478	457	578
15	8	12	7	349	49	1249	123459	6
4	127	1267	3689	369	5	12789	12379	2378
19	12349	5	349	7	1249	2489	6	28
8	23479	2347	3469	5	2469	2479	2479	1
179	6	1247	49	8	1249	3	24579	257
567	3457	34678	1	46	468	267	237	9
2	13459	1346	4569	469	7	16	8	3
1679	179	1678	689	2	3	5	17	4

H4Ca5 A6Ra6 C3Ba6 C4Ba8 E4Ba6 H9Rb3 J4Rb9
F4Cb4 D4Bb3 G6Ca8 H2Ra9 J1Ra6 J3Ra8 B6Ca4
J8Ra7 H7Ba1 G8Rb2 H3Rb4 J2Rb1 H5Cb6 G7Cb6
G5Bb4 C8Ra1 B8Ba3 B5Rb9 C5Cb3 B7Cb2 B3Bb1
C9Bb7 A2Ca7 E7Ca7 B1Ra5 C2Ra2 C7Ra9 G2Ba5
D2Rb4 G1Rb7 E2Cb3 G3Cb3 D7Cb8 A7Bb4 E3Bb2
D9Bb2 F3Ca7 F6Ca2 E8Ca4 A9Ca8 A8Ra5 E6Ra9
F1Ra1 D1Ba9 D6Ba1 F9Ba5 F8Ba9

3	237	8	1	2679	4	569	2569	256
9	1247	5	3	2678	278	68	1246	2468
14	6	124	289	5	28	89	3	7
568	789	3	4	2789	278	56789	25679	1
4568	4789	4679	25789	1	2378	356789	25679	23568
2	1789	179	5789	3789	6	4	579	358
7	5	1269	2	4	123	36	8	36
3468	2348	246	278	2378	5	1	467	9
1348	1348	14	6	378	9	2	457	345

G6Ca1 B8Ca1 G3Ra9 B9Ba4 A1Rb3 G4Rb2 H3Ca2
E6Ca3 C6Ra2 F2Ra1 F9Ra3 H1Ra6 J9Ra5 E3Ba6
D5Ba2 G7Ba3 F3Rb7 G9Rb6 A9Cb2 A2Bb7 E9Bb8
B2Ca2 E8Ca2 B6Ca8 B5Ra7 C7Ra8 A5Ba6 H4Ba7
B7Rb6 C4Rb9 D6Rb7 H8Rb4 E4Cb5 J8Cb7 E1Bb4
F4Bb8 D1Ca5 J2Ca4 F5Ca9 E7Ca7 D8Ca6 C3Ra4
D2Ra8 E2Ra9 F8Ra5 J5Ra3 C1Ba1 A7Ba5 D7Ba9
H2Ba3 J1Ba8 H5Ba8 A8Rb9 J3Rb1

8	2469	469	2369	5	1	2369	7	2369
3	5	1679	269	679	4	8	12	1269
1247	12469	14679	2369	8	23679	123569	12345	12369
12	128	138	126	167	2678	4	9	5
6	1248	148	12459	3	2589	12	128	7
9	7	5	1246	16	268	1236	1238	1236
1457	14689	146789	13569	2	3569	13579	135	139
157	19	2	8	19	359	13579	6	4
15	3	169	7	4	569	1259	125	8

D3Ca3 C8Ca4 C7Ra5 F4Ra4 G1Ca4 F5Rb1 H5Cb9
H2Bb1 G4Ca1 D1Ra1 J1Rb5 H1Cb7 J6Cb6 C1Bb2
J3Bb9 H7Bb3 E4Ca5 G7Ca7 F8Ca3 G8Ca5 E6Ra9
F6Ra8 G6Ra3 G9Ra9 H6Ra5 A7Ba9 E8Ba8 C6Rb7
E3Rb4 E2Cb2 A3Cb6 B5Cb6 D6Cb2 A2Bb4 C2Bb9
C3Bb1 D2Bb8 D4Bb6 D5Bb7 E7Bb1 G3Bb8 G2Ca6
B3Ca7 B4Ca9 F7Ca6 B9Ca1 B8Ra2 C9Ra6 F9Ra2
J8Ra1 A4Ba2 A9Ba3 J7Ba2 C4Rb3

4	1	2579	5789	2789	2789	25678	3	25689
2579	8	3	6	279	1279	12457	147	1259
2579	6	2579	145789	3	12789	124578	147	12589
1239	39	8	379	5	4	1267	167	1236
6	7	29	389	1	389	28	5	4
135	345	145	2	6	378	9	17	138
13578	35	1567	1378	4	123678	156	9	156
1789	49	14679	1789	789	5	3	2	16
1359	2	14569	139	9	1369	1456	8	7

C4Ca4 D8Ca6 G6Ra2 A4Ba5 J6Ba6 J7Ba4 J5Rb9
B8Ca4 F2Ca5 E6Ca3 F3Ra4 H2Ba4 G2Rb3 D2Cb9
E3Bb2 D4Bb7 J4Ca3 E4Ca9 E7Ra8 F8Ra7 F6Ba8
H5Ba7 B5Rb2 C8Rb1 A5Cb8 C1Ca2 B6Ca1 C9Ca8
J3Ra1 B9Ba9 J1Ba5 B1Rb7 G1Cb8 A3Cb9 B7Cb5
C3Bb5 A6Bb7 C7Bb7 H1Bb9 H3Bb6 G4Bb1 G3Ca7
H4Ca8 C6Ca9 D7Ca1 G9Ca5 D9Ra2 F1Ra1 G7Ra6
H9Ra1 A7Ba2 A9Ba6 D1Ba3 F9Ba3

147	5	6	2489	249	23489	1278	189	12379
8	2	7	59	1	6	4	9	379
14	149	3	24589	2459	7	12568	1689	1269
147	8	147	3	4679	49	167	2	5
123457	1347	12457	24569	8	2459	167	1469	14679
9	6	2457	245	2457	1	78	3	47
123456	134	12458	7	2456	2458	9	146	1246
2456	4	9	1	3	245	26	7	8
12467	147	12478	24689	2469	2489	3	5	1246

C2Ca9 A6Ca3 C7Ca5 B9Ra3 B4Ra5 F7Ra8 B3Rb7
B8Rb9 H2Rb4 E9Ca9 D1Rb7 J2Ca7 F5Ca7 E7Ra7
F3Ra5 A9Ba7 E6Ba5 F9Rb4 H6Rb2 F4Cb2 H7Cb6
D7Bb1 H1Bb5 G5Ca5 A7Ca2 G8Ca4 C9Ca6 C5Ra2
D5Ra6 G1Ra6 D6Ba9 E8Ba6 G2Ba3 J4Ba6 D3Rb4
E2Rb1 E4Rb4 G6Rb8 J1Rb2 E1Cb3 E3Cb2 G3Cb1
C4Cb8 J6Cb4 J9Cb1 A4Bb9 C8Bb1 J3Bb8 J5Bb9
G9Bb2 A1Ca1 A5Ca4 A8Ca8 C1Ra4

1248	1237	123478	5	23679	124679	2469	24	2469
5	6	1247	1247	279	12479	249	3	8
24	23	9	2346	8	246	1	245	7
26	8	5	9	267	267	2467	1	2346
1269	12379	1237	12678	4	12567	2567	257	2356
126	4	127	1267	2567	3	8	9	256
7	29	6	24	1	2459	3	2458	2459
3	5	248	247	279	2479	2479	6	1
1249	129	124	23467	235679	8	24579	2457	2459

A1Ca8 E4Ca8 G8Ca8 C8Ra5 D9Ra3 H3Ra8 D7Ba4
F5Ca5 G6Ba5 A2Ca7 A8Ca4 F3Ra7 G9Ra4 G4Rb2
H7Rb2 G2Cb9 B7Cb9 J8Cb7 A7Bb6 E8Bb2 J7Bb5
E1Ca9 E7Ca7 A9Ca2 E9Ca5 J9Ca9 E6Ra6 F1Ra2
C4Ba6 D1Ba6 F4Ba1 F9Ba6 C1Rb4 J4Rb3 J1Cb1
J5Cb6 C6Cb2 C2Bb3 B5Bb7 D6Bb7 J2Bb2 E2Ca1
B3Ca2 E3Ca3 J3Ca4 H4Ca7 D5Ca2 A5Ca3 A6Ra9
B6Ra1 H6Ra4 A3Ba1 B4Ba4 H5Ba9

2478	2478	278	45789	1	4789	3	6	2458
5	4678	678	3	47	2	14789	489	148
23478	1	9	4578	6	478	24578	2458	2458
9	234678	23678	478	347	5	248	1	2468
1	23468	2368	48	9	468	2458	2458	7
4678	5	678	2	47	14678	489	489	3
23	23	1235	1459	8	149	6	7	1245
278	278	12578	6	457	3	12458	2458	9
3678	9	4	157	2	17	158	358	158

D5Ca3 H5Ca5 J8Ca3 D9Ca6 C1Ra3 F6Ra1 J1Ra6
E6Ba6 G3Ba5 G1Rb2 J6Rb7 G2Cb3 J4Cb1 B2Ca6
H3Ca1 E3Ca3 B7Ca1 B8Ra9 F3Ra6 G9Ra1 C7Ba7
F7Ba9 C9Ca2 B9Ba4 B5Rb7 B3Cb8 F5Cb4 E4Bb8
F8Bb8 A1Ca4 H1Ca8 D4Ca7 J7Ca8 C6Ra8 D2Ra8
F1Ra7 H2Ra7 J9Ra5 A3Ba7 C4Ba4 C8Ba5 A9Ba8
E2Ba4 A2Rb2 A6Rb9 D3Rb2 E8Rb2 G4Rb9 A4Cb5
G6Cb4 D7Cb4 E7Cb5 H8Cb4 H7Bb2

2	14589	14567	15789	3	1789	1567	15679	56
17	159	1567	4	159	1279	1567	8	3
178	1589	3	15789	1589	6	4	1579	2
3	6	12457	1578	1458	1478	9	25	58
9	145	145	1568	2	1348	3568	356	7
7	25	8	5679	569	379	356	4	1
5	148	9	3	1468	148	2	167	468
6	7	124	1289	1489	5	138	13	48
148	12348	124	1268	7	1248	13568	1356	9

J1Ca4 J2Ca3 D8Ca2 B6Ra2 F2Ra2 G8Ra7 G2Ba8
F1Rb7 B1Cb1 C1Bb8 E2Ca1 C4Ra7 D6Ba7 A2Ca4
J6Rb8 D5Ca8 A4Ra8 D4Ra1 D3Ra4 E7Ra8 E3Ba5
E6Ba4 H9Ba8 D9Rb5 E4Rb6 G6Rb1 J4Cb2 A6Cb9
E8Cb3 A9Cb6 A3Bb7 B5Bb5 B7Bb7 F6Bb3 F7Bb6
J3Bb1 H4Bb9 G9Bb4 H8Bb1 C2Ca5 H3Ca2 B3Ca6
F4Ca5 C5Ca1 H5Ca4 G5Ca6 F5Ca9 A7Ca1 H7Ca3
J8Ca6 C8Ca9 A8Ra5 B2Ra9 J7Ra5

1479	4	147	8	2	5	6	3	147
134578	2	13478	137	347	6	9	78	1478
1346789	346	13478	1379	3479	479	1478	5	12478
3457	8	347	6	4579	479	2	1	3579
234567	3456	2347	279	1	24789	3578	678	356789
2567	1	9	27	57	3	578	4	5678
12348	7	12348	239	369	29	13458	268	1234568
1238	3	5	4	367	27	1378	9	123678
234	9	6	5	8	1	347	27	2347

E2Ca5 E6Ca8 A1Ra9 B1Ra5 C9Ra2 A2Rb4 H2Rb3
C2Cb6 H6Ra2 H5Ba7 F5Rb5 G6Rb9 G4Cb3 G5Bb6
G7Ca5 E8Ca6 D9Ra5 F1Ra6 H9Ra6 E9Ba9 F4Ca2
C4Ca9 J9Ca3 D5Ra9 E7Ra3 E4Ra7 B4Ba1 C6Ba7
D6Ba4 D1Ca7 D3Ra3 C1Ba3 C5Rb4 B5Cb3 J7Ca4
B9Ra4 G3Ra4 J8Ra7 A9Ba7 E1Ba4 J1Ba2 G8Ba2
A3Rb1 B8Rb8 E3Rb2 F9Rb8 B3Cb7 C3Cb8 C7Cb1
F7Cb7 G9Cb1 G1Bb8 H7Bb8 H1Ca1

27	12347	12347	9	246	8	2367	1267	5
6	1237	12378	5	2	3	2378	9	4
258	2345	9	7	1	346	2368	268	368
579	8	357	36	569	1369	4	1567	2
259	23459	2345	23468	7	13469	5689	1568	1689
1	24579	6	248	24589	49	5789	3	89
2589	259	258	468	3	7	1	24568	689
3	6	158	48	489	2	589	458	7
4	279	278	1	689	5	23689	268	3689

E9Ca1 D6Ra1 H3Ra1 A8Ba1 B5Rb2 B6Rb3 B2Ca1
D8Ca7 F2Ra7 J3Ba7 B3Rb8 B7Cb7 A1Ca7 G1Ca8
F4Ra2 D1Ca9 C6Ca6 A7Ra6 C2Ra4 C1Ba5 A5Ba4
E3Ba4 E8Ba6 E1Rb2 E6Rb9 F6Cb4 J2Ca9 H8Ca5
G9Ra9 H4Ra4 F7Ba9 H5Ba9 G8Ba4 J9Ba6 F9Rb8
G4Rb6 H7Rb8 J5Rb8 D4Cb3 F5Cb5 E7Cb5 J8Cb2
C9Cb3 C7Bb2 C8Bb8 D3Bb5 E2Bb3 D5Bb6 E4Bb8
J7Bb3 G2Ca5 A3Ca3 A2Ra2 G3Ra2

124569	1249	1256	1359	3457	13457	5789	5789	245689
14569	3	7	8	45	2	59	59	4569
2459	249	8	59	6	457	1	3	2459
135	6	135	135	357	8	4	2	1359
8	124	1235	12356	9	1356	35	15	7
1235	7	9	4	235	135	358	6	1358
3679	5	4	36	1	36	2	789	389
123	128	123	7	2358	9	6	4	1358
123679	1289	1236	2356	23458	3456	35789	15789	13589

134	9	134	2	3458	6	135	7	13
12347	12467	123467	3579	3459	1357	123569	8	1239
8	1267	5	379	39	137	12369	4	1239
2357	27	8	4	1	35	23579	359	6
9	12	123	3568	7	358	1235	135	4
6	147	1347	35	2	9	8	135	137
127	3	12679	6789	689	278	4	169	5
1247	5	124679	36789	3689	2378	13679	1369	13789
7	8	679	1	3569	4	3679	2	379

B1Ra1 C6Ra7 D5Ra7 D9Ra9 E2Ra4 B9Ra6 G9Ra8
F7Ba8 A7Rb7 B5Rb4 A8Cb8 J6Ca4 J3Rb6 A3Cb5
C1Bb4 A5Bb3 A1Ca6 A9Ca4 A2Ra2 C4Ra5 C2Ba9
A4Ba9 C9Ba2 A6Rb1 J4Rb2 D1Ca5 F5Ca2 E3Ra2
F9Ra1 D3Ba1 E7Ba3 H1Ba2 J8Ba1 D4Rb3 E8Rb5
F1Rb3 H3Rb3 H9Rb5 J2Rb8 H2Cb1 G4Cb6 H5Cb8
J5Cb5 E6Cb6 F6Cb5 J7Cb9 B8Cb9 J9Cb3 B7Bb5
E4Bb1 J1Bb7 G6Bb3 G8Bb7 G1Ca9

D1Ca5 H9Ca8 A5Ra8 E4Ra6 J5Ra5 B5Ba4 E6Ba8
D6Rb3 J1Rb7 F4Cb5 D8Cb9 F2Ca4 G4Ca8 B6Ca5
E8Ca5 F9Ca7 A7Ra5 D2Ra7 G6Ra7 B3Ba7 C6Ba1
H6Ba2 H7Ba7 D7Rb2 C4Ca7 B2Ca1 F3Ca1 J3Ca6
E7Ca1 F8Ca3 A9Ra1 B7Ra6 E3Ra3 C2Ba6 E2Ba2
A3Rb4 A1Cb3 H3Cb9 B1Bb2 G3Bb2 H4Bb3 H1Ca4
B4Ca9 C5Ca3 C9Ca2 B9Ra3 C7Ra9 G5Ra9 H8Ra1
G1Ba1 H5Ba6 J7Ba3 G8Ba6 J9Ba9

1456	14679	1679	4679	467	3	2	8	145
134568	123469	12689	2469	46	24569	1459	7	1345
345	23479	279	1	8	2459	459	3459	6
7	6	5	468	9	1	3	24	248
2	136	168	4678	5	468	148	14	9
18	19	4	3	2	8	6	15	7
9	1246	126	2468	3	7	1458	12456	12458
146	5	1267	24689	146	24689	14789	123469	12348
146	8	3	5	146	2469	1479	12469	124

249	8	149	25	2457	3	147	149	6
7	1249	1469	8	246	249	5	149	13
5	3	469	6	467	1	478	2	78
2689	2579	3	4	12678	278	12678	1568	1578
1	257	5678	236	9	278	23678	568	4
2468	247	4678	1236	123678	5	9	168	1378
489	6	14589	7	1458	48	148	3	2
48	1457	2	135	13458	6	148	1458	9
3	145	1458	9	12458	248	1468	7	158

A5Ca7 E2Ra3 E4Ra7 F8Ra5 F2Ra9 J7Ra7 H3Ba7
D2Rb6 F6Rb8 F1Cb1 D4Cb4 E3Bb8 E6Bb6 D8Bb2
B1Ca8 C2Ca7 B9Ra3 D9Ra8 C1Ba3 H8Ba3 A1Ca5
G9Ca5 A9Ca4 A2Ra1 C6Ra4 B2Ba4 B6Ba5 B7Ba1
G3Ba1 B5Rb6 C8Rb9 E7Rb4 G2Rb2 C3Cb2 A4Cb9
C7Cb5 G7Cb8 E8Cb1 A3Bb6 B3Bb9 B4Bb2 G4Bb6
H7Bb9 J8Bb6 H1Ca6 H4Ca8 J6Ca9 G8Ca4 H5Ra4
J9Ra2 J1Ba4 J5Ba1 H6Ba2 H9Ba1

B6Ca9 E7Ca3 B9Ra3 C3Ra9 H2Ra7 J7Ra6 B3Ba6
A8Ba9 D7Ba2 G1Ba9 C4Rb6 E4Cb2 A4Bb5 E2Bb5
D2Ca9 J6Ca2 E8Ra6 G6Ca4 C9Rb8 H1Rb8 D1Cb6
D5Bb1 H4Ca1 F5Ca6 G7Ca8 F4Ra3 G3Ra1 H5Ra3
J5Ra8 B2Ba1 J3Ba5 G5Ba5 J9Ba1 A3Rb4 B8Rb4
F9Rb7 H7Rb4 J2Rb4 A1Cb2 F2Cb2 F3Cb8 B5Cb2
C7Cb7 H8Cb5 D9Cb5 A5Bb7 C5Bb4 A7Bb1 E3Bb7
F1Bb4 D8Bb8 F8Bb1 D6Ca7 E6Ca8

1479	1459	6	8	3	24	1457	7	1457
1348	1458	1345	7	9	4	2	368	13458
13478	2	134	146	16	5	9	3678	13478
12689	7	129	5	1	239	13	4	12389
5	149	1249	1234	8	2349	137	2379	6
12489	3	1249	124	17	6	17	5	12789
2346	456	7	9	56	38	3456	1	2345
13469	14569	8	36	2	7	3456	369	3459
2369	569	2359	36	4	1	8	23679	23579

B2Ca8 G5Ca5 F5Ca7 G6Ca8 A6Ra2 B8Ra6 D1Ra6
F1Ba8 A8Rb7 B6Rb4 D5Rb1 F7Rb1 C5Cb6 D7Cb3
C4Bb1 D6Bb9 E7Bb7 C1Ca7 E6Ca3 C8Ca8 J9Ca7
D9Ra8 D3Rb2 G1Ca3 G9Ra2 E8Ba2 J1Ba2 B1Rb1
E4Rb4 F9Rb9 F3Cb4 F4Cb2 C3Bb3 E3Ca1 A9Ca1
B9Ca3 B3Ra5 C9Ra4 E2Ra9 H2Ra1 A1Ba9 A7Ba5
J2Ba5 A2Rb4 H1Rb4 H9Rb5 J3Rb9 G2Cb6 H7Cb6
J8Cb3 H4Bb3 J4Bb6 G7Bb4 H8Bb9

2679	3567	2379	35678	25678	1	4	2378	238
4	357	1	3578	9	23578	237	6	238
8	367	237	3467	267	23467	1	5	9
3	467	79	45679	2567	245679	8	1	245
1679	4678	789	1456789	3	2456789	257	2479	245
179	2	5	14789	178	4789	37	3479	6
5	9	6	378	78	378	23	2348	1
2	1	238	3568	4	3568	9	238	7
7	378	4	2	15678	356789	356	38	358

J7Ca6 G8Ra4 J5Ra1 J6Ra9 J9Ba5 H1Rb2 J1Rb7
F7Ca3 E7Ca5 A8Ca2 B6Ra2 G7Ra2 C3Ba2 B7Ba7
D5Ba2 D9Rb4 E9Cb2 E2Ca4 A5Ca5 B2Ra5 E3Ba8
C5Rb6 H3Rb3 J2Cb8 H8Cb8 J8Bb3 E8Ra9 F8Ba7
E6Rb7 F5Rb8 G5Cb7 F6Cb4 C6Bb3 G4Bb3 A2Ca3
C4Ca4 G6Ca8 A1Ra6 B9Ra3 C2Ra7 A3Ba9 A4Ba7
A9Ba8 D2Ba6 D3Ba7 B4Rb8 D6Rb5 E1Rb1 F1Cb9
D4Cb9 E4Cb6 H6Cb6 F4Bb1 H4Bb5

14569	12459	7	149	3	249	8	256	2456
13489	12489	349	5	1247	6	247	237	247
3456	245	3456	8	247	247	1	9	24567
349	6	349	2	47	479	5	78	1
7	1459	459	1469	8	49	269	26	3
2	159	8	1679	1567	3	679	4	679
45689	3	2	467	467	1	4679	5678	456789
4689	4789	469	3	2467	5	24679	12678	246789
4568	4578	1	467	9	2478	3	25678	245678

F5Ca5 J6Ca8 H8Ca1 B8Ca3 D8Ra8 H5Ba2 A4Ca9
B5Ca1 G5Ca6 A1Ca1 E3Ca5 H2Ca7 J2Rb4 J4Cb7
G4Bb4 B2Ca8 G8Ca7 E6Ra4 C5Ba4 D6Ba9 A6Rb2
D5Rb7 G7Rb9 A2Cb5 C6Cb7 C2Bb2 A8Bb6 J8Ca5
F9Ca9 A9Ra4 C9Ra5 E2Ra9 F7Ra7 G1Ra5 J9Ra2
B7Ba2 B9Ba7 F2Ba1 E7Ba6 H1Ba8 H7Ba4 E4Rb1
E8Rb2 F4Rb6 G9Rb8 H9Rb6 J1Rb6 C1Cb3 H3Cb9
B3Bb4 C3Bb6 D1Bb4 B1Ca9 D3Ca3

389	5	7	123469	2346	13469	138	123	1248
4	39	36	8	23567	135679	137	1235	1257
38	1	2	347	3457	3457	9	6	4578
6	23	13	5	9	37	4	8	127
2389	23489	348	3467	1	3467	67	259	2567
19	7	5	46	8	2	16	19	3
1358	6	9	134	345	1345	2	7	18
12357	234	134	1234567	234567	8	136	13	9
12378	238	138	123679	2367	13679	5	4	168

B3Ca6 A7Ca8 C1Ra8 F4Ra4 B2Ca9 E7Ca7 D6Ra7
F7Ra6 G9Ra8 A1Ba3 J9Ba6 H3Rb4 H2Cb2 E3Cb8
D2Bb3 E2Bb4 E1Ca2 J2Ca8 J3Ca3 D9Ra2 E8Ra9
F1Ba9 F8Ba1 E9Ba5 A8Rb2 D3Rb1 H8Rb3 H7Cb1
B8Cb5 B6Bb1 B7Bb3 J4Ca2 A9Ca1 B5Ra2 J1Ra1
J6Ra9 A4Ba9 C9Ba4 H1Ba7 G4Ba1 B9Rb7 G1Rb5
H4Rb6 J5Rb7 E4Cb3 H5Cb5 C4Bb7 C5Bb3 E6Bb6
A5Ca6 G6Ca3 C6Ca5 A6Ra4 G5Ra4

3	2	47	6	479	4789	1	5	4789
1467	16	8	2	14579	479	467	3467	34679
1467	9	5	3	147	478	4678	2	4678
14568	7	2	145	13456	346	9	146	456
1456	1356	134	14579	8	34679	467	1467	24567
1456	156	9	1457	124567	467	3	8	24567
17	4	137	78	367	2	5	9	3678
579	35	37	4789	34679	1	2	3467	34678
279	8	6	479	3479	5	47	347	1

```
J1Ca2 D1Ca8 A2Ca2 F5Ca2 C7Ca8 A6Ra8 B5Ra5
E9Ra2 C5Ba1 H1Ba9 H2Ra5 E2Ca3 D6Ca3 B7Ca6
C1Ra6 F2Ba6 B2Rb1 D5Rb4 F6Cb7 C6Bb4 E6Ca6
C9Ra7 E4Ra9 A5Ba7 J5Ba9 A3Rb4 B6Rb9 B1Cb7
E3Cb1 A9Cb9 G1Bb1 D8Ca1 D9Ra6 E1Ra5 F4Ra1
J8Ra3 B9Ba3 F1Ba4 D4Ba5 F9Ba5 H8Ba6 B8Rb4
G9Rb8 H5Rb3 H3Cb7 G4Cb7 G5Cb6 E8Cb7 H9Cb4
E7Bb4 G3Bb3 H4Bb8 J4Bb4 J7Bb7
```

9	347	347	5	1	3468	247	236	2347
2	6	134	7	34	349	8	1359	349
5	1347	8	369	346	2	1479	1369	3479
1347	9	6	1238	23478	3478	1257	1258	27
8	12347	12347	1239	5	3479	1279	129	6
17	1257	127	12689	2678	6789	3	4	279
137	12378	12379	4	2378	378	6	239	5
346	234	5	236	236	1	249	7	8
3467	23478	2347	2368	9	5	24	23	1

```
F2Ca5 G3Ca9 D7Ca5 D8Ca8 A6Ra8 B8Ra5 H7Ra9
J7Ba4 F6Ca6 A8Ca6 B3Ra1 G2Ca1 G5Ra8 F4Ba8
J2Ba8 G6Ba7 G1Rb3 G8Cb2 J8Bb3 D4Ca1 F1Ra1
F9Ra9 C8Ba9 E8Rb1 E4Ca9 C7Ca1 B6Ra9 D6Ra3
E3Ba3 E6Ba4 A3Rb4 D1Ca4 H2Ca4 D5Ra7 E7Ra7
H4Ra2 F3Ba7 F5Ba2 D9Ba2 J3Ba2 H5Ba3 A7Rb2
B5Rb4 E2Rb2 H1Rb6 J4Rb6 J1Cb7 C4Cb3 C5Cb6
B9Cb3 C2Bb7 A9Bb7 A2Ca3 C9Ca4
```

279	3	79	4	6	8	12	129	5
24789	1	45679	257	259	79	3	269	2469
249	24569	4569	25	1259	3	8	1269	7
12478	245678	14567	9	23	6	124567	123567	123468
248	2468	3	1	7	5	9	26	2468
12789	256789	15679	28	23	4	12567	123567	12368
5	479	8	6	149	179	127	12379	1239
13479	479	2	57	1459	179	1567	8	1369
6	79	179	3	8	2	157	4	19

```
H1Ca3 F4Ca8 D6Ca6 D7Ca4 B1Ra8 J7Ra5 C5Ba1
B9Ba4 J3Ba1 J9Rb9 J2Cb7 C3Ca4 E1Ca4 E8Rb2
B8Cb6 B3Bb5 C8Bb9 F3Ca6 H5Ca5 G9Ca2 B4Ra2
C4Ra5 C2Ra6 E9Ra6 F1Ra9 G8Ra3 H2Ra4 A3Ba9
B6Ba7 A7Ba2 D1Ba1 D9Ba8 G2Ba9 G5Ba4 H7Ba6
A1Rb7 A8Rb1 B5Rb9 C1Rb2 D3Rb7 E2Rb8 G6Rb1
H4Rb7 H9Rb1 H6Cb9 G7Cb7 D8Cb5 F9Cb3 D2Bb2
F5Bb2 F7Bb1 F8Bb7 F2Ca5 D5Ca3
```

3	467	146	8	5	1269	12679	124679	1469
47	5	146	12469	12469	1269	3	8	1469
48	2	9	7	146	136	16	146	1456
1	479	45	234569	24679	23569	8	4679	469
6	479	3	149	8	19	5	1479	2
45789	4789	2	14569	14679	1569	1679	14679	3
289	3689	68	1269	1269	7	4	5	1689
24589	1	7	2569	269	25689	269	3	689
2589	689	568	12569	3	4	1269	1269	7

```
G2Ca3 D4Ca3 H6Ca8 C9Ca5 B1Ra7 C6Ra3 C1Ra8
H1Ra4 F2Ba8 G9Ba8 G3Rb6 J2Cb9 G1Bb2 F1Ca9
A2Ca6 J3Ca8 H4Ra5 D3Ba5 J1Ba5 F6Ca5 H7Ca9
H5Ra2 D6Ba2 J4Ba6 H9Rb6 B4Ca2 B6Ca6 G4Ca1
C5Ca1 E6Ca1 D8Ca9 C8Ra4 D5Ra6 E4Ra9 G5Ra9
B5Ba4 A6Ba9 C7Ba6 F4Ba4 F5Ba7 D9Ba4 A9Rb1
B3Rb1 D2Rb7 E8Rb7 F7Rb1 E2Cb4 A3Cb4 J7Cb2
A8Cb2 F8Cb6 B9Cb9 A7Bb7 J8Bb1
```

578	579	59	12789	1259	6	3	189	1489
3678	679	2	1789	19	14789	68	5	14689
1	4	59	89	59	3	7	689	2
25	3	8	1269	7	1259	4	269	569
257	12579	159	12369	4	1259	2568	23689	5689
245	259	6	239	8	259	1	7	59
9	126	7	5	126	128	268	4	3
2456	8	145	12367	1236	127	9	126	1567
256	1256	3	4	1269	12789	2568	1268	15678

B1Ca3 H3Ca4 H5Ca3 B6Ca4 E8Ca3 A9Ra4 C8Ra6
F4Ra3 F1Ra4 B2Ba6 A1Ba8 B7Rb8 E1Ca7 E3Ca1
C4Ca8 J8Ca8 B4Ra7 E9Ra8 G6Ra8 A2Ba7 J9Ca7
H6Ra7 H8Ba1 A8Rb9 H4Rb2 A3Cb5 A4Cb1 D8Cb2
B9Cb1 C3Bb9 A5Bb2 B5Bb9 D1Bb5 J1Ca2 J2Ca5
C5Ca5 D6Ra1 G7Ra2 H9Ra5 J6Ra9 E7Ba5 G2Ba1
H1Ba6 J7Ba6 E6Rb2 F9Rb9 G5Rb6 J5Rb1 E2Cb9
F2Cb2 F6Cb5 D9Cb6 D4Bb9 E4Bb6

45679	246789	245678	358	258	2358	24589	2456789	1
4567	24678	3	58	1	9	2458	245678	578
1	289	258	7	4	6	2589	3	589
2	478	9	3458	58	3458	3458	1	6
46	468	1468	345689	7	123458	34589	4589	3589
3	5	1468	4689	89	148	7	489	2
59	1	5	2	6	7	3589	589	4
4579	2479	2457	1	3	458	6	25789	5789
8	234679	24567	459	59	45	12359	2579	3579

J2Ca3 A5Ca2 J7Ca1 D2Ra7 E6Ra2 G7Ra3 J3Ra6
F6Ba1 E9Ba3 H6Ba8 G3Rb5 G1Cb9 G8Bb8 E3Ca1
F4Ra6 J8Ra2 J9Ra7 A1Ca5 B4Ba5 A6Rb3 B9Rb8
A4Cb8 D4Ca3 J4Ca4 D6Ca4 D5Ra5 J5Ra9 F5Ba8
E4Ba9 J6Ba5 D7Rb8 F3Rb4 E1Cb6 A3Cb7 E7Cb5
F8Cb9 B1Bb4 A8Bb6 E2Bb8 E8Bb4 H3Bb2 H8Bb5
H1Ca7 H2Ca4 B2Ca6 C3Ca8 A7Ca4 B8Ca7 C9Ca5
A2Ra9 B7Ra2 H9Ra9 C2Ba2 C7Ba9

9	1238	123578	1237	6	12378	1238	28	4
268	12368	12368	4	128	12389	5	268	7
268	4	123678	1237	128	5	12368	9	12368
268	5	23689	126	4	128	2368	7	2368
1	268	268	2567	3	278	2468	24568	9
2468	7	2368	256	9	28	23468	1	2368
256	9	1256	8	125	124	12467	3	126
7	128	4	12359	125	6	1289	28	128
3	1268	1268	129	7	1249	124689	2468	5

F1Ca4 G1Ca5 D3Ca9 G7Ca7 E8Ca5 A3Ra5 B6Ra9
E7Ra4 F4Ra5 G6Ra4 H4Ra3 C3Ba7 A6Ba3 F3Ba3
H5Ba5 J4Ba9 J8Ba4 B2Ca3 E6Ca7 H7Ca9 B8Ca6
A4Ra7 C1Ra6 B1Ca8 D4Ca6 D6Ra1 C5Ba8 F6Ba8
G5Ba1 B5Rb2 D1Rb2 E4Rb2 J6Rb2 B3Cb1 C4Cb1
A2Bb2 G3Ca2 H8Ca2 H9Ca1 A7Ra1 G9Ra6 H2Ra8
J2Ra1 A8Ba8 E3Ba8 F7Ba6 J3Ba6 J7Ba8 D7Rb3
E2Rb6 F9Rb2 C7Cb2 C9Cb3 D9Cb8

8	245	6	3	457	257	9	1	245
12345	9	235	1246	456	125	7	2456	8
12345	12345	2357	1246789	45678	125789	3456	2456	2345
3459	345	35	48	2	6	345	7	1
2345	23456	1	47	9	37	8	2456	2345
7	8	23	5	1	3	346	2469	2349
1235	1235	2358	126789	35678	1235789	145	4589	4579
6	125	4	12789	578	125789	15	3	579
135	7	9	18	358	4	2	58	6

D1Ca9 E2Ca6 C3Ca7 G3Ca8 D4Ra8 E4Ba4 J8Ba8
F6Rb3 J4Rb1 F3Cb2 E6Cb7 A5Ra7 D2Ba4 A9Ra4
F9Rb9 G8Ca9 G7Ra4 F8Ba4 H7Ba1 F7Rb6 B6Ca1
G2Ca3 G1Ra1 J5Ra3 C2Ba1 H2Ba2 A2Rb5 J1Rb5
E1Cb3 B3Cb3 A6Cb2 B4Bb6 D3Bb5 E9Bb2 G6Bb5
G4Ca2 G5Ca6 C7Ca5 C8Ca6 C9Ca3 H9Ca5 B5Ra5
C1Ra2 D7Ra3 E8Ra5 G9Ra7 H4Ra7 B1Ba4 C5Ba4
B8Ba2 H6Ba9 C4Rb9 C6Rb8 H5Rb8

14678	14678	67	2	378	9	134567	345	1356
46789	3	5	1	78	478	467	249	269
1479	2	79	37	5	6	1347	8	139
3	9	2	6	128	5	148	24	7
127	17	4	3789	123789	12378	1358	6	123589
5	167	8	4	12379	1237	13	239	1239
24678	45678	2367	378	23678	2378	9	1	3568
689	568	1	389	4	38	2	7	3568
26789	678	23679	5	1236789	12378	368	3	4

B6Ca4 A8Ca5 F2Ra6 D3Rb2 J8Rb3 D8Cb4 G3Ca3
E7Ca5 D7Ra8 D5Rb1 J7Rb6 B7Cb7 B5Bb8 A3Ca6
G5Ca6 J6Ca1 B9Ra6 H1Ra6 B8Ba2 B1Rb9 F8Rb9
C3Cb7 C4Bb3 J3Bb9 G4Ca7 E5Ca9 C9Ca9 A5Ra7
H6Ra3 H4Ra9 F5Ba3 F6Ba7 G6Ba8 E4Rb8 E6Rb2
F7Rb1 G9Rb5 J5Rb2 G2Cb4 C7Cb4 E9Cb3 F9Cb2
H9Cb8 C1Bb1 A7Bb3 A9Bb1 G1Bb2 H2Bb5 A1Ca4
E2Ca1 A2Ra8 E1Ra7 J2Ba7 J1Ba8

489	3	479	145	45689	1489	14569	2	14579
1	247	5	3	469	249	8	47	479
2489	6	249	145	7	12489	1459	345	13459
346	5	346	9	2	48	7	1	348
24	1247	8	6	3	147	245	9	245
2349	1247	123479	147	48	5	24	6	2348
2456	9	1246	8	45	47	3	457	12457
7	48	34	2	1	6	459	458	4589
23458	1248	1234	457	459	3479	12459	4578	6

J6Ca3 A7Ca6 C8Ca3 B5Ra6 H3Ra3 J5Ba9 H8Ca5
H2Ra8 J8Ba8 B8Rb4 G8Cb7 G6Bb4 E6Ca7 E2Ra1
J4Ra7 F4Ba1 F5Ba4 G5Ba5 A5Rb8 D6Rb8 F7Rb2
F2Cb7 J7Cb1 D9Cb3 B2Bb2 F3Bb9 F9Bb8 G9Bb2
F1Ca3 J1Ca5 C1Ca8 J2Ca4 G3Ca1 J3Ca2 A3Ca7
C6Ca2 B9Ra7 C9Ra1 E1Ra2 G1Ra6 A1Ba9 A6Ba1
D3Ba6 A9Rb5 B6Rb9 C3Rb4 D1Rb4 A4Cb4 C4Cb5
C7Cb9 E9Cb4 E7Bb5 H7Bb4 H9Bb9

1369	4	139	1356	13578	2	35679	3567	15679
5	7	1239	136	13	36	2369	8	12469
1236	1236	8	9	4	3567	23567	23567	12567
1237	123	6	135	1235	4	2357	9	8
12379	1239	5	13	123	8	4	2367	267
4	2389	239	7	6	359	235	1	25
23678	2368	2347	3456	9	3567	1	2567	2567
23679	5	2379	8	37	1	2679	4	2679
16789	1689	1479	2	57	567	56789	567	3

G4Ca4 A5Ca8 F6Ca9 J7Ca8 B9Ca4 F2Ra8 J3Ra4
C6Ba7 G1Ba8 A3Ca1 C9Ra1 A4Ba5 B4Ca6 B5Ra1
B6Ba3 D5Ba5 J5Rb7 H5Cb3 E5Bb2 B3Ca9 B7Ra2
F9Ba2 F3Rb3 F7Cb5 D2Ca2 G8Ca2 G9Ca5 C1Ra2
C8Ra5 G2Ra3 G3Ra7 J6Ra5 A1Ba3 H3Ba2 H1Ba6
G6Ba6 C2Rb6 J8Rb6 C7Cb3 A8Cb7 D7Bb7 E8Bb3
E1Ca7 D4Ca3 A7Ca6 H9Ca7 A9Ra9 D1Ra1 E9Ra6
E2Ra9 H7Ra9 E4Ba1 J2Ba1 J1Ba9

6	1789	1479	2	3578	578	13459	3589	1359
1458	178	147	9	6	578	2	358	135
2589	289	3	58	1	4	569	7	569
7	6	29	35	2359	1	8	2359	4
1239	4	8	356	2359	2569	35679	23569	23569
239	239	5	7	23489	2689	369	1	2369
12389	5	1279	4	2789	26789	1369	2369	12369
12489	1289	6	58	2589	3	159	259	7
239	2379	279	1	2579	25679	3569	4	8

E4Ca6 F5Ca4 A7Ca4 E7Ca7 E1Ra1 F6Ra8 H1Ra4
B3Ba4 A5Ba3 D4Ca3 G8Ca6 J6Ra6 C4Ba8 H4Rb5
J7Ra5 G7Ca3 G3Ra1 H7Ba1 G5Ra7 H5Ba8 J2Ca7
B6Ra7 G1Ra8 J1Ra3 A3Ba7 A6Ba5 F2Ba3 B1Rb5
F7Ca9 C9Ca5 C7Ra6 F9Ra6 D3Ba9 F1Rb2 J3Rb2
C1Cb9 H2Cb9 J5Cb9 C2Bb2 G6Bb2 H8Bb2 E6Ca9
A8Ca9 E9Ca2 A2Ra8 D5Ra2 E8Ra3 G9Ra9 B2Ba1
B9Ba3 B8Ba8 E5Ba5 D8Ba5 A9Rb1

235	1259	1359	7	8	259	249	239	6
2567	4	579	3	2569	2569	2789	1	2789
2367	12679	8	169	1269	4	5	239	279
4	8	59	569	2569	1	3	7	29
1	2579	3579	569	245679	25679	2489	25689	2489
257	2579	6	8	24579	3	1249	259	1249
5678	1567	2	4	15679	56789	1789	89	3
5678	3	157	2	15679	56789	1789	4	1789
9	17	147	1	137	78	6	28	5

J3Ca4 J5Ca3 E8Ca6 A7Ra4 E3Ra3 J8Ra2 F8Ba5
J4Rb1 J2Cb7 J6Bb8 B3Ca7 C5Ca1 G8Ca8 C9Ra7
H1Ra8 F1Ba7 C1Ca2 A6Ca2 C8Ra3 A1Ba3 A8Ba9
C4Rb6 C2Cb9 F2Bb2 G2Ca6 D3Ca9 H6Ca6 B1Ra6
D4Ra5 D5Ra6 G7Ra1 E2Ba5 E5Ba2 F9Ba1 H3Ba1
H7Ba7 A2Rb1 A3Rb5 D9Rb2 E4Rb9 F7Rb9 G1Rb5
H9Rb9 F5Cb4 H5Cb5 E6Cb7 E7Cb8 B9Cb8 B5Bb9
B7Bb2 E9Bb4 G6Bb9 G5Ca7 B6Ca5

4589	1	3458	6	489	2	3589	7	3489
7	459	4568	4589	489	3	2	458	1
24589	3459	3458	45789	4789	1	6	458	3489
1	4579	4578	2345789	2346789	4579	89	268	2789
4589	4579	4578	1245789	1246789	4579	189	3	2789
3	6	2	1789	1789	79	4	18	5
45	8	9	1234	1234	6	7	1245	234
6	347	1347	12347	5	47	138	9	2348
45	2	13457	13479	13479	8	135	145	6

C1Ca2 B3Ca6 D8Ca6 E5Ra6 G8Ca2 G1Ra5 H4Ra2
D5Ba2 D9Rb7 J1Rb4 E9Cb2 D4Ra3 F6Ca9 J5Ca3
H6Ca7 H9Ca4 G9Ra3 H7Ra8 J3Ra7 J4Ra9 A7Ba3
E2Ba7 F8Ba8 H3Ba1 D7Rb9 H2Rb3 E7Cb1 J7Bb5
C3Ca3 J8Ca1 A3Ra5 D3Ra8 E1Ra9 A1Ba8 D2Ba5
E4Ba8 A9Rb9 D6Rb4 E3Rb4 A5Cb4 E6Cb5 C9Cb8
B4Bb5 G5Bb1 F4Ca1 G4Ca4 B5Ca8 C8Ca5 B2Ra9
C2Ra4 F5Ra7 C4Ba7 C5Ba9 B8Ba4

25	6	12	129	7	1259	124	8	3
4	1257	3	1268	256	12568	126	9	1267
25	8	9	1236	2356	4	126	157	1267
2369	12479	12467	2679	8	2679	123469	1347	5
8	2479	2467	5	1	2679	23469	347	267
269	12479	5	2679	2469	3	124689	147	12678
569	459	468	13689	3569	15689	7	2	18
7	3	268	12689	269	12689	5	1	4
1	25	28	4	235	2578	38	6	9

D1Ca3 F5Ca4 C8Ca5 A7Ra4 C9Ra7 J6Ra7 B2Ba7
J7Ba3 C1Rb2 H8Rb1 A1Cb5 A3Cb1 F8Cb7 G9Cb8
D8Bb4 D4Ca7 F7Ca8 E8Ca3 E3Ra7 J3Ra8 E2Ba4
G3Ca4 H6Ca8 B4Ra8 G1Ca6 D3Ca6 H4Ca6 H5Ca9
F9Ra6 G2Ra9 H3Ra2 F1Ba9 E6Ba6 D7Ba1 J2Ba5
J5Ba2 C7Rb6 D2Rb2 E9Rb2 F4Rb2 F2Cb1 A4Cb9
C5Cb3 D6Cb9 B7Cb2 E7Cb9 B9Cb1 A6Bb2 B6Bb5
C4Bb1 G5Bb5 G4Ca3 B5Ca6 G6Ca1

7	4	69	2	368	689	138	5	18
1	2359	259	3589	358	7	6	34	248
356	235	8	1356	356	4	137	9	127
8	12579	12579	4567	4567	256	13479	13467	14579
459	579	579	45678	1	3	2	467	4579
45	6	3	457	9	25	147	8	1457
369	8	1679	34679	2	69	5	147	1479
2	579	4	56789	5678	1	789	7	3
359	13579	1579	345789	34578	589	14789	2	6

C4Ca1 E4Ra8 F6Ra2 H8Rb7 E8Ra6 G8Ca1 G6Rb9
G9Cb4 E9Bb5 B4Ca9 D9Ca9 A3Ra9 B8Ra4 E1Ra4
C1Ba6 F1Ba5 E2Ba9 D8Rb3 E3Rb7 G1Rb3 H2Rb5
J1Cb9 G3Cb6 J3Cb1 G4Cb7 H4Cb6 D3Bb2 F4Bb4
J2Bb7 H5Bb8 J5Bb4 J7Bb8 D2Ca1 B3Ca5 J4Ca3
A5Ca6 D5Ca7 A6Ca8 D7Ca4 H7Ca9 A7Ra3 B9Ra8
C5Ra5 D6Ra6 J6Ra5 B5Ba3 A9Ba1 C9Ba2 D4Ba5
B2Rb2 C2Rb3 C7Rb7 F9Rb7 F7Cb1

6	2	3579	389	1	78	4	3589	359
4	159	1359	2389	269	268	368	235689	7
39	79	8	239	5	2467	1	2369	239
58	1568	156	4	26	3	9	1278	12
7	1469	2	19	8	16	5	134	13
3589	14589	1359	7	29	125	38	12348	6
1	579	4	6	3	257	7	579	8
2589	56789	5679	1258	247	124578	367	135679	1359
58	3	567	158	7	9	2	1567	4

H1Ca2 H5Ca4 C6Ra4 D8Ra7 G6Ra2 A6Ba7 F6Ba5
G7Rb7 J5Rb7 H3Ca7 C8Ra6 C2Ra7 H7Ba6 J3Ra6
B5Ca9 B7Ca3 B6Ra6 E4Ra9 E6Ba1 D5Ba6 E9Rb3
F5Rb2 F7Rb8 H6Rb8 E8Cb4 E2Bb6 F8Bb1 F2Ca4
D2Ca8 B8Ca2 H8Ca3 H9Ca1 B4Ra8 C4Ra2 D3Ra1
D9Ra2 H2Ra9 J4Ra1 J1Ra8 B2Ba1 A4Ba3 A8Ba8
D1Ba5 G2Ba5 H4Ba5 G8Ba9 B3Rb5 C9Rb9 J8Rb5
C1Cb3 A3Cb9 A9Cb5 F1Bb9 F3Bb3

7	2356	2356	1268	9	4	156	58	568
56	8	1	3	56	7	4569	2	4569
256	4	2569	1268	2568	12568	15679	3	5689
3568	7	3568	4	568	15689	3569	59	2
4	256	256	2679	3	2569	8	1	569
9	1	23568	2678	2568	2568	34567	457	3456
23568	2356	235678	2689	1	23689	23459	4589	34589
23568	9	4	268	7	2368	235	58	1
1238	23	238	5	248	2389	2349	6	7

J1Ca1 G3Ca7 C3Ca9 J5Ca4 F8Ca7 C7Ra7 D6Ra1
E4Ra7 A7Ba1 E6Ba9 C4Ca1 G4Ca9 G8Ca4 J7Ra9
B9Ba9 D8Ba9 B7Rb4 F9Ca4 G9Ca3 H8Ba8 A8Rb5
G2Ca5 E9Ca5 H7Ra5 G7Ba2 C9Ca6 B5Ra6 C5Ra8
C6Ba5 A9Ba8 F4Ba8 A4Rb2 B1Rb5 C1Rb2 D5Rb5
H4Cb6 F5Cb2 F6Bb6 H1Bb3 G6Bb8 G1Ca6 D1Ca8
A2Ca3 F3Ca5 J6Ca3 D7Ca6 A3Ra6 D3Ra3 F7Ra3
H6Ra2 J3Ra8 E2Ba6 J2Ba2 E3Rb2

1	2358	23	278	9	238	4	6	357
346	2368	234	24678	5	2368	137	17	9
3456	3569	7	46	1	36	8	2	35
57	1259	129	3	26	12568	15679	145789	14567
8	4	6	125	2	7	159	3	15
357	135	13	1568	4	9	2	1578	1567
9	136	8	12567	2367	4	13567	157	123567
2	136	5	1679	8	136	13679	1479	13467
346	7	134	12569	236	12356	13569	1459	8

D3Ca9 G5Ca7 G9Ca2 C2Ra9 E7Ra9 D2Ba2 D5Rb6
E5Rb2 J5Cb3 F9Ra6 J6Ca5 E4Ra5 J4Ra2 D6Ba1
H4Ba9 E9Rb1 F4Rb8 H6Rb6 A4Cb7 G4Cb1 C6Cb3
C9Bb5 G8Bb5 D7Ca5 D8Ca8 J8Ca9 A2Ra5 D9Ra4
B2Ba8 F1Ba5 F8Ba7 H8Ba4 A9Rb3 B6Rb2 B8Rb1
D1Rb7 F2Rb1 H2Cb3 A3Cb2 F3Cb3 A6Cb8 B7Cb7
H9Cb7 B3Bb4 G2Bb6 H7Bb1 B1Ca3 J1Ca4 J3Ca1
C4Ca4 G7Ca3 J7Ca6 B4Ra6 C1Ra6

2	17	3	469	679	467	8	5	4679
5678	9	5678	1	2367	4678	247	2367	2467
4	178	678	3689	23679	5	1279	123679	2679
58	6	24589	7	15	3	1249	129	2489
578	24578	24578	456	156	9	1247	1267	3
7	347	1	2	8	46	5	679	4679
3	578	5678	5689	5679	2	79	4	1
9	12457	2457	35	1357	17	6	8	27
1678	1278	2678	689	4	1678	3	279	5

J1Ca1 F2Ca3 D3Ca9 D9Ca8 A2Ra1 D7Ra4 D1Rb5
F1Rb7 E1Cb8 D5Cb1 B1Bb6 D8Bb2 H6Ca1 B3Ra5
F6Ra4 A4Ba4 H9Ba2 B9Ca4 B6Ra8 J6Ca7 A9Ca7
A5Ra9 B5Ra7 C5Ba2 G7Ba7 A6Rb6 B7Rb2 B8Rb3
E7Rb1 J8Rb9 C4Cb3 C7Cb9 E8Cb7 F8Cb6 C8Bb1
C9Bb6 F9Bb9 H4Bb5 G2Ca5 G4Ca9 H5Ca3 E5Ca5
E4Ra6 G3Ra8 C2Ba8 J3Ba6 G5Ba6 J4Ba8 C3Rb7
J2Rb2 E2Cb4 H3Cb4 E3Bb2 H2Bb7

3	2678	2678	5	4	1	278	689	6789
4578	9	278	237	6	37	124578	1458	1578
457	124567	267	8	9	7	12457	1456	3
2	78	4	367	135	35678	9	1358	158
6	3	5	49	1	48	148	7	2
1	78	789	3479	35	2	6	3458	58
4578	245678	23678	1	235	9	3578	3568	5678
4589	4568	3689	346	7	3456	1358	2	15689
579	2567	1	236	8	356	357	3569	4

C2Ca1 G5Ca2 E4Ra9 J2Ra2 B4Ba2 F3Ba9 C6Rb7
E5Rb1 B6Cb3 A2Ca6 C8Ra6 C3Rb2 A7Ca2 G2Ca4
H2Ba5 H6Rb4 H4Cb3 E6Cb8 D6Bb6 E7Bb4 H3Bb6
J4Bb6 G3Ca3 F4Ca4 J6Ca5 B8Ca4 G9Ca6 C1Ra4
F2Ra7 J7Ra3 B1Ba5 D2Ba8 D4Ba7 G7Ba7 C7Rb5
G1Rb8 J8Rb9 H1Cb9 J1Cb7 A8Cb8 G8Cb5 A3Bb7
B7Bb1 F8Bb3 B3Ca8 D5Ca3 H7Ca8 D8Ca1 B9Ca7
A9Ca9 D9Ra5 F9Ra8 H9Ra1 F5Ba5

2	36	4	1	368	7	5	69	369
35	7	1356	456	9	235	12346	146	8
8	136	9	456	23456	235	7	146	12346
1	2389	358	4589	7	6	2349	459	2349
357	4	3578	2	158	1589	1369	15679	1369
6	29	57	3	145	159	8	14579	1249
9	1368	2	5678	13568	4	16	168	16
347	1368	13678	6789	1368	1389	1469	2	5
4	5	168	689	1268	1289	1469	3	7

G8Ca8 A5Ra8 G4Ra7 G5Ba5 E5Rb1 J1Rb4 F5Cb4
H2Ca8 G2Ra3 H7Ra4 J7Ba9 A2Rb6 H1Rb7 C2Cb1
A8Cb9 A9Bb3 B6Rb2 J5Ca2 D7Ca2 C9Ra2 D3Ra3
F2Ra2 B1Ba3 E3Ba8 D2Ba9 E7Ba3 B3Rb5 D9Rb4
E1Rb5 F3Cb7 E6Cb9 D8Cb5 D4Bb8 F6Bb5 E9Bb6
F8Bb1 C4Ca5 H4Ca9 J6Ca8 E8Ca7 G9Ca1 F9Ca9
B7Ra1 C8Ra4 G7Ra6 J3Ra1 B4Ba4 B8Ba6 H3Ba6
H6Ba1 C6Rb3 H5Rb3 J4Rb6 C5Cb6

12678	1478	12467	1278	9	1248	168	5	3
1278	3	12457	6	2478	12458	9	78	178
16789	15789	1567	1378	378	1358	2	678	4
189	6	134	138	5	138	7	2	8
5	178	1237	4	23678	12368	368	368	9
278	478	2347	2378	23678	9	34568	1	58
167	2	8	5	346	346	134	3479	17
3	15	156	9	2468	7	1458	48	1258
4	57	9	238	1	238	358	378	6

C2Ca9 G8Ca9 H9Ca2 D3Ra4 D1Ra9 A2Ba4 F7Ba4
D9Rb8 F9Cb5 H8Ca4 F5Ra6 G6Ba6 H5Rb8 B6Ca4
E8Ca3 B3Ra5 E7Ra6 G7Ra3 G5Ra4 H3Ra6 C6Ba5
C8Ba6 F3Ba3 A1Ca6 C5Ca3 E5Ca7 B5Rb2 F1Ca2
A3Ra2 E6Ra2 F2Ra7 E2Ba8 F4Ba8 G1Ba7 J4Ba2
E3Rb1 G9Rb1 J2Rb5 J6Rb3 H2Cb1 C3Cb7 D6Cb1
H7Cb5 J7Cb8 B9Cb7 A6Bb8 C4Bb1 A7Bb1 B8Bb8
D4Bb3 J8Bb7 B1Ca1 C1Ca8 A4Ca7

267	267	4	12	9	3	8	125	2567
26	5	269	1248	7	1468	126	123	236
3	2678	1	28	5	68	267	9	4
1247	1247	27	124789	1248	145789	3	6	2589
9	3	5	1248	12468	1468	12	7	28
8	1267	267	12379	126	15679	4	125	259
5	1479	79	6	148	2	79	348	3789
12467	124679	8	5	3	1479	2679	24	2679
2467	24679	3	4789	48	4789	25679	2458	1

C2Ca8 F4Ca3 J7Ca5 B3Ra9 C7Ra7 C4Rb2 C6Rb6
G3Rb7 G7Rb9 D3Cb2 A4Cb1 F3Bb6 E5Ca6 H9Ca7
F5Ba2 H7Ba6 A8Rb5 G9Rb3 F8Cb1 B8Bb3 F2Bb7
E7Bb2 A1Ca7 B7Ca1 E6Ra1 E4Ba4 G5Ba1 B4Rb8
D5Rb8 E9Rb8 G2Rb4 D2Cb1 J5Cb4 B6Cb4 G8Cb8
D1Bb4 H6Bb9 J8Bb2 H1Ca1 J2Ca9 D4Ca9 J6Ca8
H8Ca4 D6Ra7 F9Ra9 H2Ra2 J1Ra6 J4Ra7 B1Ba2
A2Ba6 F6Ba5 D9Ba5 A9Rb2 B9Rb6

156	7	156	13569	8	2	369	4	1359
9	68	1568	13567	3567	4	368	2	1357
12456	2468	3	15679	567	1567	689	6789	1579
246	24689	24689	34567	234567	3567	1	36789	3479
7	2468	12468	346	2346	9	5	368	34
3	5	2469	467	1	8	269	679	479
46	346	467	2	9	1367	3	5	8
8	1	2459	345	345	35	7	39	6
56	369	5679	35678	3567	3567	4	1	2

```
J4Ca8 F7Ca2 E3Ra1 G6Ra1 H3Ra2 H8Ba9 G7Rb3
A1Ca1 J2Ca3 G3Ca7 J3Ra9 D2Ba9 J1Ba5 F9Ra9
C7Ca8 C4Ra9 B4Ba1 A7Ba9 B7Rb6 C8Rb7 E9Rb4
B2Cb8 F8Cb6 D9Cb7 B3Bb5 F3Bb4 D3Ca8 F4Ca7
J6Ca7 C9Ca1 B5Ra7 E8Ra8 J5Ra6 A3Ba6 A4Ba3
A9Ba5 D8Ba3 B9Rb3 C5Rb5 E4Rb6 E2Cb2 C6Cb6
D6Cb5 C2Bb4 D1Bb6 D4Bb4 E5Bb3 H6Bb3 C1Ca2
G1Ca4 G2Ca6 H4Ca5 D5Ca2 H5Ca4
```

34567	3567	456	34589	356789	2	679	189	1678
4567	8	1	459	5679	45679	2	9	3
2367	9	26	38	1	367	67	5	4
23469	36	2469	7	2369	1369	8	12349	5
235679	3567	8	2359	4	13569	369	1239	16
1	356	24569	23589	235689	3569	3469	7	6
589	4	59	6	23579	3579	1	38	78
569	156	7	3459	359	8	345	34	2
58	2	3	1	57	457	457	6	9

```
H2Ca1 C4Ra8 G5Ra2 H1Ra6 J1Ra8 F5Ba8 B8Rb9
F9Rb6 E9Cb1 D6Ca1 A8Ca1 A9Ra8 G9Ba7 G8Ba8
G6Ra3 C1Ra3 C3Ba2 F4Ra2 C7Ca6 C6Ra7 A7Ba7
J5Ba7 B1Rb7 E2Ca7 E6Ra6 B5Ba6 F6Ba9 D5Rb3
D2Cb6 E4Cb5 A5Cb9 A2Bb5 A4Bb3 B4Bb4 E1Bb2
H5Bb5 G1Ca5 F2Ca3 A3Ca6 H4Ca9 J6Ca4 B6Ca5
J7Ca5 E7Ca9 D8Ca2 A1Ra4 E8Ra3 F3Ra5 G3Ra9
D3Ba4 D1Ba9 F7Ba4 H7Ba3 H8Rb4
```

359	3469	456	2	3458	7	489	389	1
235	2347	1	3458	3458	9	6	238	248
239	8	4	134	34	6	5	7	24
4	269	568	1389	7	1238	1289	125689	2568
2589	29	58	6	2489	1248	124789	12589	3
7	1	3	489	2489	5	2489	2689	2468
138	5	2	3489	34689	348	18	168	7
138	37	9	3578	23568	238	128	4	2568
6	47	478	4578	1	248	3	258	9

```
J3Ca7 E7Ca7 B2Ra7 C4Ra1 C1Ra9 H4Ra7 B1Ba2
J2Ba4 C3Rb4 H2Rb3 A2Cb6 C5Cb3 C9Cb2 A3Bb5
A1Ca3 E1Ca5 D3Ca6 B8Ra3 E3Ba8 G8Rb6 H9Cb5
D9Bb8 H5Bb6 B5Ca5 D8Ca5 F9Ca6 B4Ra8 F7Ra4
J4Ra5 A5Ba4 B9Ba4 F5Ba8 F4Rb9 G5Rb9 D4Cb3
E5Cb2 F8Cb2 E2Bb9 D6Bb1 G4Bb4 J8Bb8 D2Ca2
G6Ca3 E6Ca4 H6Ca8 H7Ca2 A7Ca8 E8Ca1 A8Ca9
D7Ra9 G1Ra8 H1Ra1 J6Ra2 G7Ba1
```

1267	1267	156	138	13578	9	4	123567	2578
17	4	9	6	2	13578	3578	1357	578
1267	3	8	1	157	4	2567	9	257
1479	5	14	1234	1347	1237	237	8	6
467	8	46	234	9	23567	2357	23457	1
3	1679	2	148	14578	15678	57	457	579
5	269	46	2489	48	28	1	267	3
124689	1269	7	5	1348	1238	268	26	28
128	12	13	7	6	1238	9	25	4

```
J3Ca3 A3Ca5 G4Ca9 F9Ca9 D1Ra9 G8Ra7 J8Ra5
H2Ba9 C4Rb1 F8Rb4 F4Cb8 A4Bb3 D3Ca1 J1Ca8
D4Ca4 D7Ra2 E4Ba2 C7Rb6 E8Rb3 H7Cb8 B8Cb1
B1Bb7 A8Bb2 B7Bb3 H9Bb2 C1Ca2 F2Ca7 H8Ca6
F6Ra6 F5Ba1 E7Ba7 E6Rb5 F7Rb5 B6Cb8 A5Bb7
B9Bb5 G6Bb2 J2Ca2 C5Ca5 G5Ca8 D6Ca7 C9Ca7
A9Ca8 D5Ra3 G3Ra4 J6Ra1 E1Ba4 H1Ba1 G2Ba6
H6Ba3 H5Ba4 A1Rb6 A2Rb1 E3Rb6
```

125	8	1237	235	6	12359	4	12379	137
9	235	1237	4	12358	12358	178	6	1378
1246	2346	1236	7	1238	12389	189	1239	5
568	1	4	9	3578	35678	78	57	2
7	2569	2689	2568	12458	12568	3	159	168
2568	23569	23689	23568	123578	1235678	1789	4	1678
3	2	12	25	9	257	6	8	4
1268	7	12689	2368	238	4	5	13	13
468	46	5	1	378	3678	2	37	9

```
E5Ca4 G3Ra1 G6Ra7 H3Ra9 G4Ba5 J8Ba7 D8Rb5
G2Rb2 A4Ca3 D1Rb6 H1Cb8 J1Bb4 H5Bb2 C2Ca4
C3Ca6 C8Ra3 H4Ra6 A8Ba2 J2Ba6 H9Ba3 A3Rb7
H8Rb1 E8Cb9 A9Cb1 A1Bb5 E2Bb5 C1Ca1 F2Ca9
F7Ca1 C7Ca9 A6Ra9 C6Ra2 E6Ra1 F3Ra3 B3Ba2
B2Ba3 B5Ba1 E3Ba8 F6Ba6 C5Rb8 E4Rb2 E9Rb6
F1Rb2 F4Cb8 J5Cb3 B6Cb5 D5Bb7 D6Bb3 F9Bb7
J6Bb8 F5Ca5 B7Ca7 B9Ca8 D7Ra8
```

24567	1456	4567	145679	1479	1469	3	127	8
23457	9	457	1457	147	8	12457	127	6
45678	14568	45678	2	147	3	1457	9	1457
4578	458	3	1479	6	149	12579	127	1257
467	46	4679	8	5	2	1679	1367	17
567	2	1	79	3	9	8	4	57
9	3468	468	1346	1248	5	12467	12678	1247
34568	34568	2	1346	148	7	146	168	9
1	7	468	469	2489	469	246	5	3

```
E3Ca9 E8Ca3 B1Ra3 F1Ra6 A1Ba2 E7Ba6 D7Ba9
E2Rb4 F6Rb9 E1Cb7 F4Cb7 E9Bb1 F9Bb5 A2Rb1
A8Cb7 C9Bb4 D8Bb2 H1Ca4 D6Ca1 G7Ca7 B8Ca1
G9Ca2 B7Ra2 C5Ra1 D4Ra4 D9Ra7 H2Ra5 J5Ra2
B5Ba7 C7Ba5 D1Ba5 G2Ba3 J4Ba9 H7Ba1 J7Ba4
B4Rb5 C1Rb8 D2Rb8 H5Rb8 J6Rb6 C2Cb6 B3Cb4
J3Cb8 A4Cb6 G4Cb1 H4Cb3 G5Cb4 A6Cb4 H8Cb6
A3Bb5 C3Bb7 A5Bb9 G3Bb6 G8Bb8
```

13789	2379	1379	4	35678	156	1369	1269	123
134	23	5	9	36	16	1346	7	8
134789	6	13479	1378	378	2	5	149	13
2	4	1369	358	35689	569	13689	1569	7
35679	3579	3679	2358	1	4569	3689	569	35
13569	359	8	35	3569	7	2	1569	4
45679	579	2	157	4579	8	14	3	15
3459	8	349	125	2459	1459	7	1245	6
457	1	47	6	2457	3	4	8	9

```
A9Ca2 B2Ra2 E4Ra2 E6Ra4 G1Ra6 J5Ra2 H8Ba2
J7Rb4 J3Cb7 G7Cb1 J1Bb5 G9Bb5 C8Ca4 C9Ca1
B1Ra4 E7Ra8 G5Ra4 H3Ba4 G4Ba7 E9Rb3 G2Rb9
H1Cb3 H4Ca1 B6Ra1 E3Ca6 C3Ca9 B7Ca3 B5Ra6
D6Ba6 A6Rb5 D7Rb9 F5Rb9 F1Cb1 H5Cb5 H6Cb9
A7Cb6 E8Cb5 A8Bb9 D3Bb3 E2Bb7 D8Bb1 F8Bb6
E1Ca9 A2Ca3 F2Ca5 A3Ca1 C5Ca3 C1Ra7 D4Ra5
F4Ra3 A1Ba8 A5Ba7 D5Ba8 C4Rb8
```

13569	4	8	1236	1236	1369	2359	59	7
7	369	39	5	2368	34689	2349	1	2389
2	1359	1359	134	7	13489	3459	6	3589
13569	7	1359	136	13568	13568	359	2	4
13456	1356	2	13467	9	13456	8	57	135
13459	13589	13459	1347	1358	2	6	579	1359
359	359	359	236	4	7	1	589	2589
1459	2	6	8	15	15	4579	3	59
8	135	13457	9	1235	135	2457	457	6

```
F2Ca8 J3Ca7 J8Ca4 G8Ca8 G4Ra6 H1Ra4 H7Ra7
F3Ba4 J2Ba1 J5Ba2 J7Rb5 J6Cb3 H9Cb9 G9Bb2
A4Ca2 B7Ra2 C7Ba4 E4Ca4 B6Ra4 E8Ra7 F4Ba7
C6Ca9 C9Ra8 B5Ba8 A8Ba5 B9Rb3 F8Rb9 B3Cb9
A7Cb9 D7Cb3 B2Bb6 D4Bb1 G2Ca9 C3Ca1 C4Ca3
D6Ca8 A1Ra3 C2Ra5 D1Ra9 E2Ba3 E1Ba6 F5Ba3
G3Ba3 D3Rb5 E6Rb5 G1Rb5 F1Cb1 D5Cb6 H6Cb1
E9Cb1 A5Bb1 A6Bb6 F9Bb5 H5Bb5
```

23479	347	234	1689	12469	124689	5	1278	1267
279	6	1	89	29	5	4	3	27
245	8	245	16	7	3	26	12	9
1567	17	56	1569	12569	12679	3	4	8
13457	1347	9	1358	12345	12478	27	6	1257
134567	2	8	13569	134569	14679	79	1579	157
8	9	236	4	356	6	1	257	23567
12346	5	2346	7	8	169	269	29	236
136	13	7	2	13569	169	689	589	4

J7Ca8 B4Ra8 A8Ba8 E6Ba8 G6Rb6 J1Ra6 D3Ba6
C3Ca5 C1Ra4 E2Ba4 H3Ba4 G8Ca7 H9Ca3 H7Ra6
A9Ba6 B9Rb7 C7Rb2 E5Rb1 E7Cb7 C8Cb1 C4Bb6
F7Bb9 A4Ca1 F5Ca6 H8Ca2 F9Ca1 E9Ra2 F6Ra4
G3Ra2 H6Ra9 A5Ba4 D6Ba7 F8Ba5 J2Ba3 J6Ba1
J8Ba9 A2Rb7 A3Rb3 A6Rb2 D2Rb1 F4Rb3 G9Rb5
H1Rb1 J5Rb5 A1Cb9 D1Cb5 F1Cb7 E4Cb5 B5Cb9
G5Cb3 B1Bb2 E1Bb3 D4Bb9 D5Bb2

35	1	235	7	2568	2356	28	4	9
8	234579	234579	246	24569	23456	1	567	256
457	24579	6	124	124589	1245	3	57	258
9	458	145	14	3	14	6	2	7
3467	2347	12347	5	1246	8	49	139	14
3456	23458	12345	1246	7	9	48	135	1458
347	6	8	9	124	1247	5	17	124
1	4579	4579	3	2456	24567	2479	8	246
2	4579	4579	8	1456	14567	479	1679	3

D2Ra8 G1Ra3 A1Rb5 D3Ra5 F4Ca6 G6Ca7 E1Ra6
E5Ba2 F1Rb4 G8Rb1 C1Cb7 G5Cb4 F7Cb8 A7Bb2
C8Bb5 G9Bb2 B8Ca7 F9Ca5 C9Ca8 A5Ra8 B9Ra6
F3Ra1 H6Ra2 A6Ba6 F2Ba2 E9Ba1 J8Ba6 A3Rb3
F8Rb3 H9Rb4 E3Cb7 E8Cb9 E2Bb3 E7Bb4 H3Bb9
B3Ca2 H5Ca6 B6Ca3 J7Ca9 B5Ra5 C4Ra2 H2Ra5
J2Ra7 C5Ba9 J3Ba4 J6Ba5 H7Ba7 B4Rb4 C2Rb4
J5Rb1 B2Cb9 D4Cb1 C6Cb1 D6Bb4

12589	1256	568	1278	4	1578	3	1269	1679
1238	12346	3468	1278	9	178	5	1246	1467
1259	1245	7	6	25	3	29	8	149
237	2347	1	5	6	7	2789	2349	34789
6	8	35	4	1	9	27	235	37
357	3457	9	37	8	2	67	13456	13467
4	9	3568	138	35	1568	68	7	2
3578	3567	2	3789	357	45678	1	369	3689
1378	1367	368	123789	237	1678	4	369	5

B3Ca4 H6Ca4 C9Ra4 F4Ba3 D6Rb7 E7Ca7 E8Ra2
C7Ba2 F8Ba5 C5Rb5 E9Rb3 F1Rb7 F7Rb6 C2Cb1
F2Cb4 E3Cb5 G5Cb3 G7Cb8 F9Cb1 C1Bb9 D7Bb9
G3Bb6 G4Bb1 H5Bb7 J1Ca1 J2Ca7 J3Ca3 J5Ca2
G6Ca5 J6Ca6 D8Ca4 D9Ca8 H8Ra3 J4Ra8 H1Ba8
H4Ba9 H9Ba6 A3Rb8 B9Rb7 H2Rb5 J8Rb9 B4Cb2
A6Cb1 A9Cb9 B1Bb3 A4Bb7 B6Bb8 A8Bb6 A1Ca5
D2Ca3 B2Ca6 B8Ca1 A2Ra2 D1Ra2

2	47	6	479	3479	1	389	5	378
357	9	157	257	8	2357	4	6	137
8	1457	1457	6	234579	23457	1239	1379	137
579	457	3	245789	24579	6	1589	179	14578
5679	8	24579	24579	1	2457	359	379	34567
1	4567	4579	3	4579	4578	589	2	45678
567	3	1578	12578	2567	2578	15	4	9
4	2	15	15	356	9	7	8	135
579	157	15789	14578	3457	34578	6	13	2

B1Ca3 F2Ca6 E3Ca2 C7Ca2 E9Ra6 H5Ra6 G1Ba6
H9Ra3 G7Ba5 J8Rb1 C2Ca1 D7Ca1 A9Ca8 B9Ra1
D4Ra8 C9Ba7 D5Ba2 F7Ba8 G5Rb7 H4Ca5 H3Ra1
G4Ba1 G3Rb8 J4Rb4 J5Cb3 G6Cb2 J6Bb8 B4Ca2
C6Ca3 A7Ra3 E6Ra4 C8Ba9 E8Ba3 D8Rb7 E7Rb9
E4Cb7 A4Bb9 E1Bb5 F6Bb5 J1Ca7 J2Ca5 C5Ca5
F5Ca9 B6Ca7 D9Ca5 A2Ra7 B3Ra5 C3Ra4 D2Ra4
D1Ra9 F3Ra7 J3Ra9 A5Ba4 F9Ba4

89	258	3	569	7	4	569	1	2589
179	1257	2579	8	259	23569	4	23679	2359
6	2578	245789	359	259	1	3579	23789	23589
89	4	589	159	6	2589	359	239	7
2	567	5679	4	3	579	8	69	1
3	5678	1	579	2589	25789	569	2469	2459
478	9	4678	367	1	3678	2	5	348
5	23678	24678	3679	89	36789	1	34789	3489
178	1378	78	2	4	35789	379	3789	6

G1Ca4 D4Ca1 C3Ra4 J6Ra5 D7Ra5 D8Ba3 D6Ra2
J8Ra9 F7Ba9 A7Rb6 E8Rb6 B6Ra6 E6Ra9 F2Ra6
C4Ba3 C7Rb7 J7Cb3 B8Cb2 C8Bb8 F8Bb4 G9Bb8
H2Ca3 H3Ca2 C5Ca2 H8Ca7 F9Ca2 B9Ca3 H9Ca4
A2Ra2 C9Ra9 G6Ra3 H4Ra6 A1Ba8 A9Ba5 G3Ba6
G4Ba7 H5Ba9 A4Rb9 B5Rb5 C2Rb5 D1Rb9 F4Rb5
H6Rb8 E2Cb7 D3Cb8 F5Cb8 F6Cb7 B2Bb1 E3Bb5
J3Bb7 J1Ca1 B1Ca7 J2Ca8 B3Ca9

1247	467	12468	9	2478	3	5	1478	1478
457	4567	4568	5678	4578	1	2	4789	3
12457	3457	9	2578	24578	458	147	6	1478
8	3459	2345	1	459	7	6	2349	249
2479	3479	234	8	6	489	13479	5	12479
6	1	45	3	459	2	8	479	479
3	2	15	4	15789	6	179	1789	1789
1459	4569	7	258	3	589	149	12489	124689
149	8	146	27	1279	9	13479	123479	5

B4Ca6 H9Ca6 B8Ra9 C2Ra3 J3Ra6 A2Ba6 E4Rb8
J6Rb9 E6Cb4 B1Ca5 G3Ra5 D2Ba5 D5Rb9 F3Rb4
B3Cb8 F5Cb5 F8Cb7 F9Bb9 A3Ca1 G7Ca9 H7Rb4
H2Cb9 E2Bb7 H1Bb1 E1Ca9 B2Ca4 B5Ra7 J1Ra4
J4Ba7 J7Rb3 E7Cb1 C7Bb7 E9Bb2 A1Ca7 D3Ca2
D8Ca3 C9Ca1 G9Ca7 A5Ra2 C5Ra4 D9Ra4 E3Ra3
C1Ba2 C6Ba8 A8Ba4 H4Ba2 A9Rb8 C4Rb5 H6Rb5
H8Rb8 J5Rb1 G5Cb8 G8Cb1 J8Cb2

59	6	4	389	1389	2	135	13	7
8	137	137	5	136	16	9	1346	234
2	135	139	369	7	4	8	136	35
679	4	3679	236789	13689	16789	367	5	389
679	237	5	2346789	34689	6789	367	346789	1
1	37	8	34679	3469	5	367	2	349
567	9	2	678	568	678	4	1378	358
4567	578	67	1	45689	3	257	789	2589
3	1578	17	4789	2	789	157	1789	6

H1Ca4 E2Ca2 H7Ca2 B9Ra2 D4Ra2 G8Ra1 J4Ra4
A7Ba1 B8Ba4 G9Ba3 A8Rb3 C9Rb5 C8Cb6 C2Ca1
J7Ca5 F9Ca4 A1Ra5 C4Ra3 E5Ra4 J3Ra1 C3Ba9
H2Ba5 J2Rb8 G5Ca5 E7Ra3 J6Ca9 J8Ra7 H5Rb6
H3Cb7 B5Cb1 B3Bb3 B6Bb6 G1Bb6 F2Ca3 D3Ca6
D6Ca1 B2Ra7 D5Ra3 E4Ra6 E6Ba8 F7Ba6 D7Rb7
E8Rb9 F5Rb9 G6Rb7 D1Cb9 E1Cb7 F4Cb7 G4Cb8
A5Cb8 H8Cb8 D9Cb8 A4Bb9 H9Bb9

1	5	2367	8	9	34	367	2347	2467
4	2378	2379	5	6	13	1378	2378	1278
367	3678	367	147	147	2	13678	9	5
5	9	2367	12467	1247	8	367	347	467
8	1	367	467	457	456	2	3457	4679
267	267	4	3	257	9	5678	1	678
2679	267	25679	1269	3	156	4	2578	12789
239	234	8	1249	1245	7	159	6	129
2679	2467	1	2469	2458	456	5789	2578	3

G3Ca5 J5Ca8 B3Ra9 E9Ra9 A6Rb3 C3Rb6 C1Cb3
B6Cb1 C2Bb8 G6Bb6 H2Ca3 C7Ra1 E4Ra6 J2Ba4
J6Rb5 E6Cb4 F2Ca6 E8Ca5 E3Ra3 F5Ra5 H7Ra5
J1Ra6 J7Ba9 E5Rb7 J4Rb2 D4Cb1 C5Cb4 J8Cb7
C4Bb7 D5Bb2 G4Bb9 H5Bb1 H1Ca9 A3Ca2 H4Ca4
G9Ca1 F1Ra2 G8Ra8 H9Ra2 B2Ba7 B8Ba2 D3Ba7
G2Ba2 A8Rb4 B9Rb8 G1Rb7 B7Cb3 D8Cb3 F9Cb7
A9Bb6 D7Bb6 F7Bb8 A7Ca7 D9Ca4

249	246	236	2469	7	2469	1	8	359
12489	248	1238	5	2489	12489	6	7	39
14789	4678	5	1469	4689	3	49	4	2
1247	3	127	8	5	124679	79	126	169
6	2578	1278	3	29	1279	789	12	4
12478	2478	9	12467	246	12467	378	5	1368
5	1	2678	2467	23468	24678	348	9	368
3	9	678	467	468	5	2	146	168
28	268	4	269	1	2689	358	36	7

E2Ca5 G5Ca3 J7Ca5 J8Ca3 A9Ca5 A3Ra3 B9Ba3
C8Rb4 C7Cb9 D7Bb7 F7Ca3 G7Ca4 D9Ca9 E7Rb8
E6Ra7 E5Ba9 B3Ca8 C5Ra8 D1Ba4 G6Ba8 G9Rb6
H5Rb4 G3Cb7 H4Cb7 B5Cb2 H8Cb1 F9Cb1 B2Bb4
F5Bb6 E8Bb2 H3Bb6 G4Bb2 H9Bb8 D3Ca2 C4Ca1
D8Ca6 B1Ra1 C2Ra6 D6Ra1 E3Ra1 F6Ra2 C1Ba7
A1Ba9 F4Ba4 A2Rb2 A4Rb6 B6Rb9 F1Rb8 J1Cb2
F2Cb7 J2Cb8 J4Cb9 A6Cb4 J6Cb6

467	567	467	2	1347	8	1679	1459	145679
2478	1	3	47	6	9	27	245	457
2467	9	2467	5	147	147	3	124	8
5	267	9	1478	12478	3	12678	1248	1467
1267	4	1267	178	12578	127	126789	12389	1679
3	8	127	9	1247	6	5	124	147
12469	236	8	1346	12349	5	19	7	19
12679	267	1267	1678	12789	127	4	1589	3
1479	37	5	13478	134789	147	189	6	2

B1Ca8 A2Ca5 E5Ca5 E8Ca3 A5Ra3 H8Ra5 B9Ba5
J7Ba8 D8Ca8 A8Ca9 E4Ra8 H5Ba8 H1Ra9 J5Ra9
F8Ca1 A1Rb7 C8Rb4 A3Cb4 B8Cb2 B7Bb7 J6Ca4
B4Ra4 G1Ra4 G5Rb2 J1Rb1 E3Ca1 E6Ca2 E9Ra7
F3Ra2 C1Ba2 D2Ba7 D7Ba2 E7Ba9 H2Ba2 C3Rb6
D4Rb1 E1Rb6 F9Rb4 G7Rb1 J2Rb3 G2Cb6 H3Cb7
J4Cb7 D5Cb4 F5Cb7 A7Cb6 D9Cb6 G9Cb9 C5Bb1
A9Bb1 G4Bb3 H4Bb6 H6Bb1 C6Ca7

3	2456	24568	4589	24569	24569	12589	1568	7
24568	9	7	458	2456	1	258	3568	3568
2568	1	2568	589	3	7	2589	568	4
2456	234567	2456	1	8	3456	57	9	356
56	3567	9	2	56	356	4	135678	13568
456	8	1	34579	4569	34569	57	2	356
12589	25	258	359	7	2359	6	4	1589
12459	245	245	6	12459	8	3	157	159
7	456	3	459	1459	459	1589	158	2

F4Ca7 H8Ra7 J2Ra6 D7Ba7 F7Rb5 E2Ca7 G4Ca3
B8Ca3 E6Ra3 D2Ba3 G3Ba8 D9Rb6 F9Cb3 F6Ca6
B5Ra6 E1Ra6 F5Ra9 D6Ba4 E5Rb5 F1Rb4 B4Ra4
J5Ba4 A5Rb2 H5Cb1 H1Bb9 G1Ca1 G6Ca2 G9Ca9
G2Ra5 A2Rb4 H9Rb5 H2Cb2 B9Cb8 B7Bb2 E9Bb1
H3Bb4 C1Ca8 J7Ca8 A4Ra8 B1Ra5 C3Ra2 E8Ra8
J8Ra1 A3Ba6 A7Ba1 D1Ba2 D3Ba5 A8Rb5 C7Rb9
C4Cb5 A6Cb9 C8Cb6 J4Bb9 J6Bb5

15	17	4	5678	3	128	125678	12567	9
1359	2	13579	56789	15679	4	15678	13567	368
6	1379	8	579	12579	129	4	12357	23
134	1346	123	7	8	12	126	9	5
7	14689	129	3	129	5	1268	1246	268
1389	5	1239	9	4	6	128	123	7
14589	14789	6	4589	59	89	3	257	2
34589	34789	3579	2	569	389	5679	567	1
2	39	359	1	569	7	569	8	4

G4Ca4 H6Ca3 E8Ca4 D4Ra7 F8Ba3 G6Ba8 F4Rb9
G9Rb2 C4Cb5 C9Cb3 C6Ca9 H3Ca7 G8Ra7 A1Ba5
J3Ca5 G5Ra5 J2Ra3 G1Ca1 G2Ra9 E3Ba9 B3Rb3
F1Rb8 B1Cb9 H1Cb4 E2Cb6 D1Bb3 D2Bb4 E9Bb8
H2Bb8 B9Ca6 A4Ra6 D7Ra6 B4Ba8 H8Ba6 H5Rb9
J7Rb9 J5Cb6 H7Cb5 B7Bb7 C5Ca7 A7Ca8 B8Ca5
A2Ra7 B5Ra1 C8Ra2 C2Ba1 A6Ba2 A8Ba1 D6Ba1
D3Rb2 E5Rb2 F3Cb1 E7Cb1 F7Bb2

1258	2358	9	6	238	278	4	1358	135
128	6	1238	389	5	4	1389	1389	7
7	3458	3458	389	1	89	2	35689	356
4	2358	2358	1358	7	1568	1368	1368	9
8	7	6	2	9	18	5	1348	134
589	1	358	3458	368	568	3678	2	346
3	258	7	1589	4	125689	169	1569	1256
12568	2458	12458	1589	268	3	1679	145679	12456
1256	9	1245	7	26	1256	136	13456	8

F1Ca9 F4Ca4 A6Ca7 H8Ca7 F7Ra7 A5Ba2 E1Rb8
J5Rb6 H5Cb8 E6Cb1 F5Bb3 H1Ca6 F6Ra8 G2Ra8
D6Ba6 C6Rb9 D4Rb5 F3Rb5 F9Rb6 G7Ca6 A8Ra8
C8Ra6 D7Ba8 D8Rb1 A1Ca5 A9Ra1 C9Ra5 H2Ra5
A2Rb3 G9Rb2 C2Cb4 D2Cb2 G6Cb5 H9Cb4 C3Bb8
D3Bb3 E9Bb3 J6Bb2 G8Bb9 B1Ca2 J3Ca4 B4Ca8
H4Ca9 B7Ca9 E8Ca4 J8Ca5 B3Ra1 B8Ra3 C4Ra3
G4Ra1 H3Ra2 J7Ra3 J1Ba1 H7Ba1

2	138	9	13468	13468	7	5	456	345
136	13	5	12346	12346	3469	8	4679	2347
4	7	38	5	2368	3689	2	1	23
1378	12348	6	9	13458	348	1257	578	12578
1378	1238	1378	13678	13568	368	4	578	9
5	1489	1478	1478	148	2	6	3	178
138	6	1348	348	7	5	9	2	148
789	4589	2	468	468	1	3	4578	4578
1378	13458	13478	2348	9	348	157	4578	6

B1Ca6 H1Ca9 B8Ca9 B9Ra7 C6Ra9 E2Ra2 F2Ra9
J4Ra2 A8Ba6 A7Rb5 C7Rb2 C9Cb3 C3Bb8 A9Bb4
B5Ca2 E6Ca6 D9Ca2 C5Ra6 H8Ra7 D7Ba7 H4Ba6
J8Ba4 J7Rb1 G9Cb8 F9Bb1 H9Bb5 J2Ca5 J6Ca8
H2Ra8 G3Ba4 G4Ba3 D2Rb4 F3Rb7 G1Rb1 H5Rb4
J3Cb3 F5Cb8 D6Cb3 B6Bb4 D1Bb8 E3Bb1 F4Bb4
J1Bb7 E1Ca3 E4Ca7 A4Ca8 A5Ca3 E8Ca8 A2Ra1
B2Ra3 D5Ra1 E5Ra5 B4Ba1 D8Ba5

134	2348	1248	1468	9	48	12368	7	5
134	5	6	1478	7	2	138	1348	9
149	7	12489	14568	3	458	1268	12468	148
4579	46	4579	345789	57	345789	1358	13458	2
8	24	3	457	1	457	5	9	6
459	1	2459	34589	25	6	7	3458	348
357	38	578	35679	567	1	4	23568	38
2	34	1457	35679	8	3579	13569	1356	13
6	9	158	2	4	35	1358	1358	7

D2Ca6 F5Ca2 G5Ca6 H7Ca9 E2Ra2 G8Ra2 G4Ra9
H8Ra6 D6Ba9 B5Rb7 E7Rb5 D5Cb5 J8Ca5 J6Rb3
A1Ca3 A4Ra1 C4Ba6 B4Rb4 C7Rb2 B1Cb1 E4Cb7
A6Cb8 A7Cb6 A2Bb4 C6Bb5 E6Bb4 H4Bb5 D1Ca4
G2Ca8 A3Ca2 H6Ca7 C3Ra8 D3Ra7 G9Ra3 H3Ra4
J7Ra8 C1Ba9 B8Ba8 J3Ba1 H2Ba3 G1Ba7 H9Ba1
B7Rb3 C9Rb4 F1Rb5 G3Rb5 F3Cb9 D7Cb1 C8Cb1
F9Cb8 F4Bb3 D8Bb3 D4Ca8 F8Ca4

1	36	7	8	3459	59	2	34569	456
238	2368	5	249	12349	129	1489	1346789	1467
4	9	8	2	6	7	158	1358	15
6	157	19	279	8	4	159	1259	3
58	1458	2	3	59	569	7	1459	145
57	457	3	1	259	259	6	2459	8
9	12456	146	246	7	8	3	12456	12456
23578	12345678	1468	2469	1249	1269	1458	1245678	124567
278	124678	1468	5	124	3	148	124678	9

D3Ca9 D4Ca7 C4Ra2 C8Ra3 D8Ra2 E6Ra6 C3Rb8
B7Ca9 B8Ra8 B9Ba7 B4Rb4 B6Rb1 G4Cb6 B5Cb3
B1Bb2 H4Bb9 H1Ca3 A2Ra3 B2Ra6 H6Rb2 F5Ca2
G9Ca2 J2Ra2 G3Ca4 D7Ra5 G8Ra1 C9Ba5 E9Ba1
C7Rb1 D2Rb1 G2Rb5 H9Rb6 H3Cb1 J8Cb7 A9Cb4
A8Bb6 J1Bb8 J3Bb6 H5Bb4 H8Bb5 F1Ca7 E2Ca8
J5Ca1 J7Ca4 H7Ca8 E8Ra4 F6Ra5 H2Ra7 A5Ba5
F2Ba4 E1Ba5 E5Ba9 F8Ba9 A6Rb9

234567	34569	23479	1469	14569	8	2456	23569	34569
34568	345689	3489	2	4569	46	7	3569	1
24568	45689	1	3	4569	7	24568	2569	4569
1234	7	5	1469	13469	1346	1246	8	346
1348	348	348	1467	2	5	9	136	346
9	34	6	14	8	134	1245	1235	7
3568	2	389	168	7	136	156	4	569
467	469	479	5	146	1246	3	169	8
34568	1	348	468	346	9	56	7	2

A3Ca2 E4Ca7 H6Ca2 C7Ca8 A1Ra7 C8Ra2 D1Ba2
H3Ba7 E1Ca1 F7Ca2 F8Ra5 D7Ba1 A7Ca4 H8Ca1
H2Ra9 B3Ba9 G9Ba9 A5Ca1 A8Ca9 C5Ra9 B5Ba5
D4Ba9 A4Rb6 B6Cb4 C1Rb4 H1Cb6 H5Bb4 F4Ca4
D9Ra4 F6Ra1 J3Ra4 E2Ba4 G4Ba1 F2Rb3 J4Rb8
A2Cb5 E3Cb8 C2Bb6 A9Bb3 G3Bb3 B1Ca3 B2Ca8
D6Ca3 E8Ca3 C9Ca5 E9Ca6 B8Ra6 D5Ra6 G1Ra8
J5Ra3 J1Ba5 G6Ba6 G7Rb5 J7Rb6

39	7	34	2359	8	2569	12359	1369	259
6	389	1	4	3579	2579	23589	379	25789
389	2	5	379	3679	1	389	4	789
3578	6	378	3579	3579	45789	489	2	1
4	18	78	1279	1679	26789	89	5	3
123578	1358	9	12357	1357	24578	6	7	78
15789	14589	478	1579	1579	3	1259	19	6
13579	1359	2	6	4	579	1359	8	59
1359	1359	36	8	2	59	7	139	4

F1Ca2 G2Ca4 J3Ca6 D7Ca4 A8Ca6 A7Ra1 A3Ra4
C5Ra6 F6Ra4 G7Ra2 E6Ba6 E7Ba9 F8Rb7 F9Cb8
D3Ca3 D6Ca8 E4Ra2 H1Ca1 J8Ca1 H6Ra7 H7Ba3
C7Rb8 G8Rb9 H2Rb9 B7Cb5 B8Cb3 H9Cb5 B2Bb8
G1Ca8 J2Ca3 F5Ca3 E3Ra8 G3Ra7 J6Ra9 D1Ba7
J1Ba5 B6Rb2 E2Rb1 F2Cb5 E5Cb7 A6Cb5 B5Bb9
F4Bb1 C4Ca7 D4Ca9 G5Ca1 A9Ca2 A1Ra9 B9Ra7
C1Ra3 D5Ra5 G4Ra5 A4Ba3 C9Ba9

6	38	5	2378	238	4	9	1	2378
13	1348	1348	123578	9	23678	34578	245678	2378
2	13489	7	1358	13568	368	3458	4568	38
39	3479	349	358	358	1	2	4578	6
139	5	123469	238	7	23689	348	48	138
8	12367	1236	4	2356	236	357	9	137
4	2389	2389	6	238	2378	1	278	5
7	12368	12368	1238	12348	5	8	28	9
15	128	128	9	128	278	6	3	4

J1Ca5 H5Ca4 E6Ca9 C2Ra9 E3Ra6 J6Ra7 H2Ba6
G3Ba9 G8Ba7 H7Rb8 H8Cb2 D1Ca9 D2Ra7 E4Ra2
D3Ba4 B2Ca4 D8Rb5 F6Rb6 F5Cb5 C5Ca6 B8Ra6
C4Ra1 B4Ba5 J5Ba1 H4Rb3 H3Cb1 D4Cb8 A4Bb7
D5Bb3 F2Ca1 C7Ca5 B1Ra1 C8Ra4 E9Ra1 F3Ra2
G2Ra3 B3Ba3 E1Ba3 E7Ba4 E8Ba8 J2Ba2 A2Rb8
B7Rb7 J3Rb8 A5Cb2 F7Cb3 B6Bb8 A9Bb3 F9Bb7
G5Bb8 G6Ca2 C6Ca3 B9Ca2 C9Ca8

3689	2689	268	23689	7	268	4	15689	12569
46789	24689	5	1	28	268	2689	3	2679
36789	1	2678	5	238	4	2689	689	2679
1468	7	3	28	128	9	168	1568	1456
5	48	148	38	6	7	1389	2	1349
168	268	9	4	5	128	7	168	136
2	45689	1468	68	148	3	169	7	169
1678	3	1678	2678	9	1268	5	4	126
14679	4569	1467	267	124	1256	12369	169	8

A4Ca9 C5Ca3 J6Ca5 A1Ra3 F9Ra3 G2Ra5 J7Ra3
F2Ba2 E4Ba3 H9Ba2 C8Ca9 B5Rb8 B9Ra7 C7Ba8
C1Rb7 C9Rb6 C3Cb2 B7Cb2 B6Bb6 A6Ca2 H1Ca8
G4Ra8 H6Ra1 D5Ba1 F6Ba8 D4Rb2 D7Rb6 G5Rb4
D1Cb4 J5Cb2 F8Cb1 B1Bb9 A8Bb5 E2Bb8 F1Bb6
D9Bb5 E7Bb9 J8Bb6 J1Ca1 A2Ca6 J2Ca9 J3Ca4
A3Ca8 H4Ca6 G7Ca1 D8Ca8 E9Ca4 G9Ca9 A9Ra1
B2Ra4 E3Ra1 G3Ra6 H3Ra7 J4Ra7

1247	5	2469	147	16	1467	3	8	69
8	147	46	13457	2	9	56	567	56
37	79	69	357	368	3567	1	4	2
1457	14789	4589	6	139	135	458	2	13458
1245	6	245	1235	7	8	45	9	1345
125	3	2589	1259	4	15	7	156	1568
6	48	7	1349	139	2	4589	135	134589
9	24	1	8	5	3467	246	36	346
245	248	3	149	169	146	245689	156	7

C1Ca3 C5Ca8 B8Ca7 B4Ra3 H6Ra7 A9Ba9 J1Ba5
G5Ba3 D6Ca3 G7Ca9 H8Ca3 B2Ra1 E9Ra3 B3Ra4
F8Ca6 G4Rb1 J8Rb1 G8Cb5 E1Ra1 D1Ba4 E7Rb4
F1Rb2 A1Cb7 E3Cb5 C2Bb9 A4Bb4 E4Bb2 D2Ca7
A3Ca2 C4Ca7 J6Ca4 C6Ra5 J5Ra6 C3Ba6 A6Ba6
F4Ba5 J4Ba9 A5Rb1 F6Rb1 D5Cb9 F9Cb8 D3Bb8
F3Bb9 D7Bb5 G9Bb4 H2Ca4 J7Ca8 D9Ca1 B9Ca5
B7Ra6 G2Ra8 H7Ra2 J2Ra2 H9Ba6

2358	3568	3568	12569	23569	169	4	2389	7
2348	3468	9	246	2346	467	238	1	5
2345	7	1	8	23459	49	239	6	23
3479	1346	2	469	8	5	1367	37	36
3458	34568	34568	7	1	46	2368	2358	9
5789	1568	568	3	69	2	1678	578	4
1	348	348	2469	2469	4689	5	234789	2368
3458	9	7	12456	2456	1468	2368	2348	2368
6	2	458	459	7	3	89	489	1

B6Ca7 G8Ra7 D8Rb3 D9Cb6 H7Ca6 J3Ra8 H1Ba5
C9Rb2 J7Rb9 C7Cb3 J8Cb4 C1Bb4 B7Bb8 J4Bb5
H8Bb2 E7Ca2 A8Ca9 C5Ra5 H9Ra3 C6Ba9 G9Ba8
H5Rb4 H4Cb1 G6Cb6 A6Bb1 E6Bb4 H6Bb8 G3Ca4
B4Ca4 D2Ra4 G2Ra3 F2Ba1 F5Ba6 B2Rb6 D4Rb9
F3Rb5 F7Rb7 D1Cb7 F1Cb9 E2Cb8 A3Cb3 G4Cb2
D7Cb1 F8Cb8 A2Bb5 B1Bb2 A4Bb6 A5Bb2 E1Bb3
E3Bb6 E8Bb5 G5Bb9 A1Ca8 B5Ca3

5	4	9	7	8	36	236	136	1236
2	1368	1368	1356	4	356	3567	9	136
7	1368	1368	13569	2	3569	3456	134568	1346
3	1269	1256	12569	15679	45679	2456	1456	8
8	7	4	12569	3	569	256	156	126
16	126	1256	12568	156	4568	9	13456	7
46	368	3678	3568	567	2	1	3467	9
1469	5	13678	3689	679	36789	3467	2	346
69	2369	2367	4	679	1	8	367	5

C8Ca8 B7Ra7 F8Ra3 C7Ba5 D2Ba9 C9Ra4 F6Ra4
F4Ba8 H6Ca8 D6Ca7 G4Ca3 G5Ra5 H4Rb6 H9Cb3
B9Bb6 H7Bb4 G1Ca4 A7Ca3 D8Ca4 A9Ra2 A6Ra6
F3Ra5 A8Ba1 F2Ba2 E8Ba5 E6Rb9 E9Rb1 J2Rb3
J3Cb2 E4Cb2 C6Cb3 B6Bb5 D4Bb5 E7Bb6 B3Ca3
C4Ca9 D7Ca2 B2Ra8 B4Ba1 G3Ba8 G2Rb6 J1Cb9
C2Cb1 G8Cb7 C3Bb6 H1Bb1 J5Bb7 J8Bb6 F1Ca6
D3Ca1 H3Ca7 H5Ca9 D5Ra6 F5Ra1

14579	145	6	137	8	1347	2	1345	135
1245	12458	2458	1236	234	9	3458	134568	7
3	1248	2478	5	247	1467	9	1468	16
257	2358	1	9	237	378	6	357	4
6	2345	23457	237	1	347	357	3579	8
47	9	3478	367	347	5	37	137	2
8	2356	9	4	357	37	1	23567	356
1245	123456	2345	137	3579	137	34578	2345678	356
145	7	345	8	6	2	345	345	9

A1Ca9 H5Ca9 C6Ca6 D6Ca8 E8Ca9 B8Ra6 F8Ra1
F4Ra6 F3Ra8 J1Ra1 C3Ba7 G5Ba5 C9Rb1 E7Ra7
D8Ba5 F7Rb3 C8Ca8 B2Ra8 H7Ra8 A2Ba1 H6Ca1
A9Ra5 B4Ra1 A8Ba3 J7Ba5 A4Rb7 B7Rb4 J8Rb4
J3Cb3 H4Cb3 A6Cb4 C5Bb2 E4Bb2 E6Bb3 G6Bb7
H9Bb6 D2Ca3 G2Ca6 B5Ca3 F5Ca4 H8Ca7 G9Ca3
C2Ra4 D1Ra2 F1Ra7 G8Ra2 B3Ba2 E3Ba4 D5Ba7
B1Rb5 E2Rb5 H3Rb5 H1Cb4 H2Cb2

6	1345	1345	8	7	14	345	9	2
13	123489	13489	1346	1246	5	34678	1468	1378
135	123458	7	1346	9	1246	34568	14568	1358
4	1358	1358	16	168	9	2358	7	1358
9	1358	2	14	148	7	3458	1458	6
17	6	18	2	5	3	48	148	189
157	1457	1456	1467	12468	12468	9	3	578
8	3479	3469	5	246	246	1	26	7
2	1579	1569	1679	3	168	5678	568	4

J4Ca9 D7Ca2 H8Ca2 F9Ca9 F1Ra7 G4Ba7 H9Rb7
J2Ca7 B7Ca7 G3Ca6 A7Ca3 D9Ca3 E2Ra3 G2Ra4
H3Ba3 H2Rb9 B3Ca9 A3Ba4 A6Rb1 A2Cb5 J6Cb8
G6Bb2 G1Ca5 B5Ca2 C2Ra2 D3Ra5 G5Ra1 G9Ra8
J3Ra1 B2Ba8 D2Ba1 B9Rb1 D4Rb6 F3Rb8 B1Cb3
D5Cb8 F7Cb4 C9Cb5 C1Bb1 B4Bb4 E5Bb4 F8Bb1
E4Ca1 C4Ca3 H5Ca6 H6Ca4 C8Ca4 B8Ra6 C7Ra8
C6Ba6 E8Ba8 J7Ba6 E7Rb5 J8Rb5

5	379	23789	12348	12348	6	1249	1247	249
2679	3679	4	5	123	123	8	127	269
268	1	28	9	248	7	246	3	2456
14789	2	5	6	134789	138	149	148	349
14789	479	789	123478	12345789	12358	12469	1248	23469
3	49	6	1248	12489	128	7	5	249
247	8	237	237	2357	9	24	6	1
269	369	1	238	2368	4	5	2	7
2467	4567	27	127	12567	125	3	9	8

J2Ca5 C9Ca5 G5Ra5 J1Ra4 E6Ba5 G7Ba4 H8Rb2
J5Ca6 C5Ra4 G3Ra3 F6Ca8 D6Rb3 E9Ca3 E7Ra6
B9Ba6 F9Ba2 C7Rb2 C3Cb8 C1Bb6 H2Ca6 H1Ra9
B2Ra9 D5Ra7 A2Ba3 E3Ba9 E5Rb2 F2Rb4 E2Cb7
E4Cb4 F4Cb1 F5Bb9 H4Ca3 B5Ra3 H5Ra8 J6Ra1
A5Ba1 A4Ba8 A7Rb9 B6Rb2 B1Cb7 D7Cb1 A9Cb4
A3Bb2 A8Bb7 B8Bb1 D1Bb8 D9Bb9 E8Bb8 G1Bb2
E1Ca1 J3Ca7 J4Ca2 D8Ca4 G4Ra7

1	3679	369	26789	2679	26789	5	378	4
3459	3479	8	279	24579	1	6	37	237
45	2	456	3	4567	45678	9	178	17
23489	3489	7	5	1249	249	1238	1389	6
2589	689	569	12679	12679	3	4	15789	127
23459	1	34569	2679	8	24679	23	3579	237
7	5	2	169	3	69	1	146	8
348	348	134	12678	12567	25678	13	1346	9
6	389	139	4	19	89	7	2	5

D7Ca8 G8Ra4 B9Ba2 H8Ba6 G7Rb1 H7Cb3 F7Bb2
F9Ca3 H3Ca1 A4Ca8 C8Ra8 J5Ra1 J6Ra8 C9Ba1
E4Ba1 E9Rb7 H4Ca2 D8Ca1 F4Ca7 B4Rb9 G4Cb6
G6Bb9 E2Ca6 E1Ra8 F6Ra6 C3Ba6 D1Ba2 H2Ba8
A6Rb2 D6Rb4 H1Rb4 C1Cb5 A5Cb6 D5Cb9 B1Bb3
C6Bb7 D2Bb3 F1Bb9 E5Bb2 B2Ca4 J3Ca3 F3Ca4
H5Ca7 H6Ca5 A8Ca3 E8Ca9 A2Ra7 B5Ra5 B8Ra7
C5Ra4 E3Ra5 F8Ra5 J2Ra9 A3Ba9

3469	169	5	134679	1347	3469	137	2	8
39	19	8	1379	1357	2359	6	135	4
2	7	134	13468	13458	34568	9	135	15
3478	1258	12347	3478	9	3458	1578	6	1257
3789	1589	1379	2	6	358	1578	4	157
46789	25689	2479	478	4578	1	578	589	3
789	4	6	1389	138	389	2	1358	15
1	89	9	5	2	34689	348	7	6
5	3	2	1468	148	7	148	18	9

B6Ca2 F8Ca9 D9Ca2 H9Ca6 G1Ra7 J3Ra2 J4Ra6
A7Ba7 F2Ba2 H2Ba8 H3Rb9 A2Ca6 H7Ca3 E9Ca7
C6Ra6 F1Ra6 H6Ra4 J7Ba4 F7Ca5 G6Ca8 G4Ra9
J8Ra8 A6Ba9 G5Ba3 J5Rb1 A5Cb4 A1Bb3 D1Ca4
A4Ca1 C3Ra4 D7Ra8 F4Ra4 B2Ba1 E1Ba8 F5Ba8
E7Ba1 B1Rb9 C5Rb5 D2Rb5 E3Rb3 F3Rb7 E2Cb9
D3Cb1 B5Cb7 D6Cb3 E6Cb5 C9Cb1 B4Bb3 C8Bb3
D4Bb7 G9Bb5 C4Ca8 G8Ca1 B8Ca5

149	8	6	129	5	3	179	279	129
5	79	137	1289	189	4	6	23789	1239
2	9	13	7	1689	189	4	3589	1359
48	24	9	5	1478	6	137	2347	1234
3	456	45	149	2	179	1579	45679	8
7	1	245	3	489	89	59	24569	2459
469	3	8	2469	469	259	59	1	7
1469	245679	12457	12469	14679	12579	8	3459	3459
149	4579	1457	1489	3	15789	2	459	6

D1Ca8 D7Ca3 A1Ra4 C5Ra6 F8Ra6 E2Ba6 C2Rb9
B2Cb7 G6Ca2 G7Ra5 F7Rb9 F6Cb8 C6Bb1 F5Bb4
B3Ca1 G4Ca4 B5Ca8 C8Ra8 G1Ra6 J4Ra8 C3Ba3
C9Ba5 H4Ba6 F9Rb2 G5Rb9 F3Cb5 E3Bb4 H3Ca2
E4Ca1 E6Ca9 E8Ca5 D9Ra1 D2Ra2 E7Ra7 J1Ra1
A7Ba1 A8Ba7 D5Ba7 D8Ba4 J3Ba7 H1Ba9 H5Ba1
A9Rb9 H8Rb3 J6Rb5 J8Rb9 J2Cb4 A4Cb2 H6Cb7
B8Cb2 B9Cb3 H9Cb4 B4Bb9 H2Bb5

3	578	9	2	1467	14567	1478	178	14
167	7	67	3679	8	13467	5	2	149
4	578	2	579	17	157	3	1789	6
2	358	4568	3568	136	9	148	138	7
789	1	478	378	237	2378	2489	6	5
56789	35789	5678	4	12367	1235678	1289	1389	129
5789	6	1	378	2347	23478	279	579	29
578	4	578	678	9	2678	1267	157	3
79	279	3	1	5	267	2679	4	8

B1Ca1 J2Ca2 B3Ba6 B2Rb7 F1Ca6 F2Ca9 E7Ra9
D2Ba3 D7Ba4 E3Ca4 F8Ca3 J1Ra9 A5Ca4 A6Ra6
B9Ra4 G6Ra4 C8Ba9 H4Ba6 A9Rb1 B6Rb3 J6Rb7
B4Cb9 J7Cb6 F9Cb2 G9Bb9 D5Ca6 A2Ra5 C2Ra8
D8Ra1 F7Ba8 H7Ba1 A7Rb7 G7Cb2 A8Cb8 G5Bb3
E4Ca3 E5Ca2 E1Ra7 H6Ra2 D3Ba8 F5Ba7 H3Ba7
G4Ba8 C5Rb1 D4Rb5 E6Rb8 F3Rb5 G1Rb5 H8Rb5
H1Cb8 C4Cb7 C6Cb5 F6Cb1 G8Cb7

1	3458	9	7	2348	38	6	2345	3458
4568	3458	345	234689	1	3689	234589	2345	7
7	348	2	34689	3489	5	3489	34	1
3	12459	1457	1689	89	1689	12458	24567	4568
4	6	147	138	5	2	1348	9	348
25	1259	8	1369	7	4	1235	2356	356
9	23458	345	23458	2348	378	345	1	3456
2458	123458	1345	123458	6	138	7	345	9
45	7	6	13459	349	139	345	8	2

B1Ca6 G6Ca7 D8Ca7 C4Ra6 E3Ra7 G9Ra6 D6Ba6
F8Ba6 E1Rb4 J1Cb5 F1Bb2 H1Ca8 D7Ra2 D9Ba4
J6Ca1 H6Rb3 A6Cb8 B6Bb9 C7Ca9 E9Ca8 C2Ra8
J7Ra3 B7Ba8 F9Ba3 A9Rb5 E7Rb1 E4Cb3 F7Cb5
G7Bb4 H8Ca5 G4Ra5 G5Ba8 D5Rb9 G3Rb3 G2Cb2
F4Cb1 J5Cb4 C5Bb3 F2Bb9 D4Bb8 H4Bb2 J4Bb9
B4Ca4 A5Ca2 B8Ra2 C8Ra4 A2Ba4 A8Ba3 B3Rb5
H2Rb1 B2Cb3 D2Cb5 D3Cb1 H3Cb4

1	24	3	456	9	56	4568	7	256
47	247	5	467	8	367	9	2346	1236
6	8	2479	457	2347	1	345	2345	235
579	179	1789	3	167	4	1567	2569	12567
2	3	1478	1678	167	9	14567	456	1567
479	1479	6	2	5	7	1347	349	8
3479	5	1479	146789	13467	3678	2	36	367
8	2467	247	4567	3467	3567	3567	1	9
379	1679	179	15679	1367	2	3567	8	4

D1Ca5 C5Ca2 G6Ca8 A7Ca8 B9Ra1 C3Ra9 D3Ra8
B6Ba3 E4Ba8 F6Rb7 H3Ca2 C4Ra7 J7Ra5 J2Ca6
B1Ca7 E3Ba7 F1Rb4 J3Rb1 G3Cb4 J4Cb9 H2Bb7
J1Bb3 G4Bb1 G1Ca9 H5Ca4 D7Ca7 H7Ra3 J5Ra7
F8Ba3 G5Ba3 G9Ba7 C7Rb4 F7Rb1 G8Rb6 F2Cb9
E7Cb6 B8Cb2 C8Cb5 B2Bb4 A9Bb6 C9Bb3 D2Bb1
E5Bb1 D8Bb9 D9Bb2 E8Bb4 E9Bb5 A2Ca2 A4Ca4
D5Ca6 H6Ca6 A6Ra5 B4Ra6 H4Ra5

2	3	45	1	7	48	468	468	9
8	6	4579	3	459	249	1247	14	1257
45	457	1	2458	4569	2489	234678	3468	2567
3	9	568	578	15	178	1678	2	4
7	1248	2468	248	134	12348	9	5	16
145	12458	2458	24578	1459	6	178	18	3
146	1247	23467	47	8	1347	5	13469	126
1456	1458	34568	9	2	134	1346	7	16
9	1247	2347	6	134	5	1234	134	8

B3Ca9 C5Ca6 G8Ca9 A3Ra5 C6Ra9 F5Ra9 C2Ba7
C1Rb4 A8Ca6 B9Ca7 B5Ra5 J3Ra7 C9Ba5 D5Rb1
G9Rb2 D4Ra5 J2Ra2 G1Ca6 E9Ca1 E3Ra6 F3Ba2
D7Ba6 D3Rb8 F8Rb8 H9Rb6 E2Cb4 D6Cb7 F7Cb7
C8Cb3 E5Bb3 F4Bb4 G2Bb1 F1Ca1 H2Ca8 G4Ca7
J5Ca4 H6Ca1 F2Ra5 G3Ra4 H1Ra5 J7Ra3 H3Ba3
G6Ba3 J8Ba1 H7Ba4 A7Rb8 B8Rb4 A6Cb4 B6Cb2
C7Cb2 C4Bb8 B7Bb1 E6Bb8 E4Ca2

3456	256	25	2358	1	258	9	348	7
357	9	1	4	2378	2578	38	6	38
347	8	7	379	6	79	2	134	5
5679	4	5789	1256789	2789	256789	1368	1389	23689
2	156	3	15689	489	45689	7	1489	4689
679	167	789	126789	24789	3	168	5	24689
1	27	6	23789	5	2789	4	3789	389
579	3	579	6789	4789	1	568	2	689
8	257	4	23679	2379	2679	356	379	1

A3Ca2 E6Ca4 C8Ra1 F9Ra4 H5Ra4 A8Ba4 D9Ba2
C3Rb7 C6Cb9 C4Bb3 C1Ca4 J5Ca3 A1Ra3 A2Ba6
B1Rb5 E9Ra6 J4Ca9 G9Ca9 G8Ra3 D7Ba3 J8Ba7
H9Ba8 B7Rb8 B9Rb3 F7Cb1 F2Bb7 H1Ca7 E2Ca1
D4Ra1 E4Ra5 H3Ra9 A6Ba5 D3Ba5 J2Ba5 A4Rb8
F3Rb8 G2Rb2 H4Rb6 J7Rb6 F4Cb2 G4Cb7 J6Cb2
H7Cb5 B6Bb7 F5Bb9 G6Bb8 D1Ca9 B5Ca2 D5Ca7
D6Ca6 D8Ra8 E8Ra9 F1Ra6 E5Ba8

8	257	2457	6	1239	12379	1245	12479	2579
27	6	9	278	5	4	3	127	27
2457	1	3	279	29	279	2456	8	25679
1	27	267	5	2689	26789	2468	2469	3
235679	8	2567	2379	4	23679	256	269	1
23569	4	256	2389	123689	123689	7	269	2569
2367	9	2678	238	2368	5	126	12367	4
23467	237	1	23489	23689	23689	26	5	267
23456	235	2456	1	7	236	9	236	8

G3Ca8 H4Ca4 D7Ca8 B8Ra1 B4Ra8 D8Ra4 G7Ba1
H2Ra3 C4Ca9 G8Ca7 B9Ra7 C6Ra7 H1Ra7 C5Ba2
E4Ba7 G1Ba6 J8Ba3 B1Rb2 G5Rb3 G4Cb2 A5Cb1
A6Bb3 F4Bb3 F5Bb8 J6Bb6 E1Ca3 D5Ca6 F6Ca1
H6Ca8 D6Ra9 E8Ra9 H5Ra9 A9Ba9 F1Ba9 E6Ba2
A8Rb2 F8Cb6 E7Bb5 F3Ca5 E3Ca6 H7Ca2 C9Ca5
A2Ra5 C7Ra6 F9Ra2 H9Ra6 A3Ba7 A7Ba4 J1Ba5
C1Rb4 D3Rb2 J2Rb2 D2Cb7 J3Cb4

12358	12345	23458	9	136	12368	12468	12458	7
1278	6	2478	27	5	128	1248	12489	3
123578	1235	9	2367	1367	4	1268	1258	56
6	2349	2347	347	379	5	248	23489	1
379	8	347	347	2	139	5	6	49
2359	23459	1	8	369	369	7	2349	49
1358	135	3568	356	4	7	9	15	2
12359	12359	2356	2356	8	2369	146	1457	456
4	7	256	1	69	269	3	5	8

H8Ca7 B8Ra9 E6Ra1 J8Rb5 G8Cb1 C9Ca5 H9Ca6
H7Ra4 A8Ba4 B3Ra4 D4Ca4 E9Ra4 F2Ba4 F9Ba9
E1Rb9 H1Cb1 D2Cb2 F1Bb5 D7Bb8 H2Bb9 J6Ca9
C8Ca8 B7Ra1 D5Ra9 F8Ra2 J3Ra2 E4Ba7 D8Ba3
G3Ba6 B4Rb2 D3Rb7 E3Rb3 H3Rb5 J5Rb6 G2Cb3
A3Cb8 H4Cb3 F5Cb3 B6Cb8 B1Bb7 C2Bb1 A5Bb1
C4Bb6 F6Bb6 G1Bb8 G4Bb5 H6Bb2 A2Ca5 C5Ca7
A6Ca3 A7Ca6 A1Ra2 C1Ra3 C7Ba2

69	56	2	1	4589	34569	7	3468	368
67	3	4	57	578	56	268	1268	9
8	1	79	2	479	3469	5	346	36
5	248	3	6	29	7	489	489	1
14679	4678	1789	59	3	159	4689	456789	2
12679	267	179	4	1259	8	369	35679	356
3	2458	6	59	12459	12459	289	2589	7
1247	24578	1578	3579	124579	123459	23689	235689	3568
27	9	57	8	6	235	1	235	4

H4Ca3 B8Ca1 B7Ra2 J8Ra3 A2Ba5 H5Ba7 B4Ca7
F7Ca3 B5Ra8 C3Ra7 A1Ba9 B6Ba5 J1Ba7 A5Rb4
B1Rb6 J3Rb5 J6Rb2 C5Cb9 D5Bb2 C8Ra4 F1Ra2
F3Ca9 F5Ra1 E4Ba5 G6Ba1 E6Rb9 G4Rb9 G5Rb5
H6Cb4 G7Cb8 H1Bb1 G8Bb2 E1Ca4 H2Ca2 E3Ca1
A9Ca8 A6Ra3 D7Ra4 E8Ra8 G2Ra4 H3Ra8 C6Ba6
C9Ba3 D2Ba8 F8Ba7 D8Ba9 A8Rb6 E7Rb6 F2Rb6
E2Cb7 H7Cb9 H8Cb5 F9Cb5 H9Bb6

12346	124	12467	5	2378	2478	3468	14678	9
2346	24	2467	9	1	2478	3468	5	3478
13459	1459	8	6	37	47	34	2	1347
7	3	5	2	89	6	489	1489	148
149	6	149	378	35789	5789	2	1489	13458
29	289	29	4	3589	1	7	689	358
2569	259	269	78	4	3	1	789	578
12459	7	3	18	2589	2589	4589	489	6
8	1459	1469	17	5679	579	459	3	2

F2Ca8 E4Ca3 J5Ca6 F9Ra3 F8Ra6 E9Ba5 C9Ra1
F5Ra5 D8Ra1 J4Ca7 H4Ba1 G4Rb8 G9Cb7 G8Bb9
D7Ca9 A8Ca7 B3Ra7 D9Ra4 E8Ba8 B9Rb8 D5Rb8
H8Rb4 H1Cb9 J7Cb5 C1Bb5 F1Bb2 H5Bb2 J6Bb9
H7Bb8 G2Ca5 C2Ca9 F3Ca9 E5Ca9 H6Ca5 A6Ca8
E6Ra7 G3Ra2 B6Ba2 C5Ba7 G1Ba6 A5Rb3 B2Rb4
C6Rb4 A1Cb1 B1Cb3 J2Cb1 C7Cb3 A2Bb2 A3Bb6
B7Bb6 E1Bb4 J3Bb4 E3Ca1 A7Ca4

156	156	4	689	679	679	3	1267	56789
56	8	3	2	1	4679	45679	467	5679
7	2	19	689	3	5	14689	146	689
145	9	15	1356	4567	13467	14567	8	2
1245	3	7	156	456	8	1456	9	56
1458	145	6	1359	2	13479	1457	1347	357
9	4567	258	356	56	236	678	367	1
1236	167	12	4	8	12369	679	5	3679
13568	156	158	7	569	1369	2	36	4

C3Ca9 A8Ca2 E1Ra2 F1Ra8 G2Ra4 B6Ba4 D1Ba4
H2Ba7 G7Ba8 J3Ca8 E5Ca4 G8Ra7 F9Ba3 B8Rb6
B1Cb5 J8Cb3 C9Cb8 C4Bb6 H1Ca3 A4Ca8 A9Ra5
E9Rb6 H9Cb9 B9Bb7 H7Bb6 F4Ca9 B7Ca9 F6Rb7
A6Cb9 A5Bb7 J6Bb1 A1Ca1 J5Ca9 D7Ca7 A2Ra6
H3Ra1 J2Ra5 F2Ba1 D3Ba5 G3Ba2 J1Ba6 D5Rb6
F8Rb4 H6Rb2 G5Cb5 D6Cb3 F7Cb5 C8Cb1 C7Bb4
D4Bb1 E7Bb1 G4Bb3 G6Bb6 E4Ca5

4	135	1357	2	15789	6	158	35789	1379
135	135	8	4	1579	79	125	6	12379
156	9	2	3	1578	78	1458	578	147
9	8	4	67	2367	5	126	237	1237
12356	12356	1356	678	4	378	1268	23789	12379
7	236	36	9	2368	1	2468	238	5
2358	2345	35	578	3578	3478	9	1	6
12568	7	1569	1568	15689	89	3	4	2
1356	13456	13569	156	13569	2	7	5	8

A3Ca7 G6Ca4 C9Ca4 C1Ra6 F7Ra4 J2Ra4 H9Ba2
J8Ba5 E6Ca3 B7Ra2 F3Rb3 G3Cb5 E3Bb1 H4Ca5
H1Ra1 G1Ba8 J4Ba1 G4Rb7 J1Rb3 B1Cb5 G2Cb2
D4Cb6 G5Cb3 E1Bb2 F2Bb6 E4Bb8 D7Bb1 E2Ca5
D5Ca7 E7Ca6 A7Ca8 A5Ra5 C5Ra1 C6Ra8 D8Ra2
F8Ra8 B6Ba7 C7Ba5 F5Ba2 D9Ba3 H5Ba8 B5Rb9
C8Rb7 H6Rb9 H3Cb6 J5Cb6 E8Cb9 B9Cb1 B2Bb3
A8Bb3 A9Bb9 E9Bb7 J3Bb9 A2Ca1

9	46	47	678	5	2	1478	1478	3
345	8	2347	37	17	13	6	12457	12459
356	2356	1	3678	4	9	578	2578	25
48	149	489	589	1289	6	3	1458	7
7	1349	5	389	189	138	2	148	146
2	13	6	4	178	1358	158	9	15
4568	7	2489	1	3	458	459	245	2459
3458	23459	23489	589	89	7	1459	6	12459
1	34569	349	2	69	45	4579	3457	8

D5Ca2 J5Ca6 J8Ca3 E9Ca6 B9Ra9 F5Ra7 G1Ra6
J7Ra7 B5Rb1 B6Cb3 B4Bb7 H3Ca3 A3Ca7 E4Ca3
C8Ra7 F2Ra3 C1Ba3 A7Ca4 G7Ca9 A8Ra1 C7Ba8
A2Rb6 C4Rb6 A4Cb8 E8Ca8 D2Ra1 E2Ra4 F6Ra8
D3Ba9 E6Ba1 D4Ba5 D8Ba4 H5Ba8 D1Rb8 E5Rb9
H4Rb9 J3Rb4 H1Cb5 B3Cb2 J6Cb5 B1Bb4 C2Bb5
B8Bb5 G3Bb8 H2Bb2 J2Bb9 G6Bb4 H7Bb1 F7Ca5
G8Ca2 F9Ca1 H9Ca4 C9Ra2 G9Ra5

8	4	1239	569	1569	156	5679	13567	135
5	19	6	3	189	7	489	2	14
139	7	139	5689	4	2	5689	13568	135
26	5	28	678	3678	3468	1	368	9
169	169	7	5689	2	134568	4568	3568	345
1269	3	4	5689	15689	1568	2568	568	7
12367	126	1235	4	35678	3568	257	9	125
12479	8	1259	257	57	5	3	157	6
2367	26	235	1	3567	9	257	4	8

H1Ca4 D3Ca8 H4Ca2 G9Ca2 A3Ra2 D1Ra2 D6Ra4
H3Ra9 F7Ba2 J2Ba2 H8Ba1 H6Rb5 H5Cb7 D4Ca7
A8Ca7 A9Ra3 B5Ca9 A7Ra9 B7Ra8 C1Ba9 C4Ba8
B9Ba4 B2Rb1 C7Rb6 E9Rb5 G2Cb6 C3Cb3 E7Cb4
C8Cb5 C9Cb1 E2Bb9 J3Bb5 G3Ca1 F4Ca9 G5Ca8
G7Ca5 F5Ra5 G1Ra7 J5Ra6 A4Ba5 J1Ba3 G6Ba3
J7Ba7 A5Rb1 D5Rb3 E4Rb6 E1Cb1 A6Cb6 D8Cb6
F1Bb6 E6Bb8 F8Bb8 F6Ca1 E8Ca3

12569	7	24569	4568	3	5689	248	24589	245
8	5	459	2	479	579	34	6	1
2569	25	3	4568	469	1	7	24589	245
23567	9	256	134567	8	23567	12346	1245	23456
4	235	256	9	26	2356	1236	7	8
23567	2358	1	34567	2467	23567	2346	245	9
129	128	7	68	269	2689	5	3	246
235	4	258	3678	1	23678	9	28	26
1239	6	289	38	5	4	128	128	7

G2Ca1 D4Ca1 D9Ca3 A1Ra1 B7Ra3 E7Ra1 F2Ra8
G9Ra4 J8Ba1 H9Ba6 B2Rb5 C2Cb2 C9Bb5 E2Bb3
A9Ca2 G1Rb2 J4Rb3 J1Cb9 H4Cb7 C1Bb6 J3Bb8
H6Bb2 H1Ca3 F6Ca3 A7Ca8 C4Ra8 H3Ra5 H8Ra8
J7Ra2 G6Ba8 F7Rb6 G4Rb6 G5Cb9 D7Cb4 C5Bb4
F4Ca4 E5Ca6 A8Ca4 A6Ra6 B3Ra4 C8Ra9 D3Ra6
E3Ra2 E6Ra5 A3Ba9 A4Ba5 B6Ba9 F5Ba2 B5Rb7
D6Rb7 F8Rb5 D1Cb5 F1Cb7 D8Cb2

234567	1	23469	2479	24	8	23457	2459	23479
8	23579	2349	2479	124	479	123457	2459	6
2467	2679	2469	5	3	4679	1247	249	8
23456	2356	7	2348	9	345	246	1	24
245	25	8	6	24	1	9	3	247
9	236	12346	2348	7	34	246	2468	5
12367	23679	12369	3479	5	3479	8	2469	2349
23	2389	239	1	6	349	2345	7	2349
367	4	5	3789	8	2	36	69	1

G1Ca1 H2Ca8 B5Ca1 J5Ca8 D6Ca5 C6Ca6 F8Ca8
C7Ra1 D4Ra8 E9Ra7 F3Ra1 H7Ra5 J7Rb3 A9Ca3
B6Ca9 J4Ra9 J8Rb6 J1Cb7 C1Bb2 C2Ca7 G6Ca7
H1Rb3 H6Cb4 F6Bb3 G4Bb3 G2Ca9 B3Ca3 D2Ra3
G3Ra6 H9Ra9 A1Ba6 H3Ba2 B2Rb5 D1Rb4 E1Cb5
E2Cb2 D9Cb2 F2Bb6 E5Bb4 D7Bb6 G9Bb4 A5Ca2
A8Ca5 A3Ra9 F4Ra2 F7Ra4 G8Ra2 C3Ba4 B7Ba2
C8Ba9 A7Rb7 B8Rb4 A4Cb4 B4Cb7

7	158	6	38	13589	189	1258	4	158
1458	9	145	2	7	1468	3	1568	1568
3	158	1245	468	1568	1468	7	9	1568
1589	4	157	78	189	3	6	158	2
12589	6	12357	78	4	12789	1589	158	15789
1289	178	127	5	12689	126789	1489	3	14789
145	2	8	9	36	467	145	156	1456
6	13	9	348	238	5	1248	7	148
45	57	457	1	268	24678	24589	2568	3

H2Ca3 E3Ca3 C4Ca6 J8Ca2 A7Ra2 C3Ra2 G5Ra3
G6Ra7 H5Ra2 J7Ra9 A4Ba3 G1Ba1 H4Ca4 G9Ca4
C6Ra4 F7Ra4 G8Ra6 B9Ba6 G7Ba5 J2Ca5 J3Ra7
F2Ba7 J1Ba4 F3Rb1 F9Rb9 D3Cb5 F5Cb6 E9Cb7
B3Bb4 D1Bb9 E4Bb8 F6Bb2 J5Bb8 E1Ca2 B1Ca5
D4Ca7 A5Ca9 J6Ca6 H7Ca8 E8Ca5 A9Ra5 D8Ra8
E6Ra9 F1Ra8 H9Ra1 C5Ba5 B8Ba1 C9Ba8 D5Ba1
E7Ba1 B6Rb8 C2Rb1 A2Cb8 A6Cb1

5	378	4	189	6	2	139	39	1379
67	7	167	4	1579	3	1269	259	8
2	378	9	158	1578	78	1346	345	1367
78	6	2578	3	25789	789	289	1	4
1	23578	23578	5689	4	6789	23689	2389	2369
9	4	238	168	128	68	5	7	236
3468	2389	2368	689	389	5	7	23489	1239
3478	35789	3578	2	389	1	3489	6	39
3468	1	2368	7	389	4689	23489	23489	5

B3Ca1 J6Ca4 G9Ra1 B1Ba6 G4Ba6 B2Rb7 J3Ca6
A9Ra7 A4Ca9 A7Ra1 A2Ra8 C2Ba3 A8Rb3 B5Rb5
C9Rb6 C7Cb4 C8Bb5 E4Ca5 E7Ca6 G8Ca4 D3Ra5
F6Ra6 H1Ra4 H2Ba5 H3Ba7 E2Rb2 G2Cb9 D1Ca7
G3Ca2 F9Ca2 H9Ca9 D5Ra2 E6Ra7 F3Ra3 J5Ra9
C5Ba7 E3Ba8 D6Ba9 E9Ba3 C6Rb8 D7Rb8 E8Rb9
F5Rb1 C4Cb1 F4Cb8 H7Cb3 B8Cb2 B7Bb9 H5Bb8
J7Bb2 J8Bb8 G1Ca8 G5Ca3 J1Ra3

2	359	1359	1459	1459	6	8	7	345
1589	4	6	3	1579	179	2	15	5
159	7	1359	12459	1459	8	1459	13456	345
158	6	12578	1245	14578	1247	3	1458	9
1589	2589	125789	12459	1345789	123479	1457	1458	6
3	589	4	1569	156789	179	157	2	578
4	1	235	8	36	3	57	9	2357
7	2389	2389	149	1349	5	6	348	2348
5689	3589	3589	7	2	349	45	3458	1

J1Ca6 F4Ca6 C7Ca9 C8Ca6 B1Ra8 C4Ra2 G5Ra6
B8Ba1 B9Rb5 G6Rb3 E1Ca9 E5Ca3 H4Ca9 H5Ra1
A4Ba1 J6Ba4 J7Rb5 G7Cb7 F7Bb1 G9Bb2 E7Ca4
F9Ca7 G3Ra5 H8Ra4 J8Ba3 E4Rb5 F6Rb9 H9Rb8
D4Cb4 F5Cb8 B6Cb7 E8Cb8 B5Bb9 E2Bb2 F2Bb5
D5Bb7 D8Bb5 C1Ca5 J2Ca8 H3Ca2 E3Ca7 D6Ca2
A5Ra5 C3Ra1 D3Ra8 E6Ra1 H2Ra3 J3Ra9 A3Ba3
A2Ba9 C5Ba4 D1Ba1 A9Rb4 C9Rb3

18	6	19	3	159	7	2	58	4
5	23489	12349	2489	1469	1268	138	7	36
1248	23478	12347	2458	1456	12568	1358	3568	9
3	259	12569	57	8	15	4	2569	567
248	2458	245	6	35	9	3578	2358	1
7	589	1569	5	2	4	3589	35689	356
9	23457	23457	1	345	2358	6	345	357
24	1	23457	2459	34569	2356	3579	3459	8
6	345	8	459	7	35	359	1	2

D4Ca7 E7Ra7 F3Ra1 G6Ra8 D3Ba6 D6Ba1 E5Ba3
G9Ba7 A3Rb9 D9Rb5 F4Rb5 C2Ca7 H3Ra7 H1Rb4
G8Ca4 J4Ra4 G5Rb5 J7Rb9 A5Cb1 J6Cb3 A1Bb8
J2Bb5 C1Ca1 F2Ca8 E3Ca5 C6Ca5 A8Ra5 B7Ra1
E2Ra4 E8Ra8 F8Ra9 C7Ba8 D2Ba9 D8Ba2 F9Ba6
H7Ba5 B9Rb3 C4Rb2 E1Rb2 F7Rb3 H8Rb3 B2Cb2
H4Cb9 B6Cb6 C8Cb6 B3Bb4 B4Bb8 C5Bb4 G2Bb3
H5Bb6 H6Bb2 G3Ca2 C3Ca3 B5Ca9

3	1256	1568	1279	29	19	267	56789	4
2456	7	56	2349	249	8	1	3569	2359
248	124	9	6	5	134	237	378	237
56789	1569	4	189	689	2	367	135679	3579
5679	1569	2	19	3	169	8	4	579
689	3	168	5	4689	7	26	169	29
2457	8	357	234	1	345	9	37	6
24569	24569	356	23489	7	34569	34	3	1
1	469	367	349	469	3469	5	2	8

A4Ca7 H7Ca4 F5Ra4 H4Ra8 J3Ra7 D5Ba8 G4Ba2
G8Ba7 H8Rb3 C8Cb8 F1Ca8 G3Ca3 J5Ca6 A3Ra8
E6Ba6 F3Rb1 D8Ca1 E4Ra1 D4Ba9 A6Rb1 C2Ca1
J2Ca4 G6Ra4 J6Ra9 B4Ba4 J4Ba3 H6Ba5 C6Rb3
G1Rb5 H3Rb6 B3Cb5 C7Cb7 C9Bb2 D7Bb3 C1Ca4
F7Ca2 A8Ca5 B9Ca3 A5Ra9 F8Ra6 B5Ba2 A7Ba6
B8Ba9 F9Ba9 A2Rb2 B1Rb6 D1Cb7 H2Cb9 E1Bb9
E2Bb5 D9Bb5 H1Bb2 D2Ca6 E9Ca7

1	8	2369	7	26	4	236	5	236
7	3456	2356	2356	1	9	23468	68	2368
245	3456	2356	2356	8	236	12346	167	9
3	5679	569	1	25679	2678	25689	6789	4
59	2	4	569	3	678	15689	16789	5678
8	1	569	24569	245679	267	2569	3	2567
459	3459	13589	3469	4679	1367	35689	2	3568
6	39	12389	239	29	5	7	4	38
2459	3459	7	8	2469	236	3569	69	1

D2Ca7 G6Ca1 A3Ra9 C8Ra7 G5Ra7 H3Ra1 C7Ba1
E1Ba9 J1Ba2 G3Ba8 B7Ca4 E8Ca1 H9Ra8 B8Ba8
E4Rb6 D8Ca6 F3Ra6 D3Ba5 D5Rb9 J8Rb9 F4Cb4
H5Cb2 A5Bb6 F5Bb5 J5Ca4 J6Ca6 G7Ca6 F7Ca9
C2Ra6 C1Ba4 B9Ba6 B2Rb5 C6Rb3 G1Rb5 J2Cb3
C3Cb2 B4Cb2 G9Cb3 B3Bb3 C4Bb5 A9Bb2 H2Bb9
G4Bb9 J7Bb5 G2Ca4 H4Ca3 D7Ca2 A7Ca3 E9Ca5
D6Ra8 E6Ra7 F6Ra2 F9Ba7 E7Ba8

148	6	89	7	2359	1249	23589	2589	12359
3	2	789	459	59	149	5789	5789	6
17	17	5	39	8	6	4	279	1239
9	578	278	1	4	28	25678	3	25
2578	578	4	6	29	3	25789	1	259
128	138	6	89	7	5	289	2489	249
24567	3457	1	3459	3569	479	23569	24569	8
45678	34578	378	2	1	4789	3569	4569	3459
24568	9	238	3458	356	48	1	2456	7

B6Ra1 D7Ra6 F2Ra3 A1Ba4 F1Ba1 E7Ba7 C1Rb7
C2Cb1 B8Ca7 A9Ca1 B4Ra4 J4Ca8 D6Ra8 E5Ba2
G4Ba5 D9Rb5 F4Rb9 J6Rb4 D2Cb7 C4Cb3 E9Cb9
C9Bb2 D3Bb2 G2Bb4 H3Ca7 A6Ca2 H9Ca3 A7Ra3
C8Ra9 G5Ra3 G6Ra7 H8Ra4 F9Ba4 J3Ba3 J5Ba6
H6Ba9 H7Rb5 H2Cb8 B7Cb8 J8Cb2 B3Bb9 A8Bb5
E2Bb5 F7Bb2 F8Bb8 H1Bb6 J1Bb5 G7Bb9 G8Bb6
G1Ca2 E1Ca8 A3Ca8 B5Ca5 A5Ca9

5	14679	4679	379	8	367	1346	1347	2
289	3	6789	1	2679	4	56	578	5678
1248	14678	4678	5	2367	2367	1346	9	4678
348	5	1	6	2347	2378	9	2347	47
7	469	3469	34	234	5	8	1234	46
348	2	3468	3478	1	9	3456	3457	4567
1489	14789	4789	2	5	178	4	6	3
13489	1489	2	3489	3469	1368	7	458	4589
6	4789	345789	34789	3479	378	2	458	1

J3Ca5 H9Ca9 E8Ra1 H8Ra5 D8Ba2 H1Ba3 J8Ba8
B8Rb7 G7Rb4 C6Ca2 B1Ra2 E5Ra2 G1Ca9 C1Ca1
A7Ra1 E3Ca3 E2Ra9 F3Ba6 E4Rb4 H4Cb8 E9Cb6
F4Bb7 D6Ca8 D9Ca7 D5Ra3 D1Ra4 F1Ra8 C7Ra3
B7Ba6 F8Ba3 A8Rb4 B5Rb9 F7Rb5 B3Cb8 A4Cb3
C9Cb8 F9Cb4 B9Bb5 G3Bb7 J4Bb9 G2Ca8 C3Ca4
A3Ca9 J6Ca3 G6Ra1 J5Ra7 A6Ba7 H2Ba1 H5Ba4
A2Rb6 C5Rb6 H6Rb6 J2Rb4 C2Cb7

6	359	4	2589	123589	23	7	158	18
125	57	1257	24578	1258	6	9	1458	3
8	3579	1357	4579	1359	347	6	145	2
239	36789	2367	2678	4	5	138	13789	1789
23459	35789	2357	1	28	27	348	6	789
4	1	67	3	68	9	2	478	5
7	4	9	256	2356	8	135	1235	16
135	356	1356	24569	7	234	1358	123589	1689
35	2	8	569	3569	1	35	3579	4

E7Ca4 F1Ra4 J8Ra7 F8Rb8 F5Cb6 F3Bb7 H7Ca8
J4Ra6 A9Ba8 G9Ra6 J5Ra9 G7Ca1 D9Ca1 D4Ra7
C6Ba7 E5Ba8 E9Ba7 J7Ba5 D7Rb3 E6Rb2 H9Rb9
J1Rb3 A6Cb3 D8Cb9 D1Bb2 H6Bb4 E1Ca9 B2Ca7
D2Ca8 B3Ca2 B4Ca8 G5Ca3 B8Ra4 D3Ra6 G4Ra5
H8Ra3 C4Ba4 H2Ba6 H4Ba2 G8Ba2 A4Rb9 A2Cb5
B1Bb1 A8Bb1 E2Bb3 H1Ca5 C2Ca9 H3Ca1 C3Ca3
C5Ca1 A5Ca2 C8Ca5 B5Ra5 E3Ra5

38	3468	36	2	1347	14	1478	5	9
358	7	236	134	9	145	148	12468	26
59	245	1	8	457	6	47	247	3
2	368	4	369	35	59	35789	3789	1
137	9	367	136	8	125	357	237	4
138	138	5	1349	1234	7	6	2389	2
1579	125	279	1479	1247	3	1459	1469	8
6	1235	2379	1479	1247	12489	13459	1349	5
4	13	8	5	6	19	2	139	7

H6Ca8 H9Ca5 B9Ca6 C1Ra9 G8Ra6 F9Rb2 E6Ca2
E7Ra5 E8Rb3 H7Ca3 J2Ra3 F1Ba3 A1Rb8 B1Cb5
G2Ca5 D6Ca5 C5Ra5 A5Ba7 D5Rb3 A3Ca3 B4Ca3
J6Ca9 A2Ra6 J8Ra1 C2Ba4 E3Ba6 B3Rb2 C7Rb7
D2Rb8 E4Rb1 E1Cb7 F2Cb1 F5Cb4 D7Cb9 C8Cb2
D4Bb6 F4Bb9 D8Bb7 F8Bb8 G1Bb1 H2Bb2 G7Bb4
H4Ca4 H5Ca1 G5Ca2 B7Ca8 B8Ca4 H8Ca9 A6Ra4
B6Ra1 G3Ra9 H3Ra7 A7Ba1 G4Ba7

8	5	3479	367	236	1	369	69	349
6	349	1349	38	38	5	1389	2	7
237	23	137	3678	4	9	13568	1568	358
349	3469	34689	2	1356	347	56789	5689	589
49	469	2	45679	56	47	56789	3	1
1	7	5	369	36	8	69	4	29
3459	3469	3469	13458	1358	34	2	7	3589
2357	1	37	358	9	6	4	58	358
23459	8	349	1345	7	234	1359	159	6

C2Ca2 D3Ca8 A5Ca2 J6Ca2 F9Ca2 A9Ca4 D5Ra1
E7Ra8 H1Ra2 D7Ba7 H3Ba7 C1Ca7 G3Ca6 E6Ca7
A4Ra7 G4Ra1 C4Ba6 G6Ca3 H9Ra3 J1Ba3 J4Ba4
D6Rb4 J3Rb9 D1Cb9 G2Cb4 A3Cb3 B2Bb9 C3Bb1
E1Bb4 E2Bb6 D9Bb5 G1Bb5 D2Ca3 B3Ca4 E5Ca5
F5Ca6 C7Ca3 J8Ca1 A8Ca9 G9Ca9 A7Ra6 B7Ra1
C8Ra5 D8Ra6 E4Ra9 F4Ra3 G5Ra8 J7Ra5 B5Ba3
B4Ba8 C9Ba8 F7Ba9 H4Ba5 H8Ba8

1	2348	37	6	2347	9	5	478	3478
457	6	3579	1357	8	35	37	47	2
4578	23458	357	2357	2347	235	6	9	1
2	3458	135	1389	139	38	13789	1578	6
568	7	1356	12389	12369	4	12389	1258	389
9	38	136	1238	5	7	4	128	38
3	59	4	25789	2679	1	2789	2678	789
567	59	2	5789	679	568	1789	3	4789
67	1	8	4	23679	236	279	267	5

B3Ca9 B4Ra1 D2Ra4 F3Ra6 H7Ra1 H9Ra4 E5Ba6
D5Ca1 F8Ra1 G8Ra6 E3Ba1 F4Ra2 G9Ca7 G7Ra8
J7Ba9 G4Rb5 J8Rb2 G2Cb9 H2Bb5 G5Bb2 H5Ca9
C6Ca2 E7Ca2 E9Ca9 A2Ra2 D4Ra9 E4Ra3 B6Ba5
D6Ba8 B1Rb4 C4Rb7 H6Rb6 H1Cb7 H4Cb8 J6Cb3
B8Cb7 B7Bb3 D8Bb5 J1Bb6 J5Bb7 C3Ca5 A3Ca7
D7Ca7 A8Ca4 F9Ca3 A5Ra3 A9Ra8 C5Ra4 D3Ra3
E1Ra5 F2Ra8 C2Ba3 C1Ba8 E8Ba8

124	127	5	9	14	6	3	248	278
1246	8	12367	2345	1345	124	24567	9	257
246	26	9	23458	7	248	1	2468	258
3	1567	1678	46	2	4	4568	1468	9
12569	12569	1268	7	469	3	24568	12468	1258
269	4	26	1	8	5	26	7	23
8	12569	126	2356	13569	1279	27	123	4
126	3	4	268	16	1278	9	5	1278
7	1259	12	23458	13459	12489	28	1238	6

E1Ca5 B3Ca3 F9Ca3 C4Ra3 D7Ra5 F1Ra9 A2Ba7
C6Ba8 E5Ba9 D6Rb4 D4Cb6 D2Bb1 D3Ca7 C9Ra5
D8Ra8 A9Ba8 E3Ba8 J7Ca8 H4Ra8 B9Rb7 G7Ca7
E9Ra1 H6Ra7 H9Ba2 H1Rb6 H5Cb1 A5Bb4 F3Ca6
J4Ca4 G5Ca6 B6Ca1 A1Ra1 B4Ra2 B7Ra6 F7Ra2
G8Ra3 C2Ba6 B5Ba5 C8Ba4 E2Ba2 E8Ba6 J5Ba3
J8Ba1 A8Rb2 B1Rb4 C1Rb2 E7Rb4 G4Rb5 J3Rb2
G2Cb9 G3Cb1 J6Cb9 J2Bb5 G6Bb2

9	2457	2478	68	3	2678	4568	268	1
235	6	1238	4	18	9	358	7	258
237	1247	123478	168	5	12678	3468	23689	268
1	79	379	2	6789	5	3678	368	4
4	8	237	136	167	167	1367	5	9
357	579	6	1389	14789	1478	2	138	78
267	3	1279	15689	1689	168	15678	4	25678
26	1249	1249	7	14689	3	1568	1268	2568
8	147	5	16	2	146	9	16	3

G4Ca5 C8Ca9 E3Ra2 J2Ra7 D2Rb9 F2Cb5 B1Ca5
F4Ca9 A7Ra5 B9Ra2 J6Ra4 C7Ba4 E4Ba3 F5Ba4
H8Ba2 H9Ba5 H1Rb6 G1Cb2 B7Ra3 B3Ca8 C9Ca6
A4Ra6 B5Ra1 C4Ra8 J8Ra6 A8Ba8 D8Rb3 J4Rb1
D3Cb7 F8Cb1 A3Bb4 F1Bb3 F6Bb8 C1Ca7 H2Ca4
C3Ca3 E5Ca7 E6Ca1 G9Ca8 A6Ra7 C2Ra1 D7Ra8
E7Ra6 F9Ra7 G7Ra7 H5Ra8 A2Ba2 C6Ba2 D5Ba6
G5Ba9 H7Ba1 G3Rb1 G6Rb6 H3Rb9

4	3567	567	1278	2357	123578	3678	678	9
1	367	8	7	9	37	2	467	5
359	3579	2	6	357	4	1	78	37
7	1256	156	3	8	9	6	1256	4
2389	12349	19	5	247	6	378	12789	1237
23589	234569	569	247	1	27	3678	256789	2367
6	1279	3	12479	247	127	5	1247	8
25	8	4	127	2567	1257	9	3	1267
259	12579	1579	124789	234567	123578	467	12467	1267

J7Ca4 B8Ra4 C8Ra8 B4Rb7 D7Rb6 B6Cb3 B2Bb6
C5Bb5 F3Ca6 J5Ca3 A8Ra6 H5Ba6 A5Rb2 J9Ca6
H6Ra7 E5Ba7 J6Ba5 F6Rb2 G5Rb4 H1Rb5 F4Cb4
G6Cb1 A6Bb8 H4Bb2 E2Ca4 A4Ca1 J4Ca8 E9Ca2
D2Ra2 H9Ra1 J1Ba2 G4Ba9 G2Rb7 J8Rb7 G8Cb2
J2Ca1 A3Ca7 F9Ca3 A2Ra5 C9Ra7 E1Ra3 F7Ra7
J3Ra9 C2Ba3 A7Ba3 D3Ba5 F1Ba8 E7Ba8 C1Rb9
D8Rb1 E3Rb1 F2Rb9 E8Cb9 F8Cb5

12345	1456	12567	3568	2369	23569	24689	5679	46789
235	9	256	4	236	7	268	1	68
8	456	2567	56	1	2569	2469	5679	3
59	3	569	2	8	1	69	4	679
19	7	1689	36	5	3469	13689	2	1689
129	168	4	367	3679	369	5	3679	16789
1459	2	3	156	46	456	7	8	1469
6	148	189	137	2347	234	1349	39	5
7	145	15	9	346	8	1346	36	2

A4Ca8 D9Ra7 E6Ra4 F1Ra2 J2Ca5 H8Ca9 G1Ra9
H2Ba4 C2Rb6 D1Rb5 E1Rb1 J3Rb1 B1Cb3 A2Cb1
F2Cb8 H3Cb8 C4Cb5 A1Bb4 C8Bb7 F9Bb1 B3Ca5
A3Ca7 G6Ca5 H7Ca1 A8Ca5 G9Ca4 C7Ra4 G4Ra1
J5Ra4 C3Ba2 G5Ba6 B5Rb2 C6Rb9 A5Cb3 A6Bb6
H5Bb7 F4Ca7 F5Ca9 H6Ca2 A7Ca2 A9Ra9 F8Ra6
H4Ra3 F6Ba3 E4Ba6 E7Ba3 J7Ba6 B7Rb8 D7Rb9
E3Rb9 E9Rb8 J8Rb3 D3Cb6 B9Cb6

8	79	357	4679	2	4569	356	3567	1
6	179	157	3	59	8	25	57	4
135	2	4	167	56	156	9	8	567
245	48	9	268	1	2356	7	356	568
125	3	1258	2689	7	2569	1568	4	5689
15	6	1578	89	4	359	1358	2	589
12349	1489	12368	5	369	7	2468	69	2689
12349	149	1236	12469	8	123469	2456	5679	25679
7	5	268	2469	69	2469	2468	1	3

G5Ca3 B7Ra2 C1Ra3 F3Ra7 H3Ba3 A3Rb5 B3Cb1
G2Ca1 H2Rb4 D2Cb8 E3Bb2 D1Ca4 G7Ra4 J5Ra9
B5Rb5 C5Cb6 B8Cb7 B2Bb9 C6Bb1 C9Bb5 A2Ca7
H4Ca1 H6Ca6 H9Ca7 C4Ra7 H1Ra2 G1Ba9 G9Ba2
D9Rb6 G8Rb6 H7Rb5 G3Cb8 D4Cb2 J7Cb8 A8Cb3
H8Cb9 A7Bb6 D8Bb5 E7Bb1 J3Bb6 J4Bb4 F1Ca1
E4Ca6 J6Ca2 A6Ca4 F7Ca3 A4Ra9 D6Ra3 E9Ra8
F6Ra5 E1Ba5 F4Ba8 E6Ba9 F9Ba9

1258	123589	235789	3478	2456	2345	13457	134678	34567
58	4	3578	9	56	1	357	2	3567
6	12358	23578	3478	245	2345	13457	13478	9
125	1259	4	13	8	359	6	379	357
3	25689	25689	4	7	459	2459	49	1
7	159	59	2	1459	6	3459	349	8
248	7	2368	14	1249	249	1349	5	346
24	236	236	5	1249	8	13479	134679	3467
9	5	1	6	3	7	8	4	2

E7Ca2 J8Ra4 J2Ra5 F7Ba4 E4Rb4 E8Rb9 G4Cb1
E6Cb5 F8Cb3 D4Bb3 D8Bb7 F5Ca1 A9Ca4 F3Ra5
D6Ba9 D9Ba5 F2Rb9 A3Ca9 E2Ca8 E3Ra6 H2Ba6
H8Rb1 C8Cb8 C4Bb7 A8Bb6 B3Ca7 A4Ca8 B5Ca6
G9Ca6 A7Ra7 B1Ra8 A1Ba5 C7Ba1 G3Ba8 H9Ba7
A5Rb2 B9Rb3 A6Cb3 B7Cb5 A2Bb1 C6Bb4 D1Ca1
C2Ca3 C5Ca5 G6Ca2 C3Ra2 D2Ra2 G7Ra3 H1Ba2
H3Ba3 H7Ba9 G1Rb4 H5Rb4 G5Cb9

23469	13567	123459	1359	23589	1238	1234678	12467	12489
23469	8	12349	139	239	123	123467	5	1249
239	135	12359	4	6	7	1238	12	1289
7	9	23	35	1	234	24	8	6
236	136	123	8	2345	9	1247	1247	1245
5	4	128	6	7	26	12	9	3
489	2	7	169	489	1468	5	3	148
3489	35	34589	13679	3489	13468	12468	1246	1248
1	3	6	2	348	5	9	4	7

A2Ca7 H4Ca7 E9Ca5 B7Ra7 D4Ra5 F3Ra8 J5Ra8
A5Ba5 A6Ba8 E8Ba7 F4Rb6 J2Rb3 J8Rb4 H2Cb5
F6Cb2 C2Bb1 F7Bb1 E2Ca6 E3Ca1 C3Ca5 B5Ca2
B1Ra6 G6Ra6 C8Rb2 H9Ca2 B6Rb1 G4Rb1 G9Cb8
C9Bb9 H7Bb6 H1Ca8 C7Ca8 A8Ca6 A9Ca1 C1Ra3
H8Ra1 A7Ba3 B9Ba4 D3Ba3 A4Rb9 B3Rb9 D6Rb4
E1Rb2 A1Cb4 H3Cb4 B4Cb3 E5Cb3 H6Cb3 D7Cb2
E7Cb4 A3Bb2 G1Bb9 H5Bb9 G5Ca4

4	6	29	278	3	78	789	1	5
158	18	3	4678	9	15678	2	468	467
7	128	1259	2468	2468	1568	4689	4689	3
13689	5	1469	2368	268	689	1469	7	12469
13689	13478	14679	23678	5	6789	1469	23469	12469
2	37	679	1	6	4	569	369	8
16	1247	12467	5	468	3	146789	24689	124679
136	9	1246	468	7	68	1468	5	1246
56	47	8	9	1	2	3	46	467

C3Ca5 F7Ca5 B6Ra5 H1Ra3 J1Ra5 A3Ba9 C6Ba1
F5Rb6 F3Cb7 F2Bb3 H6Ca6 E8Ca3 A4Ra2 D4Ra3
F8Ra9 C2Ba2 C7Ba9 D5Ba2 G8Ca2 G9Ca9 E9Ra2
H3Ra2 G5Ca8 C8Ca8 A6Ra8 C4Ra6 H7Ra8 B4Ba7
E4Ba8 H4Ba4 H9Ba1 A7Rb7 C5Rb4 D6Rb9 D1Cb8
E6Cb7 G7Cb4 B1Bb1 J8Bb6 E1Ca9 B2Ca8 B8Ca4
J9Ca7 B9Ra6 G2Ra7 J2Ra4 D9Ba4 G3Ba1 D3Rb6
E2Rb1 G1Rb6 E3Cb4 D7Cb1 E7Cb6

14569	356	13469	2	13689	7	145689	4568	1458
8	356	13469	3569	1369	1359	124569	456	7
15679	567	2	569	4	1589	3	568	158
56	9	368	1	23	4	58	7	358
2	4	378	357	3	35	158	9	6
57	1	37	8	39	6	45	2	345
3	2	468	46	7	8	4568	1	9
1469	68	5	3469	123689	12389	7	3468	2348
14679	678	146789	3469	5	12389	2468	3468	2348

E4Ca7 B7Ra2 D5Ra2 E7Ra1 F5Ra9 G7Ra5 A7Ba9
E6Ba5 D7Rb8 E5Rb3 F7Rb4 G6Rb8 E3Cb8 J7Cb6
A5Ca8 A2Ca3 A8Ra5 H2Ca6 G4Ra6 B5Ba6 J2Ba8
B2Rb5 B8Rb4 G3Rb4 H5Rb1 H1Cb9 C2Cb7 J8Cb3
A9Cb1 A3Bb6 C1Bb1 C9Bb8 H8Bb8 A1Ca4 D1Ca6
J3Ca1 B3Ca9 C4Ca5 B6Ca1 C8Ca6 B4Ra3 C6Ra9
D9Ra5 J1Ra7 F1Ba5 F3Ba7 F9Ba3 H6Ba3 J4Ba9
D3Rb3 H4Rb4 J6Rb2 H9Cb2 J9Cb4

3	17	1467	159	2	14569	4567	1679	8
12458	1278	14678	13589	3469	134569	34567	1679	34679
1458	9	1468	1358	7	13456	3456	2	346
6	4	189	1279	9	179	278	3	5
12	123	5	4	36	8	9	67	267
7	238	389	239	5	369	2468	68	1
489	378	2	3579	349	34579	1	6789	3679
89	5	3789	6	1	2	378	4	379
149	6	13479	379	8	3479	237	5	2379

F7Ra4 D5Rb9 F3Ra9 D3Rb8 D7Cb2 F2Ca3 F4Ca2
H7Ca8 J9Ca2 E5Ra3 F6Ra6 F8Ra8 B5Ba6 G5Rb4
H1Rb9 G1Cb8 G2Bb7 B2Ca8 B1Ra2 C4Ra8 H9Ra7
C1Ba5 E2Ba2 E8Ba7 A2Rb1 E1Rb1 E9Rb6 H3Rb3
J7Rb3 J1Cb4 C7Cb6 A8Cb9 G9Cb9 C3Bb4 A4Bb5
B8Bb1 J3Bb1 G8Bb6 A3Ca6 D4Ca1 G6Ca5 B7Ca5
B9Ca4 A6Ra4 A7Ra7 B3Ra7 C6Ra1 D6Ra7 G4Ra3
B6Ba3 C9Ba3 J4Ba7 B4Rb9 J6Rb9

13458	1568	14568	38	7	68	1469	12468	1248
2	678	468	1	368	9	467	4678	5
18	9	168	5	4	2	167	3	178
458	3	2458	6	28	1	457	9	478
14589	12568	1245689	7	289	3	1456	1468	148
14589	1568	7	489	89	458	2	1468	1348
189	4	1289	2389	123689	678	137	5	1237
6	1258	1258	2348	1238	478	1347	1247	9
7	12	3	249	5	4	8	124	6

A1Ca3 B2Ca7 F6Ca5 A7Ca9 B5Ra3 F9Ra3 J4Ra9
A6Ba6 F4Ba4 A4Rb8 J6Rb4 G5Ca6 H8Ca7 G6Ra7
H7Ra4 H5Ba1 G7Ba3 B7Rb6 G4Rb2 H6Rb8 H4Cb3
G9Cb1 J8Bb2 A9Ca2 C3Ra6 J2Ra1 A2Rb5 H2Cb2
H3Bb5 D3Rb2 D5Cb8 F5Bb9 G1Ca9 E5Ca2 E3Ra9
G3Ra8 C1Ba8 F1Ba1 B3Rb4 C9Rb7 A3Cb1 C7Cb1
B8Cb8 D9Cb4 A8Bb4 D1Bb5 E7Bb5 E9Bb8 F8Bb6
E1Ca4 E2Ca6 F2Ca8 D7Ca7 E8Ca1

67	2567	3	4	157	9	8	267	167
9	25678	278	125	157	257	1247	2467	3
1	27	4	6	37	8	9	27	5
38	289	289	7	4	1	5	5689	69
478	14789	6	589	2	5	3	45789	1479
5	14789	1789	389	389	36	147	46789	2
4678	3	789	2589	5789	2457	2457	1	479
2	1479	5	139	1379	347	6	3479	8
478	14789	1789	123589	6	23457	2457	234579	479

D1Ca3 F6Ca6 C5Ra3 G1Ra6 F4Ba3 A1Rb7 D7Rb5
E6Rb5 C2Cb2 B3Bb8 C8Bb7 D3Ca2 J8Ca5 A8Ra2
J6Ra3 H8Ba3 B7Ca4 A9Ba1 A5Rb5 B8Rb6 D9Rb6
E9Rb7 A2Cb6 B2Cb5 E2Cb1 G5Cb8 F7Cb1 F5Bb9
G4Bb5 J3Ca1 E4Ca8 E8Ra9 D2Ba9 F8Ba4 D8Rb8
E1Rb4 F3Rb7 J1Cb8 F2Cb8 G3Cb9 G9Bb4 H6Ca4
J9Ca9 H4Ra9 J2Ra4 H2Ba7 H5Ba1 B5Rb7 J4Rb2
B4Cb1 B6Cb2 G6Cb7 J7Cb7 G7Bb2

3	456	8	5	2	16	9	145	7
469	2456	2459	589	7	1689	13568	13458	156
1	567	579	3	5689	4	568	58	2
48	3458	6	1	3589	7	2	589	59
48	9	2345	2458	358	238	1578	6	15
7	258	1	2589	5689	2689	4	589	3
4689	134678	3479	2789	1389	12389	13567	123579	1569
2	1378	379	6	1389	5	137	1379	4
5	1367	379	279	4	1239	1367	12379	8

E4Ca4 E7Ra7 E9Ba1 A4Rb5 E1Rb8 D1Cb4 C8Rb5
B9Cb6 B1Bb9 C7Bb8 G1Ca6 G7Ca5 C5Ra9 J7Ra6
A6Ba6 D9Ba5 A2Rb4 B4Rb8 C3Rb7 D2Rb3 G9Rb9
C2Cb6 D5Cb8 B6Cb1 A8Cb1 B7Bb3 D8Bb9 G3Ca4
F5Ca6 G6Ca8 H7Ca1 B8Ca4 F8Ca8 F2Ra5 H2Ra8
H3Ra9 J2Ra1 B3Ba5 E3Ba2 E5Ba5 J3Ba3 G2Ba7
G5Ba1 B2Rb2 E6Rb3 G4Rb2 H5Rb3 F4Cb9 J6Cb9
G8Cb3 H8Cb7 F6Bb2 J4Bb7 J8Bb2

8	4567	467	3	14567	9	147	457	2
2579	3	2479	2478	12457	1457	1478	6	157
257	1	2467	24678	24567	4567	3478	9	57
27	2467	3	9	467	8	5	27	167
1	25679	26789	67	3567	567	36789	2378	4
579	45679	46789	1	34567	2	36789	378	679
4	279	1279	5	12679	3	679	7	8
379	8	5	467	4679	467	2	1	679
6	279	1279	247	8	147	479	457	3

H1Ca3 C7Ra3 D9Ra1 J8Ra5 B7Ba8 J7Ba4 G8Rb7
A8Cb4 D8Cb2 D1Bb7 C4Ca8 A7Ca1 G2Rb2 J4Rb2
J6Rb1 G3Cb1 E3Ca2 B5Ca1 B1Ra2 E8Ra8 B3Ba9
C5Ba2 F3Ba8 F8Ba3 C1Rb5 J3Rb7 F1Cb9 J2Cb9
A3Cb6 C9Cb7 A2Bb7 C3Bb4 B9Bb5 F9Bb6 E5Ca3
E6Ca5 G7Ca6 H9Ca9 A5Ra5 C6Ra6 E7Ra9 F2Ra5
G5Ra9 D2Ba4 F7Ba7 D5Rb6 E2Rb6 F5Rb4 E4Cb7
H5Cb7 B4Bb4 H6Bb4 H4Ca6 B6Ca7

5789	2578	24578	12479	14679	12469	12358	1345	1248
6	3	2458	124	14	124	1258	9	7
79	1	247	5	3	8	2	6	24
2	78	9	13478	1478	134	6	1347	5
1578	5678	13578	1234789	146789	123469	12379	1347	1249
17	4	137	12379	5	12369	12379	8	129
1578	578	6	1389	2	1359	4	157	189
4	9	158	6	18	7	158	2	3
3	2578	12578	1489	1489	1459	15789	157	6

E2Ca6 C1Ra9 F6Ra6 A5Ba6 C7Rb2 C9Cb4 C3Bb7
A4Ra7 A6Ba9 A3Ca4 A2Ra2 J3Ba2 A8Ca5 A7Ra3
B3Ra5 H7Ra5 A1Ba8 A9Ba1 E1Ba5 B7Rb8 J7Ca9
G9Ca8 G4Ra9 E5Ba9 G6Ba3 E9Rb2 G2Rb5 F9Cb9
F3Ca3 D5Ca7 B6Ca2 J6Ca5 D6Ra1 E7Ra7 F4Ra2
F1Ba7 E6Ba4 F7Ba1 D2Rb8 E8Rb3 G1Rb1 J2Cb7
E3Cb1 H3Cb8 D4Cb3 E4Cb8 D8Cb4 G8Cb7 H5Bb1
J8Bb1 B4Ca1 J5Ca8 B5Ra4 J4Ra4

36	7	9	45	35	348	1	2	3458
8	234	5	1249	1239	12349	6	49	7
13	234	1234	124579	6	1234789	3489	4589	34589
9	23	8	1247	1237	12347	5	47	6
1357	235	1237	1245679	8	123479	3479	479	349
4	6	37	579	3579	379	3789	1	2
67	489	467	3	1279	5	24789	46789	489
2	359	37	8	4	6	79	579	1
567	1	467	279	279	279	24789	3	4589

G2Ca8 E4Ca6 G8Ca6 A1Ra6 F7Ra8 G5Ra1 J3Ba6
H2Ba9 J9Ba8 G1Rb7 H7Rb7 J1Cb5 G3Cb4 H3Cb3
H8Cb5 F3Bb7 G9Bb9 E2Ca5 C8Ca8 A6Ra8 G7Ra2
J7Ra4 C1Ca3 C3Ra1 D2Ra3 A9Ba3 E1Ba1 E3Ba2
A5Rb5 C7Rb9 E9Rb4 A4Cb4 E6Cb7 E7Cb3 B8Cb4
D8Cb7 C9Cb5 B2Bb2 C6Bb2 D5Bb2 E8Bb9 C2Ca4
J4Ca2 F4Ca5 J5Ca7 D6Ca4 C4Ra7 D4Ra1 J6Ra9
B6Ba1 F5Ba9 B4Rb9 B5Rb3 F6Rb3

1348	1348	7	3489	1345	1589	6	248	2458
3468	9	368	2	3456	7	48	1	458
2	5	68	468	146	168	478	3	9
134568	13468	35689	34679	123456	12569	124789	246789	12468
7	146	569	469	8	12569	1249	2469	3
13468	2	3689	34679	1346	169	14789	5	1468
368	3678	2368	5	9	4	128	268	1268
568	68	1	68	7	268	3	24689	2468
9	68	4	1	26	3	5	268	7

G2Ca7 G3Ca2 D8Ca7 C7Ra7 F4Ra7 G1Ra3 H1Ra5
H8Ra9 H9Ba4 H6Ra2 D5Ba2 H4Ba8 J8Ba2 H2Rb6
J5Rb6 J2Cb8 E7Ca2 A9Ca2 B9Ba5 A5Ca5 B5Rb3
C3Rb8 B3Cb6 A4Cb9 B1Bb4 A6Bb8 D4Ca3 G8Ca8
A2Ra3 A8Ra4 B7Ra8 F3Ra3 G9Ra6 A1Ba1 E8Ba6
G7Ba1 E4Rb4 E2Cb1 C4Cb6 F5Cb1 C5Bb4 C6Bb1
D2Bb4 F9Bb8 D1Ca8 F7Ca4 D9Ca1 D6Ra6 F6Ra9
F1Ba6 E6Ba5 D7Ba9 D3Rb5 E3Rb9

1468	1456	1468	3	15679	2	4678	168	468
7	12456	12346	146	8	145	2346	1236	9
12468	9	123468	1467	167	147	234678	5	3468
3	7	169	169	1569	1589	5689	4	2
1246	8	12469	1269	13569	159	3569	7	356
5	26	269	2679	4	789	3689	368	1
9	146	146	8	2	3	456	6	7
2468	246	5	479	79	479	1	2368	3468
1248	3	12478	5	17	6	248	9	48

J3Ca7 E5Ca3 E9Ca5 A5Ra9 G7Ra5 B6Ba5 J5Ba1
G8Rb6 H5Rb7 C5Cb6 D5Bb5 A2Ca5 A9Ca6 A7Ra7
G2Ca4 G3Ra1 E1Ba1 A1Rb4 C1Rb2 E6Rb9 J1Cb8
A3Cb8 H6Cb4 E7Cb6 C3Bb3 A8Bb1 E4Bb2 H1Bb6
H4Bb9 J9Bb4 B2Ca1 F3Ca2 E3Ca4 H9Ca3 B3Ra6
F7Ra9 H8Ra8 J7Ra2 B8Ba2 F2Ba6 D3Ba9 F8Ba3
D7Ba8 H2Ba2 B4Rb4 C7Rb4 C9Rb8 D6Rb1 F4Rb7
C4Cb1 D4Cb6 C6Cb7 F6Cb8 B7Cb3

1456	2	467	146	468	468	368	9	13478
146	46	9	3	5	7	2	168	148
8	3467	467	12469	2469	2469	36	1367	5
7	1	468	469	4689	34689	3689	5	2
2456	4568	2468	245679	1	2345689	3689	3678	3789
256	9	3	2567	2678	2568	1	4	78
2469	46	5	8	2469	1	7	23	39
2469	4678	24678	245679	3	24569	589	128	189
3	78	1	2579	279	259	4	28	6

C2Ca3 E2Ca5 H7Ca5 A1Ra5 B1Ba1 C7Rb6 B8Cb8
A7Bb3 B9Bb4 J8Bb2 E8Ca6 B2Ra6 D6Ra3 J2Ra8
E9Ba3 H9Ba8 F9Rb7 G2Rb4 G8Rb3 G9Rb9 H8Rb1
H2Cb7 C8Cb7 A9Cb1 C3Bb4 E1Ca4 H1Ca9 A3Ca7
C4Ca1 J5Ca7 E4Ra7 J4Ra9 J6Ba5 F4Ca5 G1Ca2
E3Ca2 H4Ca2 E7Ra8 F5Ra2 G5Ra6 H6Ra4 C6Ba2
D3Ba8 F6Ba8 D7Ba9 H3Ba6 A6Rb6 C5Rb9 D5Rb4
E6Rb9 F1Rb6 A4Cb4 D4Cb6 A5Cb8

1578	78	9	12357	6	1278	4	135	1238
3	48	2	159	14589	148	6	15	7
145678	4678	15678	123579	134589	12478	12358	135	12389
6789	5	3678	1279	189	1278	1378	4	1368
4789	1	78	6	89	3	578	2	8
678	2	3678	4	18	5	1378	9	1368
156	9	1356	135	7	146	123	8	12346
15678	3678	4	135	2	16	9	1367	136
2	367	1367	8	134	9	137	1367	5

G9Ca4 C9Ca9 E1Ra4 E7Ra5 G7Ra2 J5Ra4 A9Ba2
D1Ba9 E9Rb8 E3Cb7 E5Cb9 B4Ca9 C5Ca3 F7Ca7
C7Ca8 A8Ra3 B5Ba5 A4Rb1 B8Rb1 A1Cb5 C8Cb5
G3Ca5 G4Ra3 H4Ra5 H1Ca8 F1Rb6 G1Cb1 C1Bb7
J3Bb6 G6Bb6 C2Ca6 C3Ca1 D4Ca7 H6Ca1 H8Ca6
D9Ca6 A6Ra7 C6Ra4 D6Ra2 H2Ra7 J7Ra1 B2Ba4
C4Ba2 B6Ba8 F9Ba1 J2Ba3 H9Ba3 J8Ba7 A2Rb8
D7Rb3 F5Rb8 D3Cb8 F3Cb3 D5Cb1

14689	5	16789	4789	478	479	12479	3	2467
3	4679	6789	2	478	1	479	479	5
2	479	179	4579	6	34579	1479	479	8
89	279	4	1578	1278	257	6	5789	37
5	27	278	3	9	6	478	478	1
689	1	36789	4578	478	457	345789	2	347
1469	2469	12569	1479	12347	23479	234578	4578	2347
49	3	259	6	247	8	2457	1	247
7	8	12	14	5	234	234	6	9

F3Ca3 G5Ca3 A9Ca6 A7Ra2 C6Ra3 D9Ra3 F1Ra6
J7Ra3 C4Ba5 C7Ba1 D5Ca1 F7Ra9 D6Ba2 D8Ba5
J6Rb4 J4Cb1 J3Bb2 E2Ca2 H5Ca2 F6Ca5 G9Ra2
D1Ca8 H9Ca4 D2Ra9 H7Ra7 E3Ba7 G7Ba5 B7Rb4
C3Rb9 D4Rb7 F9Rb7 G8Rb8 H1Rb9 H3Cb5 G4Cb9
E7Cb8 C8Cb7 E8Cb4 C2Bb4 B8Bb9 G6Bb7 G1Ca4
B2Ca7 A6Ca9 A5Ra7 B3Ra6 G3Ra1 A1Ba1 A3Ba8
A4Ba4 G2Ba6 B5Rb8 F4Rb8 F5Cb4

123678	1368	136789	267	4	36	235689	3589	2589
236	4	369	1	5	8	2369	7	29
5	368	3678	267	9	36	2368	348	1
4	168	1678	2569	1268	1569	5789	589	3
68	9	5	3	68	7	1	2	48
1378	2	1378	459	18	1459	5789	6	45789
1368	13568	2	5679	1367	13569	4	3589	5789
36	7	346	8	36	2	359	1	59
9	1358	1348	457	137	1345	23578	358	6

D5Ca2 C8Ca4 E9Ra4 H3Ra4 J7Ra2 G9Ba7 J5Ca7
C4Ra2 A4Ba7 F1Ca7 C3Ra7 D7Ra7 F3Ra3 E5Ca8
E1Ra6 D4Ba6 G2Ba6 F5Rb1 H1Rb3 B1Cb2 G5Cb3
H5Cb6 B9Bb9 G8Bb8 A1Ca8 J2Ca5 A3Ca9 J8Ca3
D8Ca9 A9Ca2 A2Ra1 B7Ra3 C7Ra8 D6Ra5 H7Ra9
J3Ra8 C2Ba3 B3Ba6 A7Ba6 D3Ba1 D2Ba8 F9Ba8
G1Ba1 G4Ba5 H9Ba5 A6Rb3 A8Rb5 C6Rb6 F7Rb5
G6Rb9 J4Rb4 F4Cb9 F6Cb4 J6Cb1

2469	23679	3469	5	23478	1	2478	23478	2378
8	1237	5	234	2347	2347	9	2347	6
2469	123679	13469	234689	23478	234789	2478	234578	12378
7	4	69	2389	238	2389	268	1	5
1	25	8	24	6	247	3	27	9
3	269	69	1289	5	2789	2678	2678	4
46	8	7	1234	1234	234	5	9	23
4569	13569	13469	12348	12348	23458	24678	234678	2378
45	35	2	7	9	6	1	348	38

C4Ca6 H6Ca5 C8Ca5 C9Ca1 B2Ra1 E2Ra5 F4Ra1
G1Ra6 C6Ba9 F2Ba2 H3Ba1 J1Ba5 J2Rb3 C2Cb7
H2Cb9 J9Cb8 A2Bb6 H1Bb4 J8Bb4 A1Ca9 D4Ca9
G5Ca1 F3Ra9 C1Ba2 D3Ba6 H4Ca8 B5Ca4 B8Ra7
A5Ba7 F7Ba7 E8Rb2 F6Rb8 E4Cb4 D7Cb8 F8Cb6
C7Bb4 E6Bb7 H8Bb3 A3Ca4 C5Ca8 G6Ca4 H7Ca6
A8Ca8 A9Ca3 H9Ca7 A7Ra2 C3Ra3 G4Ra3 H5Ra2
B6Ba3 D6Ba2 G9Ba2 B4Rb2 D5Rb3

1259	1569	12569	3	12689	7	4689	49	4689
4	7	1569	1568	1689	569	689	2	3
8	69	3	46	269	2469	1	479	5
13579	4	1579	167	12679	269	259	8	129
6	8	19	14	5	249	249	3	7
1579	2	1579	1478	3	49	459	6	149
257	56	25678	9	4	1	235678	57	268
579	3	45679	2	67	8	45679	1	469
12579	1569	12456789	567	67	356	23456789	4579	24689

D1Ca3 J6Ca3 C8Ra7 F4Ra8 G7Ra3 J4Ba5 G8Rb5
G2Cb6 C2Bb9 A2Ca5 D4Ca7 B6Ca5 J2Rb1 B3Ca6
C4Ca6 D6Ca6 B4Ra1 C6Ra4 C5Ba2 D5Ba1 E4Ba4
F6Rb9 E6Cb2 E7Bb9 F9Ca1 B5Ra9 D3Ra9 E3Ra1
F7Ra4 A1Ba1 A5Ba8 D7Ba5 A3Rb2 A7Rb6 B7Rb8
D9Rb2 H7Cb7 G9Cb8 G3Bb7 H5Bb6 J7Bb2 G1Ca2
F1Ca7 J3Ca8 J5Ca7 J9Ca6 F3Ra5 J8Ra4 A9Ba4
H3Ba4 H1Ba5 H9Ba9 A8Rb9 J1Rb9

7	12	4	5	6	9	3	27	28
5679	1259	1256789	3	127	4	1256789	2679	258
5679	12359	125679	12	8	127	125679	24679	245
2	459	5679	4689	3479	3567	689	369	1
4679	8	679	12469	123479	12367	269	5	23
1	59	3	2689	29	256	4	269	7
3	7	125	1246	124	126	25	8	9
8	12459	1259	1249	12349	123	257	2347	6
49	6	29	7	5	8	2	1	234

C2Ca3 B3Ca8 A2Ra1 A9Ra8 F4Ra8 J9Ra3 D8Ba3
D7Ba8 H8Ba4 A1Rb7 E9Rb2 J7Rb2 J3Cb9 G7Cb5
A8Cb2 B9Cb5 C9Bb4 J1Bb4 H7Bb7 C1Ca5 D2Ca4
E3Rb7 F5Rb2 B2Ra2 B1Ba9 C3Rb6 E1Rb6 H2Rb5
F2Cb9 D3Cb5 E7Cb9 C7Bb1 F8Bb6 F6Ca5 B7Ca6
C8Ca9 B5Ra1 C6Ra7 C4Ba2 B8Ba7 D5Ba7 D6Rb6
G5Rb4 D4Cb9 E5Cb3 E6Bb1 H4Bb1 H5Bb9 G3Ca1
E4Ca4 G4Ca6 H6Ca3 G6Ra2 H3Ra2

12369	123469	2349	8	26	7	1349	124569	13456
2689	5	2489	1	26	3	489	7	468
123689	1234679	23489	269	5	49	13489	124689	13468
1269	8	2459	5679	167	159	1479	3	1456
169	169	59	3	4	2	1789	15689	1568
1369	13469	7	569	168	1589	2	145689	14568
4	23	6	2	9	18	5	18	7
5	23	238	4	12378	6	138	18	9
7	39	1	5	38	58	6	48	2

C2Ca7 D4Ca7 C6Ca4 E7Ra7 G2Ra3 H5Ra7 J8Ra4
J2Ra9 C4Ba9 F1Ba3 H3Ba8 G6Ba1 G4Ba2 J5Ba3
H7Ba3 G8Rb8 H2Rb2 H8Rb1 J4Rb5 F4Cb6 J6Cb8
D5Bb1 F5Ca8 E9Ra8 F9Ba1 F2Rb4 B9Rb4 A3Ca4
D7Ca4 A9Ra3 C3Ba3 A8Ba5 C9Rb6 F8Rb9 F6Cb5
C8Cb2 E8Cb6 D9Cb5 E2Bb1 D6Bb9 A2Ca6 E3Ca5
B5Ra6 D1Ra6 E1Ra9 B3Ba9 A5Ba2 D3Ba2 A1Rb1
B7Rb8 B1Cb2 C1Cb8 A7Cb9 C7Cb1

4589	4589	3	6	2	1	7	259	49
457	1456	1567	9	237	8	2456	1235	1346
2	1469	1679	347	5	347	469	139	8
34579	459	8	237	2367	2367	1	239	3469
3	2	1	5	4	9	68	7	36
6	49	79	2378	1	237	2489	2389	5
589	3	2569	1278	26789	2567	589	4	179
589	5689	4	1278	26789	2567	3	1589	179
1	7	59	348	389	345	589	6	2

G3Ca2 E3Ra1 E7Ra8 F4Ba8 H2Ba6 H8Ba8 A5Rb2
E1Rb3 E9Cb6 A2Ca8 J5Ra8 G1Ba8 C7Rb6 B3Ca6
J7Ra9 H1Ba9 G7Ba5 G6Rb6 H5Rb7 J3Rb5 G4Cb1
B5Cb3 G5Cb9 H9Cb1 B9Bb4 D5Bb6 H4Bb2 G9Bb7
H6Ca5 F7Ca4 D9Ca3 A1Ra4 B1Ra7 C8Ra3 F6Ra3
B2Ba5 B8Ba1 D2Ba4 F3Ba7 D6Ba2 J4Ba3 A9Rb9
B7Rb2 C3Rb9 D1Rb5 D4Rb7 D8Rb9 F2Rb9 J6Rb4
C2Cb1 C4Cb4 C6Cb7 A8Cb5 F8Cb2

2489	289	6	1	24	3	5	4789	4789
7	1	589	458	456	46	49	3	2
2458	2358	58	9	2456	7	14	468	468
5689	4	3	5	2569	269	7	1	89
1	789	2	347	3479	49	6	489	5
569	5679	579	3457	8	12469	2349	249	349
3	256789	5789	47	479	49	249	245679	1
259	2579	1579	6	13479	8	2349	24579	3479
69	679	4	2	1379	5	8	679	3679

C2Ca3 H3Ca1 B4Ca8 F6Ca1 C7Ca1 J5Ra1 H5Ba3
D4Rb5 D6Ca2 F7Ca3 D5Ra6 E4Ra3 F8Ra2 J9Ra3
B6Ba6 C9Ca6 F3Ca7 E5Ra7 E6Ba9 G4Ba7 E2Rb8
F4Rb4 G5Rb9 G6Rb4 G7Rb2 D1Cb9 E8Cb4 F9Cb9
C8Bb8 D9Bb8 J1Bb6 A1Ca8 F2Ca6 G3Ca8 B3Ca9
G8Ca6 A8Ra9 B5Ra5 F1Ra5 G2Ra5 C1Ba4 C3Ba5
A9Ba7 H8Ba5 H7Ba9 A2Rb2 B7Rb4 C5Rb2 H1Rb2
H9Rb4 J8Rb7 H2Cb7 J2Cb9 A5Cb4

25689	679	25678	3678	4	35678	1379	238	123789
468	3	4678	2	1	9	47	5	78
1	79	24578	378	578	3578	3479	238	6
7	1	3568	368	2568	3568	35	9	4
3568	4	9	3678	5678	35678	2	1	3578
358	2	358	134789	5789	134578	357	6	3578
3469	679	1	5	679	2	8	3	39
2469	5	246	14689	3	1468	169	7	129
2369	8	2367	1679	679	167	13569	4	12359

D5Ca2 G1Ra4 G8Rb3 G9Cb9 J4Ca9 F5Ra9 H1Ra9
J6Ba1 F6Rb4 F4Cb1 H6Cb8 H4Bb4 G2Ca6 G5Ra7
H7Ra6 J3Ba7 J5Ba6 H9Ba1 B9Rb7 H3Rb2 J7Rb5
J1Cb3 A3Cb5 B7Cb4 D7Cb3 A9Cb3 J9Cb2 A1Bb2
C3Bb4 C7Bb9 F7Bb7 A2Ca9 F3Ca3 A7Ca1 C8Ca2
D6Ra5 C2Ba7 C5Ba5 A8Ba8 C6Rb3 E5Rb8 C4Cb8
D4Cb6 E9Cb5 A4Bb7 D3Bb8 E1Bb6 E6Bb7 F9Bb8
F1Ca5 B1Ca8 B3Ca6 E4Ca3 A6Ca6

5	7	68	136	126	23	123	4	9
2469	3	469	1467	124567	2457	127	8	25
24	4	1	9	2457	8	6	2357	235
34679	45689	45689	2	4789	1	38	356	34568
347	48	2	5	478	6	9	13	348
1	45689	45689	348	489	349	238	2356	7
6	2	3	1678	15678	57	4	9	68
8	4569	4569	467	3	24579	27	267	1
469	1469	7	1468	124689	249	5	236	2368

J2Ca1 E8Ca1 A3Ra8 C2Rb4 G1Rb6 C1Cb2 E2Cb8
G9Cb8 B1Bb9 B3Ba6 J1Rb4 D7Ca3 H7Ca7 C8Ra7
D5Ra8 E1Ra3 C9Ba3 D1Ba7 E5Ba7 F7Ba8 J4Ba8
C5Rb5 E9Rb4 G5Cb1 G4Bb7 G6Ca5 B6Ca7 J8Ca3
B9Ra5 D3Ra4 F8Ra2 D8Ba5 J9Ba2 D9Rb6 H8Rb6
J6Rb9 D2Cb9 H4Cb4 J5Cb6 A5Bb2 B4Bb1 F3Bb5
F4Bb3 H2Bb5 H6Bb2 F2Ca6 H3Ca9 A4Ca6 F5Ca9
A6Ca3 F6Ca4 A7Ca1 B7Ca2 B5Ra4

459	489	2	14789	14	1478	6	38	1348
1	489	3	4689	5	468	7	8	2
4	6	7	1248	3	1248	5	9	148
6	1278	9	12378	12	12378	4	2378	5
2347	5	48	234678	9	234678	238	1	3678
2347	12478	148	1234678	1246	12345678	2389	23678	3678
24579	12479	1456	12346	1246	12346	1238	235678	13678
247	1247	146	5	8	9	123	2367	1367
8	3	156	126	7	126	12	4	9

F6Ca5 F7Ca9 G8Ca5 A1Ra5 J3Ra5 B8Rb8 C1Rb4
B2Cb9 A8Cb3 C9Cb1 A2Bb8 A9Bb4 G1Ca9 A4Ca9
A6Ra7 A5Ba1 D5Rb2 D8Cb7 D2Bb1 F4Ra1 E4Ba7
H2Ra4 F5Ca6 E9Ra6 F3Ra4 E3Ba8 E6Ba4 H8Ba6
B6Rb6 F8Rb2 G5Rb4 H3Rb1 F2Cb7 G3Cb6 B4Cb4
E7Cb3 E1Bb2 F1Bb3 F9Bb8 G2Bb2 H7Bb2 H1Ca7
J4Ca6 G7Ca8 H9Ca3 G6Ra1 G9Ra7 J6Ra2 C4Ba2
G4Ba3 J7Ba1 C6Rb8 D4Rb8 D6Cb3

4	258	257	9	1	6	28	278	3
1258	3	12567	4578	278	2578	2468	9	1678
9	268	1267	3478	2378	278	2468	1278	5
125	2459	12459	6	2789	3	2589	2578	789
6	259	8	57	279	2579	1	2357	4
1235	7	1259	158	4	12589	23589	6	89
7	1	569	38	3689	89	35689	4	2
28	24689	3	18	5	189	7	18	1689
58	5689	569	2	36789	4	35689	1358	1689

F1Ca3 D3Ca4 D1Ra1 E8Ra3 H2Ra4 J5Ra7 H1Ba2
G5Ba6 C5Ca3 H9Ra6 J7Ra3 G4Ba3 H6Ra9 H4Ba1
G6Rb8 H8Rb8 F6Ca1 J1Ca5 G7Ra5 J2Ra8 B1Ba8
D8Ba5 J3Ba6 J9Ba9 B5Rb2 F9Rb8 G3Rb9 J8Rb1
F4Cb5 E5Cb9 C6Cb7 D9Cb7 B4Bb4 B6Bb5 B9Bb1
C8Bb2 F3Bb2 D5Bb8 E4Bb7 E6Bb2 A2Ca2 C2Ca6
D2Ca9 C3Ca1 A3Ca5 C4Ca8 D7Ca2 C7Ca4 A7Ca8
A8Ca7 B7Ra6 B3Ra7 E2Ra5 F7Ra9

4789	4589	1	45	2	78	6	3789	378
3	6	479	14	478	78	1789	5	2
78	2	57	3	5678	9	178	4	178
124789	134589	234579	29	38	238	124578	13678	135678
6	1348	234	7	38	5	1248	138	9
2789	3589	23579	6	1	4	2578	378	3578
149	7	3469	45	3456	36	1589	2	1568
1249	149	8	245	4567	267	3	1679	1567
5	3	236	8	9	1	7	67	4

B4Ca1 D4Ca9 C5Ra6 J3Ra2 A4Ba5 D6Ba2 G3Ba6
G4Rb4 G6Rb3 J2Rb3 J7Rb7 H4Cb2 G5Cb5 J8Cb6
H5Bb7 F1Ca2 B5Ca4 H6Ca6 D9Ca6 C3Ra5 E7Ra2
H9Ra5 D7Ba4 E3Ca4 F7Ca5 D2Ra5 G1Rb9 H8Rb9
B7Ca9 A2Ra9 B6Ra8 A1Ba4 A6Ba7 F3Ba9 B3Rb7
F2Rb8 H1Rb1 C1Cb8 D1Cb7 E2Cb1 H2Cb4 D3Cb3
C7Bb1 D5Bb8 E5Ca3 G7Ca8 D8Ca1 F8Ca7 G9Ca1
C9Ra7 E8Ra8 F9Ra3 A8Ba3 A9Ba8

59	3	589	6	458	1	579	2	79
125	1268	7	3	258	9	4	1	16
1259	126	4	257	25	27	8	137	13679
12457	12678	12568	12789	1238	2378	123679	1378	123679
127	12678	1268	4	1238	5	123679	1378	123679
3	9	128	1278	6	278	127	5	4
6	4	123	125	7	23	123	9	8
8	127	123	12	9	2346	1237	1347	5
1279	5	1239	128	12348	2348	1237	6	1237

D1Ca4 D4Ca9 H6Ca6 A7Ca5 H8Ca4 A5Ra4 A9Ra7
D3Ra5 G4Ra5 B5Ba8 C9Ba9 J6Ba4 A1Rb9 B8Rb1
A3Cb8 C8Cb3 B9Cb6 B2Bb2 E3Ca6 J3Ca9 C5Ca5
E7Ca9 B1Ra5 C2Ra6 D7Ra6 J4Ra8 C1Ba1 F6Ra8
C6Ca7 C4Ra2 F4Ra7 H4Rb1 H2Cb7 J1Bb2 E1Ca7
F3Ca2 J7Ca7 D8Ra7 F7Ra1 H7Ra2 J9Ra1 J5Ra3
D6Ba3 E8Ba8 G3Ba1 G6Ba2 G7Ba3 D9Rb2 E2Rb1
H3Rb3 D2Cb8 D5Cb1 E5Cb2 E9Cb3

3	6	58	2459	249	245	248	1	7
47	4	9	8	3	1	5	246	24
1478	2	1578	457	46	4567	3468	9	348
9	3458	23568	23457	24	234578	2468	245678	1
148	7	1258	6	24	9	248	3	2458
468	3458	23568	23457	1	234578	24689	245678	2458
5	13	1367	1234	8	2346	1234	24	9
168	1389	4	1239	5	236	7	28	238
2	1389	138	1349	7	34	1348	458	6

C5Ca6 A5Ca9 F7Ca9 B8Ra6 B1Ra7 G3Ra7 J8Ra5
D7Ba6 H1Ba6 B2Rb4 B9Cb2 F3Ca6 G6Ca6 G7Ca2
F8Ca2 E9Ca5 H6Ra2 A4Ba2 D8Ba7 J7Ba1 G8Rb4
H8Rb8 H9Cb3 C7Ca3 D5Ra4 E5Ba2 D3Ca2 J3Ca3
G4Ca3 G2Ra1 J2Ra8 H2Ba9 H4Ba1 D4Rb5 J6Rb4
D2Cb3 F4Cb7 J4Cb9 A6Cb5 A3Bb8 C4Bb4 C6Bb7
F2Bb5 D6Bb8 C3Ca5 F6Ca3 E7Ca8 F9Ca4 A7Ra4
C1Ra1 C9Ra8 E1Ra4 F1Ra8 E3Ba1

23578	12568	235678	459	1249	1245	1356	13678	12568
235	4	235	8	7	6	135	9	125
9	12568	25678	5	3	125	156	1678	4
345	59	1	2	46	7	8	346	569
6	258	2358	1	48	9	345	34	7
3458	7	358	3456	468	3458	134569	2	1569
28	3	9	46	12468	1248	7	5	168
578	568	4	3679	1689	138	2	168	1689
1	268	2678	4679	5	248	469	468	3

D2Ca9 C4Rb5 F6Ca5 F4Ba3 F3Rb8 F1Cb4 F5Bb6
H6Ca3 E5Ra8 D5Ba4 H8Ca1 C7Rb6 H5Rb9 A4Ca9
D8Ca6 F9Ca9 A6Ra4 D1Ra3 F7Ra1 J7Ra9 B9Ba1
G4Ba4 J8Ba4 D9Rb5 E8Rb3 E7Cb4 A9Cb2 A5Bb1
C2Ca1 G5Ca2 G6Ca1 C8Ra8 G9Ra6 C6Ba2 A8Ba7
J6Ba8 H9Ba8 C3Rb7 G1Rb8 A1Cb5 B1Bb2 A7Bb3
H1Bb7 A2Ca8 B3Ca3 E3Ca5 J4Ca7 B7Ca5 A3Ra6
E2Ra2 H2Ra5 J3Ba2 J2Ba6 H4Ba6

35679	13579	1567	4	3689	2	1356	15678	13567
236	23	4	5	7	1	9	68	36
35679	8	1567	369	369	36	1356	2	134567
5789	6	578	129	149	4	125	3	1257
4	35	5	7	136	8	1256	156	9
1	379	2	369	5	36	4	67	8
2568	1245	9	136	1346	3456	7	1456	123456
2567	12457	3	16	146	4567	8	14569	12456
567	1457	1567	8	2	9	1356	1456	13456

D3Ca8 D4Ca2 A5Ca8 H6Ca7 H8Ca9 B8Ra8 C9Ra4
E7Ra2 G1Ra8 G6Ba5 D6Rb4 E3Rb5 E2Cb3 B2Bb2
H1Ca2 G9Ra2 A7Ca6 B1Ra6 H9Ra6 A1Ba3 J3Ba6
A3Rb1 B9Rb3 H4Rb1 H5Rb4 H2Cb5 C3Cb7 A2Bb9
C1Bb5 J1Bb7 D1Ca9 F2Ca7 J7Ca3 C7Ra1 D9Ra7
F4Ra9 C5Ba9 A8Ba7 F6Ba3 E8Ba1 D7Ba5 A9Rb5
C6Rb6 D5Rb1 E5Rb6 F8Rb6 G8Rb4 G2Cb1 C4Cb3
G5Cb3 J8Cb5 J9Cb1 J2Bb4 G4Bb6

12589	1589	6	3489	389	249	7	3459	359
59	4	3	679	1	79	2	8	59
7	89	28	34689	5	249	3469	3469	1
3	1568	1258	69	7	159	159	1259	4
4	157	157	2	39	8	1359	1359	6
1256	1567	9	346	36	145	8	1235	2357
15689	1356789	14578	789	2	79	134569	134569	3589
1689	2	18	5	4	3	169	7	89
589	35789	4578	1	89	6	3459	23459	23589

F5Ca6 F9Ca7 B4Ra6 D2Ra6 B6Ba7 D3Ba8 C3Rb2
D4Rb9 G6Rb9 H3Rb1 E5Cb3 J5Cb8 C6Cb4 A5Bb9
A6Bb2 F4Bb4 G4Bb7 F1Ca2 J9Ca2 A8Ra4 D8Ra2
F8Ra3 A1Ca1 J8Rb5 J1Cb9 B1Bb5 C2Ca9 A9Ca5
A4Ra3 B9Ra9 C4Ra8 A2Ba8 C7Ba3 H7Ba9 C8Rb6
H9Rb8 J7Rb4 H1Cb6 J3Cb7 G8Cb1 G9Cb3 E3Bb5
E8Bb9 G1Bb8 G2Bb5 J2Bb3 G7Bb6 E2Ca7 G3Ca4
D7Ca5 D6Ra1 E7Ra1 F6Ra5 F2Ba1

478	1248	6	347	2358	234578	9	2378	138
3	248	4789	4679	1	2478	267	2678	5
5	128	1789	3679	23689	2378	12367	23678	4
4689	14568	14589	1349	7	2348	12346	23469	1369
46789	1468	2	1349	389	348	5	34679	1369
479	14	3	5	29	6	8	2479	19
68	7	58	2	4	9	36	1	368
1	9	48	367	36	37	346	5	2
2	3456	45	8	356	1	346	3469	7

J2Ca3 A6Ca5 G3Ra5 H3Ra8 J8Ra9 D2Ba5 J3Ba4
G1Ba6 J5Ba5 G9Ba8 G7Rb3 J7Rb6 H7Cb4 E2Ca6
D9Ca6 H6Ca7 A4Ra7 A1Rb4 D3Rb1 F2Cb4 D7Cb2
B7Bb7 F8Bb7 E1Ca7 C3Ca7 E4Ca1 C7Ca1 A2Ra1
F9Ra1 F5Ra2 B3Ba9 D1Ba8 E9Ba9 A9Rb3 F1Rb9
A5Cb8 A8Bb2 E5Bb3 C5Ca9 C6Ca3 E6Ca8 D8Ca3
C2Ra2 D4Ra9 E8Ra4 H4Ra3 B2Ba8 B6Ba2 D6Ba4
H5Ba6 B8Rb6 C4Rb6 B4Cb4 C8Cb8

39	2	139	5	6	7	189	4	18
3459	134579	13459	2489	189	12349	15689	25689	1268
459	6	8	249	19	1249	3	7	12
8	349	23469	49	7	149	146	36	5
1	45	7	3	58	6	2	8	9
34569	3459	34569	489	2	1459	14678	368	14678
7	159	12569	269	4	259	5689	25689	3
234569	3459	234569	1	59	8	45679	2569	2467
24569	8	24569	2679	3	259	45679	1	2467

B2Ca7 J4Ca7 B6Ca3 C1Ra5 D3Ra2 E2Ra4 G4Ba6
E8Rb8 E5Cb5 H5Bb9 G2Ca1 B5Ca8 F4Ra8 G7Ra8
A9Ba8 C5Rb1 C9Cb2 B4Ca2 F8Rb3 F1Cb6 D8Cb6
F3Bb5 H2Ca5 D2Ra3 F2Ba9 G3Rb9 H8Rb2 G8Cb5
B8Bb9 G6Bb2 J1Ca2 A1Ca9 J6Ca5 B7Ca5 J7Ca9
A3Ra3 B9Ra6 B3Ba1 A7Ba1 H1Ba3 H7Ba6 B1Rb4
D7Rb4 H3Rb4 J9Rb4 J3Cb6 D4Cb9 F7Cb7 H9Cb7
C4Bb4 D6Bb1 F9Bb1 F6Ca4 C6Ca9

8	7	236	4	2	1	3	5	9
2345	349	2359	6	258	7	1348	1238	1248
2345	34	1	2358	9	235	6	2378	2478
6	1489	7	159	45	459	2	18	3
1234	13489	2389	1259	2456	24569	14578	1678	14678
124	5	2	7	3	8	14	9	146
9	1368	368	238	24678	2346	1378	123678	5
357	368	4	2358	1	2356	9	23678	2678
1357	2	3568	3589	5678	3569	1378	4	1678

E7Ca5 A3Ra6 F9Ra6 A5Rb2 A7Rb3 F3Rb2 H9Ba2
H1Ra7 C2Rb4 E5Rb6 J6Ca6 J4Ra9 G2Ba1 G3Rb8
H2Cb6 G7Cb7 G5Bb4 H8Bb3 J5Ca7 C6Ca3 D6Ca4
G8Ca6 D2Ra9 G4Ra3 H4Ra8 B3Ba9 B5Ba8 E2Ba8
E6Ba9 G6Ba2 H6Ba5 B2Rb3 C4Rb5 D5Rb5 E3Rb3
C1Cb2 J3Cb5 D4Cb1 B1Bb5 E4Bb2 D8Bb8 J1Bb3
J7Ca8 B8Ca2 C9Ra8 J9Ra1 B7Ba1 C8Ba7 B9Rb4
E8Rb1 F7Rb4 E1Cb4 F1Cb1 E9Cb7

1	7	3	59	89	589	2	6	4
569	2	5689	35679	34689	3589	3578	1	378
4	568	568	23567	1368	12358	3578	357	9
8	1469	12469	39	7	139	1349	2349	5
2579	3	1259	4	19	6	179	8	27
5679	14569	14569	359	2	13589	13479	3479	367
3	4569	24569	8	69	7	459	2459	1
29	89	7	1	5	4	6	239	238
2569	145689	1245689	2369	369	239	345789	234579	2378

B5Ca4 F9Ca6 F6Ra8 F4Ba5 A4Rb9 D4Cb3 A5Cb8
A6Cb5 B6Bb3 J5Ca3 H9Ca3 H2Ra8 E9Ca2 D3Ra2
D2Ba6 H1Ba2 C2Rb5 H8Rb9 D8Cb4 G8Ca2 B7Ra5
J8Ba5 G7Rb4 G2Cb9 J1Bb6 G5Bb6 E1Ca5 E5Ca9
D7Ra9 E7Ra7 G3Ra5 J6Ra9 F1Ba7 D6Ba1 F7Ba1
J4Ba2 J9Ba7 B1Rb9 B9Rb8 C5Rb1 C6Rb2 E3Rb1
F2Rb4 F8Rb3 J7Rb8 J2Cb1 B3Cb6 F3Cb9 J3Cb4
C7Cb3 C8Cb7 C3Bb8 B4Bb7 C4Bb6

6	28	12378	125	9	12357	12357	1257	4
9	24	5	124	37	1237	6	127	8
1247	24	1237	8	37	6	123579	12579	12357
457	3	679	156	2	157	14579	8	1567
24578	1	26789	56	678	578	24579	3	2567
2578	2568	2678	3	4	9	1257	12567	12567
3	7	1268	26	5	28	12	4	9
1258	25689	12689	7	368	4	1235	1256	12356
25	2569	4	269	1	23	8	2567	23567

B4Ca4 J4Ca9 C8Ca9 B2Rb2 A2Cb8 C2Cb4 H2Ca9
D4Ca1 B6Ba1 A7Ba3 J6Ba3 B8Rb7 B5Cb3 A8Cb1
A3Bb7 C5Bb7 C3Ca3 F7Ca7 H9Ca3 C1Ra1 F9Ra1
J9Ra7 D9Ca6 C7Ra5 D6Ra5 A4Ba5 C9Ba2 E6Ba7
E9Ba5 A6Rb2 D3Rb9 E1Rb4 E4Rb6 F8Rb2 G7Rb1
D1Cb7 E3Cb2 G4Cb2 E5Cb8 G6Cb8 D7Cb4 E7Cb9
H7Cb2 G3Bb6 H5Bb6 J1Ca2 F2Ca6 H3Ca1 J8Ca6
F1Ra5 H1Ra8 J2Ra5 F3Ba8 H8Ba5

3458	12358	2345	7	1268	9	24568	24568	246
4589	2589	6	28	3	8	1	245789	2479
7	1289	29	5	1268	4	268	2689	3
2	368	1	4	8	7	9	68	5
345689	356789	34579	128	128	138	23468	124678	12467
348	378	347	9	5	6	2348	12478	1247
1	5679	579	3	4	2	56	569	8
569	4	2579	168	16789	158	256	3	1269
3569	23569	8	16	169	15	7	124569	12469

H5Ca7 E6Ca3 D2Ra3 F7Ba3 J1Ba3 J5Ba9 B6Rb8
D5Rb8 B4Cb2 D8Cb6 E4Bb1 A3Ca3 H4Ca8 E5Ca2
J4Ba6 F3Ca4 F2Ra7 F1Ba8 G3Ba7 J2Ca2 C3Ba2
C8Ra9 H9Ba9 G8Rb5 H3Rb5 H1Cb6 E3Cb9 H6Cb1
G7Cb6 C7Bb8 E1Bb5 G2Bb9 J6Bb5 H7Bb2 B1Ca9
B2Ca5 E2Ca6 A2Ca8 A7Ca5 E8Ca8 A9Ca6 A5Ra1
A8Ra2 C5Ra6 E9Ra7 C2Ba1 A1Ba4 B8Ba7 F9Ba2
E7Ba4 B9Rb4 F8Rb1 J8Cb4 J9Cb1

13689	7	1289	1346	1246	1248	168	5	1248
5	168	128	7	1246	9	168	12468	3
1368	1368	4	1356	1256	128	9	12678	128
16789	15689	15789	146	3	1247	1568	12468	12458
4	1369	19	8	1269	5	136	1236	7
13678	2	1578	146	146	147	13568	9	1458
2	1459	1579	145	8	14	1357	137	6
178	1458	3	9	145	6	2	178	158
189	1589	6	2	7	3	4	18	1589

E5Ca9 G7Ca7 J9Ca9 C8Ra7 E8Ra2 G8Ra3 H1Ra7
J2Ra5 D6Ba2 H9Ba5 E3Rb1 G3Cb9 D2Ca9 C5Ca5
F6Ca7 A1Ra9 C9Ra2 D3Ra7 G4Ra5 F3Ba5 D7Ca5
A4Ra3 H2Ca8 C6Ca8 J8Ca8 H5Ra4 J1Ra1 A6Ba4
G2Ba4 G6Ba1 H8Ba1 B8Ra4 D8Rb6 D1Cb8 E7Cb3
E2Bb6 C1Ca6 C2Ca3 C4Ra1 F1Ra3 B2Ba1 F5Ba1
D4Rb4 F7Rb8 F4Cb6 B7Cb6 D9Cb1 F9Cb4 B5Bb2
A7Bb1 A9Bb8 A3Ca2 B3Ca8 A5Ca6

4	2	18	38	7	168	36	5	9
5	3	6	245	259	245	1	8	27
158	15789	189	23458	235689	124568	23467	23467	237
1356	1569	7	235	4	256	8	12369	235
2	568	38	9	1	7	356	36	4
13568	145689	13489	2358	23568	2568	23567	123679	2357
368	468	2348	1	258	9	23457	2347	23578
7	48	5	6	28	3	9	24	1
9	148	12348	24578	258	2458	23457	2347	6

C2Ca7 J4Ca7 G9Ca8 B9Ra7 B5Ra9 C3Ba9 J6Ba4
B1Rb5 B6Cb2 B4Bb4 G8Ca7 F7Ra7 C1Ca8 E2Ca5
C6Ra1 E3Ra8 A3Ba1 C4Ba5 C9Rb3 C5Cb6 A7Cb6
A6Bb8 F5Bb3 E7Bb3 A4Ca3 F4Ca8 J8Ca3 E8Ca6
D1Ra3 F9Ra2 J2Ra1 F1Ba1 D4Ba2 D9Ba5 G3Ba3
H2Ba8 D6Rb6 F3Rb4 F8Rb9 G1Rb6 H5Rb2 J3Rb2
D2Cb9 F2Cb6 G2Cb4 G5Cb5 F6Cb5 J7Cb5 D8Cb1
H8Cb4 C8Bb2 J5Bb8 G7Bb2 C7Ca4

5	278	29	4	238	6	2378	379	1
134678	12478	12469	2358	2358	238	2378	35679	456789
3468	248	246	9	1	7	238	356	4568
14	6	3	7	48	5	9	2	8
17	9	8	123	23	123	6	4	57
147	12457	124	12368	234689	123489	1378	1357	578
9	18	5	1368	3678	138	4	167	2
2	148	7	168	4689	1489	5	169	3
146	3	146	1256	245679	1249	17	8	679

F2Ca5 D1Ra1 E9Ra5 F3Ba2 A3Rb9 D9Rb8 E1Rb7
F1Cb4 D5Cb4 F9Cb7 J1Bb6 C8Ra5 J9Rb9 B8Ca9
C2Rb2 A2Cb7 A8Bb3 F7Ca3 G8Ca7 B7Ra7 C1Ra3
F8Ra1 J5Ra7 B1Ba8 A7Ba2 J4Ba5 J7Ba1 H8Ba6
A5Rb8 C7Rb8 J3Rb4 C3Cb6 H5Cb9 J6Cb2 B3Bb1
B6Bb3 C9Bb4 F5Bb6 B2Ca4 G4Ca6 B5Ca5 H6Ca4
F6Ca9 B9Ca6 B4Ra2 F4Ra8 G5Ra3 E5Ba2 E4Ba3
G6Ba8 E6Rb1 G2Rb1 H4Rb1 H2Cb8

8	9	2345	235	125	13	145	6	7
1357	1245	23457	23589	6	1379	14589	13459	2589
13567	1256	23567	23589	4	1379	1589	1359	2589
4	2568	25678	269	3	69	56789	579	1
16	1268	9	7	12	5	3	4	68
1567	3	567	4	19	8	5679	2	569
9	568	3568	1	578	2	567	57	4
356	4568	1	35689	5789	34679	2	579	569
2	7	456	569	59	469	1569	8	3

E8Ra4 G3Ra3 J7Ra1 D3Ca8 E9Ra8 A6Ca1 A4Ra3
H6Ba3 J6Ca4 F9Ca6 H2Ra4 G2Ba8 G7Ba6 D6Rb6
G5Rb7 H9Rb9 H5Cb8 G8Cb5 H8Cb7 D8Bb9 J4Ca9
D7Ca7 D2Ra5 F5Ra9 J3Ra6 E2Ba2 E5Ba1 F7Ba5
H1Ba5 H4Ba6 A7Rb4 B2Rb1 D4Rb2 E1Rb6 F3Rb7
J5Rb5 F1Cb1 C2Cb6 A5Cb2 B8Cb3 A3Bb5 B1Bb7
C8Bb1 C1Ca3 B3Ca4 C6Ca7 B9Ra2 C7Ra9 C3Ba2
B6Ba9 C9Ba5 B7Ba8 B4Rb5 C4Rb8

2	1567	1467	13678	34567	1345	148	348	9
456	156	9	12368	23456	12345	7	2348	148
3	8	147	127	247	1249	124	5	6
6	4	12367	5	237	8	126	9	17
689	267	5	27	1	24	3	24678	478
8	1237	12378	9	2347	6	12458	2478	14578
456	9	2346	236	8	235	456	1	457
1	256	268	4	256	7	5689	68	3
7	356	3468	136	9	135	4568	468	2

E1Ca9 C6Ca9 H7Ca9 G9Ra7 D1Rb6 D9Rb1 F1Rb8
D7Cb2 B8Ca2 F8Ca7 F9Ca5 E6Ra4 E8Ra6 F7Ra4
A8Ba3 E9Ba8 J8Ba4 B9Rb4 C7Rb1 H8Rb8 B1Cb5
A7Cb8 G1Bb4 J3Ca8 B4Ca8 G6Ca2 G7Ra5 J7Ba6
B6Ca3 B2Ra1 F3Ba1 B5Rb6 H5Cb5 J6Bb1 J2Ca5
H3Ca2 A4Ca1 G4Ca6 A6Ca5 G3Ra3 H2Ra6 J4Ra3
A3Ba6 F2Ba3 A2Rb7 D3Rb7 F5Rb2 E2Cb2 C3Cb4
E4Cb7 A5Cb4 D5Cb3 C4Bb2 C5Bb7

9	12	3	7	26	4	8	126	5
14	8	124	5	236	9	34	7	1246
457	6	245	8	23	1	34	9	24
2	14579	1456	14	145678	568	457	1458	3
3	1457	1456	124	1245678	2568	457	12458	9
1457	1457	8	1234	9	235	6	1245	1247
14568	1345	7	1349	13458	358	2	34568	468
458	2345	9	6	23458	7	1	3458	48
14568	12345	12456	12349	123458	2358	34579	34568	4678

D2Ca9 J7Ca9 C1Ra7 G4Ra9 J9Ra7 C3Ba5 F2Ra7
C9Ba2 C5Rb3 C7Cb4 B7Bb3 H2Ca2 B3Ca2 A5Ra2
B1Ra4 H8Ra3 A2Ba1 B5Ba6 A8Rb6 B9Rb1 F9Cb4
H9Bb8 G9Ca6 H5Ra4 J1Ra6 G1Ba8 H1Rb5 F1Cb1
F8Bb2 E2Ca5 J3Ca1 F6Ra5 G5Ra1 F4Ba3 D7Ba5
J5Ba5 E7Rb7 G6Rb3 J4Rb2 J8Rb4 G2Cb4 J2Cb3
E5Cb8 J6Cb8 G8Cb5 D5Bb7 D6Bb6 E8Bb1 E3Ca6
D4Ca1 E6Ca2 D8Ca8 D3Ra4 E4Ra4

6	1259	3	129	12	12459	8	9	7
1258	1259	1589	1236789	123678	1234579	23469	369	239
7	4	89	23689	2368	239	2369	5	1
1258	1257	145678	12379	1237	12379	12369	13689	23589
125	3	156	4	12	8	1269	7	259
9	127	178	5	1237	6	123	138	4
13	179	2	13678	4	137	5	1389	389
4	8	157	137	9	137	137	2	6
13	6	179	12378	5	1237	1379	4	389

D3Ca4 B7Ca4 A6Ra4 G4Ra6 H3Ra5 B6Ba5 E3Ba6
J4Ba8 A8Rb9 A2Ra5 B4Ra7 J6Ra2 C7Ca2 C5Ra6
F2Ra2 B1Ba2 B5Ba8 B8Ba6 B9Rb3 C3Rb8 E1Rb5
D1Cb8 J9Cb9 E9Bb2 J3Bb7 G9Bb8 D2Ca7 B3Ca9
A5Ca2 D7Ca6 H7Ca7 E7Ca9 F8Ca8 D9Ca5 A4Ra1
B2Ra1 D4Ra2 E5Ra1 F5Ra7 G6Ra7 G2Ra9 F3Ba1
D5Ba3 D6Ba9 H6Ba1 C6Rb3 D8Rb1 F7Rb3 H4Rb3
C4Cb9 J7Cb1 G8Cb3 G1Bb1 J1Bb3

569	689	4	3	2	7	1	5689	589
369	13689	2	48	5	49	7	3689	389
359	389	7	1	89	6	4	23589	3589
2469	2469	9	7	4689	3	289	124589	14589
2469	5	1	2468	4689	249	3	7	489
8	23479	39	245	1	2459	29	2459	6
23457	2347	35	9	3467	8	6	1346	1347
23479	234789	6	24	347	124	5	13489	134789
1	34789	3589	456	3467	45	689	34689	2

B2Ca1 J3Ca8 H6Ca1 C8Ra2 F2Ra7 F3Ba3 H4Ba2
D3Rb9 G3Rb5 G7Rb6 J7Cb9 F7Bb2 E6Ca2 D7Ca8
J5Ra7 J4Ba6 F4Ca5 J6Ca5 D5Rb6 E1Rb6 A2Ca6
B8Ra6 C2Ba8 C5Rb9 E5Cb8 B6Cb4 B4Bb8 E4Bb4
F6Bb9 H2Ca9 A8Ca9 A9Ra8 B1Ra9 E9Ra9 F8Ra4
C1Ba3 C9Ba5 H8Ba8 A1Rb5 B9Rb3 D9Rb1 J8Rb3
J2Cb4 D8Cb5 G8Cb1 D2Bb2 H1Bb7 G1Ca2 D1Ca4
G2Ca3 G9Ca7 G5Ra4 H5Ra3 H9Ba4

126	1268	5	13468	9	1238	7	1348	3468
1269	7	1239	13468	123468	1238	3468	5	34689
4	1689	139	13678	1368	13578	368	1389	2
3	2459	6	489	248	289	1	248	7
127	124	8	5	1234	6	9	234	34
1259	12459	129	13489	7	12389	3468	2348	34568
159	3	4	1789	18	1789	2	6	89
8	269	29	3679	5	379	34	3479	1
169	169	7	2	1368	4	5	389	389

E1Ca7 C6Ca5 H8Ca7 F9Ca5 C4Ra7 D2Ra5 F7Ra6
G1Ra5 H7Ra4 G6Ba7 E5Ca3 E2Ra1 F8Ra3 F2Ba4
D8Ba8 J1Ba1 J9Ba3 E9Rb4 J8Rb9 J2Cb6 C8Cb1
E8Cb2 A9Cb6 G9Cb8 A1Bb2 A8Bb4 B9Bb9 G5Bb1
J5Bb8 B1Ca6 F1Ca9 H2Ca2 B3Ca1 B7Ra3 C5Ra6
G4Ra9 H4Ra6 C3Ba3 C7Ba8 F3Ba2 D6Ba9 H3Ba9
H6Ba3 A2Rb8 C2Rb9 D4Rb4 B4Cb8 D5Cb2 A6Cb1
A4Bb3 B5Bb4 B6Bb2 F4Bb1 F6Bb8

45	9	457	8	1347	2	1347	6	137
458	3	45678	1456	1479	15679	1479	2	179
245	2567	1	3456	3479	35679	8	34579	379
1	6	2	7	39	8	5	39	4
35	4	3569	136	2	1369	1379	8	1379
7	8	389	134	5	139	1239	139	6
9	1278	3478	123	1378	137	13467	1347	5
6	1578	34578	135	1378	1357	13479	13479	2
2358	12578	3578	9	6	4	137	137	1378

G4Ca2 F7Ca2 G7Ca6 C8Ca5 J9Ca8 D2Ra6 F4Ra4
B3Ba6 F2Rb8 B1Ca8 J2Ca5 J1Ra2 C2Ba2 J3Ba3
C1Rb4 F3Rb9 J7Rb1 A1Cb5 E3Cb5 J8Cb7 A3Bb7
E1Bb3 F8Ca1 F6Ra3 D8Ba3 D5Rb9 G8Rb4 G3Cb8
H8Cb9 H3Bb4 H7Bb3 C4Ca3 H5Ca8 A9Ra3 C6Ra6
G5Ra3 B6Ba9 B9Ba1 E4Ba6 A7Rb4 B4Rb5 C5Rb7
E6Rb1 H4Cb1 A5Cb1 B5Cb4 G6Cb7 B7Cb7 C9Cb9
E7Bb9 E9Bb7 G2Bb1 H2Bb7 H6Bb5

9	568	458	1	48	2	567	7	3
2358	2358	23458	7	348	6	259	129	125
7	2356	1	359	3	39	8	29	4
23568	235689	23589	4	1236	7	2359	1239	125
236	23679	2379	8	1236	5	23479	123479	127
4	1	2357	23	9	3	2357	6	8
238	4	6	239	238	389	1	5	27
1	2358	2358	236	7	348	2346	2348	9
238	23789	23789	2369	5	13489	23467	23478	267

C4Ca5 J6Ca1 J9Ca6 C2Ra6 G9Ra7 H4Ra6 C6Ba9
A7Ba6 H6Ba4 A8Rb7 C5Rb3 C8Rb2 F6Rb3 F4Cb2
G6Cb8 G5Bb2 G4Ra9 J4Ba3 G1Rb3 D1Ca5 D5Ra6
F7Ra5 B9Ba5 E1Ba6 E5Ba1 E7Ba7 B7Rb9 E9Rb2
F3Rb7 J3Cb9 D7Cb3 B8Cb1 D9Cb1 E3Bb3 D8Bb9
J2Bb7 H7Bb2 B2Ca3 E2Ca9 J7Ca4 H8Ca3 E8Ra4
J1Ra2 B3Ba2 J8Ba8 B1Rb8 D3Rb8 A2Cb5 D2Cb2
H3Cb5 B5Cb4 A3Bb4 A5Bb8 H2Bb8

4	56	156	2369	289	35689	1259	1259	7
8	567	9	26	27	56	3	125	4
2	3	57	1	79	4	59	8	6
5	24678	23678	234	248	38	1246	12346	9
39	2489	238	7	6	1	245	2345	2358
369	1	2368	2349	5	389	246	7	238
169	2569	1256	8	3	7	124569	124569	125
13679	679	4	5	19	2	8	1369	13
13679	256789	1235678	469	149	69	1245679	1234569	1235

J7Ca7 B8Ra1 A3Ba1 D7Ba1 H1Ca7 F7Ca6 D3Ra6
F4Ra4 H8Ra6 D2Ba7 F6Ba9 G1Ba6 J5Ba4 H9Ba3
F1Rb3 H2Rb9 J6Rb6 E1Cb9 J1Cb1 J4Cb9 H5Cb1
B6Cb5 B2Bb6 E2Ca4 J3Ca3 C3Ca7 A4Ca6 G9Ca1
A6Ra3 B5Ra7 C7Ra5 D8Ra4 E8Ra3 J2Ra8 A2Ba5
B4Ba2 A5Ba8 D4Ba3 E9Ba5 G7Ba4 C5Rb9 D5Rb2
D6Rb8 E7Rb2 G2Rb2 J9Rb2 E3Cb8 G3Cb5 A7Cb9
J8Cb5 F9Cb8 A8Bb2 F3Bb2 G8Bb9

1	349	8	349	5	469	2	3469	7
2369	3459	24569	1	8	7	469	3469	34569
23679	34579	24569	2349	23469	469	4689	13469	134569
3679	2	4569	459	149	1459	4679	8	13469
69	459	4569	8	7	3	469	12469	1469
3789	34789	1	6	49	2	5	3479	349
4	189	7	59	169	15689	3	69	2
289	6	29	23479	12349	1489	479	5	49
5	9	3	2479	2469	469	1	4679	8

G2Ca1 C7Ca8 E8Ca2 E9Ra1 G6Ra8 C8Ba1 H1Ba8
G4Ba5 J2Rb9 H3Cb2 F2Ca8 D6Ca5 B1Ra2 D5Ra1
H6Ba1 C2Ca7 A6Ra6 C6Ba9 C1Rb6 J6Rb4 E1Cb9
B3Ca9 A8Ra9 G8Rb6 G5Cb9 J8Cb7 F5Bb4 H5Bb3
J4Bb2 H4Ca7 D4Ca9 C5Ca2 J5Ca6 D7Ca7 B8Ca4
F1Ra7 F9Ra9 D1Ba3 H7Ba9 B7Rb6 F8Rb3 H9Rb4
E7Cb4 D9Cb6 D3Bb4 E2Bb5 A2Ca4 C3Ca5 E3Ca6
A4Ra3 B9Ra5 C4Ra4 B2Ba3 C9Ba3

1458	148	1349	1578	6	578	235789	23589	234579
7	8	2	4	58	3	6	589	1
14568	1468	1346	2	1578	9	3578	358	3457
26	5	8	37	237	67	1	4	2379
3	247	47	9	24578	1	257	25	6
9	12467	1467	357	23457	4567	2357	235	8
12468	9	146	1358	13458	458	2358	7	235
18	178	5	6	13789	2	4	1389	39
1248	3	147	1578	145789	4578	2589	6	259

A3Ca9 H8Ca1 B8Ra9 D9Ra9 E5Ra8 C3Ba3 J7Ba9
B2Rb8 B5Rb5 H1Rb8 H9Rb3 H2Cb7 H5Bb9 G7Ba8
C8Ca8 A1Ra5 C7Ba5 E8Ra5 D5Ca2 D4Ra3 D6Ba7
G5Ba3 A6Rb8 D1Rb6 F4Rb5 F5Rb4 G4Cb1 F6Cb6
A4Bb7 J5Bb7 C2Ca6 G3Ca6 J4Ca8 C5Ca1 C9Ca7
A2Ra1 C1Ra4 A9Ba4 F3Ba1 J3Ba4 E3Rb7 F2Rb2
G1Rb2 J6Rb5 J1Cb1 E2Cb4 G6Cb4 E7Cb2 F8Cb3
G9Cb5 J9Cb2 A7Bb3 A8Bb2 F7Bb7

7	269	236	4	8	1	29	2369	5
4	12569	2356	236	7	36	129	12369	8
168	1268	2368	9	36	5	124	12367	2347
68	2468	9	1368	5	3468	7	128	24
568	245678	1	68	469	4689	3	2589	249
3	458	458	7	49	2	14589	1589	6
589	4589	7	358	1	3489	6	23589	239
2	3	568	568	69	6789	589	4	1
15689	145689	4568	3568	2	346789	589	35789	379

E2Ca7 D4Ca1 B4Ca2 C5Ca3 D6Ra3 H6Ra7 B6Ba6
D2Ba2 D8Rb8 D9Rb4 D1Cb6 C7Ca4 A7Ca2 C3Ra2
C9Rb7 J8Ca7 E5Ca4 E4Ra6 E6Ba8 H5Ba6 E1Rb5
F5Rb9 H7Ra9 J7Ba8 B7Rb1 J9Rb3 J4Cb5 F7Cb5
C8Cb6 G9Cb2 E9Bb9 F8Bb1 H4Bb8 G8Bb5 B2Ca5
F3Ca8 G4Ca3 E8Ca2 B8Ra9 F2Ra4 H3Ra5 A2Ba9
A8Ba3 J3Ba4 A3Rb6 B3Rb3 G2Rb8 J6Rb9 G1Cb9
J1Cb1 C2Cb1 G6Cb4 C1Bb8 J2Bb6

13689	2	135689	39	4	36	3589	7	35689
36789	35679	35689	239	1	236	3589	24568	235689
369	4	369	8	7	5	39	1	2369
2	3569	7	359	35689	368	4	568	1
689	1	5689	2579	25689	2468	5789	3	56789
3689	3569	4	13579	35689	1368	2	568	56789
5	8	136	123	23	123	137	9	4
1347	37	13	6	2358	9	13578	258	23578
139	39	2	4	358	7	6	58	358

H1Ca4 E6Ca4 B8Ca4 C9Ra2 G3Ra6 G7Ra7 J1Ra1
A3Ba1 H2Ba7 J2Ba9 H7Ba1 H8Ba2 H3Rb3 C3Cb9
C7Bb3 B1Ca7 J9Ca3 C1Ra6 E5Ca6 D5Ca9 E4Ra2
B6Ba2 F4Ba7 F5Rb3 D4Cb5 G5Cb2 D6Cb8 F6Bb1
D8Bb6 A1Ca3 F2Ca6 G4Ca1 A6Ca6 E9Ca7 B4Ra3
B9Ra6 D2Ra3 G6Ra3 B3Ba8 A4Ba9 E3Ba5 B2Rb5
B7Rb9 E7Cb8 A7Bb5 E1Bb9 F8Bb5 F1Ca8 J8Ca8
H9Ca5 F9Ca9 A9Ra8 H5Ra8 J5Ra5

34678	2	13678	69	3689	38	1789	5	13789
378	3	5	1	2389	4	6	23789	23789
368	136	9	5	2368	7	4	1238	1238
3589	7	238	29	23459	135	1289	6	12489
35689	3569	2368	279	234579	135	12789	12789	124789
1	9	4	8	279	6	3	279	5
2	45	7	3	1	9	578	78	6
35679	13569	1367	4	5678	2	15789	13789	13789
35679	8	1367	67	567	5	12579	4	12379

A1Ca4 G2Ca4 A6Ca8 G7Ra5 H5Ba8 B2Rb3 F2Rb9

G3Rb7 J6Rb5 G8Cb8 B1Ca7 B9Ra8 C1Ba8 J7Ca2

F8Ca2 B5Ra2 F5Ra7 A5Ba9 C9Ba2 J4Ba7 A4Rb6

B8Rb9 J1Rb9 J5Rb6 A3Cb1 C5Cb3 C2Bb6 A7Bb7

C8Bb1 J3Bb3 H2Ca1 H3Ca6 H8Ca3 A9Ra3 E1Ra6

H1Ra5 H9Ra7 J9Ra1 D1Ba3 E2Ba5 E8Ba7 H7Ba9

D6Rb1 E5Rb4 D5Cb5 E6Cb3 D7Cb8 E9Cb9 D3Bb2

E4Bb2 D9Bb4 E7Bb1 E3Ca8 D4Ca9

1	45678	4589	4579	59	479	3468	4678	2
3	245678	458	2457	125	147	1468	14678	9
2479	2457	459	8	3	6	14	147	457
5	9	1	267	4	17	6	3	8
6	48	7	3	89	5	2	49	1
248	3	148	2679	12689	1789	469	5	467
4789	14578	134589	4569	5689	3489	134689	124689	346
489	148	2	469	7	3489	5	14689	346
489	458	6	1	589	2	7	489	34

G3Ca3 G8Ca2 C9Ca5 A7Ra3 D4Ra2 J9Ra3 B5Ba2

F1Ba2 F9Ba7 H6Ba3 D3Rb1 D7Rb6 D6Cb7 C2Ca2

F5Ca1 F4Ra6 B6Ba1 G5Ba6 G9Rb4 H9Cb6 A6Ca4

H4Ba4 C3Ca9 H2Rb1 C8Ca1 C1Ra7 E5Ra9 G7Ra1

A4Ba9 B7Ba8 F6Ba8 F7Ba9 G2Ba7 A5Rb5 C7Rb4

E8Rb4 F3Rb4 G4Rb5 G6Rb9 G1Cb8 E2Cb8 A3Cb8

B3Cb5 B4Cb7 J5Cb8 A2Bb6 B8Bb6 H1Bb9 J8Bb9

J1Ca4 J2Ca5 A8Ca7 H8Ca8 B2Ra4

23469	123469	12369	14567	8	1457	1459	124679	5679
2468	7	126	1456	9	145	145	3	56
469	5	169	3	67	2	149	8	679
3469	13469	8	47	5	347	2	1469	369
234	234	237	9	1	6	3458	4	358
23469	123469	5	248	23	348	7	1469	3689
1	8	369	67	4	379	39	5	2
7	239	4	258	23	3589	6	9	1
5	2369	2369	12678	2367	13789	389	79	4

B1Ca8 E3Ca7 A8Ca2 B3Ra2 J8Ba7 J7Ba8 E8Rb4

H8Rb9 G7Cb3 E7Bb5 C5Ca7 A9Ra7 E9Ra8 B9Ba5

J5Ca6 C9Ca6 B4Ra6 G3Ra6 G4Rb7 D4Cb4 G6Cb9

D6Ca7 E1Ca2 D9Ca3 E2Ra3 F9Ba9 J3Ba3 H2Rb2

J6Rb1 J2Cb9 J4Cb2 H5Cb3 B6Cb4 A6Bb5 B7Bb1

F4Bb8 F5Bb2 A1Ca3 A4Ca1 H4Ca5 F6Ca3 H6Ca8

A2Ra6 C3Ra1 D1Ra9 C1Ba4 A3Ba9 F1Ba6 A7Rb4

C7Rb9 D2Rb1 F8Rb1 F2Cb4 D8Cb6

1235	1359	8	4	25	7	6	2359	259
2567	567	26	1	9	3	457	24578	24578
23567	4	236	256	258	568	3579	1	25789
1347	2	9	57	1457	45	8	6	457
1347	1378	134	579	6	4589	34579	234579	24579
467	678	5	3	478	2	1	479	479
3456	356	7	8	45	1	2	459	4569
9	156	1246	2567	2457	456	457	4578	3
8	56	246	25679	3	4569	4579	4579	1

A2Ca9 D5Ca1 G9Ca6 A1Ra1 D1Ra3 G8Ra9 H8Ra8

C3Ba3 G2Ba3 E7Ca3 A8Ra3 B9Ra8 F9Ra9 C7Ba9

B3Rb6 F8Rb7 F1Ca6 H5Ca7 C9Ca7 D4Ra7 F5Ra4

J7Ra7 E6Ba8 D6Rb5 F2Rb8 G5Rb5 G1Cb4 E4Cb9

A5Cb2 C6Cb6 D9Cb4 C4Bb5 C5Bb8 A9Bb5 E1Bb7

J3Bb2 H6Bb4 B1Ca5 B2Ca7 E3Ca4 H4Ca2 J6Ca9

B7Ca4 H7Ca5 E9Ca2 B8Ra2 C1Ra2 E2Ra1 E8Ra5

H2Ra6 J8Ra4 J2Ra5 H3Ba1 J4Ba6

237	12357	1237	8	13579	4	12369	1269	2369
4	1378	1378	2	1379	6	139	189	5
238	9	6	1	135	135	7	4	238
23789	123478	123478	14679	134679	137	12369	125679	2369
6	1237	1237	5	1379	8	1239	1279	4
379	1347	5	14679	2	137	8	1679	369
278	6	9	147	1478	127	5	3	28
1	2348	2348	46	4568	25	2469	2689	7
5	2478	2478	3	4678	9	246	268	1

A2Ca5 D8Ca5 C4Rb1 A9Ca9 B5Ra9 A5Ba7 H4Rb6
J5Cb8 H5Bb5 D5Ca6 C6Ca5 C5Ra3 E5Rb1 H6Rb2
G5Cb4 G4Bb7 G6Ca1 F9Ca6 A1Ca3 D9Ca3 B7Ra3
F6Ba3 D6Rb7 D1Cb9 F1Bb7 D4Bb4 F4Ca9 E8Ca7
E7Ra9 F2Ra4 D7Ba2 H8Ba9 F8Rb1 H7Rb4 J7Cb6
B8Cb8 A7Bb1 C9Bb2 J8Bb2 G1Ca2 E2Ca2 J3Ca4
A8Ca6 G9Ca8 A3Ra2 C1Ra8 E3Ra3 J2Ra7 B3Ba7
H2Ba3 B2Rb1 H3Rb8 D2Cb8 D3Cb1

189	2	1679	48	489	789	147	3	4579
139	5	1379	2	349	6	147	8	479
389	4	379	1	389	5	27	6	279
1359	1379	4	356	2359	239	8	127	267
6	79	2	48	1	89	5	47	3
135	13	8	3456	7	23	9	124	246
123589	1389	1359	7	6	4	23	259	2589
7	3689	3569	358	2358	238	2346	2459	1
23458	368	356	9	2358	1	23467	2457	245678

J1Ca4 A6Ca7 A9Ra5 A3Ra6 G1Ba2 G7Rb3 A4Rb8
G9Rb8 E4Cb4 E8Bb7 C1Ca8 D2Ca7 E6Ra8 D6Ba9
E2Rb9 G2Cb1 F2Bb3 B1Ca3 B3Ca1 H6Ca3 A7Ra1
C5Ra3 D4Ra3 J3Ra3 C3Ba7 F4Ba6 A1Rb9 C7Rb2
F6Rb2 H4Rb5 H3Cb9 A5Cb4 D5Cb5 C9Cb9 F9Cb4
B5Bb9 B9Bb7 D1Bb1 F8Bb1 G3Bb5 F1Ca5 J7Ca7
H8Ca4 J8Ca5 G8Ca9 D9Ca6 B7Ra4 D8Ra2 H5Ra2
J2Ra6 H2Ba8 J5Ba8 J9Ba2 H7Ba6

139	4	1367	3	8	79	3579	2	157
2389	2789	2378	1	6	5	3479	348	478
12389	12789	5	234	23479	2479	6	1348	1478
1258	6	128	9	124	3	245	7	2458
7	2589	4	258	2	26	1	568	3
1258	3	128	2458	1247	2467	245	9	24568
6	28	238	7	5	1	234	34	9
12345	1257	1237	6	2349	8	23457	1345	12457
12345	1257	9	234	234	24	8	13456	124567

A3Ca6 E2Ra9 H5Ra9 A4Rb3 E5Rb2 E6Cb6 H1Ca4
J5Ca3 J8Ca6 F9Ra6 J1Rb1 A1Cb9 A6Bb7 C2Ca1
F5Ca7 C6Ca9 B7Ca9 A9Ra1 C4Ra2 C9Ra7 F3Ra1
C5Ba4 A7Ba5 D5Ba1 J6Ba2 H8Ba1 H7Ba7 F6Rb4
J4Rb4 J9Rb5 J2Cb7 F7Cb2 H9Cb2 D7Bb4 H2Bb5
H3Bb3 B3Ca7 G7Ca3 E8Ca5 B9Ca4 D1Ra5 E4Ra8
G8Ra4 D3Ba2 F4Ba5 D9Ba8 F1Rb8 G3Rb8 C1Cb3
G2Cb2 B1Bb2 B2Bb8 C8Bb8 B8Ca3

5	19	6	7	19	8	2	49	3
79	4	2	359	3569	3569	1	8	5679
789	13789	178	123459	13569	234569	46	45679	5679
3	156789	1578	459	579	4579	468	14567	2
27	12567	4	235	8	2357	9	13567	1567
2789	25789	578	6	3579	1	348	3457	57
1	25	9	35	4	356	7	236	8
2478	2578	578	13589	135679	35679	36	12369	169
6	78	3	189	2	79	5	19	4

H1Ca4 C2Ca3 A8Ra4 C7Rb6 H7Cb3 F7Ra4 D7Ba8
F1Ca2 E1Rb7 B1Cb9 A2Bb1 C1Bb8 D3Ca1 C5Ca1
C9Ca9 A5Ra9 B9Ra7 C8Ra5 C3Ba7 F9Ba5 F3Rb8
F2Cb9 H3Cb5 G2Bb2 H8Ca2 J8Ba9 G8Rb6 J6Rb7
J2Cb8 H5Cb6 D8Cb7 H9Cb1 D5Bb5 E9Bb6 F8Bb3
H2Bb7 H6Bb9 J4Bb1 E2Ca5 D2Ca6 H4Ca8 D4Ca9
B5Ca3 F5Ca7 B6Ca6 E8Ca1 B4Ra5 D6Ra4 C4Ba4
G6Ba5 C6Rb2 G4Rb3 E4Cb2 E6Cb3

6	8	5	49	34	39	1	7	2
1	379	347	246789	34678	23689	348	3489	5
2	379	347	4789	5	1389	348	3489	6
57	3567	9	1	68	4	2	3568	38
45	1256	146	3	9	7	4568	14568	148
45	1356	8	56	2	56	7	134569	1349
578	1567	2	45678	134678	13568	9	134568	1348
5789	4	167	56789	13678	135689	3568	2	138
3	1569	16	245689	1468	125689	4568	14568	7

H1Ca9 E2Ca2 F9Ca9 C6Ra1 D5Ba8 G1Ba8 D9Rb3
D1Ca7 F2Ra3 E3Ba1 F1Rb4 J3Rb6 E1Cb5 H3Cb7
F8Cb1 D2Bb6 D8Ra5 E9Ca8 H9Rb1 G9Cb4 J8Bb8
A4Ca4 A6Ra9 J5Ra4 A5Ba3 G5Ba1 J4Ba9 G2Rb5
H5Rb6 J6Rb2 J7Rb5 J2Cb1 G4Cb7 B5Cb7 G6Cb3
H7Cb3 B2Bb9 C4Bb8 G8Bb6 C2Ca7 B4Ca2 H6Ca8
E7Ca6 B7Ca8 C8Ca9 B6Ra6 C3Ra3 E8Ra4 H4Ra5
B3Ba4 B8Ba3 C7Ba4 F6Ba5 F4Ba6

25	7	125	3	4	8	29	6	29
9	3458	23458	257	567	567	2478	2578	1
258	458	6	1257	1579	1579	3	25789	279
4	59	259	6	157	3	1279	279	8
3568	1	358	9	57	2	67	4	367
2368	3689	7	148	1	14	5	239	2369
1	34689	3489	47	2	4679	6789	3789	5
7	2	359	5	8	569	69	1	4
3568	345689	34589	1457	135679	145679	26789	23789	23679

A3Ca1 F4Ca8 J5Ca3 D7Ca1 B7Ca4 A1Ra5 C2Ra4
F6Ra4 H3Ra3 B2Ba3 F5Ba1 G8Ba3 H4Rb5 B5Ca6
C5Ca9 C9Ba7 J1Rb6 F2Ca6 F8Ra9 D8Ba2 F9Rb3
J8Rb7 F1Cb2 E9Cb6 C1Bb8 E7Bb7 E1Ca3 B3Ca2
E3Ca8 D5Ca7 B8Ca8 B6Ra5 C4Ra2 E5Ra5 C6Ba1
B4Ba7 C8Ba5 G4Rb4 J6Rb9 G3Cb9 J4Cb1 H6Cb6
J9Cb2 A9Bb9 D3Bb5 G2Bb8 G6Bb7 H7Bb9 J7Bb8
J2Ca5 D2Ca9 J3Ca4 A7Ca2 G7Ca6

4568	2458	1	2467	3	246	9	25	457
7	2345	9	124	12	124	8	1235	6
46	234	346	5	12679	8	1234	123	347
2	7	3458	89	89	59	345	6	1
1568	58	568	3	4	7	25	258	589
14568	9	34568	1268	1268	1256	2345	7	3458
4589	458	4578	1246789	126789	123469	1356	1358	358
48	1	2	468	5	346	7	9	38
3	6	578	1789	1789	19	15	4	2

G1Ca9 G7Ca6 E9Ca9 C5Ra9 E1Ra1 A4Ba7 D5Rb8
D4Cb9 D6Bb5 F5Ca6 J6Ca9 C9Ca7 E3Ra6 A6Ba6
C1Ca6 H4Ca6 C3Rb4 D3Cb3 D7Bb4 G2Ca4 A9Ca4
F1Ra4 H6Ra4 B4Ba4 G6Ba3 H1Rb8 A1Cb5 H9Cb3
B2Bb3 A8Bb2 C2Ca2 E2Ca5 F3Ca8 E7Ca2 C8Ca3
A2Ra8 B8Ra5 C7Ra1 E8Ra8 F7Ra3 J4Ra8 F9Ba5
G8Ba1 G9Ba8 G4Rb2 J7Rb5 J3Cb7 F4Cb1 G5Cb7
F6Bb2 G3Bb5 J5Bb1 B5Ca2 B6Ca1

9	3	1268	128	78	27	128	5	4
4	126	12568	12589	3589	239	12389	12689	7
12578	127	1258	124589	6	23479	12389	1289	1238
125	1246	123456	2489	4789	2479	125789	1289	1258
12	9	124	6	478	5	1278	3	128
25	8	7	3	9	1	6	4	25
3	124	1249	7	459	8	1245	12	6
178	147	1489	459	2	3469	13458	18	1358
6	5	248	4	1	34	2348	7	9

D3Ca3 B5Ca3 H6Ca6 B8Ca6 A3Ra6 D2Ra6 F5Ra9
E3Ba4 J6Ba3 H4Ba9 J4Rb4 G5Cb5 G3Ca9 D5Ca4
G7Ca4 C6Ra4 H2Ra4 B6Ba9 H1Ba7 C1Rb8 C2Ca7
J3Ca8 H8Ca8 H3Ra1 J7Ra2 B2Ba1 G2Ba2 G8Ba1
B7Rb8 D8Rb9 A7Cb1 C8Cb2 C3Bb5 C9Bb3 E7Bb7
B3Ca2 C4Ca1 B4Ca5 A5Ca7 H7Ca3 C7Ca9 A4Ra8
D6Ra7 H9Ra5 A6Ba2 D4Ba2 E5Ba8 D7Ba5 D1Rb1
F9Rb2 E1Cb2 F1Cb5 D9Cb8 E9Cb1

2367	5	1237	4	36	9	137	8	1237
237	279	4	57	8	357	6	2379	123579
3678	679	3789	2	356	1	34579	3479	3579
1	247	27	3	9	8	457	47	6
3467	4679	5	167	146	467	2	3479	3789
23467	8	2379	567	2456	24567	34579	1	3579
9	3	278	158	125	25	17	6	4
2457	247	6	159	12345	2345	8	2379	12379
248	1	28	689	7	2346	39	5	239

H1Ca5 A3Ca1 E9Ca8 B9Ra1 D7Ra5 C9Ba5 G7Ba1
C1Ra8 G3Ra7 J3Ba8 D3Rb2 G4Rb8 A9Ra2 H8Ba2
H2Rb4 J1Cb2 D2Cb7 H5Cb1 H6Cb3 B1Bb3 C2Bb6
E5Bb4 D8Bb4 H4Bb9 F1Ca4 A1Ca7 B2Ca2 F3Ca3
E4Ca1 A5Ca6 J6Ca4 C7Ca4 A7Ra3 B8Ra9 C8Ra7
E8Ra3 H9Ra7 J4Ra6 C3Ba9 C5Ba3 E1Ba6 E2Ba9
F7Ba7 J9Ba3 E6Rb7 F4Rb5 F9Rb9 J7Rb9 B4Cb7
F5Cb2 B6Cb5 F6Bb6 G5Bb5 G6Bb2

3568	9	368	4	156	2	368	7	138
23568	12357	23678	35679	15679	1359	23468	1239	13489
236	1237	4	3679	8	139	5	1239	139
289	6	5	279	3	89	1	4	7
7	4	239	259	1259	159	23	8	6
238	23	1	2567	2567	458	9	235	357
2359	8	2379	2359	4	359	37	6	13579
1	357	379	8	59	6	347	359	2
234569	235	2369	1	259	7	348	359	34589

J1Ca4 F6Ca4 F1Ra8 G9Ra1 H7Ra4 J3Ra6 B9Ba4
D6Ba8 G7Ba7 D9Rb7 A5Ra1 E6Ba1 A1Ra5 A7Ra6
E5Ca5 H5Rb9 J5Cb2 C4Ra7 F5Ba7 B5Rb6 F4Rb6
B1Cb3 A3Bb8 C1Bb6 G4Ca3 J9Ca8 A9Ra3 B7Ra8
G6Ra5 J8Ra9 C6Ba3 B4Ba5 C9Ba9 H8Ba5 B6Rb9
F9Rb5 J7Rb3 J2Cb5 E7Cb2 E4Bb9 F8Bb3 H2Ca3
G3Ca9 D4Ca2 D1Ra9 E3Ra3 F2Ra2 G1Ra2 H3Ra7
B3Ba2 B2Ba7 B8Rb1 C2Rb1 C8Cb2

123	1279	1379	6	257	8	127	247	1247
126	4	167	3	27	9	12678	5	1278
126	8	5	127	4	17	9	3	127
124568	1269	14689	79	379	367	12378	24789	1234789
7	169	1469	8	39	2	13	49	5
28	3	89	4	1	5	278	6	2789
348	5	3478	279	6	347	2378	1	23789
1368	167	2	1579	35789	137	4	789	3789
9	17	13478	1257	23578	1347	23578	278	6

D1Ca5 D6Ca6 J7Ca5 B7Ca6 A5Ra5 B9Ra8 C1Ra6
H2Ba6 H4Ba5 G1Ca4 E3Ca6 E8Ra4 J6Ra4 A9Ba4
D3Ba4 A1Ca3 A7Ca1 D9Ca1 E2Ra1 J3Ra3 H1Ba1
B1Rb2 E7Rb3 J2Rb7 F1Cb8 A2Cb9 G3Cb8 B5Cb7
E5Cb9 A3Bb7 B3Bb1 C6Bb1 D2Bb2 F3Bb9 D4Bb7
D5Bb3 H5Bb8 J4Ca1 G4Ca9 J5Ca2 D7Ca8 H8Ca7
A8Ra2 C9Ra7 D8Ra9 G6Ra7 H9Ra9 J8Ra8 C4Ba2
F7Ba7 H6Ba3 G9Ba3 F9Rb2 G7Rb2

56	7	3	268	48	24568	1	9	245
1	59	4	239	379	259	6	25	8
569	2	8	169	149	4569	7	3	45
2459	3	259	7	489	1	4589	6	2459
24679	1469	2679	5	489	3	489	12478	12479
8	14569	5679	69	2	469	459	1457	3
34679	4689	1	389	5	89	2	478	4679
23569	5689	2569	4	1389	7	3589	158	1569
234579	4589	2579	12389	6	289	34589	14578	14579

B5Ca7 B4Ra3 H5Ba3 C5Ca1 J7Ca3 G1Ra3 J4Ba1
A4Ca2 B8Ra2 J6Ba2 G4Rb8 G6Cb9 B6Bb5 A6Ca8
A1Ra6 B2Ra9 C1Ba5 C4Ba9 A5Rb4 C9Rb4 F4Rb6
C6Cb6 F6Cb4 A9Cb5 J9Rb9 D9Cb2 H1Ra9 H3Ba2
D1Rb4 E3Rb6 J1Cb7 E2Cb1 E1Bb2 F2Bb5 E9Bb7
J3Bb5 F3Ca7 E7Ca4 H8Ca5 G8Ca7 H9Ca1 D7Ra5
E5Ra9 F8Ra1 F7Ra9 G2Ra4 H2Ra6 D3Ra9 D5Ba8
E8Ba8 J2Ba8 J8Ba4 G9Ba6 H7Rb8

3467	3479	8	59	13459	135	2	13569	569
234	2349	34	7	123459	6	135	13589	589
5	239	1	289	239	38	4	3689	7
9	4578	457	1	6	2	57	4578	3
1347	6	3457	589	59	578	157	2	458
17	1578	2	3	5	4	9	15678	568
123467	123457	34567	256	8	135	3567	345679	24569
12346	12345	9	256	7	135	8	3456	2456
8	2357	3567	4	235	9	3567	3567	1

E6Ca7 C8Ra6 A1Ba6 E4Ba8 F9Ba6 F5Rb5 E5Cb9
C6Ca8 B9Ca8 A2Ra7 H4Ra6 A4Ba5 A9Rb9 G4Rb2
C4Cb9 J5Cb3 C5Bb2 B2Ca9 A6Ca3 G8Ca9 H9Ca2
A5Ra4 B1Ra2 C2Ra3 J2Ra2 B3Ba4 B5Ba1 A8Rb1
E7Ca1 E9Ca5 D3Ra5 E1Ra4 E3Ba3 F1Ba7 D8Ba4
D2Rb8 D7Rb7 F8Rb8 G9Rb4 H8Rb3 H1Cb1 F2Cb1
G7Cb6 B8Cb5 B7Bb3 G1Bb3 G2Bb5 G3Bb7 H6Bb5
J7Bb5 J8Bb7 H2Ca4 J3Ca6 G6Ca1

234	9	234	7	28	5	346	1	346
23457	2357	1	2349	29	2469	8	3467	3456
8	357	6	134	1	14	2	347	9
9	126	24	1245	3	124	46	2468	7
123467	12367	8	1249	1279	12479	5	23469	2346
2347	237	5	6	279	8	1	2349	234
127	4	27	8	6	3	9	5	12
123567	1235678	237	1259	4	1279	369	23689	12368
12356	123568	9	125	125	12	7	23468	123468

J5Ca5 A5Ca8 B6Ca6 B9Ca5 C2Ra5 D4Ra5 D8Ra8
G7Ra9 H1Ba5 H6Ba7 C5Rb1 C6Cb4 C4Bb3 G3Ca7
E4Ca4 E6Ca9 C8Ra7 F8Ra9 H4Ra9 B5Ba9 D6Ba1
B4Rb2 J6Rb2 J4Cb1 D2Ca2 D7Ra6 A9Ba6 F9Ba4
H8Ba6 D3Rb4 H7Rb3 H3Cb2 A7Cb4 J8Cb4 J9Cb8
A3Bb3 B8Bb3 G1Bb1 H9Bb1 A1Ca2 B1Ca4 E2Ca1
H2Ca8 E8Ca2 E9Ca3 B2Ra7 E1Ra6 F5Ra2 G9Ra2
F1Ba7 E5Ba7 J2Ba6 F2Rb3 J1Rb3

4589	145789	145689	379	2	1	156789	1356789	13679
29	3	1269	5	179	8	12679	4	12679
2589	125789	12589	6	1379	4	125789	135789	12379
7	59	59	2	4	3	169	169	8
589	6	3	9	19	15	4	2	179
1	249	249	8	69	7	69	369	5
23458	2458	2458	1	3678	9	25678	5678	267
24589	124589	7	4	68	26	3	15689	1269
6	1289	1289	37	5	2	12789	1789	4

G1Ca3 H4Ca4 E6Ca5 H6Ca6 E9Ra7 E1Ra8 F8Ra3
J4Ra3 C5Ba3 E5Ba1 F5Ba6 J6Ba2 G5Ba7 A6Rb1
B5Rb9 E4Rb9 F7Rb9 H5Rb8 B1Cb2 A4Cb7 A1Ca4
C2Ca7 A9Ca3 B7Ra7 J8Ba7 C1Ca9 A8Ra9 H9Ba9
H1Rb5 H8Cb1 D8Bb6 H2Bb2 J7Bb8 J2Ca1 F3Ca2
C8Ca8 D7Ra1 F2Ra4 G2Ra8 J3Ra9 A3Ba8 D2Ba9
G3Ba4 A2Rb5 D3Rb5 G8Rb5 C3Cb1 A7Cb6 B3Bb6
B9Bb1 C9Bb2 G7Bb2 C7Ca5 G9Ca6

7	29	18	1249	3	49	59	1589	6
5	2369	136	7	29	8	39	139	4
1369	4	1368	169	5	69	379	2	1789
246	2567	4567	3	79	1	24569	4589	2589
1236	8	1356	59	4	59	23569	7	259
34	357	9	8	6	2	1	345	5
8	5679	4567	24569	1	45679	24579	459	3
349	1	2	459	79	34579	8	6	579
3469	35679	34567	24569	2789	345679	24579	1459	12579

J5Ca8 F2Ra7 D5Ba7 F9Rb5 H5Rb9 B5Cb2 H9Cb7
C7Ca7 A2Ra2 E9Rb2 D1Ca2 J2Ca3 H6Ra3 H4Ba5
E4Rb9 H1Rb4 F1Cb3 E6Cb5 F8Bb4 C3Ca3 D3Ca4
B8Ca3 B3Ra1 C9Ra8 D2Ra5 E7Ra3 B2Ba6 A3Ba8
A8Ba1 E1Ba1 D7Ba6 D8Ba8 A4Rb4 B7Rb9 C1Rb9
D9Rb9 E3Rb6 G2Rb9 J1Cb6 A6Cb9 C6Cb6 A7Cb5
G8Cb5 J9Cb1 C4Bb1 G3Bb7 J4Bb2 J8Bb9 J3Ca5
G4Ca6 J6Ca7 G7Ca2 G6Ra4 J7Ra4

678	5	467	3	24678	468	689	1	6789
1	478	2	9	45678	468	568	5678	3
9	78	3	12678	125678	168	4	25678	5678
678	3789	679	5	13468	13468	2	34678	6789
4	2378	567	268	9	368	3568	35678	1
2568	2389	1	2468	23468	7	35689	34568	5689
57	479	8	467	3467	3469	1	356	2
3	19	59	168	168	2	7	568	4
27	6	47	1478	13478	5	38	9	8

H2Ca1 G6Ca9 C8Ca2 A5Ra2 H3Ra9 J1Ra2 G1Ba5
J9Rb8 J7Cb3 G8Bb6 E3Ca5 G5Ra3 H8Ra5 J3Ra7
G2Ba4 G4Ba7 D3Rb6 F1Cb8 A3Cb4 A6Bb8 D1Bb7
A1Ca6 E7Ca8 A9Ca7 A7Ra9 C2Ra8 D5Ra8 E8Ra7
B2Ba7 B8Ba8 D6Ba1 H4Ba8 C6Rb6 D9Rb9 H5Rb6
D2Cb3 C4Cb1 F5Cb4 B6Cb4 E6Cb3 C9Cb5 B5Bb5
C5Bb7 B7Bb6 E2Bb2 D8Bb4 F8Bb3 F9Bb6 J4Bb4
J5Bb1 F2Ca9 F4Ca2 E4Ca6 F7Ca5

3579	1357	2	1349	489	138	3567	145	34567
37	6	4	5	2	123	237	9	8
359	8	139	12349	6	7	235	1245	2345
1	4	367	237	257	9	8	25	2356
23679	237	36789	2347	1	2358	23569	245	234569
239	23	5	6	248	238	239	7	1
2457	1257	17	8	3	125	2579	6	2579
8	9	67	27	257	4	1	3	257
23567	12357	1367	1279	2579	1256	4	258	2579

G1Ca4 E3Ca8 J6Ca6 J8Ca8 B6Ra1 F5Ra4 H3Ra6
E1Ba6 F6Ba8 J4Ba1 A6Rb3 B5Rb2 C3Ca9 A5Ca8
A7Ca6 A4Ra9 C8Ra1 D9Ra6 A2Ba1 C4Ba4 F1Ba9
J5Ba9 J1Ca2 G3Ca1 F2Ca2 F7Ra3 C9Ba3 B7Rb7
C1Rb5 A1Cb7 B1Cb3 C7Cb2 J2Ra5 J3Ba3 D3Rb7
G2Rb7 J9Rb7 E2Cb3 D5Cb5 E4Bb7 E6Bb2 D8Bb2
H5Bb7 H4Ca2 D4Ca3 G6Ca5 A8Ca5 A9Ra4 E7Ra5
G9Ra2 H9Ra5 E8Ba4 E9Ba9 G7Ba9

58	48	4578	24579	1	3	2589	25	6
2	138	13578	6	579	7	13589	4	589
156	9	13456	245	8	24	1235	1235	7
1589	7	124589	29	29	6	12458	125	3
1689	1268	12689	3	4	5	12678	1267	28
3	1246	12456	8	27	127	124567	9	245
7	126	1269	245	3	24	24569	8	2459
68	5	2368	247	27	9	23467	2367	1
4	238	2389	1	6	278	23579	2357	259

B5Ca5 F6Ca1 J6Ca8 A4Ba9 F5Ba7 G4Ba5 B6Rb7
D4Rb2 H5Rb2 C4Cb4 D5Cb9 G6Cb4 C6Bb2 H4Bb7
E1Ca9 A3Ca7 F9Ca4 A2Ra4 D3Ra4 H7Ra4 J9Ca5
H3Ra8 H1Rb6 H8Cb3 E8Ca6 C3Ra6 E7Ra7 G7Ra6
F2Ba6 J8Ba7 F3Ca5 A8Ca2 C7Ra3 F7Ra2 G9Ba2
E9Rb8 G2Rb1 J7Rb9 E2Cb2 G3Cb9 B7Cb1 B9Cb9
B3Bb3 C8Bb5 E3Bb1 D7Bb5 J2Bb3 C1Ca1 A1Ca5
B2Ca8 J3Ca2 A7Ca8 D8Ca1 D1Ra8

12368	12378	12378	5	2369	236	279	4	1267
12346	123	5	2469	7	2346	29	169	8
246	9	27	1	26	8	257	3	2567
9	2357	237	8	236	2346	1	57	23457
1238	12378	4	29	5	123	6	78	237
12358	12358	6	24	123	7	2458	58	9
158	4	18	3	168	9	578	2	1567
7	1258	1289	26	4	126	3	15689	156
1238	6	12389	27	128	5	4789	1789	147

J4Ca7 A5Ca9 C1Ra4 E4Ra9 D6Ra6 F4Ba4 B6Ca4
J7Ca4 A1Ra6 D9Ra4 A6Ba3 E9Ba3 J9Rb1 H9Cb5
H4Ca2 B7Ca9 B8Ca1 A9Ca2 A7Ra7 B4Ra6 C7Ra5
C3Ra7 G1Ra5 H8Ra6 C5Ba2 C9Ba6 F7Ba2 G5Ba6
G9Ba7 J8Ba9 D5Rb3 G7Rb8 H3Rb9 H6Rb1 J5Rb8
H2Cb8 D3Cb2 G3Cb1 F5Cb1 E6Cb2 A2Bb1 A3Bb8
J3Bb3 E1Ca1 B2Ca2 B1Ra3 E8Ra8 J1Ra2 F2Ba3
F1Ba8 D8Ba7 D2Rb5 E2Rb7 F8Rb5